ಬಿ

Planning Latin America's Capital Cities, 1850–1950

ಚಿ

Planning, History and the Environment series

Editor:
Emeritus Professor Dennis Hardy, High Peak, UK

Editorial Board:
Professor Arturo Almandoz, Universidad Simón Bolívar, Caracas, Venezuela and Pontificia Universidad Católica de Chile, Santiago, Chile
Professor Gregory Andrusz, London, UK
Professor Nezar AlSayyad, University of California, Berkeley, USA
Professor Robert Bruegmann, University of Illinois at Chicago, USA
Professor Meredith Clausen, University of Washington, Seattle, USA
Professor Robert Freestone, University of New South Wales, Sydney, Australia
Professor John Gold, Oxford Brookes University, Oxford, UK
Professor Sir Peter Hall, University College London, UK
Professor Peter Larkham, University of Central England, Birmingham, UK
Emeritus Professor Anthony Sutcliffe, Nottingham, UK

Technical Editor
Ann Rudkin, Alexandrine Press, Marcham, Oxon, UK

Planning Latin America's Capital Cities, 1850–1950

edited by Arturo Almandoz

Routledge
Taylor & Francis Group
LONDON AND NEW YORK

First published 2002 by Routledge

This paperback edition first published 2010
by Routledge
2 Park Square, Milton Park, Abingdon, Oxon, OX14 4RN

Simultaneously published in the USA and Canada
by Routledge
270 Madison Avenue, New York, NY 10016

Routledge is an imprint of the Taylor & Francis Group, an informa business

© 2002, 2010 selection and editorial material, Arturo Almandoz; individual chapters, the contributors

Typeset in Garamond by PNR Design, Didcot, Oxfordshire

Printed and bound in Great Britain by TJ International Ltd, Padstow, Cornwall

This book was commissioned and edited by Alexandrine Press, Marcham, Oxfordshire

British Library Cataloguing in Publication Data
A catalogue record for this book is available from the British Library

Library of Congress Cataloging-in-Publication Data
A catalog record has been requested for this book

ISBN10: 0–415–55308–3 (pbk)
ISBN13: 978–0–415–55308–7 (pbk)

☙ Contents ❧

III THE CARIBBEAN RIM AND CENTRAL AMERICA

෬ Foreword ๙

The hardback edition of *Planning Latin America's Capital Cities 1850–1950* was published in 2002. Edited by Arturo Almandoz, it reflected the rise of planning history in South and Central America in which Almandoz had played a leading role, if not *the* leading role. This paperback edition reflects the continuing growth of interest in the history of urban planning in central and southern America.

Visitors to Buenos Aires or Rio de Janeiro will appreciate why 'Paris Goes West' was once considered a possible title for this book. French architecture and planning were the dominant foreign influences on Latin America from the time of Haussmann in the 1850s until the 1920s, when North American ideas started to take over. Even later, French influence in the United States was part of the process. France offered a combination of grandiose architecture and urban design which reached its peak in Paris between 1860 and 1914. French colonialism and industrialization were beginning to rival Britain's, while French 'taste' was seen as superior throughout the world. French architects and planners won competitions in Latin America and were invited to lecture there, culminating in Le Corbusier's influential visits in the 1930s. Thus, while the planning debate in Europe was led by Germany and Britain, Latin America saw a more equal exchange between a number of countries which developed rapidly from colonial status after achieving spectacular independence from Spain and Portugal in the early nineteenth century. The survival of slavery and continuing immigration from Europe produced a unique climate for urbanization and urban policy until 1900 and beyond.

The first 'capital cities' volume in this series was Thomas Hall's *Planning Europe's Capital Cities: aspects of nineteenth century urban development* (1997 and now also in paperback). Since then there have been two volumes on Middle Eastern capitals and one on twentieth-century capitals, while works on the capitals of Central and Southeastern Europe and of Pacific Asia are in preparation. Arturo Almandoz's proposal was first put to the series editors in 1999 and it quickly materialized under his creative and energetic guidance. Like the other regional collections it does not attempt to cover all the countries in the region or the whole of their planning history, nor does it review a history which goes back to the ancient civilizations of the Mayas and other peoples. Instead, it identifies a period in which modern urban planning is exported to Latin America from Europe from about 1860 to 1930.

During these years almost every capital city in Latin America was influenced by Beaux-

Arts architecture and planning. The visits and advice of French experts are well known but less familiar are the studies of Latin American students and visitors in France, especially in Paris. Rapid urbanization tended to reproduce conditions which Europe had already encountered and to some extent mastered. Reforms created a basis for city government which could draw on European example. The result was a series of impressive cities, some of which, like Buenos Aires, bid fair to surpass Paris in scale and grandeur.

This may look like a standard process of diffusion of planning ideas but the editor and his authors draw something more from the specifically Latin culture of *urbanismo* which is used to contextualize both planning and architecture. Drawn partly from French literary and sociological thinking since the late nineteenth century, *urbanismo* is a comprehensive means of understanding the city. As an amalgam of ideas and images it can easily be diffused within and between countries. In Latin America this self-conscious *urbanismo* has given a real strength and richness to planning debates. The onset of American influence around 1930 affected it but it is still a big feature of Latin American culture. Arturo Almandoz is to be congratulated on bringing all this together.

Anthony Sutcliffe
2009

cs Contributors so

Arturo Almandoz is Associate Professor in the Urban Planning Department, Simón Bolívar University, Caracas, where he was Chairman of the Urbanism programme (1996–1998). Among other books, he has published *Urbanismo europeo en Caracas (1870-1940)* (1997), which received three national and local awards, and an international mention. He has written on the emergence of modern urbanism and metropolitan culture. almandoz@usb.ve

Margareth da Silva Pereira teaches on the Post-Graduate Programme in Urbanism (PROURB) in the Faculty of Architecture at the Federal University of Rio de Janeiro. Among many publications on the arrival of modern urbanism in Brazilian cities, she is co-author of *Le Corbusier e o Brasil* (1987), which won an award from the Brazilian Institute of Architects. spmarg@terra.com.br

Lorenzo González Casas is Professor in the Urban Planning Department, Simón Bolívar University, Caracas, where he has been Director of the Institute of Urban and Regional Studies since 1997. He was also Chairman of the Urbanism programme (1988–1991). His doctoral thesis at Cornell University was on Modernity and the City: Caracas 1935–1958 (1996). lgonza@usb.ve

Ramón Gutiérrez is Senior Researcher at the National Council of Scientific Research (CONICET), Argentina, consultant of UNESCO on the issues of Latin American heritage, a member of the Academies of History and Fine Arts in Argentina, Spain and Latin American countries. He has written widely on Latin American architecture and urbanism, including his book *Buenos Aires. Evolución histórica* (1992). ramongut@ interserver.com.ar.

Carol McMichael Reese teaches in the School of Architecture at Tulane University, New Orleans. She was an organizer and co-curator of the 1999–2000 exhibition 'Buenos Aires 1910, Memories of the World to Come', which appeared at venues in Buenos Aires, Washington, and New York. Her current research includes studies of nineteenth- and twentieth-century Latin American architecture and urbanism, particularly in Mexico and Panama. creese1@ tulane.edu

Fernando Pérez Oyarzun is Professor at the Catholic University of Santiago de Chile, where he was Director of the School of Architecture (1987–1990) and Dean of its Faculty of Architecture and Fine Arts. He has published extensively on the influence of the modern movement in Chile and Latin America, including *Le Corbusier y Sudamérica* (1991) of which he was the editor. fperez@puc.cl

Florencia Quesada is a doctoral candidate at the École des Hautes Études en Sciences Sociales, Paris. She is also a researcher at the University of Costa Rica and at the Ibero-American Center, University of Helsinki. Her book *En el barrio Amón. Arquitectura, familia y sociabilidad del primer residencial de la elite urbana de San José, 1900–1935* was published in 2001. quesada@helsinki.fi

Gabriel Ramón Joffré is Director of the Historical Archive, Higher National University of San Marcos and member of the Riva Agüero Institute, Lima. He has written on Peruvian history and archaeology, including his book *La muralla y los callejones. Intervención urbana y proyecto político en Lima durante la segunda mitad del siglo XIX* (1999). garajo@eudoramail.com

José Rosas Vera is Director of the 'Carlos Raúl Villanueva' School of Architecture, Central University of Venezuela, Caracas. He also was Director of the School of Architecture at the Catholic University of Santiago de Chile (1997–2000). He has written articles on the modern architecture and planning in Chile in the first part of the twentieth century. jrosas@villanueva.arq.ucv.ve

Roberto Segre is Chairman of the Post-Graduate Programme in Urbanism (PROURB) in the Faculty of Architecture at the Federal University of Rio de Janeiro. He has written widely on Latin American and Caribbean Architecture and Urbanism. His most recent publications include a new edition of *Havana: Two Faces of the Antillean Metropolis* (2002), written with Joseph Scarpaci and Mario Coyula. bobsegre@uol.com.br

᎒ᏻ Acknowledgements ᏽ᎒

I and my contributors would like to thank the following institutions which have provided primary material or services helpful in the creation of this book:

Archivo Audiovisual de Venezuela, Biblioteca Nacional, Caracas
Archivo Centro de Documentación de Arquitectura Latinoamericana (CEDODAL), Buenos Aires
Archivo Fotográfico Universidad de Chile, Santiago
Archivo Nacional de Costa Rica, San José
Archivo del Instituto Riva Agüero, Lima
Archivo Roberto Segre, Rio de Janeiro
Arquivo Nacional, Rio de Janeiro
Biblioteca Nacional de Chile, Santiago
Bilbioteca Nacional, Rio de Janeiro
Centro de Informaciones Sergio Larraín García Moreno, Facultad de Arquitectura, Diseño y Estudios Urbanos, Pontificia Universidad Católica de Chile, Santiago
Cinemateca Brasileira, São Paulo
Consejo Nacional de Investigaciones Científicas de la Argentina (CONICET)
Decanato de Investigación y Desarrollo (DID), Universidad Simón Bolívar (USB), Caracas
Departamento de Geografía y Meteorología, Mapoteca Orozco y Berra, Mexico

Departamento de Planificación Urbana (DPU), USB, Caracas
Dirección de Servicios Multimedia, USB
Equinoccio, editorial of the USB, Caracas
Fundación John Boulton, Caracas
Fundarte, Alcaldía de Caracas
Instituto de Estudios Regionales y Urbanos (IERU), USB, Caracas
Library of Congress, Washington, D.C.

And I would like, personally, to express my thanks to the following persons: Professor Anthony Sutcliffe, whose initial invitation to submit a book proposal on this subject was a way of encouraging me to go further into the vast domain of Latin America's urban and planning history. As I have mentioned to him sometimes, Professor Sutcliffe has become a mentor of my academic career during the recent years. Ann Rudkin, Alexandrine Press, for her support, advice and dedication far beyond the production of this book. To all the contributors, who from the beginning believed in the project and responded patiently to all my requests. In particular to Drs Pérez Oyarzun and Rosas Vera, for allowing of the images of their chapter to be used on the cover of the book. To Professor Rubena Saint Louis, Departamento de Idiomas, Universidad Simón Bolívar (USB), Caracas, for translating the first versions of chapters 3, 7, 8 and 9. Urbanist Douglas Llanos, Arquitect Mónica González Picó, Melissa López, assistants in the Theory and History Section of the Departamento de Planificación Urbana, USB, who collaborated in the pro ject; Douglas's supervision of the graphic material and logistics has been fundamental. Professor Jorge Villota, Departamento de Diseño, Arquitectura y Artes Plásticas, USB, for his kind help with the translation of some Portuguese terms. To Shila Díaz, my secretary, for her kind help. Lorenzo Bassoni, Carlos Delgado, Teresa De Vincenzo, Jahnmary Díaz, Fernando Gómez, Melissa López, Luidelia Marcano, María C. Rodríguez, students of the course 'Modernización urbana en América Latina (1850–1950)', USB, April–July 2001. And to David Ashurst, for his continuous support since the genesis of this project.

Margareth da Silva Pereira would like to thank José Eduardo Ribeiro Moretzsohn, for the translation of her chapter; Flávio Ferreira, Marcos London and Milton Fefferman, Facultade de Arquitectura e Urbanismo (FAU), Universidade Federal de Rio de Janeiro (UFRJ), as well as Cecilia Rodrigues dos Santos, Centro Cultural São Paulo, for providing primary sources for the illustrations. Carlos Roberto de Souza, Cinemateca Brasileira, for helping with images; Fausto Fleury, photographer; Marguerite David Roy and Dominique Delaunay, who have made possible the use of nineteenth-century material. And Flavio Coddou, Dr. da Silva Pereira's assistant, who has helped to realize the chapter.

Ramón Gutiérrez wishes to thank Graciela María Viñuales, Jorge Tartarini, Dora Castañé, Elisa Radovanovic, Patricia Méndez and Rodrigo Gutiérrez Viñuales, for their collaboration in his chapter.

Fernando Pérez Oyarzun and José Rosas Vera want to express their thanks to Catalina Griffin, for her valuable contribution in the research process as well as in her efforts in collecting the graphic material.

Florencia Quesada is grateful to Lara Elizabeth Putnam and Jussi Pakkasvirta for their comments and encouragement, especially to Lara, for her excellent and efficient revision on the English versions of her chapter.

Gabriel Ramón wishes to thank Dr. Sandra Vallejo.

Arturo Almandoz
Caracas, May 2002

Europe offers the Latin American democracies what the latter demand of Anglo-Saxon America, which was formed in the school of Europe. We find the practical spirit, industrialism and political liberty in England; organization and education in Germany; and in France inventive genius, culture, wealth, great universities and democracy. From these ruling peoples the new Latin world must indirectly receive the legacy of Western civilization.

F. García Calderón, *Latin America: its Rise and Progress* (1913)

The urban history of the second half of the 19th century and the early decades of the 20th is virtually unknown, in spite of the extremely rich material left to us by the innumerable travelers, scientists and men of state; chronicles and articles published by newspapers and periodicals; and certain valuable specialized studies undertaken in those decades.

J.E. Hardoy, Two Thousand Years of Latin American Urbanization (1975)

☙ Chapter 1 ❧

Introduction

Arturo Almandoz

Europa Transfer: A Historiographic Survey of Latin American Capitals[1]

When American planner and scholar Francis Violich published his book *Cities of Latin America* (1944) – in some respects an introduction, for the North American audience, to the unknown urban reality of the rest of the two continents – he repeatedly praised the gracious 'Old World'character of the main Latin American metropolises, comparing it to the lack of genuine urban style in most North American cities. As major intercontinental differences, Violich also emphasized the attitude of South American public leaders, who 'in general, have made a greater effort to leave behind public works and to take an active part in planning the physical development of their cities than have those of the United States.' He highlighted the contrast at the end of the nineteenth century, when urban expansion of Latin American cities had taken place according to 'the old traditions of planning in the grand manner':

While in the United States our cities embarked upon expansion without an established nucleus, without a sense of civic form or dignity inherited from history, most Latin American cities had such a pattern for future growth. Not in every case did Latin American cities follow the old traditions of planning in the grand manner, but a general comparison today between our cities and theirs indicates a greater planlessness in the development of our urban environment. The early established civic discipline of Latin America has served to endow their cities with a better feeling of form and urban character, which goes far to counteract some of the weakness in other respects.[2]

The contrast between the cities of North and Latin America was noticeable up to the time when the book was written in the early 1940s, when most Latin capitals were still under the influence of European urbanism. But probably the contrast would not be so apparent to a Violich of today, when not only has the 'weakness' of Latin metropolises undermined their urban balance, but also North American planning skills have been widely adopted throughout the continent. Nevertheless, Violich's early impressions recall a definitely European-oriented period of Latin American urban history, not experienced in the same way by North America. Although it is past, that period informed the conspicuous 'Old World' image that some Latin capitals still offer in parts of their complex structures. Let us now review the different perspectives from which historians have approached that period,[3] in order to provide a framework which could help us to understand – in the following chapter – the different stages of the process of city development and urbanization.

The political independence of Latin American colonies from Spain and Portugal – which came about in most of the continent between 1810 and 1825 – did not imply either an economic or a cultural release from Europe. Britain assumed the economic predominance in the area, through the exploitation of those natural resources which were necessary for its expanding economy and world trading system. If Britain thereby became the economic paradigm of commercial progress and industrialization, France managed to consolidate the cultural prestige that it had acquired during the eighteenth century. Translating both the European humanism and urbanism for the young republics, France was acknowledged as the guiding muse of Latin America. With the connivance of local elites, the former colonies thus entered an era of cultural neo-colonialism, some of whose components have been described, for an English-speaking readership, in the works of W.E. Crawford, C.C Griffin and E. Bradford Burns.[4]

From the 1960s the so-called School of Dependence provided a historical matrix for understanding that neo-colonial era, whose economic, political and social dimensions were analysed by Cardoso and Faletto and the Steins at that time.[5] In relation to the urban change, the dependent urbanization of Latin America was described according to the successive predominance of blocs of power which conditioned the post-colonial stages of capitalist dependence. The results of such a succession in terms of the national patterns of cities and the structural problems of urban-

ization have been explored by Kaplan, Castells, Quijano, Rofman and Roberts, among others.[6] As a result of their materialist logic and their macro-structuralism, some of these approaches ended up overestimating the importance of economic dependence, and reducing the social changes to the imposition of cultural models from abroad.

From a geographical perspective, Richard M. Morse focused on the growth and articulation of Latin America's urban networks during the nineteenth century, when the structural weakness inherited from the colonial era had to be rectified in order to attain industrial modernization.[7] The twentieth century was reviewed in a panoramic text by J.E. Hardoy, where the urban sprawl of Latin American metropolises was set in the context of the main urban planning and design ideas coming from abroad.[8]

One of the key issues of the modernization of Latin America has to do with the importation of urban planning and design ideas from Europe, and the distinct way in which these were incorporated into the capitals of the emerging republics. This question was treated in morphological terms in the international history of urbanism by Sica and later in the work of Gutiérrez, which remains the major history of Latin American urbanism and architecture.[9] Without considering Ward's distinction between 'transference' to colonial contexts and 'diffusion' amid culturally-related but non-colonial countries,[10] the question of transfer has been explored gradually over time through partial approaches with the urban historiography of Latin America. A seminal text also by Hardoy provides an outline of the main influences arriving from Europe, on a continental scale, between 1850 and 1930, where the author concluded that the Haussmannic surgery and the *Beaux-Arts* tradition of French urbanism inspired a great many of the pro-posals for the 'bourgeois city', until the rise of the metropolises.[11] Another panoramic yet brief review of this diffusion has been produced by the Argentine architect Ramón Gutiérrez, who has completed the genealogy of the Euro-pean urbanists who visited Latin America from the first decades of the twentieth century until the years following World War II, when he recognizes that the 'European cycle' was 'toned down', while American planning had a 'growing influence' in Mexico, Central America, the Caribbean and Venezuela.[12]

Over the last ten years or so, the theoreti-cal interpretation of the urban models which arrived from Europe, both in terms of design and culture, has been explored through two main trends of historical research. On the one hand, there are studies which have reviewed in detail the urban proposals elaborated by leading European designers who visited the Latin American countries during the early decades of the twentieth century. For instance, Jean-Claude Nicholas Forestier's urban and landscape designs for Buenos Aires, Havana and other capitals were com-piled by Leclerc.[13] Le Corbusier's visits to Argentina, Brazil and Colombia were minutely reconstructed in a collective work edited by Pérez Oyarzun.[14] Karl Brunner's contributions as the pioneer of modern urbanism in Chile and Colombia have been reviewed in an issue of the *Revista de Arquitectura*.[15] Although not focused on a particular figure, different examples of the transfer of urban planning and design ideas through proposals inspired by European models were compiled by Gutiérrez in another journal issue.[16]

Another trend corresponds to the histori-cal study of how that transfer of urban design and culture informed the physical trans-formation and social change of some capitals

since the second half of the nineteenth cen-tury. Although some works on urban growth were produced in the 1970s,[17] the urban his-tory of individual cities was not published until the end of the following decade.[18] Rio was described by Needell;[19] SãoPaulo by Rodrigues Porto;[20] Buenos Aires by Gutiérrez, Berjman and Gorelik;[21] Havana by Segre, Coyula and Scarpaci;[22] Lima by Ramón and Caracas by Almandoz.[23] Featuring the role played by foreign planners and planning models in Latin American capitals, particular episodes of that transfer have been revisited in countless journal articles and collective works in recent years, some of which will be referred to in the following chapters.

European influence has been studied not only in terms of physical changes and plan-ning proposals but also in relation to the urban ideas, myths and fashions that informed the ethos of the bourgeois city in Latin America. Approaching the process of cultural diffusion in terms of social theories imported after the progressive modernization of the nineteenth century, Morse analysed the parasitic burden that some of the growing capitals were for the expanding economies of Latin America. He based his analysis on the ideas elaborated by local intellectuals who were influenced by European positivism and liberalism, a tradition that Morse recognizes as prevalent during the nineteenth century.[24] Bradford Burns emphasized the role played by local elites, whose cultural conflict with other local social groups often 'provides a useful guide for the interpretation of Latin American history.'[25]

As in the case of Europe, the portrayal of the bourgeoisie seems to be fundamental to an understanding of the urban mythology of that period, especially during the extravaganza of the so-called *Belle Époque*. In this respect, the urban historiography of Latin America provides two major approaches which recreated the social climate of the Europeanized cities. The ideological effects of European urban culture on Latin societies are to be found in José Luis Romero's wide ranging *Latinoamérica. Las ciudades y las ideas* (1976). Here he demonstrates beautifully how, until the 1930s and the eve of the emergence of the 'mass metropolises', the bourgeois city displayed an almost total imitation of Europe in terms of social customs, political ideas and literary trends. Especially during the final decades of the nineteenth century, the piecemeal implementation of the 'Haussmannic example' not only responded to the need to expand the Latin capitals, but also to the bourgeoisie's longing to appropriate the metropolitan myth coming from industrializing Europe. For the Frenchified elites of these cities, the invocation of Second-Empire Paris was thereby supposed to make possible their magic transformation from post-colonial city into real metropolis.[26]

The cultural change of the learned elites of Latin America is also portrayed in Angel Rama's *La ciudad letrada* (1984), an outstanding example of social semiology of Latin metropolises through their literature. This Uruguayan critic also pointed out the Haussmannic example as a feature of the period, but recognized the original value of that imitation. Rama insisted that rather than a mere copy of Second-Empire Paris or Victorian London, there was a genuine recreation due to the urban desire and fantasy, illusion and obsession of local elites excited by the metropolitan spirit.[27]

Also coming from a literary domain, the Peruvian critic Julio Ramos recreated the *flânerie* of some novelists and chroniclers that – as Walter Benjamin and Georg Simmel did in the European metropolises – reported the spectacle of consumerism and the 'rhetoric of walk' evinced in the public spaces of Latin America's booming capitals at the turn of the century.[28] The Venezuelan historian, Elías Pino, directed a research project into the main manifestations of modernity in Latin America during the significant period 1870 to 1930, stressing the role played by the capitals as the setting for exhibiting the progressive devices and fashions arrived from Europe.[29] More recently, Pineo and Baer compiled experiences of social movements, political changes and administrative reforms in some countries during that same period of significant urbanization.[30]

Notwithstanding their historical accuracy, most of the works referred to above fail to put into perspective Latin America's urban importation from Europe, particularly in terms of the recent debate about the international exportation of urban models. This debate has focused mainly on the twentieth century, whose latest manifestations of diffusion are close to the emerging discussion on globalization, which has been addressed from different disciplines.[31] But, as Ward has recently pointed out,[32] the overall perspective of the diffusion of urban planning since its beginnings in the late nineteenth century can only be found in the works of planning historians such as Peter Hall and Anthony Sutcliffe. They established the framework for understanding planning as an international movement whose key ideas travelled throughout different contexts.[33] Unfortunately, they have not been well known in many countries of Latin America, where the historiographic interpretation introduced by Choay and Benevolo has predominated,[34] according to which twentieth-century urbanism can be explained in terms of models and traditions shaped in industrial Europe, whose routes and means of transfer seem to be less important than the models as such.[35]

So the reconstruction of the route map of Latin America's importation of urban models from Europe, and specially from France, is a task that for the most part remains to be completed on a continental scale. In order to insert Latin America's urban genealogy within the international debate, one might use other works that have described the transfer of French *urbanisme* to colonial contexts, such as Wright's and Rabinow's,[36] as well as King's explanation for the exportation of urban models throughout the British empire.[37] However, I am inclined to consider that, in terms of the typology of 'diffusional episodes' distinguished by Ward, the recreation of some of Europe's urban ideas and models which took place in postcolonial Latin America can be seen as variants of the 'selective borrowing' and 'synthetic innovation' whereby the capitals of a peripheral bloc wanted to evince its belonging to the Western world.[38] As happened in other emerging areas of the nineteenth-century world,

such as the United States and Japan, the urban importation from Europe was part of Latin American countries' search for national identity and modernization, though the latter's economic dependence and fragility somehow recalls the imposition that took place in colonial contexts. This is the resemblance traditionally stressed by the theorists of dependence, whose differences from the actual borrowing we must distinguish from an urban perspective. On the one hand, the young republics' fascination with France and Britain was certainly due to the economic and political presence of the European powers in the booming markets of the Southern cone. But, on the other hand, far from being a cultural imposition linked to the interests of foreign capital, the urban importation proved to be an expression of the urban needs of Latin American elites, eager to strengthen their links with European metropolises.

A Cultural Approach to the Transfer of Urbanism

Following discussion of some of the works which have dealt with the republican era of Latin America from urban perspectives, the need for a cultural approach to the question of transfer of urbanism remains evident – especially when it comes to studies in English. In addition to the traditional scarcity of urban studies of Latin America, there appears to be no volume devoted to Latin American capitals as the most conspicuous recipients of the importation of urban culture and urbanism from Europe.

In order to fill this void, the aim of this book is to provide the coordinates that let us track the mainstreams of diffusion of urbanism throughout Latin American capitals, during the post-colonial era when Europeanization was most conspicuous, until the consolida-

tion of the United States' predominance in technical and cultural terms. The diffusion can be said to be pursued in terms of the three main concerns identified by Ward when revising historical studies: namely, the 'mechanisms of diffusion – for example key personalities, reformist or professional milieux, intergovernmental actions'; the 'extent to which ideas and practices are changed in their diffusion'; and the 'fundamental causation of diffusion', including political, economic and cultural factors.[39] In this respect, it must be borne in mind that, during the Europeanized era, republican Latin America while no longer colonial was still a dependent region of the world. Therefore the prevailing economic conditions under which the urban transfer took place have to be taken into consideration

when addressing the subject. These conditions will be summarized in the next chapter,
which establishes the context and historical
background of that era. However, in this
book we distance ourselves from the School
of Dependence's materialist logic and macro-
structuralism, which induced some of its representatives to overestimate the importance
of economic dependence, while reducing the
social changes to the imposition of cultural
models from abroad. So it is in contrast to
those interpretations that our approach is first
and foremost a cultural one.

Secondly, urban transfer will be seen as a
component of a cultural relationship maintained by Latin America's societies with the
most advanced countries of North Atlantic
capitalism. By exploring the nature and extent
of the urban importation resulting from the
dependent elites' cultural needs, the unidirec-
tional and determinist imposition of colonialist
concepts must be enriched by the incorporation of local elements; in other words, the notion
of cultural colonialism has to be replaced by
that of cultural re-invention, in the sense that
there is a 'synthetic innovation' in the recipient
countries. This is why, in the peculiar context
of Latin American republics, the notions of
'transference', 'exportation' and 'importation'
do not imply a colonial imposition – as it does
in the distinctions established by King and
Ward[40] – so we will not refrain from using the
terms in a wider sense.

By tracing the transfer of urban ideas from
Europe to Latin America – which remains the
core issue of this book – a parallel theme can
be explored, namely what it was that articulated
the urban debate in the capitals and underpinned modern urbanism as a discipline in
the republics, a process which apparently
occurred against that European background.
However, the development of urbanism as a
discipline cannot be explained purely in terms
of its technical contents – especially in the context of the backward nature of nineteenth-
century Latin America. It is necessary to trace
not only the diffusion of urban ideas as such,
but also the importation which took place in
other areas related to the Latin Americans'
urban culture, for example art, literature and
fashion, and this constitutes a third feature of
this book's cultural approach.

Such an approach seems to coincide with
Hardoy's comments made in 1975 in relation
to the need for an all-embracing historiography of this period – comments which I
believe are is still valid from a perspective of
Latin America in general, notwithstanding the
fact that nearly three decades have elapsed
since they were written:

The urban history of the second half of the 19th century and the early decades of the 20th is virtually
unknown, in spite of the extremely rich material left to
us by the innumerable travelers, scientists and men of
state; chronicles and articles published by newspapers
and periodicals; and certain valuable specialized studies
undertaken in those decades.[41]

The Capital City Case Studies

The order in which the capital city case studies
appear in the book is simple and illustrates
three political and economic trends which had
urban expressions and which will be explained in the next chapter:

1. Buenos Aires, Santiago, Rio and São Paulo
as emerging metropolises of the booming
economies that were favoured by their early
incorporation into the North Atlantic bloc
from the second half of the nineteenth century.

2. Former viceregal capitals like Mexico City and Lima, that lost regional importance after Independence.

3. Havana, Caracas and San José as three capitals of the Caribbean rim and Central America where diverse political and economic conditions combined with the different magnitudes of the cities, produced intriguing and relatively unexplored expressions of Latin America's Europeanization during the republican era.

Although there are considerable differences between Latin American capitals during the period studied here, it is possible to establish common traits in the way the different case study cities have been treated. Each chapter includes the essential elements of urban history that are necessary for understanding – especially by a foreign audience – the social and morphological evolution of the different cities. But the emphasis is on the aspects of urban transfer from Europe that led to the local crystallization of urbanism, including the projects, plans and the pioneers that made possible the institutionalization of the discipline. At the same time, we have incorporated those elements of urban culture and representation that help us to recreate the ethos of those capitals under the aegis of European modernity.

While maintaining those traits as the common framework of the book, each chapter also reflects the authors' background and discourse. Ramón Gutiérrez's authoritative position as one of the leading voices of the theory and history of architecture and urbanism in Latin America, enables him to produce a didactic and panoramic review of what can be said to be the most conspicuous case of Europeanization of a city throughout the Americas. Using Georges Clemençeau's impression as a *leit-*

motif, he describes the transformation of that 'great European city', recreating at the same time its intellectual climate through the combination of references drawn from travellers, literature and foreign experts. The latter were hired by the Argentine government, ambitious *intendentes* (mayors) and professional groups in their pursuit of modernization of the country's federal capital after 1880. The deep-seated Europeanization of the Argentine society did not impede local reaction to proposals from such foreign celebrities as Bouvard, Forestier, Jaussely and Le Corbusier, whose lack of consideration of context doomed their schemes to remain *'urbanismo de papel'* (paper urbanism or plans only on paper). One of Gutiérrez's major contributions in this chapter is to demonstrate how a great deal of the urban development of Buenos Aires during this period was marked by the combination of the improvement in functional components such as hygiene and transport, with the concept of *'estética edilicia'* (building aesthetic), whose essence can certainly be extended to other Latin American capitals.

Demonstrating from the very beginning of her chapter that, unlike other Latin American countries, Brazil's well-rooted notions of capital city and urban system did not start in 1889 with the proclamation of the republic, but were a legacy of the colonial and imperial periods, Margareth da Silva Pereira assumes the difficult task of combining in one chapter the different urban genealogies of two cities comparable with respect to their roles as the nation's capitals: Rio de Janeiro and São Paulo. In spite of the differences between the former's background as administrative capital from 1763, and the latter's belated yet sudden development from the 1880s, da Silva Pereira manages to distinguish common episodes in terms of urban planning: from the dynamic administrations of Prefects such as Pereira Passos in Rio and da Silva Prado in São Paulo, to the influence of visits by foreign urban planners such as Bouvard and Barry Parker to the latter; followed by the famous plans and proposals of Agache and Le Corbusier for Rio, which remained the administrative capital until 1960. Most of these proposals informed an era of academic urbanism, in a country that, after the move of the administrative capital to Brasilia, would take Latin America's lead in modernism.

A less famous example of Europeanization during the republican era, Santiago de Chile is presented by Fernando Pérez Oyarzun and José Rosas Vera as an interesting case of a secondary capital of the Spanish empire that gained importance thanks to the early political stabilization of the country, and its becoming one of Latin America's booming economies in the second half of the nineteenth century. With their combined experience as scholars in the domains of architectural and urban semiology, Pérez and Rosas provide a detailed interpretation of Santiago's major plans and buildings from the time when foreign architects were first invited to the country during Bulnes's presidency. Vicuña Mackenna's breakthroughs during the 1870s are described in detail, demonstrating not only their significance for the city's urban renewal and management up to 1900, but also the reasons why the *Intendente* of Santiago can be considered one of the Haussmanns of Latin America. The centennial celebrations of Independence are perceptively pointed out by the authors as a political occasion that helped to boost architectural and urban academicism, that in Chile was not only nurtured by French but also by Italian representatives. The development of what was perhaps Latin America's most solid

platform of urbanism during the first decades of the twentieth century is demonstrated by Pérez and Rosas by reference to the contribution of Brunner, among other pioneers who moved the emerging discipline towards a more rational and comprehensive approach, while contributing to the creation of different 'cities within the city'.

In a carefully researched chapter, Carol McMichael Reese provides an unusual approach to Mexico City, a peculiarly complex case study that she has worked from architectural and artistic perspectives in other publications. The structure of her chapter according to the city's subdivisions is different from the chronological approach followed in most of the other city studies of this book, which tend to elaborate and illustrate the phases given in the next chapter. However, the fact that McMichael Reese has her own hypothesis on Mexico City's urban growth around Porfirio Díaz's regime or 'Porfiriato' (1876–1910), makes her more comfortable with the elaboration of a discourse in terms of the different *colonias*, or residential developments. This allows her to analyse diverse aspects of the city's urban growth – the provision of public services, the creation of administrative bodies, the centennial celebrations – while she moves throughout the *colonias*. Taking the 'residential fabric' as the thread of her discourse provides a revealing way of describing Mexico City's changes, especially in the cases of working-class *colonias*. The consideration of the nearby towns of the Aztec metropolis is another feature of this chapter that deserves special recognition.

The relative loss of importance that the earliest viceregal capitals of the Spanish Empire suffered after Independence is confirmed in the case of Lima by Gabriel Ramón, a young historian and archaeologist who is one of the few to have worked on this relatively unexplored example of Europeanization during the republican era. He provides a revealing text that, with references drawn from novelists and travellers, illustrates how the Peruvian capital underwent different phases of a subtle Europeanization not only perceivable through the elite's urban culture, but also through the changes in architectural styles and the patterns adopted in the 'script of the urban surgery'.

Highlighting the importance of Spain and the United States as the powers that were present in Cuba from the beginning of the nineteenth century, in authoritative style Roberto Segre brings together all the ingredients that turned Havana into one of the most interesting expressions of urbanism in Latin America following Captain General Tacón's reforms in the 1830s. He demonstrates that Spain's longest domination in this colony has not only to be taken into account when periodizing the urban history of Cuba in relation to other countries of the continent, but also when cataloguing the intriguing mixtures of architecture and urbanism imported for Havana's expansion beyond the colonial walls – a process that many of the wealthy Catalonians living in the city associated with Cerdá's *ensanche* (expansion) for their native Barcelona. Segre reviews the typology of the palaces and hotels of the new centres; the villas, bungalows and other buildings of the new suburb of Vedado; and he finally takes us along the new boulevards resulting from Forestier's plan for the Paris of the Caribbean, which he presents as the 'maturity' of academic urbanism.

As an example of a backward capital that showed some symptoms of recuperation from the 1870s on, the case of Caracas is portrayed by Lorenzo González Casas in a comprehensive text that goes beyond the limits of the Venezuelan capital in order to provide clues for the emergence and scope of Venezuelan urbanism in terms of 'territory, architecture and urban space'. Combining his background as an architect and a town planner, González offers a revealing reading of the Caracas plans, starting from a colonial *damero* (checkerboard) that, unlike in other capitals of Latin America, remained untouched until the beginning of the 1940s. He describes and links the three episodes during the European-oriented period that put this colonial city on the brink of becoming the Americanized metropolis of an oil-producing country: Antonio Guzmán Blanco's 'recreation' in 1870s–1880s Caracas of the foreign cities he had visited or lived in, with special reference to Second-Empire Paris; the 'interlude' of the *Belle Époque*, including hygiene, traffic and housing reforms that had been traditionally neglected by Venezuela's urban historiography; and the emergence of modern urbanism through the proposals of the so-called 'Monumental Plan of Caracas', under the guidance of French planner Maurice Rotival.

A smaller case than Caracas in terms of its scale and continental significance, San José de Costa Rica proves to be another fascinating example of how the Europeanization of republican Latin America flourished in urban design, architecture and fashion. Based on a clear description of the urban structure of the Costa Rican capital and its segregation during the period considered, the change in its cultural ethos and urban scenery is well portrayed by Florencia Quesada in a chapter that, partly because of its use of travellers' impressions, reminds one of the composition of those postcard albums that were so fashionable during the *Belle Époque*.

Despite the differences between the sizes of the capital cities and the authors' approaches to their subjects, the eight case studies combine ingredients relating to urban history, urban culture and its representation, the emergence of planning and the transfer of urban ideas and models. In a continent where the capitals' primacy has been so decisive for political and economic growth, these studies shed new light on Latin America's history during one of the most significant periods of its republican life.

NOTES

1.   Parts of this chapter are taken from my book Almandoz, A. (1997) *Urbanismo europeo en Caracas (1870–1940)*. Caracas: Fundarte, Equinoccio, Ediciones de la Universidad Simón Bolívar. The book is the translation of my PhD thesis, Almandoz, A. (1996) European Urbanism in Caracas, 1870s–1930s, Architectural Association School of Architecture, Open University, London. The thesis was supervised by Dr. Nicholas Bullock, King's College, Cambridge.

2.   Violich, F. (1944) *Cities of Latin America. Housing and Planning to the South*. New York: Reinhold Publishing Corporation, pp. 34–35.

3.   Most references are taken from English and Spanish literature.

4.   Crawford, W. R. (1944, 1961) *A Century of Latin American Thought*. Cambridge, Mass.: Harvard University Press; Griffin, C. C. (1961) *The National Period in the History of the New World. An Outline and Commentary*. Mexico, D. F.: Instituto Panamericano de Geografía e Historia; Bradford Burns, E. (1979) Cultures in conflict: the implication of modernization in nineteenth-century Latin America, in Bernhard, V. (ed.) *Elites, Masses and Modernization in Latin America, 1850–1930*. Austin: University of Texas Press, pp. 11-77; Bradford Burns, E. (1982) *The Poverty of Progress. Latin America in the Nineteenth Century*. Berkeley: University of California Press.

5.   Cardoso, F. H. and Faletto, E. (1969) *Dependencia y desarrollo en América Latina*. México: Siglo XXI; Stein, S. J. and B. H. (1970) *The Colonial Heritage of Latin America. Essays on Economic Dependence in Perspective*. New York: Oxford University Press.

6.   Kaplan, M. (1972) La ciudad latinoamericana como factor de transmisión de control socioeconómico y político externo durante el período contemporáneo. *Boletín del Centro de Investigaciones Históricas y Estéticas*, **14**, pp. 90–124; Castells, M. (1973) *Imperialismo y urbanización en América Latina*. Barcelona: Gustavo Gili; Quijano, A. (1977) *Dependencia, urbanización y cambio social en Latinoamérica*. Lima: Mosca Azul; Rofman, A. B. (1974, 1977) *Dependencia, estructura de poder y formación regional en América Latina*. México: Siglo XXI; Roberts, B. (1978) *Cities of Peasants. The Political Economy of Urbanization in the Third World*. London: Edward Arnold.

7.   Morse, R. M. (1971) Latin American cities in the 19th century: approaches and tentative generalizations, in Morse, R. M., Coniff, M.L. and Wibel, J. (eds.) *The Urban Development of Latin America 1750–1920*. Stanford: Center for Latin American Studies, Stanford University, pp. 1–21; Morse, R.M. (1975) El desarrollo de los sistemas urbanos en las Américas durante el siglo XIX, in Hardoy, J.E. and Schaedel, R.P. (eds.) *Las ciudades de América Latina y sus áreas de influencia a través de la historia*. Buenos Aires: Sociedad Interamericana de Planificación (SIAP), pp. 263–290.

8.   Hardoy, J. E. (1989) Las ciudades de América Latina a partir de 1900, in *La ciudad hispanoamericana. El sueño de un orden*. Madrid: Centro de Estudios Históricos de Obras Públicas y Urbanismo (CEHOPU), Ministerio de Obras Públicas y Urbanismo (MOPU), pp. 267-274.

9.   Sica, P. (1978) *Storia dell'urbanistica: il Novecento*. Bari: Laterza, Vol. II, pp. 771–819; Gutiérrez, R. (1984) *Arquitectura y Urbanismo en Iberoamérica*. Madrid: Cátedra.

10.   Ward, S.V. (1999) The international diffusion of planning: A review and a Canadian case study. *International Planning Studies*, **4**(1), pp. 53–77.

11.   Hardoy, J.E. (1988) Teorías y prácticas urbanísticas en Europa entre 1850 y 1930. Su traslado a América Latina, in Hardoy, J.E. and Morse, R.M. (eds.) *Repensando la ciudad de América Latina*. Buenos Aires: Grupo Editor Latinoamericano, pp. 97-126. There is an English edition: Hardoy, J.E. (1990) Theory and practice of urban planning in Europe, 1850–1930: Its transfer to Latin America, in Hardoy, J.E. and Morse, R.M. (eds.) *Rethinking the Latin American City*. Washington:

The Woodrow Wilson Center, The John Hopkins University Press, pp. 20–49.

12. Gutiérrez, R. (1996) Modelos e imaginarios europeos en urbanismo americano 1900–1950. *Revista de Arquitectura*, 8, pp. 2–3.

13. Leclerc, B. (ed.) (1994) *Jean Claude Nicolas Forestier, 1861–1930. Du jardin au paysage urbain*. Paris: Picard.

14. Pérez Oyarzun, F. (ed.) (1991) *Le Corbusier y Sudamérica, viajes y proyectos*. Santiago de Chile: Escuela de Arquitectura, Pontificia Universidad Católica de Chile.

15. (1996) *Revista de Arquitectura*, 8.

16. (1995) DANA. *Documentos de Arquitectura Nacional y Americana*, 37–38.

17. For instance, the work by Scobie, J. (1971) *Buenos Aires: From Plaza to Suburb, 1870–1910*. New York: Oxford University Press.

18. As it was pointed out by Guerra, F.-X. (1989) El olvidado siglo XIX, in Vásquez de Prada, V. and Olabarri, I. (eds.) (1989) *Balance de la historiografía sobre Iberoamérica (1945–1988)*. Pamplona: Ediciones de la Universidad de Navarra, pp. 593–631.

19. Needell, J. (1987) *A Tropical Belle Époque. Elite, Culture and Society in Turn-of-the-Century Rio de Janeiro*. Cambridge: Cambridge University Press.

20. Rodrigues Porto, A. (1992) *História urbanística da cidade de SãoPaulo (1554 a 1988)*. SãoPaulo: Carthago & Forte.

21. Gutiérrez, R. (1992) *Buenos Aires. Evolución histórica*. Bogotá: Escala; Berjman, S. (1998) *Plazas y parques de Buenos Aires: la obra de los paisajistas franceses. André, Courtois, Thays, Bouvard, Forestier, 1860–1930*. Buenos Aires: Gobierno de la Ciudad de Buenos Aires, Fondo de Cultura Económica; Gorelik, A. (1999) *La grilla y el parque. Espacio público y cultura urbana en Buenos Aires, 1887–1936*. Buenos Aires: Universidad Nacional de Quilmes.

22. Segre, R., Coyula, M. and Scarpaci, J. (1997) *Havana. Two Faces of the Antillean Metropolis*. Chichester: John Wiley & Sons.

23. Ramón, G. (1999) *La muralla y los callejones. Intervención urbana y proyecto político en Lima durante la segunda mitad del siglo XIX*. Lima: Sivea, Promperú; Almandoz, *op. cit.*

24. Morse, R. M. (1978) Los intelectuales latinoamericanos y la ciudad (1860–1940), in Hardoy, J.E.,

Morse, R. M. and Schaedel, R.P. (eds.) *Ensayos histórico-sociales sobre la urbanización en América Latina*. Buenos Aires: Ediciones SIAP, pp. 91–112.

25. Bradford, Cultures in Conflict., *loc. cit.*, pp. 13–14.

26. Romero, J.L. (1976, 1984) *Latinoamérica: las ciudades y las ideas*. México: Siglo Veintiuno Editores, pp. 247–318.

27. Rama, A. (1984) *La ciudad letrada*. Hanover: Ediciones del Norte, pp. 71–104, 116.

28. Ramos, J. (1989) *Desencuentros de la modernidad en América Latina. Literatura y política en el siglo XIX*. México: Fondo de Cultura Económica, pp. 113–142.

29. (1997) *Sueños e imágenes de la modernidad. América Latina 1870–1930*. Caracas: Fundación CELARG

30. Pineo, R. and Baer, J.A. (eds.) (1998) *Cities of Hope. People, Protests and Progress in Urbanizing Latin America, 1870–1930*. Boulder: Westview Press.

31. King, A. (1991) *Global Cities*. London: Routledge.

32. Ward, *op. cit.*, pp. 54–55.

33. Hall, P. (1974, 1992) *Urban and Regional Planning*. London: Routledge; Hall, P. (1988, 1994) *Cities of Tomorrow. An Intellectual History of Urban Planning and Design in the Twentieth Century*. Oxford: Blackwell; Sutcliffe, A. (1981) *Towards the Planned City: Germany, Britain, the United States and France, 1780–1914*. Oxford: Blackwell.

34. Choay, F. (1969, 1989) *The Modern City. Planning in the 19th Century*. New York: George Braziller; (1965) *L'urbanisme, utopies et réalités. Une anthologie*. Paris: Éditions du Seuil, 1979; Benevolo, L. (1963, 1989) *L'origini dell'urbanistica moderna*. Bari: Laterza.

35. As I have pointed out in Almandoz, A. (2000) A propósito de progresismo y culturalismo. Aproximaciones historiográficas al urbanismo moderno, in *Ensayos de cultura urbana*. Caracas: Fundarte, pp. 173–183. See also Almandoz, A. (2000) Aproximación historiográfica al urbanismo moderno en Venezuela, in Rodríguez, J.A. (ed.) *Visiones del oficio. Historiadores venezolanos en el siglo XXI*. Caracas: Academia Nacional de la Historia, Comisión de Estudios de Postgrado-FHE, Fondo Editorial de Humanidades y Educación, Universidad Central de Venezuela, pp. 211–231.

36. Wright, G. (1991) *The Politics of Design in French Colonial Urbanism*. Chicago: The University of Chicago

Press; Rabinow, P. (1989) Modern French urbanism, in *French Modern. Norms and Forms of the of the Social Environment*. Cambridge, Mass.: The MIT Press.

37. King, A.D. (1990) *Urbanism, Colonialism and the World-Economy. Cultural and Spatial Foundations of the World Urban System*. London: Routledge; (1976) *Colonial Urban Development. Culture, Social Power and Environment*. London: Routledge & Kegan Paul.

38. Ward, *op. cit.*, p. 58.

39. *Ibid.*, p. 55.

40. King, *Urbanism, Colonialism and the World-Economy, loc. cit.*, pp. 7–12; Ward, *op. cit.*, pp. 55–56.

41. Hardoy, J.E. (1975) Two Thousand Years of Latin American Urbanization, in Hardoy, J.E. (ed.) *Urbanization in Latin America. Approaches and Issues*. New York: Anchor Books, pp. 3–55, p. 45.

Urbanization and Urbanism in Latin America: From Haussmann to CIAM[1]

Arturo Almandoz

To understand the transfer of urbanism from a cultural perspective, it is necessary to review the post-colonial era when European influence prevailed in most of Latin America. We shall do this in the first section of this chapter, highlighting some of the demographic, economic, political and cultural conditions that made possible that predominance, and putting emphasis on the changes in the intellectual debate concerning foreign models. The urban changes outlined in this review make possible the identification, in the second section, of the three phases that corresponded to the dependence on Europe both culturally and economically, in terms of exports, between 1850 and 1950. In spite of national differences that will become clear in each of the city case studies, these phases will be characterized, in the third section, in terms of their predominant urban models and trends. This will help to set the context for planning schemes and proposals reviewed in the following chapters.

From Colonial Cities to Teeming Metropolises, from Europeanism to Americanization

The degree of European influence in different Latin American republics depended on the level of political stability in each country and to a great extent this, in turn, influenced the penetration of foreign capital. Most of the continent, with the exception of Cuba, gained political independence from Spain and Portugal during the first decades of the nineteenth century. This was followed by a diversification of national export economies from those of late colonial times. Cattle raising in Argentina and Uruguay, mining in Chile and Mexico, and coffee growing in Brazil allowed the new republics to benefit from the competitiveness of their former colonial staples within international trade

Figure 2.1 South America's political division by the mid-nineteenth century. From *Politische Übersichtkarte von Sudamerika*, c.1850–1859. (*Source:* Archivo Audiovisual de Venezuela, Biblioteca Nacional, Caracas)

circuits, while Cuba's sugar production soared as colonial bonds to Spain weakened (figure 2.1). Boosted by European capital investment and immigration from the 1860s onwards, commercial prosperity in some republics brought about regional differences in development across the continent: on the one hand, the non-tropical Atlantic shore and Chile became the leaders of the 'era of economic expansion' that lasted until World War I; on the other hand, the remaining Andean countries were of little interest to international

capitalistic blocs, especially Britain, whose investments in that region were minimal until the end of the nineteenth century.[2]

During his journey across South America in the early 1880s, the relative prosperity among the Atlantic countries was already evident to the Argentine Miguel Cané; to him they seemed 'to have felt more rapidly and intensely' the influence of Europe, 'undoubted source of all material progress', so that they could 'get rid of the colonial hindrance.'[3] By contrast, on the other side of the continent,

M.G. Mulhall, the author of *The English in South America* (1878), summarized a pessimistic prospect for the small British capital investment in Venezuela, Bolivia, Nueva Granada and Ecuador: 'The amount of British capital in these 4 republics is trifling and consists almost wholly of loans raised in England, a great portion of which may be considered as so much money lost.'[4]

Despite economic diversification and political independence, there were no major changes in the urban geography of Latin America until the second half of the nineteenth century. Since the 1750s, there had been an obscure period of urban stagnation, whose gloomiest phase coincided with the peak of civil wars that devastated the new republics in the early years of Independence. Among other effects, the volatile political climate brought about a process of decentralization and 'ruralization' of the backward societies, that caused further stagnation.[5] From the 1860s onwards, demographic urban changes started to be noticeable both in the structure of new centres and the traditional capitals. In relation to the former, as Hardoy summarized, 'the building of railroads and the opening up of new lands, the exploitation of coal and mineral resources, and the administrative need of new political subdivisions motivated the construction of thousands of new cities and towns.' Brazil's Belo Horizonte and Argentina's La Plata became the emblematic examples of Frenchified design applied to the imposing layout of new provincial capitals. But these were exceptional new settlements: 'The majority of new cities founded, however, were simple service centers and transportation hubs for shipment of agricultural products to the ports.'[6]

With a total population of 30 million by 1850, the density of Latin America barely reached 1.5 inhabitants per square kilometre, while the capitals' population was only 3.5 per cent of the rural one. However, the national capitals' 'primacy dip' – which had plunged their growth rates below national growth during the previous obscure decades – was overcome by the middle of the century. The degree of primacy in the different Latin American countries was related 'to the extent of their connection with the world economy.' Foreign investments in general, and British in particular, 'were deployed in a way likely to increase primacy by helping to provide the administrative and economic infrastructure for exports; this infrastructure was concentrated in the major city through which exports were channelled.'[7] Latin capitals pulled ahead of the national growth rate in the following order: Havana (1840s), Rio (1850s), Lima and Buenos Aires (1860s), Bogotá (1870s), Caracas and Santiago (1880s), and Mexico City at the turn of the century. The domestic importance of the capitals must be set in perspective with the absolute gaps disparities among different countries and the general tendency of the continent. On the whole, former viceregal metropolises such as Mexico City and Lima yielded attraction to capitals of the new expanding economies – a tendency which can be confirmed by a quick look at the figures of the takeoff of the capitals' populations. Buenos Aires was about 90,000 by the 1850s and jumped to 178,000 by 1869; Rio already had 186,000 by 1854 and increased to 267,000 in 1872; Santiago was 115,000 by 1865 and jumped to 150,000 by the mid-1870s; Havana, which already had 130,000 by 1847, went up to 197,000 by 1861; mostly due to its former colonial splendour, Mexico City already had 200,000 by 1855, but only increased to 210,000 by 1862, whereas Lima had only 89,000 by 1862, and Bogotá kept its moderate 40,000 from the mid-1820s up to 1870. Meanwhile, Caracas had 47,013 by 1869 and barely rose to 48,897 by 1873.[8]

The economic and cultural relationship of nineteenth-century Latin America to Europe can be portrayed as a binomial dependence which launched an era of 'neo-colonialism' for the young republics. The historic bonds of that new dependence can be dated back to the last period of the colonial regime. Due both to the weakened position of Spain and Portugal in Europe and the pressures exerted by Creole groups, there had been gradual concessions allowing the colonies to escape from the metropolitan hegemony during the eighteenth century. Even before the Independence wars were over, Latin American colonies had expanded their commercial and cultural exchanges with other European countries, especially with Britain and France. During the years after Independence, the Pyrenees were perceived by local elites as the southern frontier of modern Europe; Britain and France were thereafter confirmed as the real alternatives to the economic, political and cultural backwardness represented by the Iberian countries.[9] Britain was chosen, so to speak, as the economic godfather of the young republics, whereas France was confirmed as their cultural godmother – a peripheral yet useful honour for the European countries, especially in restraining the emergence of the United States as a continental superpower.

Britain became the main customer for the traditional staples produced by the new republics, which not only assumed their function as suppliers of raw materials for British industrialization but also relied upon British trade and loans for their incipient economies. In terms of the investment of capital and the supply of technology, the predominance of Britain was more evident

from the 1850s to the 1900s, including two marked booms during the 1880s and in the decade following 1902. After that period, the United States was to have an increasing presence which would overtake British capital from World War I.[10]

Although they were not numerous, the British possessed an economic supremacy which was the fact that most struck and pleased Michael G. Mulhall in his report:

It may appear surprising that in a continent twice the size of Europe, where the total number of English residents is hardly equal to the population of Chester or Carlisle, and does not reach one in 800 of the inhabitants, the English element has in a few years been able to make its impress felt in a greater degree than any other foreign nationality. This appears mainly owing to the influence of British capital and trade.[11]

He certainly had reasons to be proud. The 'leading merchants' took to Latin America technological devices and manufactures which allowed those nearly-preindustrial ex-colonies to sample the coming industrial era for the first time. Among other inventions, machinery for mining, steam engines and railways was introduced in the new republics by British companies and citizens, which shared with Americans and Germans the privilege of launching most of the devices of the industrial era until the beginning of the new century.[12]

Although France was economically present in Latin America during the eighteenth century, her predominance among the former colonies was mainly social and cultural. Taking the lead in bringing the European Enlightenment to the New World, French philosophers had won over the Creole intelligentsia which championed the crusade for Independence and early republicanism. The prestige achieved by Rousseau's France was maintained throughout the nineteenth century, from Saint-Simon's social reformism and Renan's freethinking to Comte's and Taine's positivism. France was thus considered not only a philosophical power but also the main translator of contemporary European thinking for the Latin world.[13]

Even by the 1820s, Domingo Faustino Sarmiento pointed out in his *Facundo, o Civilización y Barbarie* (1845) – a literary result of the Argentine intelligentsia's opposition to Juan Manuel Rosas's tyranny (1835–1852) – that 'the Europeanization' of Argentina's urban society was already evident; all Europeans arriving in Buenos Aires believed that they were in Parisian salons, since not even the characteristic French petulance was lacking.[14] Through the foremost case of Buenos Aires, the Argentinian statesman and writer thus anticipated a French-oriented culture which spread across the continent for more than a century. This is what Manuel Ugarte, another Argentinian man of letters and Ambassador to France, would call 'the second conquest', paralleling the fifteenth-century occupation of the vast land by the Spanish and Portuguese with the nineteenth-century subjugation of its people by French thought.[15] Even though that supremacy would not be so absolute by the beginning of the twentieth century, the Peruvian writer Francisco García Calderón still proclaimed on the eve of World War I, 'France has been the teacher of social life and letters to the American democracies' – a tutelage that he praised gratefully as one of the main traits of the 'Latin spirit'.[16]

As well as being a leader in social change and philosophical thought, France also became the paradigm of fine arts and civilization, refinement and urbanity for the young republics. Though recognizing the German and Italian influences on the writing and sciences of post-colonial Latin America, the Venezuelan sociologist Gil Fortoul identified the French predominance in 'the elegant life, the fashion and the art' as a feature of the 'social race' of the new republics.[17] In a similar way, when mapping the influence of Southern-European immigration on this Latin American 'race', Ugarte accurately highlighted that spiritual yet powerful influence of France in 'embellishing the life' in the continent.[18]

Fascinated by the European prestige of France as the main representative of the classical tradition, from early republican times Latin America had also turned to French artistic canons. Especially from the second half of the nineteenth century, the emergent bourgeoisie, benefiting from the export boom, would adopt a so-called 'French style' in different aspects of domestic and public life in the cities. By the conspicuous imitation of European manners in general, Second-Empire Paris became the archetype of urban modernity and refinement for Latin American elites throughout the second part of the nineteenth century.[19]

This worship of Haussmann's Paris was one of the main features of what Romero called the 'bourgeois city' of Latin America, which bloomed in the second half of the nineteenth century in those countries which had been incorporated in the capitalistic circuits – as we shall see in the following chapters. Urban renewal was part of a more ambitious package of reforms intended to modernize the social structures, whereby countries such as Argentina, Chile, Brazil and Mexico decided to improve the image of the then untouched 'colonial cities', as well as to restructure their regional networks of urban settlements by the introduction of railways. In countries like Chile, where some political stalibity was reached relatively early, urban improvement was encouraged from the early

1840s by the relative continuity of cultural progressivism during the successive governments of Manuel Bulnes (1841–1851), Manuel Montt (1851–1861) and José Pérez (1861–1871). Countries that suffered international and domestic conflicts until the middle of the century, had to wait for autocratic and more stable regimes to support the transformation, as was the case of Porfirio Díaz's dictatorship in Mexico between 1876 and 1910; during this period, among other achievements, the length of the railway system was extended from 800 to 24,000 kilometres. Railways and foreign immigration were seen as significant manifestations of progress by regimes linked to postivism and industriousness (figure 2.2), two of the ideologies that seduced Latin America elites through the works of Comte and Spencer.[20] In this respect, Antonio Guzmán Blanco's three governments in Venezuela between 1870 and 1888 provide an example of what could be achieved, by a progressive autocrat who tried to overcome the con-

straints of an economy less attractive to international capital. In any event, the process of urban concentration in most Latin American countries led to the emergence of a new type of bourgeois city, whose Europeanism was evident in the physical transformations and the cultural ethos sponsored by economic groups, social elites and political leaders representing the liberal interests of commercial and industrial capitalism.[21]

By the turn of the century, Latin America's Europeanism was undermined by the United States's growing presence in political affairs. In addition to the latter's expulsion of Spain from Caribbean waters in 1898, the United States had decided to revive the golden rule of the so-called Monroe Doctrine – 'America belongs to the Americans', formulated by President James Monroe in 1823 – when dealing with the British Empire's territorial dispute with Venezuela in the mid-1890s. Later on, when Theodore Roosevelt rose to power in 1901, the 'Dollar Diplomacy' in the

Figure 2.2 Entrance to Ferro Central Railway Station, Rio de Janeiro. Photo: Marc Ferrez, 1880. (*Source*: Hoffenberg collection, Archivo Audiovisual de Venezuela, Biblioteca Nacional, Caracas)

Caribbean was boosted by the project of the Panama Canal and what was called 'Roosevelt's Corollary': if the United States wanted to take over from Europe as a continental superpower, the former should help to overcome political upheavals and economic crises in the Caribbean and Latin republics.[22] A great opportunity for applying Roosevelt's Corollary came when the United States had to intervene to settle the conflict at the end of 1902, when British and German ships blockaded Venezuelan coasts, after the bankrupt nation refused to pay its international debts.

The revival of the Monroe Doctrine for the sake of helping the weak republics paved the way for a new line-up of superpowers in the Americas. Changes mostly affected the supremacy of the British Empire, whose last attempts to control the Latin American republics had been blocked by the United States which, by the end of World War I, completely replaced the political influence of Europe. In the economic domain, the supremacy of English manufactures in the Latin markets was no longer safe, being challenged by American and German products from the early twentieth century. Despite relative recuperation in the decade after 1902, British investments in the area were also doomed to decrease gradually up to the late 1920s, by which time a century of financial supremacy was over.[23] Even with its strong economic presence, Germany would never defy the Monroe Doctrine again, and the possible dream of Latin America as a colonial expansion, if it ever existed, remained as such.[24] The definite supremacy of the United States was to be sealed by World War I, which reduced European trade and investments, gave an impetus to American exports in the region, and left the United States unchallenged in the New World.[25]

Before its economic and political consolidation by the time of World War I, the United States' ideological conquest of Latin America had to pass through several cultural battles. At the end of the Spanish-American war in the Caribbean in 1898, Ruben Darío – the Nicaraguan poet and essayist who fathered literary modernism in the Spanish-speaking world[26] – had declared his definitive enmity towards the 'Caliban' who defeated and humiliated 'the Daughter of Rome, the Sister of France, the Mother of the America.'[27] This hatred was fuelled by the publication of some books which justified the American takeover from Spain in the Caribbean, in view of the Anglo-Saxons' alleged superiority over tropical races. The thesis was epitomized in Benjamin Kidd's *The Control of the Tropics* (1898) – a manifesto which urged the establishment of Anglo-American protectorates in the former colonies set up by continental Europe. The British sociologist entreated the English-speaking world to define the 'principles' of its relations with pretended 'republics' plagued with 'anarchy and bankruptcy', especially Central and South American states, where unstable conditions attracted German expansionism. Britons and Yankees should assume that 'in dealing with the natural inhabitants of the tropics we are dealing with peoples who represent the same stage in the history of the development of the race that the child does in the history of the development of the individual. The tropics will not, therefore, be developed by the natives themselves.' As an alternative to the old fashioned policy of colonization carried out by continental Europe, the English-speaking world should thereafter take a grip on its responsibility of 'holding the tropics as a trust for civilization'.[28]

While the expansionism of Presidents

McKinley and Roosevelt in the Caribbean carried out the Americans' part in such a crusade, Latin intellectuals looked for arguments against Kidd's plea. One of the first answers was to acknowledge that the whole of Latin America was *El continente enfermo* (*The Sick Continent*, 1899), according to the diagnosis given by César Zumeta from New York. Though recognizing the political and economic failure of most Latin republics throughout the century which was about to end, the Venezuelan journalist and diplomat warned fellow citizens about Kidd's doctrine, exhorting them to face proudly the challenge of the new century, threatened by the 'civilizations of the Golden Calf'.[29] Just as it did for the Venezuelan modernist, so the Anglo-Saxons' 'Golden Calf' apparently became a material beast for other intellectuals throughout South America, who fought against the peril by invoking the spiritual tradition inherited from Latin Europe.

In 1900 there appeared a manifesto calling upon the cultural values of Latin America in order to face the materialistic dangers of the new century. Rapidly becoming a bedside-book for the younger generation, *Ariel*, by José E. Rodó, featured the Shakespearian character as a personification of the noble spirituality that the young republics of the South should adopt to defend themselves against the utilitarian Caliban lurking in the North. The twentieth-century combat would be highly risky because, the Uruguayan humanist argued, the Yankee conquest had already pervaded the Latin spirit. Relying on the critique of American utilitarianism provided by European thinkers such as Spencer, Renan and Taine, the writer and politician not only alerted people to the expansionism of the northern neighbour but also attacked its values. Hinting at metropolitan Buenos Aires,

Rodó finally warned about the danger looming over those Latin American cities whose 'material greatness' and 'apparent civilization' ranked them amongst the leading capitals of the world: they could become the modern equivalents of Sidon, Tyre or Carthage. The image was doubly prophetic: Latin capitals should beware not only of the materialism emerging in the markets of Chicago, but also of the dependence on New York as the Rome of the New World.[30]

French civilization was evoked once again as one of the main ingredients of Latin nobility in order to defeat the 'enemy race'. Despite its imperialist presence in other areas of the world, France was not perceived as a threat to the Latin republics, in the same way that Germany, other European countries or even Japan were.[31] At the outset of the cultural battle of the twentieth century, France still kept sound the intellectual 'puissance' which she had gained in the early years of republicanism in Latin America.[32] Additionally, for Latin intellectuals of the *Belle Époque*, France's cultural leadership was epitomized in their cult of Paris, which was a kaleidoscopic Mecca for painters, sculptors and writers who could make a living from cultural production in the '*Ville lumière*' (City of Lights). That is what Darío himself had done in the early 1900s, when he founded Latin American modernism on the basis of French influences, from symbolism to impressionism.

Ugarte's and Darío's appeal for the cultural alliance of Latin Americans with France was extended to other European countries by Francisco Garcia Calderón, one of the main heirs of the French-oriented thinking coming from Rodó. In his book *Latin America: its Rise and Progress* (originally published in French) the Peruvian writer and diplomat demanded appreciation for the inspiration offered to the

Latin republics by the great nations of Europe. Unlike the United States, he argued,

Europe offers the Latin American democracies what the latter demand of Anglo-Saxon America, which was formed in the school of Europe. We find the practical spirit, industrialism and political liberty in England; organization and education in Germany; and in France inventive genius, culture, wealth, great universities and democracy. From these ruling peoples the new Latin world must indirectly receive the legacy of Western civilization.[33]

The end of Latin America's *Belle Époque* was to a large extent determined by the transformation of the bourgeois cities into mass metropolises increasingly seduced by the progressive models of New York, Chicago, and other American counterparts.[34] In terms of urban culture, this shift tends to be associated with the 'Roaring Twenties' and the Americanization that followed World War I, whereas in the domain of the emerging urbanism, the process of transition can be said to last until the end of World War II, as we shall see in the last section and the following chapters.

Some of the bourgeois capitals of the expanding economies were replaced by real metropolises by the 1930s: Buenos Aires jumped from 663,000 people in 1895 to 2,178,000 in 1932; Santiago from 333,000 in 1907 to 696,000 in 1930; and Mexico City from 328,000 in 1908 to 1,049,000 in 1933. As a dramatic case comparable to the growth of industrial cities like Manchester and Chicago, São Paulo spiralled from 240,000 inhabitants in 1900 to 579,000 in 1920, and 1,075,000 in 1930, while the urban predominance of Rio was diminished, its population increasing from only 650,000 in 1895 to 811,433 in 1906. The expansion of the capitals was partly due to a process of industrialization by import substitution, which accelerated urbanization in Argentina, Uruguay, Chile and Cuba, which figured

among the world's most urbanized countries at the time of the Depression in 1930. Havana's population jumped from 250,000 inhabitants by the turn of the century to 500,000 in 1925. Fuelled mainly by rural-to-urban migration, other capitals of the Andean countries also underwent significant increase: Bogotá went from 100,000 people in 1900 to 330,000 in 1930, while Lima increased from 104,000 in 1891 to 273,000 in 1930. Although Caracas rose only from 72,429 inhabitants in 1891 to 92,212 in 1920, the first effects of the oil boom pushed the population from 135,253 in 1926 to 203,342 in 1936. San José de Costa Rica had only 50,580 inhabitants in 1927, but this population represented 11 per cent of the country's.[35]

As Romero has pointed out, in social terms, Latin America's new 'masses' were a mixture of traditional groups long established in the cities and incoming migrants from diverse backgrounds. At the same time, from a cultural perspective, the emergence of the mass society in the new metropolises coincided with the boom in the import of cars and other progressive products from the United States.[36] The Americans also became the new reference for sanitation, since World War I had forced Latin Americans to seek from United States sponsored organizations and programmes the advice on medicine and hygiene they had previously received from Europe.[37] In countries like Peru, Venezuela and Cuba, the replacement of Europe's technical predominance by that of the United States was encouraged by the centralized and progressive regimes of Augusto Leguía (1908–1912, 1919–1930), Juan Vicente Gómez (1908–1935) and Gerardo Machado (1925–1933), all of which favoured the implantation of American capital for modernizing the sanitary, communication and urban infrastructure in general.

Before moving to New York during the 1920s, Jesús Semprún – a journalist and writer of Gómez's Venezuela – aptly summarized the change in attitude of a great deal of Latin America's 'positivistic' intelligentsia in relation to the United States, when he revised and amended, in a retrospective way, South Americans' former misconceptions and fears regarding the formidable example of the Colossus of the North. Blinded by their thoughtless loyalty to a decadent Spain, turn-of-the-century intellectuals had been poisoned against the Yankees because they could not grasp the historic significance of the independence of Cuba, Puerto Rico and the Philippines. But the nightmare images of Caliban and the 'Golden Calf' had vanished after World War I, when the Latin youth, as a new generation of Ariels, could realize that 'yesterday's masters were mistaken'. In contrast to the pseudo-history recounted by Darío, Rodó and Ugarte – according to which all Latin Americans had been 'aggrieved by Uncle Sam's big stick' – the Americans' altruistic participation in World War I had proved, on the contrary, their international idealism. The United States had thus become the symbol of democracy, modernity, and good citizenship that could be contrasted with the European allies' hidden interests in the recent conflict. Free from fears and suspicions, the Latin American republics could follow the ideals of the Colossus of the North in order to reach 'the peaceful, harmonious and fruitful tree of freedom', concluded Semprún.[38]

With different levels of political freedom, the ideals that were now associated with the Americans were certainly pursued throughout the continent in the years before World War II, when the world predominance of the United States was confirmed. Northern liberalism was loosely adopted in different political models in order to seek goals of modernization and industrialization, as in the governments of Getulio Vargas in Brazil (1930–1945), Fulgencio Batista (1934–1959) in Cuba, and Isaías Medina Angarita in Venezuela (1941–1945). However, in spite of the United States' political, economic and technological supremacy in most of the administrations of the Latin American republics by World War II, Europe retained some degree of prestige in the domain of urbanism – as we shall see in the concluding section here and the following chapters. In short, urbanism was the last expression of European cultural dominance that dated back to the early republican era.

Three Phases of Republican Dependence

As we have just outlined, the incorporation of Latin America within modern capitalism and Western civilization has been a long journey guided by different nations and states. Spain and Portugal during the colonial era; Britain, France and other European powers during the republican period until World War I; and the United States during most of the twentieth century have set the rules of Latin America's peripheral modernization. The multiple effects of those successive types of political, economic and cultural domination have been the main reason for Latin American backwardness, according to the materialist explanation provided by the School of Dependence.[39] Although the school's Marxist premises and reductionist view of Latin America as a mere supplier of raw materials has been dismissed in historical terms, some of the urban-related postulates of that school are still worth calling upon in order to characterize the phases of Latin American dependence in the republican era.

First of all, the notion of dependence must not be mistaken for absolute backwardness or lack of progress and development – which, on the contrary, did take place in Latin America from the nineteenth century, especially in the urban field. Instead, dependence should be associated with the adjustment and orientation of economic, political and social structures to conditions established by the ruling elites which represented the foreign interests invested in the export sector of each nation. Thus, far from involving a situation of antagonism or domination, dependence consisted of a 'correspondence' between the interests of the local elites and the demands of foreign groups; a connivance which increased as commercial diversification of the national economies took place throughout the nineteenth century.[40] At the same time, dependence did not always imply a passive attitude on the part of the dependent society, but rather the latter's deliberate and conscious acceptance and recreation of the manifestations produced in the dominant bloc – a creative aspect of the relationship which is especially significant in cultural terms.[41]

Secondly, the dependence was due in most cases to an export-led economy which had important societal implications. Indeed, the assumption by Latin America of its role as raw material producer within the nineteenth-century international division of labour implied a reinforcement of the 'outward-oriented model of growth' inherited from colonial times. The Latin republics thereby settled for a different destiny from the United States, which had adopted a self-sufficient model of growth from the 1820s. Thus the

latter started to replace its dependence on foreign inputs with an internal growth based on industrialization and urbanization of central territories.[42] Clear evidence of that economic distortion is to be seen in the dependant nature of urbanization in most Latin American countries – during the early republican era, poorly developed urban networks dating from colonial times were expanded according to the requirements of foreign capital. From the nineteenth century on, this outward economic orientation also brought about the local elites' association of 'modern' with all that had to do with the export sector and everything foreign in general, whereas 'traditional' remained associated with activities linked to domestic production and consumption.[43] This nineteenth-century dependence can also be seen as the basis of the antinomy between 'official' and 'popular' culture, whose dissociation would mark the social evolution of the continent.[44]

Thirdly, from an economic perspective, two major stages have been distinguished in the post-colonial dependence of Latin America.[45] After political liberation, the 'capitalist commercial domination' was obviously different from the colonial regime, because the legitimacy of new republics for trading was internationally recognized, though their conditions of commercial exchange with the North Atlantic bloc were uneven.

These two phases of Latin America's economic dependence can be subdivided and extended when considering the effects of the urbanization which accompanied the penetration of European capitalism from the 1850s. The rise of international and rural-to-urban immigration, the increasing primacy of the Latin republics' capitals, the structural changes in their morphology and the architectural eclecticism which built on their colonial heritage, can be seen as changes associated

with a cultural Europeanization that predominated at least until the 1930s.[46] Furthermore, Europe's influence in the domain of
urbanism can be said to have lasted until the
end of World War II, in spite of the fact that
– as mentioned in the previous section – the
urban explosion in the major capitals had led
to a mass culture which erased the last
vestiges of the *Belle Époque* and its worship
of the Parisian model.

Thus, on the basis of the economic,
cultural and urban factors that shaped the
dependence of Latin America from 1850 to
1950, it is possible to distinguish three phases
of that dependence that can help us to understand the changes in urbanism during that
period:

(*a*) the second half of the nineteenth century,
which put an end to the colonial city, in the
midst of urban reforms fuelled by the increase of European capital;

(*b*) the prolonged *Belle Époque* that served as
a stage for displaying the cultural predominance
of Europe, in spite of its diminished position
in political and economic terms, specially after
World War I;

(*c*) the Americanization and urbanization of
Latin America from the 1930s, during which
phase Europe maintained a predominance in
the domain of its urban models until the end
of World War II.

As outlined in the previous section, each of
these phases represented a change in the economic, political and intellectual climate of
most of the continent. In the following section,
we characterize the urban planning ideas and
models which were predominant in each of
these three phases, and so provide a general
context for the city case studies which follow,
and in which national differences will become
evident.

Creole Haussmanns

Following the urban revival fuelled by the
penetration of European investment, by the
second half of the nineteenth century Haussmann's *grands travaux* in Paris became the
main symbol of modernization imported by
some Latin American capitals during their
republican consolidation. Eager to participate
in the capitalist-industrialist order epitomized
by Haussmannic urbanism, independent
Latin America became a devotee of what was
seen culturally as a French product *par
excellence*. However, in order to judge the
authenticity of this 'French' phenomenon, it
is necessary to examine the principles of the
urban 'surgery' undertaken by Georges-
Eugène de Haussmann while he was Prefect

of the Seine (1853–1870) during the Second
Empire.

Haussmann's *Mémoires* (1890–1893) are
perhaps the best source from which to identify
his ideas. A detailed, reflective account of his
grands travaux, rather than a theoretical work,
the *Mémoires* state the basic principles of his
approach to urban renewal. As the central
streets of Paris were previously 'impenetrable
to circulation', his surgery systematically applied
the means to satisfy the need for freer movement of traffic, always respecting the requirements of salubriousness while preserving
historic and artistic monuments.[47] Circulation,
hygiene and concern for the monumental
therefore emerged as basic principles of the

so-called 'urbanism of regularization', characterized by the 'disentanglement' of the old Parisian fabric through a new circulatory system and an opening up of space.[48]

Classified in the *Mémoires* according to their financial requirements and their articulation through different systems or *réseaux*, thoroughfares such as the Rue de Rivoli and other boulevards and avenues certainly occupied a great deal of the Prefect's endeavours and budget. The circulatory system was at the same time conceived as an instrument for spreading open spaces, from the majestic Bois de Boulogne and Bois de Vincennes, to the tiny green squares all over Paris. In terms of infrastructure, the circulatory network was used to improve the distribution of water, air, light and the basic conditions of hygiene, which 'more than ever' had to become the basis of urban organization.[49] Even though hygiene certainly inspired most of his monumental works of underground infrastructure, it is worth mentioning that the Prefect's concern for sanitation was influenced by Britain and Germany, where public health reforms had started in the 1840s.

The Baron's endeavours to regularize and equip the Parisian fabric were undertaken with due regard to the importance of monumental perspective. This can be said to have been another clue to his astonishing success: although the network of services was based on the functional rationale of the new industrial era, the 'far-sighted engineer' managed to design the layout according to the monumental principles of French baroque, thus demonstrating that the emerging capital of the industrial era could be planned beautifully as well as functionally.[50] Of all the elements that made up 'Haussmannization' – including other financial and administrative reforms not mentioned here[51] – the monumentality of the

reconstruction of Paris was to be the most influential in Latin America, since it provided a platform for displaying an architectural eclecticism that local elites were eager to adopt.

According to Sica – one of the few European historians to refer to this transfer – at least two consecutive yet different waves of 'Haussmannization' in post-colonial Latin America can be distinguished. The first led to the 'systematization' of the urban structure of the capitals, which basically took place within their colonial-era boundaries during the second half of the nineteenth century. Although the results were not comparable with the unique achievement of Paris, Haussmannesque boulevards and avenues were superimposed on the colonial layout. The second wave included the urban renewal and enlargement of Latin capitals up to World War II, always with a degree of reference to the Haussmannic model.[52] Epitomizing at the same time the metropolitan myth imported from industrializing Europe, the Haussmannic example was used by local elites – as has already been mentioned – to demonstrate the cultural transformation of their post-colonial towns into bourgeois cities. This transformation was obviously more conspicuous in the capitals of expanding economies, where a mature bourgeoisie was emerging on the basis of the activities linked to the export sector.[53]

We turn our attention now to the first of Sica's waves. Haussmann's main contributions to the biggest Latin capitals have been traced to the baroque lines of new neighbourhoods, as well as to the huge public parks and tree-lined avenues. Although the French genealogy of some of these designs is reviewed in the city case study chapters, the following are traditional examples of Hausmannesque works: the Paseo de la Reforma in Mexico City, said to be the first copy of a Parisian

Figure 2.3 Avenida de Mayo, Buenos Aires, *c.*1880. (*Source*: Hoffenberg Collection, Archivo Audiovisual de Venezuela, Biblioteca Nacional, Caracas)

boulevard in the New World; the Parque de Palermo and the Avenida de Mayo in Buenos Aires (figure 2.3); the Paseo del Prado and the Avenida Agraciada in Montevideo; the Parque Forestal and the Santa Lucía hill in Santiago (figure 2.4); and the Guzmán Blanco boulevard and Paseo El Calvario in Caracas.[54]

The rulers of some cities were compared to the Prefect of the Seine, so they can be regarded as Creole Haussmanns. Torcuato de Alvear, mayor of Buenos Aires (1883–1886), became known in his own time as the Argentine version of the Baron.[55] Benjamín Vicuña Mackenna, mayor of Santiago, had also proposed, in the early 1870s, a transformation plan for the capital, which was influenced by Haussmann's Paris; though the

plan was approved in 1892, it was not finally implemented. Guzmán Blanco's urban reforms in 1870s and 1880s Caracas were also associated with Napoleon III's *grands travaux*, though the ambitious principles of the Baron's urbanism were difficult to apply to the tiny capital. Having studied in Second-Empire Paris and taken part in the design of a planning scheme for Rio de Janeiro in the mid-1870s, Francisco Pereira Passos was also supposedly inspired by the Baron's ideas for the inauguration of the Avenida Central (1905) (figure 2.5) and other transformations of the 'Cidade Maravilhosa', when he became Prefect of Rio during the Presidency of Rodrigues Alves.[56]

But Haussmann's ideological presence in

Latin America during the nineteenth century must not be exaggerated. In fact, the Prefect of the Seine, was rarely identified as an urban inspiration in the contemporary debate of some capitals; instead, his name appeared later, and rather as an exemplar of the centralism and power required for the transformation of big capitals.[57] At the same time, it must be remembered that not all the Baron's principles had arrived in nineteenth-century Latin America. From the baroque lines of new avenues and the Bois-de-Boulogne-like pattern of some parks to the 'French style' of architecture, associations have been established on the grounds of the physical and symbolic apparatus of Haussmannization – a range which certainly mirrored the Prefect's morphological

principles. Nevertheless, his hygienic reforms were apparently not included in the first Haussmannic portfolio of ideas that arrived in Latin America; they were to be adopted only at the end of the century, and in a different way. Nor, apparently, did Latin Americans perceive the Baron's own conception of an articulated urban surgery which assembled circulation, services and monuments[58] – a surgery which would arrive even later, in the first decades of the twentieth century, when urban planning was maturing everywhere. Even then, Haussmannesque neo-baroque transformations were adopted for the sake of their progressive and civilized symbolism, whereby Latin American capitals not only strove to demonstrate their resem-

Figure 2.4 Santa Lucía hill, Santiago de Chile, *c.*1880–1890. (*Source*: Archivo Audiovisual de Venezuela, Biblioteca Nacional, Caracas)

blance to the metropolises of the emerging *Belle Époque*, but also tried to demonstrate their rejection of the *damero* (checkerboard) and architectural vocabulary inherited from colonial times.

Figure 2.5 Avenida Central, Rio de Janeiro, 1908. Photo: Marc Ferrez. (*Source*: Hoffenberg Collection, Archivo Audiovisual de Venezuela, Biblioteca Nacional, Caracas)

The Belle-Époque *Reforms, 1890s–1910s*

In the midst of the intellectuals' plea for a cultural alliance with the Old World, there were three main trends of European influence on the urban modernization of Latin American capitals: namely, sanitary reforms, proposals for urban renewal, and residential expansion. In relation to the former, it must be considered that, as industrialization was less traumatic than in Europe, sanitary concerns in nineteenth-century Latin America were less closely linked to housing problems. Building and environ-

mental ordinances in major capitals were partly an attempt to respond to European ideas on public health. The British example was prominent: the 1848 and 1875 Acts were studied in different countries, especially in Argentina, where they apparently inspired the works and reforms of Guillermo Rawson and Samuel Gache.[59] By the 1880s, Buenos Aires pioneered, with Montevideo, the creation of institutions specializing in hygienic research (figure 2.6), which were followed by similar ones in Mexico City, Santiago and Lima.[60] The exchange of experiences across the Americas also played an important role in diffusing the new ideas. The 1897 and 1902 *Conferencias Interamericanas* (Interamerican Conferences), held in Mexico City, discussed the hygiene agenda and encouraged participants to pursue international agreements, some of which were reached in the 1905 *Convención Sanitaria* (Sanitary Convention). In addition, the 1898 Congress of Hygiene and Demography, which took place in Madrid, included sections on Urban Hygiene and Urban Engineering and Architecture, and represented a unique opportunity for Spanish-speaking

countries to update their sanitary policies.[61] On the basis of such events, by the turn of the century, the advanced programmes implemented in Buenos Aires, Montevideo, Rio and Havana inspired hygiene reforms in backward capitals such as Caracas and Lima.[62]

During the first decades of the twentieth century, the debate on hygiene influenced diverse proposals for urban renewal and extension for Latin American capitals, such as the razing of the Morro do Castelo by Carlos Sampaio, Prefect of Rio.[63] There were also the 'linear proposals' for the expansion of Santiago, developed from 1909 by the Chilean engineer and architect Carlos Carvajal, on the basis of

GRAN INSTITUTO SANITARIO MODELO EN LA BARRANCA DE SANTA LUCIA

Figure 2.6 Gran Instituto Sanitario, Buenos Aires, *c.*1865–1870. Photo: Benito Panunzi. (*Source:* Hoffenberg Collection, Archivo Audiovisual de Venezuela, Biblioteca Nacional, Caracas)

the example of Arturo Soria's 1890s *Ciudad
Lineal* (Linear City) in Madrid.[64] But most of
the urban projects were closer to the lineage
of the 'academic urbanism' represented by
the *École des Beaux-Arts* and, later on, by the
Institut d'Urbanisme of the Université de Paris,
whose journal *La vie urbaine* – published
from 1919 – would become highly influential
among Latin America's new generations of
professionals.[65] The centennial Independence
celebrations were ideal occasions for organizing architectural competitions and inviting
foreign designers to propose new public works,
as was the case of Emilio Jecquier, Emilio
Doyère and Ignazio Cremonesi in Santiago in
the 1900s. Preparing the celebration of the
centenary of Argentina's Independence in 1910,
the Mayor of Buenos Aires invited Joseph
Antoine Bouvard to the city in 1907. The
Architect of the City of Paris – where he had
organized the 1900 Exhibition[66] – designed a
web of diagonals for the transformation of
central Buenos Aires, including the project
for a new Plaza de Mayo that was never
built.[67] Invited while Raymundo Duprat was
Prefect of São Paulo (1911–1914), Bouvard's
proposals for parks for the city used the same
baroque conception of monumental space, while
making evident his admiration for Camillo
Sitte's artistic principles.[68] Visiting Argentina
in 1924, Jean-Claude Nicholas Forestier designed the parks and open spaces for a 1925
plan for Buenos Aires, with echoes of Second-
Empire Paris.[69] Léon Jaussely made a similar
attempt in 1926, while Forestier laid out parks
in Havana.[70]

The urban sprawl of residential areas made
up another chapter of the urban agenda in the
major capitals of Latin America. As we have
already seen, the image and urban structure
of the most populous cities drastically changed
from the 1900s onwards: crammed since the

late nineteenth century with administrative and
commercial activities, the traditional centres
sheltered rural and foreign immigrants
attracted by incipient industrialization. The
upper and middle classes now started to look
for new residential locations, thus setting the
direction of expansion for their capitals.[71]
The arrival of the motor car broadened the
possibilities of urban expansion, up to then
limited to the capitals which already had
suburban railways or trams from the late
nineteenth century. This is the moment when
the 'garden cities' supposedly arrived. A loose
use of the term has sometimes labelled as such
some late nineteenth-century examples, from
the first *colonias* of Porfirio Díaz's Mexico City,
including the 1890s area of Higienópolis in
São Paulo, developed by Martin Burchard and
Victor Nothmann, through the *urbanización*
El Paraíso in 1900s Caracas.[72] Havana's Vedado
has also been seen as an expression of the
suburban qualities of the garden city (figure
2.7), mixed with Frederick Law Olmsted's
natural ingredients of design and Ildefonso
Cerdá's combination of activities within
blocks.[73] But others claim that Howard's
garden city concept 'was never transported to
Latin America', which was 'attracted' instead
to the ideas of the 'garden suburb' and the
dormitory garden suburb for the middle and
working classes respectively. Late examples
of this type include Mexico City's Colonia
Balbuena (1933), Rio's Realengo (1942) and
Buenos Aires's El Palomar in the 1940s.[74] The
only projects directly related to the English
garden city principles were some of São Paulo's
new areas, such as Jardim América, developed
with Barry Parker's collaboration after 1915.[75]

All in all, despite its relative backwardness
by comparison with the urban reforms in
Britain and Germany at the turn of the
century,[76] France kept the leadership which it

Figure 2.7 Avenida de Los Presidentes (G street), Vedado, Havana. View of the *parterres* of the pedestrian promenade created in the 1920s. Photo: Roberto Segre. (*Source*: Archivo Roberto Segre)

had gained in the nineteenth century by prolonging its influence on the academic repertoire of Latin American capitals. Although its predominance was to be toned down from the 1930s on, when new urban models were to be incorporated into the planning of the capitals, Paris was the permanent example of the *Beaux-Arts* rhetoric which to a great extent informed the ethos of *Belle-Époque* Latin America. Besides being an ally in Ariel's cultural battle against Caliban, the mythical presence of Paris throughout this period was decisive for the later choice of France as godparent to some of the first urban plans for major capitals – as we shall see in the next section.

Urban Plans and European Emissaries

Population growth and urban sprawl evinced the urgency of adopting new plans for the capitals, which were sponsored by local governments and new generations of professionals. Although many of the latter were still sent to study or train in Europe, some had graduated from the architectural faculties recently founded in local universities which, by that time, had started to offer their first courses on urban planning and design.[77] Confirming the specialization of the discourse and the discipline that accompanied the emergence of urbanism in industrialized countries,[78] technical journals on urban problems started to be published or were translated throughout Latin America during the first decades of the twentieth century. Among them were *La Ciudad* (1929) in Buenos Aires; *Planeación* (1927) and *Casas* (1935) in Mexico; *Ciudad y Campo* in Lima; *Zig-zag* and *Urbanismo y Arquitectura* (1939) in Chile; and *Revista Técnica del Ministerio de Obras Públicas* and *Revista Técnica del Concejo Municipal del Distrito Federal* (1939) in Caracas. The influence of European urban planners was still evident in the widespread use of books by Marcel Poëte, Pierre Lavedan and Raymond Unwin, and others that were translated or circulated in their original versions among Latin American professionals.[79]

In addition to the Inter-American Conferences and Pan-American Congresses of Architects that took place since the 1920s, technical innovations in urbanism were exchanged at international events that, from the following decade, specialized in diverse components of the emerging field. Chile held a national congress on architecture and urbanism in 1934, and the first international *Congreso de Urbanismo* (Congress of Urbanism) was held in Buenos Aires in 1935; later on, the first *Congreso Interamericano de Municipalidades* (Inter-American Congress of Municipalities) took place in Havana in 1938, and the second in Santiago in 1941. In relation to housing, the first *Congreso Panamericano de Vivienda Popular* (Pan-American Congress of Low-cost Housing) also took place in Buenos Aires in

1939, and the Sixteenth International Congress on Planning and Housing was held in Mexico City in 1938. The Fifteenth International Congress of Architects held in Washington in 1939 also represented a good opportunity for Latin American professionals to update their experiences.[80]

Confirming the importance that administrative changes had for the consolidation of planning – as Sutcliffe demonstrated had happened in industrial countries before 1914[81] – Latin America's technical planning apparatus did not take shape until the second half of the 1920s when urban problems became a public issue. Most of the national or municipal offices of urban planning in Santiago, Montevideo, Buenos Aires, Mexico City, Rio, Lima, Bogotá and Caracas were a joint effort between local and national governments, new professional associations, and urban research centres.[82] Some acting at the same time as administrative heads, urban designers and promoters, a new generation of indigeous urban planners and designers would emerge from these offices in charge of elaborating the first plans for the growing metropolises, including Carlos Contreras in Mexico City, Mauricio Cravotto in Montevideo, Carlos della Paolera in Buenos Aires, Francisco Prestes Maia in São Paulo, Pedro Martínez Inclán in Havana, and Leopoldo Martínez Olavarría in Caracas.[83] Benefiting from both the specialization and diversity of the professional milieux, other trends of European urbanism, different from those of the *Beaux-Arts* tradition, were incorporated into the planning agendas of the new institutions, which often involved the visit of famous urbanists as advisers for the first plans of Latin American capitals.

Still capitalizing on the prestige of the eclectic side of French urbanism in *Belle-*

Époque Latin America, conspicuous representatives of what Choay labelled the '*École Française d'Urbanisme*' (EFU) were invited to participate in proposals and plans for some capitals.[84] As already mentioned, Forestier visited

Habana' (Plan for the Beautification and Enlargement of Havana) was published and included in the *Ley de Obras Públicas* (Act of Public Works) issued by Gerardo Machado's new government (figure 2.8). A team made up

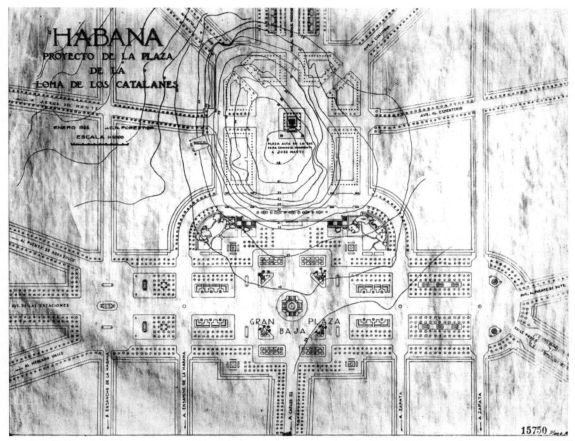

Figure 2.8 Original drawing of the Forestier Plan. Project of the Plaza de la Loma de los Catalanes, 1926. Ministerio de Obras Públicas. (*Source*: Archivo Roberto Segre)

Buenos Aires in 1924, when some of his ideas, inspired by the City Beautiful, were incorporated into the first 'Organic Project' elaborated by the *Comisión de Estética Edilicia* (Commission of Building Aesthetic), created for the Argentine capital in 1925.[85] By then, the '*Plan para el Embellecimiento y Ensanche de La*

of French and Cuban experts framed the three main chapters of the plan, namely circulation, open spaces and the general proposal which included amongst its aims converting Havana into a sort of Nice of the Americas and a Paris of the Caribbean . . . As Duverger points out, the everlasting example of Paris was still present, but this time not as Haussmann's capital but rather as the city that Forestier had analysed in his book *Grandes villes et systèmes de parcs* (1904).[86] Although modified during Forestier's second visit to Havana in 1928, and eventually cancelled in 1929, the plan stands as 'the most complete and best presented of all the efforts of the period, and it is still considered an important contribution to the growth of the city.'[87]

The *Beaux-Arts* tradition seemed to renew and enlarge its repertoire during Léon Jaussely's visit to Montevideo in 1926, when the founder of the *Sociéte Française des Urbanistes* (SFU) manifested his opposition to the colonial grid and his preference for the introduction of some garden city principles in relation to urban expansion.[88] Showing a more modernist image while in Buenos Aires, Jaussely not only spoke of the necessity of considering the future of the southern metropolis as 'a New York of South America', but also introduced zoning as a means of escaping from the centre and searching for open spaces where new buildings could be combined with parks. Jaussely's argument in the Argentine capital thus distanced itself from *Beaux-Arts* precepts, anticipating more functional issues that might be seen as preparing the local audience for Le Corbusier's visit in 1929.[89]

Invited by the Prefect Antonio Prado Junior to coordinate a technical team between 1926 and 1930, Donat-Alfred Agache masterminded a plan for Rio, which was a methodological model with many geographical surveys and an informative synthesis of the sprawling capital. As Margareth da Silva has pointed out, Agache saw the Brazilian metropolis as a laboratory, where he could experiment with circulation axes drawn from Eugène Hénard's proposals, as Le Corbusier would also do on his visits.[90] From a theoretical perspective, the

French edition of the plan – *La rémodelation d'une capitale* (1932) – claimed to combine biological concepts derived from Poëte's evolutionism with scientific methods taught at the *École Supérieure d'Urbanisme*. But the introduction to the plan made by the SFU's vice-president dwelt for too long upon his belief that the new discipline was also an art of embellishment, intuition and imagination – which probably prevented him from conveying a more definite message of modernity.[91]

A late example of the EFU's eclectic tradition can be seen in the first plan for Caracas (1939), drawn up by the Directorate of Urbanism of the capital's Federal District. Since the creation of the office in 1937, the team of local experts had been boosted by the advice of the Paris-based office of Henri Prost, whose junior associates, Jacques Lambert and Maurice Rotival, were sent to Caracas to coordinate the plan. The French advisers combined most of the ingredients of the EFU, which made possible the final arrival of Haussmannic surgery to the Venezuelan capital, after several decades of Frenchified aspirations in its urban culture.[92] The example of the Prefect of the Seine was invoked many times in the so-called '*Plan Monumental de Caracas*' (Monumental Plan of Caracas, 1939), whereas the example of Paris was often used to draw different conclusions about the plan's major dilemma between urban renewal or urban extension of the centre. The final project opted for a sort of renewal aimed at solving the growing traffic problems with the creation of eastward corridors, presided over by a monumental Champs-Elysées-like Avenida Central (figure 2.9).[93] But Haussmannic surgery arrived in Caracas too late. Playing down that delay was, perhaps, the major fault of Rotival's mission, at least in relation to the physical structure and dynamics of an embryonic

PROYECTO PARA LA AVENIDA PRINCIPAL
PERSPECTIVA

Figure 2.9 Perspective drawing of the Avenida Principal, included the first urban plan of Caracas, 1939. (*Source*: *Revista Municipal del Distrito Federal*, No. 1)

metropolis that could no longer be wrapped up in eclectic buildings and monumental axes.[94]

An alternative message of modernity is what South Americans tried to get from inviting Le Corbusier to visit Buenos Aires, Montevideo, São Paulo and Rio – a tour undertaken in 1929, while the Second *Congrès International d'Architecture Moderne* (CIAM) took place in Frankfurt. Invited and sponsored by the *Sociedad de Amigos del Arte* (Society of Friends of Art) and the School of Architecture, his visit was disregarded by the Central Society of Architects and its *Revista de Arquitectura*.[95] Le Corbusier criticized the colonial grid because it was not suitable for the destiny of Buenos Aires as a great city of the world. This has been interpreted as a 'syllogism' intended to justify his role as an 'architect-messiah' for the capital's trans-

formation.[96] The visitor presented a pre-conceived version of the 1925 '*Plan Voisin de Paris*' – which had attempted the introduction of 'a business city at the heart of town', a progressive initiative which, Le Corbusier claimed, had been rejected by Parisian academicians. But the visionary thought that the *Plan Voisin* could succeed in the New World; that with its massive city of towers dominating the Atlantic, the Buenos Aires of more than 3 million people could easily become 'one of the most deserving cities of the world', expected to replace the metropolitan role of New York, which had merely been 'the first gesture of contemporary civilization.'[97]

By focusing on his own visions for the Argentine capital, Le Corbusier probably tried to avoid any polemic with the proposals of Forestier and Jaussely; he was to do the same with Agache's plan for Rio, where he did not deliver a single lecture.[98] Whereas Agache had seen the Brazilian capital as a sort of laboratory, during his visits in 1929 and 1936 Le Corbusier conceived it as a 'manifesto', where he unfolded modernist principles drawn from Hénard's proposals – as Agache had also done – while introducing elements from the 'villes radieuses' that in some way anticipated the evolution of metropolitan Rio.[99]

In his *Précisions sur un état présent de l'architecture et de l'urbanisme* (1930), Le Corbusier reported his 1929 tour with an enthusiasm that mirrored his belief in the mission of French urbanism abroad, no matter what the differences among its representatives. Sailing back to Europe on board the liner *Lutetia* of the Compagnie Sud-Atlantique, Le Corbusier was still overexcited with fresh memories of the vast and heterodox continent – from his flights 1,000 metres high and at 200 kilometres per hour over the Parana and the Uruguay rivers, to his daring excursions into the negroes' *favellas* (squatter settlements) of Rio. Even frivolous experiences seemed to gain further meaning in the New World: in São Paulo, Le Corbusier had attended a performance by Josephine Baker 'in a silly variety show'; but this time she had sung '*Baby*' with 'such an intense and dramatic sensibility' that Le Corbusier was brought to tears. The architect then designed a choreography for the ebony goddess, when the two luminaries embarked together from São Paulo, on board the *Giulio Cesare*. In view of all these stimulating experiences, the champion of modernism confirmed that he had perceived in South America a renewed energy capable of doing away with all academic methods, '. . . in architecture, the methods from the stone age that have survived until

Haussmann . . .'[100] But, above all, the Frenchman felt proud of representing the spiritual value that the '*ville lumière*' still had in Latin America: 'This spiritual value of Paris has enabled me to say in Buenos Aires, in Montevideo, in São Paulo, in Rio, what I had to say, . . . This journey becomes a mission.' His crusade was in accordance with the South Americans' Latin vocation, which should prevent them from copying the Anglo-Saxon example of the North.[101] With such a plea, the CIAM leader seemed thus to confirm that the prestigious mission of French urbanism should prevail over his ideological differences with the EFU members – at least in the case of Latin America.

CIAM's legacy in Latin American capitals remained important during the 1940s, mainly through the visits of its representatives as advisers to new national or local planning bodies. In the second plan for Buenos Aires – prepared in 1939 by Argentine architects Kurchan and Ferrari and published in 1947 – the analysis of the 'cardiac system' of the inner city, including the integration of traditional avenues and new 'motorways', was complemented in the suburbs with the proposals *of 'villes radieuses'*, satellite towns and a green belt. The application of the principles of zoning differentiated the urban areas according to their functional coherence, putting aside the predominance traditionally given to the monumental articulation of spaces and axes like the Plaza and Avenida de Mayo.[102] Also Le Corbusier's several journeys to Bogotá crystallized in a plan in 1950.[103]

Meanwhile, the theoretical presence of CIAM would be consolidated with the Spanish edition of the *Charte d'Athènes* (1941), published in Argentina in 1954, and its Cuban adaptation in Martínez Inclán's *Código de Urbanismo*.[104] Following his role as

CIAM crusader among new generations of Cuban architects, José Luis Sert became adviser to the new *Junta Nacional de Planificación* (National Board of Planning) created by law in 1955 by Fulgencio Batista's dictatorship. In the 1957 master plan proposed by the Catalan urbanist, the former image of Havana as a Nice of the Caribbean was replaced by the myth of Las Vegas or Miami, aimed at creating a regional centre of tourism that included a complex of hotels, a business city in the style of Le Corbusier, and CIAM-inspired grids for the working-class residential suburbs.[105] Sert would also be adviser to the *Comisión Nacional de Urbanismo* (National Commission of Urbanism) – created in Venezuela by the new junta in 1946 – which became a platform for the implementation of modern principles in housing projects and public works led by Venezuelan architect Carlos Raúl Villanueva.[106] A belated example of this modern trend would be Lucio Costa's plan for Brasilia (1957), in which can be traced the influence of Le Corbusier and CIAM.[107]

Veterans of the German-speaking world also offered to foster the emerging urbanism of Latin America. Werner Hegemann, who was Editor of *Der Städtebau*, was invited to Buenos Aires in 1931, where he was hosted by '*Los Amigos de la Ciudad*' (The Friends of the City), a pragmatic society which was not satisfied with either the EFU's proposals or Le Corbusier's prefabricated plans. The man responsible for Hegemann's invitation was apparently Carlos María Della Paolera, an Argentinian engineer who had graduated at the *Institut d'Urbanisme*, was acquainted with the ideas of the *Musée Social* and the SFU, and also knew of Hegemann's combined scientific and humanist approach to planning.[108] During his four months in Buenos

Aires, Rosario and Mar del Plata, Hegemann tried to be tactful in relation to proposals by former visitors, while focusing on the unique aspects of the Argentine context. In his first lecture on 18 September 1931, he criticized the densities allowed by the urban regulations of Buenos Aires, one of the causes of its shortage of public spaces. His reappraisal of the colonial *damero* (checkerboard) was understood as a subtle criticism of Bouvard's Haussmannesque diagonals, while his new '*Plano Regulador*' (Master Plan) was a more comprehensive instrument than Le Corbusier's architectural sketches. The use of the system of parks as a structural element – not as a feature of urban design – has been interpreted as a hidden allusion and a shift in relation to the greenery of Bouvard and Forestier.[109] References to the German world were unavoidable: the projection of the film *Die Stadt von Morgen* (1930) – a silent movie produced by architects Kotzer and von Goldbeck, reporting the advantages of long-range planning in the Rühr basin – was an unsuccessful attempt to convey the importance of the regional background for local urbanism. At the same time, the *Stadtbahns* of Vienna and Berlin were recommended as examples for the inner-city railroads which should link Buenos Aires with satellite towns. Although his visit did not leave any concrete result, Hegemann's view of Buenos Aires remained as a lesson of comprehensive urbanism for the local audience, since his lectures and proposals epitomized the 'pragmatic ideal' that conciliated scientific and rational considerations in urban planning with humanist and aesthetic values.[110]

Karl Brunner was another representative of what has been labelled 'Austrian-German rationalism' in Latin America, where he came to represent the last descendant of that national lineage that dated back to Sitte and Wagner. In view of the Chilean capital's lack of urban spaces and landmarks, Brunner's 1933 plan for Santiago proposed 'to architecturalize' the space and to configure new centres and axes, while open spaces were given great importance in shaping the city.[111] In addition to his achievement in securing the approval of his plan in 1939, throughout the 1930s Brunner contributed to the consolidation of urban planning in Chile, by advising institutions and organizing events that underpinned what probably was Latin America's best professional platform, whose administrative roots dated back to the nineteenth century.[112] During the same decade, Brunner masterminded both the municipal office and plan for Bogotá, where he had translated his *Manual de Urbanismo* (1939–1940) – a very popular textbook among Latin American planners by those years. Having jumped from 100,000 inhabitants in 1900 to 300,000 in 1930, as we already mentioned, Bogotá sprawled with morphological voids and functional problems among different areas, which is why Brunner decided to introduce connections between the traditional centre, the nineteenth-century expansion and the suburban growth of the twentieth. In a 1940s proposal, he completed this task of patching and connecting the fragments of the urban structure, by introducing an alternative axis that connected the core of the city with the satellite town of El Salitre.[113] In 1941 Brunner also drew up a plan for Panama City.[114]

When celebrating, in a special issue of *L'architecture d'aujourd'hui*, the twenty years of the '*Loi Cornudet*', which since 1919 had turned planning into a statutory activity in France, Marcel Poëte regretted the political circumstances which had caused his country's urbanism to lag 'behind other European countries'; still, the urban historian and urbanist looked with great hope at the potential task of fellow countrymen who intended 'to carry out abroad what they cannot do at home.' Invoking the 'universal quality' of the French spirit hinted at by Pascal in the seventeenth century, Poëte tried to convey to the French urbanist how his work around the world should be performed 'in accordance with the genius of his country'.[115] Some years later, Gaston Bardet expressed his firm belief that the urbanist's work was a cornerstone of the 'real mission' of *la France* as an ambassador of Western civilization, not only in the colonial dependencies but also in other parts of the world. In this respect, one of France's traditional devotees still was Latin America, where Bardet had heard the clamour for the French mission 'in the streets in Buenos Aires as well as in the salons of embassies in México City, in the confidential remarks in Santiago or in Caracas . . .'[116] Despite their enthusiastic plea, these urban historians knew that French urbanism was just awaking from its prolonged *Beaux-Arts* lethargy, which Bardet aptly christened '*Haussmannisme amélioré*' (improved Haussmannization), whose diagonals, *rond-points* and academic forms still ruled in the domains of French urbanism around the world.[117]

Apart from the historians, for nearly two decades Le Corbusier had denounced this use of never-ending axes as 'a calamity of architecture'.[118] However – as we have seen – this *Haussmannisme amélioré* apparently inspired some of the proposals of the EFU members in Latin American capitals from the turn of the century. Notwithstanding the delay in its arrival and the differences between its representatives, the Haussmannic urbanism of the EFU helped to consolidate the cultural mission of *la France* in Latin America, as Le Corbusier well recognized after his first tour. When adding the contributions of the more technical tradition represented by Hegemann and Brunner, the significance and prestige of this mission can be extended to European urbanism in general, at least during the cycle that lasted until World War II. Even though CIAM architecture continued to be a seductive influence on new generations of Latin American professionals throughout the middle of the twentieth century, in the post-war era CIAM urbanism would become only one among other options of vernacular and international modernity, most of which would arrive via the United States.[119]

The end of the phase of predominance of European urbanism was clearly perceived by Violich in his tour across Latin American capitals, one of whose impressions opened the previous chapter. When he met some of the local planners on his 1941–1942 journey, the Californian planner noticed that Latin professionals were 'European-trained, or prepared for the technical field in their own country by European-trained professors.' In addition to their thorough technicality, Latin professionals frequently had 'a broader understanding of their own and related fields than would be provided in similar training in the United States.' More than their North American colleagues, Latin urbanists also tended 'to philosophize about the significance of the city's pattern, about the broad human objective of planning.' Knowing European capitals 'by heart', most of the planners Violich talked to were still influenced by the philosophical and artistic tradition of French urbanism, epitomized in books such as Poëte's *Paris. Son évolution créatrice* (1938), which the visitor found in some of the planners' libraries. Thus, even in the early 1940s,

the urbanist mission of France in Latin America was not only proclaimed by Le Corbusier, by representatives of the EFU or by the French historians, but also confirmed by a North American planner. However, the missions of European urbanism were not to last for long, at least among the 'younger practising architects and planners', who started to 'look towards the United States rather than to Europe.'[120]

This turning point was to be confirmed by Violich when called by the Venezuelan government to advise, in the late 1940s, the first National Commission of Urbanism. As he was to summarize three decades later, the dilemma before the Venezuelan urban planners in those years was 'the question of a conceptual approach on which to base the institutional process. A latter-day *Beaux Arts* movement inspired the late 1930s, and a social orientation, the mid-1940s, only to give way in the early 1950s to a functional approach drawing on North American techniques.'[121] Although it can be argued that Venezuelan society underwent a conspicuous Americanization due to the oil boom, this shift towards the United States as the main exporter of urbanism can be generalized to most countries of Latin America in those decades.[122] After nearly a century of European predominance in the urban culture and urbanism of the young republics, Paris was no longer the ideal for young planners of Latin America.

NOTES

1. Parts of this chapter are taken from my book Almandoz, A. (1997) *Urbanismo europeo en Caracas (1870–1940)*. Caracas: Fundarte, Equinoccio, Ediciones de la Universidad Simón Bolívar. The book is the translation of my PhD thesis, Almandoz, A. (1996) European Urbanism in Caracas, 1870s–1930s, Architectural Association School of Architecture, Open University,

London. The thesis was supervised by Dr. Nicholas Bullock, King's College, Cambridge.

2. Rippy, J.F. (1959) *British Investments in Latin America, 1822–1949. A Case Study in the Operations of Private Enterprise in Retarded Regions*. Minneapolis: University of Minnesota Press, pp. 12, 116.

3. Cané, M. (1883, 1942) *En viaje*. Buenos Aires: Editorial Molino, p. 11.

4. Mulhall, M.G. (1878) *The English in South America*. Buenos Aires: Standard Office, p. 530.

5. Morse, R.M. (1975) El desarrollo de los sistemas urbanos en las Américas durante el siglo XIX, in Hardoy, J.E. and Schaedel, R.P. (eds.) *Las ciudades de América Latina y sus áreas de influencia a través de la historia*. Buenos Aires: Sociedad Interamericana de Planificación (SIAP), pp. 263–290.

6. Hardoy, J.E. (1975) Two thousand years of Latin American urbanization, in Hardoy, J.E. (ed.) *Urbanization in Latin America. Approaches and Issues*. New York: Anchor Books, pp. 3–55.

7. Roberts, B. (1978) *Cities of Peasants. The Political Economy of Urbanization in the Third World*. London: Edward Arnold, pp. 47–48.

8. Most figures are taken from Morse, R.M. (1971) Latin American cities in the 19th century: approaches and tentative generalizations, in Morse, R.M., Coniff, M.L. and Wibel, J. (eds.) *The Urban Development of Latin America 1750–1920*. Stanford: Center for Latin American Studies, Stanford University, pp. 1–21.

9. Stein, S.J.and B.H. (1970) *The Colonial Heritage of Latin America. Essays on Economic Dependence in Perspective*. New York: Oxford University Press, 1970, pp.105, 137, 168. See also Pagden, A. (1995) *Lords of all the World. Ideologies of Empire in Spain, Britain and France c.1500–c.1800*. London: Yale University Press.

10. Rippy, J.F. (1944) *Latin America and the Industrial Age*. New York: Putnam's Sons, p. 239; *British Investments in Latin America, 1822–1949, loc. cit.*, pp. 11, 36.

11. Mulhall, *op. cit.*, p. 599.

12. Rippy, *Latin America and the Industrial Age, loc. cit.*, pp. 19, 189. See also Griffin, C.C. (1961) *The National Period in the History of the New World. An Outline and Commentary*. México, D.F.: Instituto Panamericano de Geografía e Historia.

13. Hussey, R.D. (1942) Traces of French enlightment in colonial Hispanic America, in Whitaker, A.P. (ed.) *Latin America and the Enlightment*. New York: D. Appleton-Century Company, pp. 23–51; Pagden, *op. cit.*, pp. 178–200.

14. Sarmiento, D.F. (1845, 1889) *Facundo, o Civilización y Barbarie*. Buenos Aires: Félix Lajouane, Editor, pp. 98–102.

15. Ugarte, M. (1911) *El porvenir de la América Latina*. Valencia: F. Sempere y Compañía, Editores, p. 77.

16. García Calderón, F. (1913) *Latin America: Its Rise and Progress* (trans. Bernard Miall). London: Fisher Unwin, p. 287.

17. Gil Fortoul, J. (1896) *El hombre y la historia. Ensayo de sociología venezolana*. París: Libreria de Garnier Hermanos, pp. 29–30.

18. Ugarte, *op. cit.*, p. 62.

19. Griffin, *op. cit.*, pp. 83–84.

20. Bradford Burns, E. (1990) *La pobreza del progreso. América Latina en el siglo XIX*. México: Siglo Veintiuno Editores, p. 29–30.

21. Romero, J.L. (1976, 1984) *Latinoamérica: las ciudades y las ideas*. México: Siglo Veintinuo Editores, pp. 274–299.

22. Munro, D. (1964) *Intervention and Dollar Diplomacy in the Caribbean, 1900–1921*. Princeton: Princeton University Press, pp. 4–7, 65–66.

23. Rippy, *British Investments in Latin America, 1822–1949, loc. cit.*, pp. 11, 36, 75; Carl, G.E. (1980) *First Among Equals: Great Britain and Venezuela 1810–1910*. Syracuse, N.Y.: Syracuse University, pp. 139–140.

24. Herwig, H. (1986) *Germany's Vision of Empire in Venezuela, 1871–1914*. Princeton: Princeton University Press, pp. 207–208.

25. Bradford Burns, *op. cit.*, p. 17.

26. Unlike the meaning it has in the history of English literature, 'modernism' was a movement launched in the 1900s by Darío, on the basis of French influences – symbolism, Parnassianism and impressionism – that gathered writers from Latin America and Spain.

27. Darío, R. (1898, 1989) El triunfo de Calibán, in *El modernismo y otros ensayos*. Madrid: Alianza, pp. 161, 166.

28. Kidd, B. (1898) *The Control of the Tropics*. New York: Macmillan & Co., pp. 41–58.

29. Zumeta, C. (1899) *El continente enfermo*. New York, p. 17.

30. Rodó, J.E. (1900, 1912) *Ariel*. Valencia: F. Sempere y Compañía, Editores, pp. 66–68, 87, 94–95.

31. Ugarte, *op. cit.*, pp. 113–145.

32. Blanc-Chaléard, M.-C. (1992) L'image de la puissance française dans les manuels d'histoire et de

géographie autour de 1900, in Milza, P. and Poidevin, R. (eds.) *La puissance française à la 'Belle Epoque'. Mythe ou réalité?*. Paris: Editions Complexe, pp. 63–79.

33. García Calderón, *op. cit.*, p. 311.

34. As it has been pointed out by Romero, *op. cit.*, pp. 370–372.

35. Most of these figures are drawn from Hardoy, J.E. (1990) Theory and practice of urban planning in Europe, 1850–1930: its transfer to Latin America, in Hardoy, J.E. and Morse, R.M. (eds.) *Rethinking the Latin American City*. Washington: The Woodrow Wilson Center, The John Hopkins University Press, pp. 20–49, 22; Hardoy, Two thousand years of Latin American urbanization, *loc. cit.*, pp. 50–51. See also Almandoz, *Urbanismo europeo en Caracas (1870–1940)*, *loc. cit.*, pp. 233, 255.

36. Romero, *op. cit.*, pp. 370–372.

37. Wilson, W.E. (1942, 1972) *Ambassadors in White. The Story of American Tropical Medicine*. New York: Kenikat Press.

38. Semprún, J. (1918, 1983) El Norte y el Sur. Los Estados Unidos y la América Latina. Divagaciones sobre un tema de actualidad (1918), in *Pensamiento político venezolano del siglo XIX. La doctrina positivista*. Caracas: Congreso de la República, Vol XIV, pp. 507–527.

39. See for instance Palma, G. (1978) Dependency: a formal theory of underdevelopment or a methodology for the analysis of concrete situations of under-development? *World Development*, 7/8, pp. 881–920. A recent review of the 'dependency school' in urban terms can be seen in Potter R.B. and Lloyd-Evans, S. (1998) *The City in the Developing World*. London: Longman, pp. 43–47.

40. Quijano, A. (1977) *Dependencia, urbanización y cambio social en Latinoamérica*. Lima: Mosca Azul, p.156.

41. Palma, *op. cit.*, p. 910.

42. Morse, El desarrollo de los sistemas urbanos en las Américas durante el siglo XIX, *loc. cit.*, pp. 270–271.

43. Cardoso, F.H. and Faletto, E. (1969) *Dependencia y desarrollo en América Latina*. México: Siglo XXI, pp. 42–48.

44. Bradford Burns, *op. cit.*, pp. 21–22.

45. Quijano, *op. cit.*, pp.158, 165–166; Bradford Burns, *op. cit.*, p.17.

46. According to the periodization and urban changes highlighted by Hardoy, Two thousand years of Latin American urbanization, *loc. cit.*, pp. 48–50. From an architectural perspective, see Fernández, R. (1999) Cartografías del tiempo. Notas sobre sociedad, territorio, ciudad y arquitectura americanas. *Astrágalo. Cultura de la arquitectura y la ciudad*, 11, pp. 121–143.

47. Haussmann, Baron G.E. de (1890–1893, 1979) *Mémoires*. Paris: Guy Durier, 2 vols, Vol. I, pp. 28–29, Vol. II, p. 53.

48. Choay, F. (1969, 1989) *The Modern City. Planning in the 19th Century*. New York: George Braziller, 1989, pp. 15–18.

49. Haussmann, *op. cit.*, Vol. I, pp. 55–100; Vol II, pp. 124–125.

50. Londei, E. (1982) *La Parigi di Haussmann. La trasformazione urbanistica di Parigi durante il secondo Impero*. Roma: Kappa, pp. 102–107; Pinkney, D.H. (1958) *Napoleon III and the Rebuilding of Paris*. Princeton: Princeton University Press, pp. 220–221.

51. In this respect, see Roncayolo, M. (1983) La production de la ville, in Agulhon. M. (ed.) *Histoire de la France urbaine. La ville de l'age industriel. Le cycle haussmannien*. Paris: Seuil, Vol. IV, pp. 77–157; Sutcliffe, A. (1970) *The Autumn of Central Paris: The Defeat of Town Planning 1850–1970*. London: Edward Arnold.

52. Sica, P. (1978) *Storia dell'urbanistica: il Novecento*. Bari: Laterza, Vol. II, pp. 773–774.

53. Romero, *op. cit.*, pp. 282–284.

54. Gutiérrez, R. (1983) *Arquitectura y Urbanismo en Iberoamérica*. Madrid: Cátedra, pp. 515–518.

55. There is a good analysis of the Haussmannian myth in Buenos Aires and other Latin American capitals in Gorelik, A. (1999) *La grilla y el parque. Espacio público y cultura urbana en Buenos Aires, 1887–1936*. Buenos Aires: Universidad Nacional de Quilmes, pp. 115–124.

56. Needell, J. (1987) *A Tropical* Belle Époque. *Elite, Culture and Society in Turn-of-the-Century*. Rio de Janeiro. Cambridge: Cambridge University Press, pp. 33–51.

57. Almandoz, *Urbanismo europeo en Caracas (1870–1940)*, *loc. cit.*, pp. 120–125.

58. Haussmann, *op. cit.*

59. Hardoy, Theory and practice of urban planning in Europe, 1850–1930, *loc. cit.* pp. 25, 31.

60. Wilson, *op. cit.*, pp. 33–35.

61. (1938) *Conferencias Internacionales Americanas*. Washington: Dotación Carnegie para la Paz Internacional, Vol . I: 1889–1936, p. 98.

62. Ronzón, J. (1997) La fiebre amarilla en los puertos de Veracruz y La Habana 1900–1910. *Tierra Firme*,

XV(57), pp. 33–56; Almandoz, A. (2000) The shaping of Venezuelan urbanism in the hygiene debate of Caracas, 1880–1910. *Urban Studies,* 37(11), pp. 2073–2089; Parker, D. (1998) Civilizing the city of kings: hygiene and housing in Lima, Peru, in Pineo, R. and Baer, J. (eds.) *Cities of Hope. People, Protests and Progress in Urbanizing Latin America, 1870–1930.* Boulder: Westview Press, pp. 153–177; Elmore, P. (1991) Lima: puertas a la modernidad. Modernización y experiencia urbana a principios de siglo. *Cuadernos Americanos,* 30, pp. 104–123.

63. Kessel, C. (2000) Carlos Sampaio and urbanism in Rio de Janeiro (1875–1930). *Planning History,* 22(1), pp. 17–26.

64. Figueroa, J. (1995) La Ciudad Lineal en Chile (1910–1930). *DANA. Documentos de Arquitectura Nacional y Americana,* 37/38, pp. 64–70.

65. Gutiérrez, R. (1996) Modelos e imaginarios europeos en el urbanismo americano 1900–1950. *Revista de Arquitectura,* 8, pp. 2–3.

66. Ragon, M. (1971–1978, 1991) *Histoire de l'archi-tecture et de l'urbanisme modernes. Naissance de la cité moderne.* Paris: Caterman, Vol. 2, p. 163.

67. Berjman, S. (1998) *Plazas y parques de Buenos Aires: la obra de los paisajistas franceses. André, Courtois, Thays, Bouvard, Forestier, 1860–1930.* Buenos Aires: Gobierno de la Ciudad de Buenos Aires, Fondo de Cultura Económica, pp. 175–213; Berjman, S. (1995) Proyectos de Bouvard para la Buenos Aires del Centenario: Barrio, plazas, hospital y exposición. *DANA. Documentos de Arquitectura Nacional y Americana,* 37/38, pp. 41–53.

68. Rodrigues Porto, A. (1992) *História urbanística da cidade de São Paulo (1554 a 1988).* São Paulo: Carthago & Forte, pp. 107–108; Segawa, H. (1995) 1911: Bouvard em São Paulo. *DANA. Documentos de Arquitectura Nacional y Americana,* 37/38, pp. 31–35.

69. Berjman, *Plazas y parques de Buenos Aires: la obra de los paisajistas franceses, loc. cit.,* pp. 215–271; Berjman, S. (1994) En la ciudad de Buenos Aires, in B. Leclerc (ed.) *Jean Claude Nicolas Forestier, 1861–1930. Du jardin au paysage urbain.* Paris: Picard, pp. 207–219.

70. Duverger, H. (1994) El maestro francés del urban-ismo criollo para La Habana, in B. Leclerc, *op. cit.,* pp. 221–240.

71. Amato, P. (1970) Elitism and settlement patterns in the Latin American city. *Journal of the American Institute of Planners,* XXXVI(2), pp. 96–105; Harris, Jr., W.D. (1971) *The Growth of Latin American Cities.* Athens: Ohio University Press.

72. Johns, M. (1997) *The City of Mexico in the Age of Díaz.* Austin: University of Texas Press; Rodrigues Porto, *op. cit.,* pp.81–82; Almandoz, *Urbanismo europeo en Caracas (1870–1940), loc. cit.,* pp. 237–240.

73. Segre, R. and Baroni, S. (1998) Cuba y La Habana. Historia, población y territorio. *Ciudad y Territorio. Estudios Territoriales,* XXX(116), pp. 351–379.

74. Hardoy, Theory and practice of urban planning in Europe, 1850–1930, *loc. cit.,* pp. 26–27; Sica, *op. cit.,* pp. 789–790.

75. Rodrigues Porto, *op. cit.,* p. 74; Segawa, *op. cit.,* pp. 34–35.

76. Sutcliffe, A. (1981) *Towards the Planned City: Germany, Britain, the United States and France, 1780–1914.* Oxford: Blackwell, pp. 190–194; Choay, Pensées sur la ville, arts de la ville, in Agulhon, *op. cit.,* pp. 158–271.

77. Among several articles that deal with different case studies in specific national contexts, we can mention two of the earliest: Caraballo, C. (1986) Del academicismo retórico al profesionalismo pragmático. Crisis recurrente de la educación venezolana de la inge-niería y la arquitectura. *Boletín del Centro de Investigaciones Históricas y Estéticas,* 27, pp. 52–77; Pavez, M.I. (1992) Precursores de la enseñanza del urbanismo en Chile. Período 1928–1953. *Revista de Arquitectura,* 3, pp. 2–11.

78. According to the distinction between 'pre-urbanism' and 'urbanism' established by Choay, F. (1965, 1979) *L'urbanisme, utopies et réalités. Une anthologie.* Paris: Éditions du Seuil, pp. 30–31.

79. Gutiérrez, Modelos e imaginarios europeos en urbanismo americano 1900–1950, *loc. cit.*

80. Hardoy, Theory and Practice of Urban Planning in Europe, 1850–1930, *loc. cit.,* pp. 22–46.

81. Sutcliffe, A. (1980) Introduction: the debate on nineteenth-century planning, in Sutcliffe, A. (ed.) *The Rise of Modern Urban Planning: 1800–1914.* London: Mansell, pp. 1–10; Sutcliffe, *Towards the Planned City, loc. cit.,* pp. 203–204.

82. Violich, F. (1944) *Cities of Latin America. Housing and Planning to the South.* New York: Reinhold Publishing Corporation, pp. 157–170.

83. Some of the works by these pioneers have been edited; see for instance Della Paolera, C.M. (1977) *Buenos Aires y sus problemas urbanos.* Buenos Aires: OIKOS; Lovera, A. (comp.) (1996) *Leopoldo Martínez Olavarría. Desarrollo urbano, vivienda y estado.* Caracas: Fondo Editorial ALEMO.

84. Choay, Pensées sur la ville, arts de la ville, *loc. cit.*

85. Gorelik, *op. cit.*, pp. 318–330.

86. Duverger, H. (1995) La insoportable solidez de lo que el viento se llevó. J.C.N. Forestier y la ciudad de La Habana. *DANA. Documentos de Arquitectura Nacional y Americana*, 37/38, pp. 71–82.

87. Préstamo, F.J. (1995) City planning in a revolution: Cuba, 1959–61. *Planning Perspectives*, 8(2), pp. 188–212, 190.

88. Gutiérrez, Modelos e imaginarios europeos en urbanismo americano 1900–1950, *loc. cit.*, p. 2.

89. Gutiérrez, R. (1995) Buenos Aires. Modelo para armar (1910–1927). *DANA. Documentos de Arquitectura Nacional y Americana*, 37/38, pp. 36–40.

90. Silva, M. da (1995) Pensando a metrópole moderna: os planos de Agache e Le Corbusier para o Rio de Janeiro. *DANA. Documentos de Arquitectura Nacional y Americana*, 37/38, pp. 97–105.

91. Agache, D.-A. (1932) *La rémodelation d'une capitale*. Paris: Société Coopérative d'Architectes, Vol. I, pp. xviii–xx, 93

92. Almandoz, A. (1999) Longing for Paris: the Europeanized dream of Caracas urbanism, 1870–1940. *Planning Perspectives,* 14(3), pp. 225–248.

93. (1939) Plan Monumental de Caracas. *Revista Municipal del Distrito Federal*, 1, pp. 17 ff.

94. Among the several works interpreting Rotival's plan for Caracas, see (1991) *El Plan Rotival. La Caracas que no fue*. Caracas: Instituto de Urbanismo, Universidad Central de Venezuela; Almandoz, A. (1999) Transfer of urban ideas: the emergence of Venezuelan urbanism in the proposals for 1930s' Caracas. *International Planning Studies* 4(1), pp. 79–94; Almandoz, *Urbanismo europeo en Caracas (1870–1940), loc. cit.*, pp. 293–308.

95. Pérez Oyarzun, F. (1991) Le Corbusier y Sudamérica en el viaje del 29, in Pérez Oyarzun, F. (ed.) *Le Corbusier y Sudamérica, viajes y proyectos*. Santiago de Chile: ARQ, Escuela de Arquitectura, Pontificia Universidad Católica de Chile, pp. 15–41.

96. Nicolini, A. (1995) Le Corbusier: Utopía y Buenos Aires. *DANA. Documentos de Arquitectura Nacional y Americana*, 37/38, pp. 106–113.

97. Le Corbusier (C.E. Jeanneret) (1930) *Précisions sur un état présent de l'architecture et de l'urbanisme*. Paris: G. Crès & Cie, pp. 167, 172–174, 202 (quotation author's translation)

98. Pérez Oyarzun, *op. cit.*, pp. 25–27.

99. Rodríguez, C., Silva, M. da, Veriano, R. and Caldeira, V. El viaje de 1936 (1991), in Pérez Oyarzun, *op. cit.*, pp. 42–49; Silva, Pensando a metrópole moderna, *loc. cit.*, pp. 102–104; Tsiomis, Y. (ed.) (1998) *Le Corbusier. Rio de Janeiro: 1929, 1936*. Rio de Janeiro: Secretaria Municipal de Urbanismo, Centro de Arquitetura e Urbanismo do Rio de Janeiro.

100. Le Corbusier, *Précisions sur un état présent de l'architecture et de l'urbanisme, loc. cit.*, pp. 12–14 (author's translation); Pérez Oyarzun, *op. cit.*, pp. 20–25.

101. Le Corbusier, *Précisions sur un état présent de l'architecture et de l'urbanisme, loc. cit.*, pp. 2, 245 (author's translation).

102. Liernur, F. and Pschepiurca, P. Le Corbusier y el plan de Buenos Aires (1991), in Pérez Oyarzun, *op. cit.*, pp. 56–71; Nicolini, *op. cit.*, pp. 110–111.

103. Bannen, P. (1991) Bogotá–Colombia: Cinco viajes y un plan, in Pérez Oyarzun, *op. cit.*, pp. 72–85; Cortés, R. (1991) Bogotá 1950: Plan Director de Le Corbusier, in Pérez Oyarzun, *op. cit.*, pp. 86–94.

104. Gutiérrez, Modelos e imaginarios europeos en urbanismo americano 1900–1950, *loc. cit.*, p. 3

105. Segre, R. (1995) La Habana de Sert: CIAM, ron y cha cha chá. *DANA. Documentos de Arquitectura Nacional y Americana,* 37/38, pp. 120–124.

106. González, L. (1996) Modernity and the City. Caracas 1935–1958. Unpublished PhD Thesis. Ithaca, Cornell University, Ithaca, N.Y.; López, M. (1995) Gestión urbanística, revolución democrática y dictadura militar en Venezuela (1945–1958). *Urbana*, 14/15, pp. 106–119.

107. Segre, R. (1998) Huellas difusas: La herencia de Le Corbisier en Brasilia. *Revista de Arquitectura*, 10, pp. 4–11; Figueroa, J. (1998) Brasilia transfer. Las raíces clásicas del Movimiento Moderno. *Revista de Arquitectura*, 10, pp. 12–15.

108. Collins, C.C. (1995) Urban interchange in the Southern Cone: Le Corbusier (1929) and Werner Hegemann (1931) in Argentina. *Journal of the Society of Architectural Historians,* 54(2), pp. 208–227; Tartarini, J.D. (1995) La visita de Werner Hegemann a la Argentina en 1931. *DANA. Documentos de Arquitectura Nacional y Americana*, 37/38, pp. 54–63.

109. Tartarini, *op. cit.*, pp. 58–59.

110. Collins, *op. cit.*, pp. 210–219; Tartarini, *op. cit.*, pp. 61–63.

111. Figueroa, J. (1995) La recomposición de la forma urbana. K.H. Brunner 1932–1942. *DANA. Documentos*

de Arquitectura Nacional y Americana, 37/38, pp. 83–91.

112. Gurovich, A. (1996) La venida de Karl Brunner en gloria y majestad. La influencia de sus lecciones en la profesionalización del urbanismo en Chile. *Revista de Arquitectura,* 8, pp. 8–13.

113. Figueroa, La recomposición de la forma urbana. K.H. Brunner 1932–1942, *loc. cit.,* pp. 88–89; Cortés, F. (1996) La construcción de la ciudad como espacio público. *Revista de Arquitectura,* 8, pp. 14–19.

114. Uribe, A. (1996) El Plan Brunner para la ciudad de Panamá. *Revista de Arquitectura,* 8, pp. 20–21.

115. Poëte, M. (1939) L'esprit de l'urbanisme français. *L'Architecture d'Aujourd'hui,* 3, pp. III–4–5 (author's translation).

116. Bardet, G. (1951) *Naissance et méconnaissance de l'urbanisme.* Paris: SABRI, p. 396 (author's translation).

117. Bardet, G. (1939) Vingt ans d'urbanisme appliqué. *L'Architecture d'Aujourd'hui,* 3, pp. III–2–3 (author's translation).

118. Le Corbusier (1923) *Vers une architecture.* Paris: Les Éditions G. Cres et Cie., p. 51 (author's translation).

119. Hardoy, Theory and practice of urban planning in Europe, 1850–1930, *loc. cit.,* pp. 37–39.

120. Violich, *Cities of Latin America, loc. cit.,* pp. 158, 169, 173.

121. Violich, F. (1975) Caracas: Focus of the New Venezuela, in H. Wentworth Elredge (ed.) *World Capitals. Toward Guided Urbanization.* New York: Anchor Press, Doubleday, pp. 246–292, 285.

122. Gutiérrez, Modelos e imaginarios europeos en urbanismo americano 1900–1950, *loc. cit.;* Almandoz, A. (1998) From urbanism to planning: the Caracas shift (1930s–1940s), in Freestone, R. (ed.) *20th Century Urban Planning Experience. 8th International Planning History Conference.* Sidney: International Planning History Society, University of New South Wales, pp. 7–12.

Buenos Aires, A Great European City

Ramón Gutiérrez

'Buenos Aires, a great European city' – these words, spoken by George Clemençeau in 1911, would mark the climax of the efforts made by Argentina's elite leaders in their search to achieve a vision which was civilized and ultimately unmistakeably European.[1]

This chapter describes the way in which this vision was achieved, tracing the ideas and work which have led to Buenos Aires being recognized even today as the most European city in Latin America.

ଔ BUENOS AIRES: FROM THE CAPITAL OF THE VICEROYALTY ଙ
OF RIO DE LA PLATA TO THE 'GRAN ALDEA'

The city of Santa María de los Buenos Aires, founded for the second time in 1580 on its present site, became the politicial capital of the viceroyalty of Río de la Plata, which had been created by the Spanish Crown in 1776 (figure 3.1). As political capital, the city's strategic importance as a port would be increased and it would be in a position to deal with the serious border conflicts which existed in the region between the kings of Spain and Portugal.[2]

The creation of this viceroyalty was intended to strengthen urban growth, and therefore the openness granted by the Free Trade Ordinace of 1778 was needed to legalize methods of exchange and so put paid to the traditional smuggling carried out between the Spanish colonies and Brazil. As the capital of this viceroyalty, the city would serve as the site for important public buildings bringing together governmental bodies and public amenities such as the Aduana (Customs), Correos (Post Office), Renta de Tobaco (Tobacco Tax Office), the Consulado de Buenos Aires (Buenos Aires Consulate), Colegios Reales (Royal Colleges), the Plaza de Toros (the Bull Ring), the Corral de Comedias (Comedy Theatre) and the Recova de Comercio (Trading Market). These helped to enhance a modest urban landscape where the main recreation site was the short tree-lined avenue along the river and beside the old fort, at that time the residence of the Viceroys.

The rapid mercantile expansion that brought about the opening of the port, together with

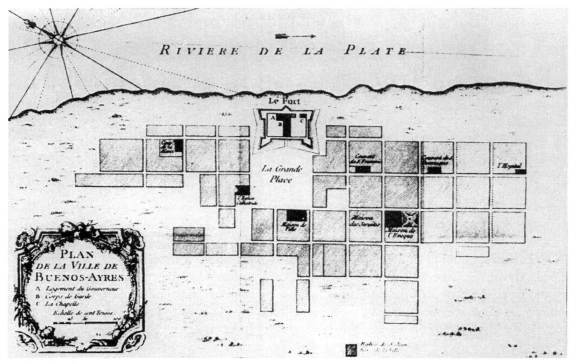

Figure 3.1 Buenos Aires in 1650. Plan by a French spy named Massiac, who gave it to Vauban. Published by Charlevoix in 1756. (*Source*: Archivo del Centro de Documentación de Arquitectura Latinoamericana, CEDODAL)

the geopolitical importance of the enclave for the dominance of the southern part of the continent – demonstrated by two unsuccessful attempts at invasion by the British in 1806 and 1807 – made possible the emergence of a Creole sector who would rapidly seize their Independence from the Spanish crown – as soon as Napoleon's invasion led to the fall of King Fernando VII in 1808.

Although reminders of the war were evident in Buenos Aires during the first years after Independence, the city soon began to establish itself, successively extending its internal borders onto those of the indigenous people, which at the end of the colonial era were little more than 40 kilometres from the city.

Urban Projects of the Nineteenth Century

For several of the leaders of the newly independent country the Spanish grid layout represented an obstacle that should be modified while, paradoxically, the recently created

Departamento de Ingenieros y Agrimensores (Engineering and Surveying Department) sought 'scientific' prestige in its geometrical designs.[3] It is also curious that the urban expansion of European cities in the nineteenth century followed the positive experience of the American checkerboard design (for example Plan Castro in Madrid and Plan Cerdá in Barcelona).

The grid as an urban symbol became part of nineteenth-century planning thought and of the first development projects in Buenos Aires on the Río de la Plata; for example that carried out by the English businessman Micklejohn in 1824, which showed signs of the desire to 'square' that curious 'new town'. The idea of Buenos Aires as the centre was accepted and, at the same time, a new and speculative division of the land into lots introduced.[4]

However, the ambitions of the leaders to transform the city into a mirror image of a European metropolis, prevailed during a large part of Bernardino Rivadavia's municipal administration as Minister and President (1826–1827), and that of the groups searching for political unification. They aimed at reproducing in Buenos Aires the image of a country they aspired to be more progressive, even if that meant that it might become smaller. At that time thoughts such as 'the bad thing about the country is its size . . .' or '. . . beyond the port, progress is impossible' were voiced. In the midst of such debate (between unionists, federalists and oligarchs), Buenos Aires was confirmed as the prestigious icon of an Europeanized elite.

In the second decade of the nineteenth century, the arrival of English, French and Italian technicians brought in by Rivadavia, would emphasize this desire to create a

Figure 3.2 *Conventillo* located in a southern neighborhood in Buenos Aires by 1890. (*Source*: Archivo del Centro de Documentación de Arquitectura Latinoamericana, CEDODAL)

European and cosmopolitan country, and this would, in itself, ensure progress and overcome colonial backwardness. A plan drawn by James Bevans around 1828, reveals a city with a checkerboard design, rectangular blocks and several plazas designed diagonally. This was a foretaste of the imagery or vision of the new cultural leaders. However, a large part of this enthusiasm for the renewal of the urban image was shipwrecked on the stormy seas of the local bureaucracies, political discontinuity, the civil wars, and the lack of funds to carry out some of the models coming from abroad, which showed little viability in the Argentine context.

There are obvious signs by which to measure the slowness of certain technological transformations and to explain why these changes were barely started in the second half of the nineteenth century. The first three-storey house was built in Buenos Aires in 1838,

which reveals the squat nature of the city whose urban landscape was still dominated by church towers and domes. The example of industrial architecture was introduced in 1857 when the roof of the Teatro Colón (Colon Theatre) was imported from Dublin. Carlos Enrique Pellegrini, the French engineer who conceived this plan, indicated that from then on the country's progress would be measured by its consumption of iron.

The scarcity of basic urban services was notorious. The search for a supply of potable water from artesian wells went on for decades without being able to meet the demands of a city with rapid commercial growth and a large immigrant population from 1860. From 1856, with the municipal organization centralized, work on the cutting, surfacing and paving of the streets began. Nevertheless, problems vital for the city, such as adequate port installations, were still unsolved.[5]

Transformations of the Urban Fabric

In the meantime, the city grew dramatically, with the surrounding territory being divided into square plots, subdividing the colonial *parcelas* (plots) and defining new types of housing. The old, large colonial houses were divided, creating the half-courtyard house (*casa chorizo* or sausage house as it is known in Argentina) in which the generous space of the family living room was replaced by a modest patio with functions being redistributed towards the interior rooms. This loss of private domestic space was compensated for by a more open urban life outside the home, helped by the growing availability of new buildings such as clubs and cafés, and new meeting places in public spaces and thoroughfares.

At the same time, many colonial houses in

the southern area of the port became densely occupied, and this led to a type of building known as the *conventillo* (tenement) or the neighbourhood house where each room housed a family (figure 3.2). Although initially the situation was one of improvisation, it was seen by speculative sectors as an adequate solution for immigrant housing and, as a result, grew exponentially in the last decades of the nineteenth century. Some groups of immigrants would create more spontaneous settlements with singular architectural types. Such was the case of the Genovese who, with their skills as river boat builders and carpenters, would populate the Boca del Riachuelo area with buildings made of wood and iron sheets.

Towards 1860, the parcelling of the city in

the central area reflected these changes due to the hereditary subdivision of plots or functional alteration of activities, with the clear predominance of the *casa chorizo*. The Beare *catastro*, a land census carried out in that year with the careful listing of the owners, reveals the transformation of the old colonial urban fabric without any specific interruption of the original urban layout.[6]

The First Projects to affect the Checkerboard Design

The first attempts to change the city's design on the basis of the opening of new roadways can be attributed to the Rivadaviano period, when avenues were laid down to help solve the new traffic problems (figure 3.3). However, these would take a century to be completed, revealing the protracted nature of urban design compared to short-term governmental enthusiasm.

Some attempts to move away from the colonial tradition can be found in the third part of the nineteenth century with the circular avenue designs proposed by José María Lagos in 1869, and those made by Carranza y Soler in 1872, which ran from the Plaza de Mayo to the Plaza Once. Of special importance was the project by Felipe Senillosa, which had been published in Paris, in which diagonal avenues were placed into the grid design of the port, in so doing complying with the new expropriation legislation. Senillosa declared that '. . . the rich build their homes in districts far from the commercial centres . . .', and that if attention was paid to his proposal, '. . . these would be the elected scenery, the "*el rendez-vous*" of the most select population'.[7]

During this period, there were also projects for the reorganization of the port zone, especially after the construction of the Nueva Aduana (New Customs house) in 1859 and the Muelle de Pasajeros (Passenger Dock) in 1855. Some of these projects were undertaken by private businesses and included the recurrent idea of filling in and dividing the river or, in its place, constructing islands.[8]

The lack of services in the city and the dynamic growth of slums in the central area – the old Barrio Sud (Southern district) – would

Figure 3.3 Calle Perú (Peru Street) in Buenos Aires in 1886. (*Source*: Archivo del Centro de Documentación de Arquitectura Latinoamericana, CEDODAL)

end tragically in 1871 with thousands of deaths from the yellow fever epidemic. The outcry which arose as a result would lead to multiple changes, from the public commitment to boost sanitary works and water supply, to the migration of those people with greater economic resources who founded a new district to the north of the city.

With a more generous parcelling of land, and an image of suburban houses surrounded by gardens, this new district marked the abandonment of the historic city as a residential area for the port aristocracy. The historic city was developing into a popular district and, along with other areas near the Plaza de Mayo, was taken over by tertiary activities until it became the commercial and financial district of the city (figure 3.4).

Buenos Aires, Capital of Argentina

Once the political divisions had been overcome, the province of Buenos Aires ceded the city of Buenos Aires to the nation in 1880 to be the capital of the country. To meet the demands for a provincial capital, La Plata, located some 50 km from the Federal capital, would be founded in 1882.

Buenos Aires would be the dominant centre of the political and economic power that the provinces had questioned for decades. At that time, its port and customs had the conditions needed for the country to enter the world market hand in hand with the British Empire. The next fifty years would see the develop-

Figure 3.4 Plaza de Mayo in 1880. In the background, the Colón Theatre (Teatro Colón) built by Carlos Enrique Pellegrini in 1857. (*Source*: Archivo del Centro de Documentación de Arquitectura Latinoamericana, CEDODAL)

ment of Argentina's economy, culminating in 1933 with the explicit recognition through a trade and investment pact between the foreign offices of Britain and Argentina.

Spurred on by the British, whose capital investment in Argentina was almost a third of the total overseas capital investment made by Great Britain between 1889 and 1930, the territory would be restructured with a railway network linking the most remote parts of the country to Buenos Aires and its port. Under the 'primary-exporter' model agricultural and ranching products from the Argentinean plains were exchanged for British manufactured products.[9] The governing aristocracy and the new commercial bourgeoisie wisely followed the British plan and formed the conservative

political power which would control the country from 1880 to 1916 when, through a universal and secret vote, these elites would be replaced by a new bourgeoisie with a wide, popular base.

The ideas from the generation which would 'modernize' the country were mirrored in the argument elaborated by one of its most eminent thinkers, Domingo Faustino Sarmiento, who put forward an exclusive option between 'Civilization' (Europe) or 'Barbarism' (America). In this context, the desire for change was the essential motive which would make new economic and cultural development possible. Buenos Aires would obviously be the privileged laboratory for this venture.[10]

❧ THE MODERN METROPOLIS, 1880–1930 ❧

With Buenos Aires as the national capital, there was the need to find construction solutions to the requirements of the new national administration. This would lead to the hiring of technicians and professionals in Europe who would be able to fulfil the needs of the State. Francisco Tamburini and his assistant Victor Meano, from Italy, would be called to take charge of a large part of the public works

that would be carried out in the last two decades of the century.[11] This initial choice of professionals from Italy would give way, towards the end of the nineteenth century, to an unchallenged preference for French technicians, reflecting the high regard in which the Baron Haussmann's public works in Paris were held.

The Paris of America

In the imagination of those leaders fascinated by the possibility of creating great public works and changing the face of the city from the vision of the *Gran Aldea* (Great Village) – an expression made popular by Lucio V. López in his novel of the same name (1882) – to the 'Modern Metropolis', Paris became the unquestionable model.

Once this institutional vision had taken root at the national and municipal level (figure 3.5), all efforts to achieve it seemed thoroughly justifiable. In the decades towards the end of the nineteenth century, the changes in the city under the auspices of this renewal project were evident. Some measures were in fact taken as a result of the grave

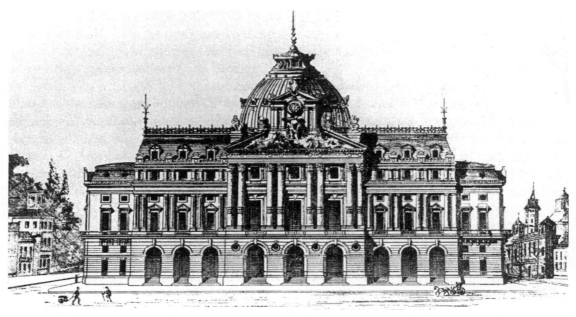

Figure 3.5 Palacio de Correos y Telégrafos (Mail and Telegraphs Palace) in 1908. Designed by the French architect Norbert Maillart. (*Source*: Archivo del Centro de Documentación de Arquitectura Latinoamericana, CEDODAL)

crisis brought about by the yellow fever epidemic of 1871, which not only caused thousands of deaths but, as mentioned above, also led to wealthier sectors of the population moving from the historic city to a new district to the north. The proposals put forward by the health campaigners indicated the urgent need to carry out sanitary works, to eliminate the *conventillos* with their residential overcrowding (12 per cent of the population lived there according to the 1887 census), and to create ample, open, green spaces which would bring oxygen to the city. It is worth mentioning the studies carried out by Émile Coni, *Progrès de l'hygiène dans la République Argentine*, published in Paris in 1887, and that by the French doctor Samuel Gache in *Les logements ouvriers à Buenos Aires,* published in Paris in 1900.

From 1874, English companies, jointly with Swedish, Norwegian, Belgian and French technicians, participated in the installation of running water and sanitation services; 'that great show of cosmopolitanism filled the *porteños* (port inhabitants) with pride to think that they were 'more European than the inhabitants of any European country', because they were Germans, English, Italians, French, Spanish and many other nations, all these nationalities at the same time.[12]

The developments in infrastructure were accompanied by the creation of large green spaces and plazas. The Bosque de Palermo mimicked the Parisian Bois de Boulogne and soon professionals from the Municipality began to push for urban changes which they considered to be close to the Haussmannic model. Through their designs for parks and plazas, the French landscape designers Eugenio Courtois and Carlos Thays, would play an outstanding role in the approach to the Parisian model.[13]

The impact of the railroad and the major works carried out at the port in the last decade of the nineteenth century reflected the euphoria unleashed by the enormous British investments in the infrastructure which would make the union of the country to the world market possible.[14] Works at the port included the construction of Puerto Madero, an unnecessary and costly undertaking which had replaced the idea of dredging the Riachuelo, which although the natural port of the city, was far from the idea of 'centrality' determined by the location of the sectors in power. Following the design by the German Fernando Moog, the Mercado Proveedor de Frutos (Fruit Supply Market) was built on the outskirts of the city, in Avellaneda; it was the largest area in the world under an iron roof.[15]

The Expansion and Formation of the Districts

The development of public transport, mainly trams first drawn by animals and later powered by electricity, would play an important role within the city. The tram car companies quickly boosted urban development by acquiring vacant suburban land and extending their services there. Once accessible, this land was auctioned in parcels for development at a correspondingly higher price.[16]

Urban expansion was clearly marked in 1887, when the jurisdiction of the Federal Capital, extended to include Buenos Aires and the old towns of Belgrano and Flores, was legalized. This set out clear plans to fill in the empty spaces between these towns, then later to expand the urban spread towards the new limits with the province of Buenos Aires (figure 3.6).[17]

The poor sanitary and housing conditions – lack of potable water networks and overcrowded *conventillos* – together with the persistence of immigration in the southern part of the city, favoured the extension in other areas of residential concentration. This gave rise to a city made up of districts each with its own characteristics in terms of urban landscape, ethnicity and social class. The steps taken by the municipality tended to strengthen this pattern of development with the provision of schools and other public facilities and infrastructure.[18] The construction of schools clearly marked one of the modernization policies of these governments who pushed literacy to a level unsurpassed by other Latin American countries at that time. To achieve this, teachers and teaching equipment were imported from the United States.[19]

Initially, the railway ran around the outskirts of the city, with the stations connecting the old arrival points of the wagons from the countryside (Plaza Once or Constitution). However, urban expansion quickly surrounded the railway lines, which acted as barriers that marked the limits of new districts, thus causing accessibility problems.[20] This urban growth increased the traffic problems caused by the new transport systems, particularly the carriages and tram cars. The streets of the old colonial city were too narrow to accommodate the large flow of pedestrians and vehicles. In the light of this, it is not surprising that proposals to widen the streets, making new avenues and creating the 'boulevards' with circulation in opposite directions allowing for tree-lined spaces, were quickly accepted.

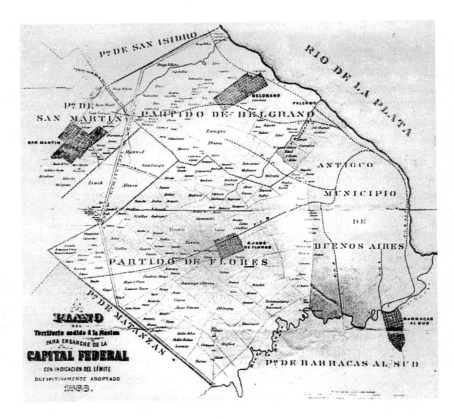

Figure 3.6 Plan of Buenos Aires with the expansion including the old Municipalities of Flores and Belgrano, 1888. (*Source*: Archivo del Centro de Documentación de Arquitectura Latinoamericana, CEDODAL)

Urban Intervention. Plaza and Avenida de Mayo

The transformation of the Plaza de Mayo – a highly symbolic space for the city – was just the starting point in the search for a new urban identity. Juan Antonio Buschiazzo, an Italian who had studied architecture in Argentina, was the person chosen by the *Intendente* (Mayor), Torcuato de Alvear, to undertake these great urban changes.[21] To do so, Buschiazzo proposed joining the spaces between the two plazas – Plaza de Mayo and the open area in front of the fort – then divided by the Recova, an arched building of shops that had been constructed at the end of the colonial period. This building was demolished in 1886 at the same time that Tamburini, on the side nearest to the river, joined two existing buildings to

form the Casa de Gobierno (Government House). At that time, the façade and tower of the old Cabildo building (Town Hall) was changed to meet with the demands of the new academic fashion.[22]

The idea of opening the Avenida Norte-Sur (North-South avenue), which would connect the train stations at Constitución with those at Retiro, was proposed in 1889. However, it was the success of the 'modern' image of the city of La Plata, founded in 1882, which was to spur major urban reconstruction in Buenos Aires.[23]

Around 1870, Sarmiento had proposed the opening of a large avenue starting at Plaza de Mayo and ending at Plaza Lorea (part of the

Congress) so providing a promenade for the city. Torcuato de Alvear joined Buschiazzo in obtaining political agreement to these ideas and to the costly acquisition of land. Between 1890 and 1896, these works shaped the image of the new metropolis and led the city's inhabitants to believe that anything was possible with power and money.

The new avenue was conceived as a 32-metre wide boulevard with central islands for pedestrians, originally with trees and broad paths some 6 metres wide, which would allow space for cafes and pedestrian meeting spots. It was seen as the great salon of the city where different social groups could show themselves off and watch the passing carriages or the social events which made up the city's cosmopolitan life.[24]

The French Presence

Perceived as a model, the Haussmannic influence became embodied in a group of design trademarks worshipped by followers of the late nineteenth-century 'building aesthetic'. A new network of widened streets and diagonal avenues that linked the city's main reference points for improving its internal control, would emerge over the old city design. All these avenues and nodes articulated the communication centres, the new railway stations, the plazas and public meeting places.

Meanwhile, the more important buildings were isolated according to that monumental vision of a new urban scenery that highlighted the reference landmarks following the old baroque tradition (figure 3.7).

This was a design with geometric axes and 'compositions' which coincided ideologically with the precepts of academicism found in architecture and revived the ideas of monumentality and hierarchy in public works. Added to this, was the nuance of the authoritarian

Figure 3.7 Ortiz Basualdo and Anchorena Palaces from when Buenos Aires wanted to be the 'American Paris'. (*Source*: Archivo del Centro de Documentación de Arquitectura Latinoamericana, CEDODAL)

Figure 3.8 Errazuriz Palace. Designed by the architect René Sergent in Paris, without visiting Buenos Aires. (*Source*: Archivo del Centro de Documentación de Arquitectura Latinoamericana, CEDODAL).

exercise of power which allowed this type of solution to be imposed on a population regarded as spectators in such urban decisions. The works of the first mayor of Buenos Aires, Torcuato de Alvear, corresponded to this profile of an enlightened governor.

But this trend in urban planning and design was stimulated by the predominance of a French cultural ambience which led the elite governing class to imitate French tastes, lifestyle and customs (figure 3.8). If Anatole France or Georges Clemençeau perceived this universal validity of the French spirit around 1910, its essence had, undoubtedly, been shaped in the last decades of the nineteenth century. Clemençeau enthusiastically claimed: 'with regard to the language, there is no difficulty. Everyone understands French, it is read, and spoken like the speaker and their actions show that all shades of meaning in the discourse have been acquired. What more can be desired? Through the grace of the diffused word the spirit of our France has emigrated to a land beyond the ocean'.[25]

Joseph Bouvard in the Vision of an Urban Renewal

Joseph Bouvard, the urbanist from Paris, would make his first, swift and dynamic visit to Buenos Aires in 1907 to present Mayor Carlos T. de Alvear with a plan for future avenues. The Haussmannic stamp would make a strong impression on the city through the potential irruption of 60 kilometres of artery and thirty-two diagonal roads which would lead to the destruction of the old foundation square.[26] Basically, this was what it was about. According to the mayor, the plan would allow the 'correction of the flaw in the strict parallelism of narrow streets and the division

of the land into square blocks which, if they were to remain that way, would in a short time turn the city into an enormous extension, antiaesthetic from all points'.[27]

Bouvard warned of the need to implement a gradual plan which would ensure steps in the same direction as well as continuity, thus avoiding short-term decisions being made. Nevertheless, this alleged scientific approach hid the misleading, if not unprincipled, nature of certain definitions of the new urban designs which were being proposed. Although the opposition questioned the proposals put forward by

Figure 3.9 French landscape design contemporary with the hygiene proposals. Rodriguez Peña Square. (*Source*: Archivo del Centro de Documentación de Arquitectura Latinoamericana, CEDODAL)

Bouvard for their high degree of flippancy, the non-existence of prior studies and the consequences they might have on the city, the official sector not only approved the carrying out of the plan, but also entrusted other urban projects to Bouvard. Among these were the transformation of the Quinta Hale in the Recoleta area, an urban design for the important Plaza del Congreso, the layout of the land for the *Exposición del Centenario* (Centenary Exhibition) in Palermo, and the construction of a 200-bed hospital.[28] Such was the high esteem that he enjoyed, that the visit would be repeated in 1909 to promote new projects.

Meanwhile, a Municipal Commission made up of Thays along with other officials and even including an auctioneer, gave their opinion with regard to Bouvard's proposals. They pointed out the need to change the checker-board design as had been done in other areas, in an attempt to create 'convergent and concentric roads in certain important points'. The design of diagonal roads, a new urban panacea which would break from the unbearable monotony of the old design, 'thus giving the ensemble a more picturesque, varied and enjoyable appearance'[29] was also needed.

In his report in 1910, Bouvard proposed the construction of 15 squares, following the guidelines set down in Forestier's treaty published in 1905 (figure 3.9). At the same time, the construction of wide avenues which joined the parks was encouraged. The communication roadways were placed in hierarchical order based on their functionality and the importance of the points they connected. In so doing they attempted to avoid crossroads as well as to increase access to public places and commercial centres. The diagonal roads created a network which set a stage for the public monuments on a stage and encouraged the construction of new buildings which would complement the wide avenues, consciously but amply deployed by the visiting architect in a compact and densely populated city such as Buenos Aires, which by 1907 had more than a million inhabitants.[30]

Local Reaction

However, the proposals put forward by the French urban planner were countered by those of the Argentinean architect Víctor Jaeschke, a graduate of the Technische Hochschule (Technical High School) in Munich, who had been promoting building improvements in the city and who, in 1904, had already proposed the need for a *Ley de Expropiación* (Expropriation Law) to make the creation of new roads and plazas possible. A declared enemy of the 'grid', Jaeschke preferred diagonals which he considered as being 'essential' for improvements in buildings and transit.[31]

Jaeschke concurred with Bouvard in his disdain for the historic city and proposed that the existing buildings be torn down to widen the streets and avenues to form a new Municipal border. This process, he believed, would give the city a new and modern look in 50 years. He imagined commercial streets with arcades and covered galleries, like those which had been created by Pellegrini in the lower areas of Avenida Alem and Paseo Colón since 1860.

His interventions on the layout suffered from the same oversimplification. He suggested that the streets be oblique or curved, never straight, and that instead of a line of continuous buildings, there should be *dentados* (recessed façades) with gardens. This model was totally different from the urban tradition in Buenos Aires. He also proposed that the design of the blocks be subdivided into two or three parts, with narrow lots and gardens in the centre. He naively believed that in this way the tenement buildings and the neighbourhood houses would disappear while these were, in fact, part of the real estate business, stemming from the growth of the immigrant population.

As a reasonable precaution against the unstemmed real estate speculation, Jaeschke advocated that no new housing developments be authorized on the outskirts of the city unless they had basic services and infrastructure. From the start, he had questioned the seriousness of the Bouvard plan which had been carried out as a result of a six-week visit to Buenos Aires. He saw the famous plan as a series of sketches and outlines which were not a solid project and warned of the spending of millions of pesos as a result of decisions which had not been carefully considered.[32]

Jaeschke's objections to Bouvard's *rond-points,* or meeting points of fast roads around certain monuments were added to a direct criticism of the tendency to flatten topographical differences (Alvear Avenue) or to straighten designs which had potential urban design value (Quinta de Hale, the Escalinatas area). Having led to twelve diagonal roads and avenues being concentrated in the Plaza del Congreso, the supreme abuse of new roads was an example of the contradictory value of what it would mean to improve substantially urban transit.[33]

Jaeschke's criticism also included the rejection of the banal dependence on what came from abroad. As Jorge Tartarini pointed out, Carlos Altgelt, who had also studied in Germany, shared this view. Altgelt wrote to Jaeschke:

You and I are Argentineans. We are not from Paris. Paris in whose boulevards and entertainment centres like those of all big capitals, you meet ten times more stupid people than talented ones, where many go with their traveling chests and return with a cigarette case, and when we were in the Mecca, we did not become bosom buddies of the pilgrims who in South America control the puppets of national, provincial, community and commercial politics.[34]

It is interesting to note, however, that Jaeschke's criticism was not made from another ideological and urbanistic stand, but rather from the same idea of major intervention in the city. Jaeschke did not hesitate in proposing the demolition of convents and colonial temples, while advocating the creation of other avenues and diagonal roadways. He insisted on the need for studies and thought, but his proposals, like Bouvard's, would open deep scars in the old Spanish design. Nor did he oppose the European urban models but insisted on the same positivist view, that any proposal for Buenos Aires should be supported by 'reason, logic and truth' and by those which were in themselves impossible, 'immutable scientific and artistic principles'.

Perhaps Bouvard's lack of knowledge of the city, the priority Jaeschke gave to solving the transit problems before the aesthetic ones, and the preference for the foreigner above those who had been struggling for a long time in the city, explain the harsh criticism by the Argentinean urban planner. Jaeschkle's proposals for avenues were made in a context of obtaining lower expropriation costs. This, however, did not prevent Congress from approving, in 1912, the proposal made by Representative Louro in 1909 for work on the Avenida Norte Sur, which would become 9 de Julio (9th of July), and that made by Bouvard for the North and South diagonal roads. These would be carried out piecemeal during the second third of the century and some, like the Diagonal Sur (South Diagonal), would remain unfinished.[35]

As Tartarini also points out, the stream of governors who had decided to go down in history for their public works, the 'speculators disguised as councillors' who Jaeschke condemned, and the weakness of a 'cosmetic' urban planning which tried to imitate the prestigious models, led to the creation of those plans which the harsh reality of daily life would lead toward failure. From these, we are left with the first underground train (1913), the Diagonal Norte (North Diagonal road), the Avenida 9 de Julio (with another width and design) and, as mentioned earlier, a part of the Diagonal Sur. The other thirty diagonal roads proposed by Bouvard and a large part of his fifteen plazas would remain on paper only.

Kept alive by professional and administrative groups, the conservative vision of academic urbanism continued, beyond the nuances, advocating a static city, under geometric norms, balances and symmetries. In short, a city that, put together in these perfect sketches, would be frozen forever. This model was so far from true city life that, had all the resources and political will been available to carry it through, it would have been a resounding failure.

The overwhelming French presence in the urban planning and architecture of Buenos Aires would, however, produce other reactions. Some of these came from the professional front, as a result of the clash between the 'national' architects (graduates from the capital's Architecture School, which was attached to the Faculty of Science at the University of Buenos Aires), and the foreign architects (with degrees which had or had not been recognized) who worked freely and controlled the *Sociedad Central de Arquitectos* (Central Society of Architects), founded in 1886. This would lead to the threat of formation of a parallel organization, a problem that would be solved after long discussions and concession making.[36]

In a wider context, the presence of a Latin American movement had been gaining ground in the field of literature with Rubén Darío, José Martí and José Enrique Rodó. This was seen in Buenos Aires in 1909 with the publishing of 'The Nationalist Restoration' by Ricardo Rojas and texts by Manuel Ugarte. This new thought led to conflicts in the minds of the new breed of intellectuals tired of mimicry and cultural underestimating by the enlightened Euro-centrics.[37]

The upheaval of the Mexican agricultural revolution in 1910, the uprising of indigenous movements in different countries, the European crisis produced by the World War I (1914–1918), the Russian Revolution (1917) and the Córdoba University Reform (1918) were Latin American and European events which left a deep mark on Argentinean society.[38] These ideas were taken up by the architectural students in Buenos Aires, who published the first issue of La Revista de Arquitectura in 1915. In the editorial, 'Rumbos nuevos' (New directions) the idea of an architectural and urban horizon centred on Latin American space was proposed.[39]

The Urban Conflict and the Political Reply

We have mentioned the attacks made by the architect Jaeschke on the proposals put forward by Bouvard and the same could be said with regard to the objections raised by Altegelt when the designs for large public buildings were handed over to Norbert Maillart. But these did not affect the promoters of the Parisian model.

In this context, we can understand the conflict that arose in June 1912, when the Concejo Deliberante (Deliberative Council) of Buenos Aires hired Francisco Benjamín Chaussemiche, an Austrian architect resident in Paris, who would be called upon to head the Municipal department responsible for implementing the urban planning which would definitely achieve the desired aesthetic transformation.[40]

Argentina's representative for the Austrian-Hungarian Empire, had been the one to handle this 'exotic' contract. Chaussemiche had remarked that he 'had no problem in coming to the capital for a six year contract' for the sum of 60,000 francs per year, with the trip paid for and besides 'with the power to charge for certain commissions apart from these professional fees'. Among these 'additional' services were no less than the Palacio Municipal (Municipal Palace) and eventually the control of the work.[41]

In the political debate, the prior experience was accepted as being an 'extremely costly contract between Mr. Bouvard, who did no more than propose initiatives that had already been found in individual projects'. Councillor Canale said: 'Barely a year or so ago, Mr. Bouvard's projects were accepted and already we are thinking of bringing another famous foreigner to repeat precisely the same mistake that we made the last time'.

It was then that, as an additional benefit, Chaussemiche was offered the opportunity to create a School of Architecture and, if in 1916 the government should decide to stage any public art exhibition, the plans and management of these would also be given to him. That is to say that funds from the city's future administration, as well as from the national one, were being compromised.

Councillor Canale pointed out to the Mayor that neither of them knew the famous Chaussemiche personally and that both trusted Dr. Pérez, the diplomat responsible for the contract, but in view of past experience, Canale needed to express his feelings. 'This gentleman is as intelligent as can be, famous, the last word in the field, but I must frankly say that I am tired of these wise foreigners and would like to know a little about the wise people who live here and have the same ideas and artistic production'. He indicated that most of the plans that were to be given to Chaussemiche were already underway and that a School of Architecture already existed 'of which the country is proud'. He ended by asking: 'Is there no countryman with as much intelligence as this gentleman who can produce something artistic for us?'

The official view was explained by the Secretary of Public Works, Atanasio Iturbe, when, on endorsing the contract, he pointed out that in Buenos Aires 'until now no one has dedicated himself to study the questions which refer essentially to public art, the beauti-fying and transforming of the cities'. The former *Intendente* Guerrico insisted: 'I am not saying that there are no intelligent Argentineans, but here among us there is no public art school because there is no environment like that found in the great European cities. Which is the best, the most beautiful city on earth? Paris. Well then, a gentleman has to be brought from Paris who has been outstanding in beautifying cities'. The impromptu nature of the proposal was brought to light when a councillor asked: 'What plans are there for the Municipal Palace if nothing has yet been solved? We don't know its site or if we are going to have enough money to carry it out'. Finally, 'Operation Chaussemiche' was rejected by the majority of voters on the Buenos Aires Council. This was the first time that a battle had been won in the long quest to obtain autonomous planning.

More Ideas for Buenos Aires.
The Landscape Designer Forestier and the Plan for Building Aesthetic

A decade after Chaussemiche, it was the turn of the landscaper Forestier, whose presence also led to harsh debates which, although they did not prevent his arrival, were enough to put a stop to a large part of his proposals.

In 1923, during the Municipal government of Carlos Noel (a graduate of the *École des Hautes Études des Sciences Sociales* in Paris), it was proposed that Jean-Claude Nicholas Forestier, at that time Director of Avenues in Paris, be hired as 'Municipal consultant for the *Plan Edilicio* (Building plan) to be developed in the Federal capital'. This was a very controversial decision, for the same reasons of improvisation and cultural dependence which had been discussed in the debate a decade earlier.[42]

Forestier himself stressed his complete ignorance of the local urban situation but insisted on the importance of gardens in city life. After travelling around Buenos Aires and meeting with Carlos Thays Jr., he announced, to win local public opinion, that 'there was no boulevard in Paris which could be compared to our winter gardens and the Rosedal'. A master in the art of eloquence, after a month in Buenos Aires, Forestier announced: 'In this city, I feel as if I were in Paris, as there is such a similarity in the surroundings that if differences were to be found, they would only be with regard to details'.[43] This was precisely what the officials who had hired him wanted to hear.

On returning to Paris to design the gardens

for the *Arts Décoratifs* Exposition of 1925, Forestier left a summary of his ideas where he expressed the need to increase the green areas, joining them to the large avenues, to eradicate the cemeteries from the city and work on the coastal area, constructing promenades and seaside resorts. In 1924, Forestier sent the plans and the report on his work which would be incorporated into the *Plan de Estética Edilicia* (Building Aesthetic Plan), to be published by the Municipal Council a year later.

Forestier proposed ideas for Buenos Aires which had been developed in 1905 in his work *Grandes villes et systémes de parcs*.[44] Sonia Berjman analysed the characteristics of his proposal which included an increase in the green areas in the city from 6 per cent to the 14 per cent of the total area. To achieve this, he proposed suburban parks on the outskirts of the city, large urban parks, open commons (fields and groves) following the British style for Avenida de Circunvalación (Ring Road Avenue), which in 1936 would become General Paez Avenue (figure 3.10).

He also suggested gardens for children and workers and cemetery parks. But Forestier's expertise was more that of a landscape designer than an urban planner. His vision of the avenues and boulevards which would run 'between the peaceful villas, bursting with greenery and flowers', were undoubtedly a bucolic version of the booming metropolis, but would have meant the destruction of consolidated urban areas.

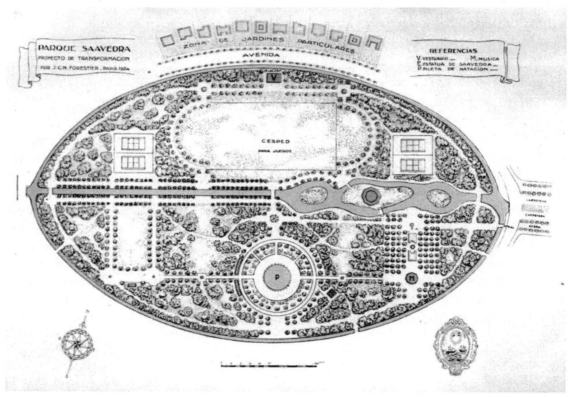

Figure 3.10   Forestier's landscape project for the Saavedra Park. (*Source*: Archivo del Centro de Documentación de Arquitectura Latinoamericana, CEDODAL)

Analysed in detail, a large part of the boulevards and parks proposed by Forestier had already been included in the 1923 project by the *Dirección de Paseos de Buenos Aires* (Buenos Aires Department of Boulevards), under Carlos Thays, Jr. and the most innovative proposal was that of the Costaneras (Coastal avenues). These were of such great magnitude that they could not be carried out with Municipality resources and Forestier used the already well-worn idea of gaining land from the Plata river for urban developments for a sector which was both economically and socially privileged. His only proposal to survive would be that of the effective use of the river banks, as would be seen in the installation of the resort on the Costanera Sur (Southern Coastal Area).

During the government of Alvear (1922–1928), the ideas of applying French urban philosophy gained strength and the old proposals made by Bouvard and Maillart, as well as the new ones put forward by Forestier, were reintroduced by the *Comisión Municipal de Estética Edilicia* (Municipal Commission for Building Aesthetic) which was appointed by the *Intendente* Carlos Noel. This Commission included the Frenchman, René Karman, the Italians Carlos Morra and Sebastián Ghigliazza and the Argentinean architect (who had studied in Paris) Martín Noel.[45]

As the name implies, the Commission's concern was focused on monumental interventions and fundamentally on the implementation of the avenues and diagonal roads, which were scattered all over the plan of the city, many times without joining well-developed areas. As a result, this was seen as a game on paper whose purpose was to achieve symmetry and a compositional balance on the plan (figure 3.11).

The relocation of groups of public buildings and particularly those of the Municipality, was one of the main tasks set out by these proposals based on the incipient decentrali-

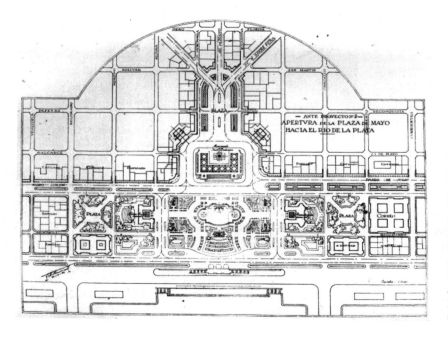

Figure 3.11 René Villeminot's project for the *Comisión de Estética Edilicia*. Proposal made in 1925. From the opening of Plaza de Mayo to Rio de La Plata. (*Source*: Archivo del Centro de Documentación de Arquitectura Latinoamericana, CEDODAL)

Figure 3.12
Transformation studies
for the central area of
Buenos Aires including
systematization, big
administrative towers
and 'promenades' by the
river. (*Source*: Archivo
del Centro de
Documentación de
Arquitectura
Latinoamericana,
CEDODAL)

zation which would allow the expanding city to establish its territorial presence. At the same time, buildings to house several ministries would be located around the Plaza de Mayo, thereby reaffirming the idea of centrality and indicating the eclectic plurality of criteria (figure 3.12). The Commission's project modified Forestier's proposals for the coastal avenues, establishing access through Sarmiento Avenue, in this way crossing the Palermo wood and breaking up the residential area into Parque

de la Rivera and another 'Belgrano Beau Rivage', divided by the presence of the fishing dock and some unfeasible hotels, restaurants and casinos.

This was the public administration's final attempt to put together an urban plan for Buenos Aires which took into consideration the French urban planning ideas, after two decades of professional advice from technical consultants.

The Visit of Léon Jaussely in 1926

Léon Jaussely's visit was slightly different, perhaps because through his former pupils, the Uruguayans Mauricio Cravotto and Jorge Hardoy, he was better acquainted with the local situation. This did not prevent him from insisting that his view of the future city as being comparable to a foreign model that,

while shifting from the traditional fascination with Paris, still predicted that Buenos Aires ought to be the 'New York of South America'.[46]

Jaussely questioned the urban dimension of 'a small city well extended' and at the same time foresaw the need for regional planning, dreaming of the El Tigre area transformed into the French Côte d'Azur. The hope of the future lay, as always, in the port, 'where activity is really intense and should be completely confident of the future', as its level of movements and trade were greater than that of Paris and similar to that of Marseilles and Antwerp.

In his report of 1926, Jaussely went into more detail with regard to urban planning and design than Forestier and underlined the conflict with the railroad in the city, favouring underground trains. He criticized the expansion of the city through addition of territory where public pressure was, in fact, behind the development of urban areas, thus reaffirming the Municipality's active role in motivating the city's growth through infrastructure and facilities development.

To set aside the building aesthetic and concern for central areas of the city, to tackle the problems of transport and construction on the outskirts, was a notorious break from the Municipal Commission's plan described above. Jaussely stressed the obsolete nature of checkerboard urban planning which lacked the public policies needed to influence a city's development by actively participating in its expansion process.

This does not mean that the notion of a 'building aesthetic' was not present. Jaussely was deeply bothered by the square and declared:

I agree that having squared blocks is comfortable for the numbering of the undoubtedly long streets. But that this is the only ideal to be pursued, seems to me to be inadmissible. This shows a very narrow ideal for a building administration, an inexplicable ideal; contrary to all beauty, all urban aesthetic value. It is the highest error committed.

Jaussely did not find any virtue in the grid other than enumeration, and this gratuitous reduction indicates the rejection *a priori* of the Hispanic model. He added:

I remember that in my international competition project in Barcelona, there as well, the eternal checkerboard plan was finally broken. This came from an era in which nothing related to urbanism was understood, at least not in Spain. I designed the new areas using a different style but unifying them with the other parts of the plan in such a natural way, even with the checkerboard, that the landscape from one part to another was seamless and the union was perfect. With the checkerboard design nothing better can be done than what is done here, given the horror of its monotony.

Today, it seems difficult to accept that at the time of Idelfonso Cerdá, 'nothing of urbanism was understood', but the French arrogance always gave rise to long academic lecture.

As translator of Raymond Unwin's work, Jaussely thought deeply about the aspects of the garden city which 'would be a charm in England' and proposed this example for Buenos Aires, while almost at the same time, from Spain there were suggestions to use Soria y Mata's design of the linear cities. Jaussely told the Municipality and the *porteños* that:

From now on you should propose to fill the spaces which are still free in your plan with new neighbourhoods with a simpler design, be it curved or straight, well proportioned lines, and gardens in front of all houses, be they for the rich or less rich, as therein lies the beauty of modern cities.

These ideas would form the basis for the layout of the Barrio Parque Chas (Parque Chas area), which was criticized by Carlos Della Paolera for the difficulties arising from combining the curved lines with an efficient subdivision of the land.

In the old academic tradition, Léon Jaussely centred his ideas on the location of the public buildings recommending that they be placed in the 'high parts of the city' – which was somewhat difficult in a city on a plain. To accomplish this, he insisted on the need to give Buenos Aires 'the public monumental character which it lacked and which was so necessary'. When considering zoning, he put forward the idea of a university city and suggested moving away from the centre in search of wider spaces where the buildings could mingle with parks.

☙ THE CITY 'WITHOUT HOPE': 1930–1940 ❧

The academic concept of 'building aesthetic' permeated a large part of 1920s opinion; under its influence, Forestier, Jaussely and Alfred Agache, and then later, in another trend, Le Corbusier, proposed different options for Buenos Aires.

The giddy, speculative growth of the city during the 1920s would lead to the creation of the *Comisión de Urbanismo y Estética Edilicia* (Urban Planning and Building Aesthetic Commission) of the Central Society of Architects, and the passing of the *Código de Edificación* (Building Code) of 1928. The Commission was comprised of prestigious professionals such as Alejandro Christophersen, the polemic Victor Jaeschke, Ernesto Vautier (recently returned from Paris where he had studied with Tony Garnier) and Alberto Gelly Cantilo. Many of the projects and initiatives of this period would be postponed when the economic Depression of 1930 crippled the dreams of aesthetic grandiloquence, although the crisis did not prevent the signs of pharaoh-like monuments which the local public offices developed.

As proof that there could be no doubt about the deep-rooted dependency on the French model, in 1937 the Argentinean ambassador in Paris contracted a professor (not necessarily an architect) on behalf of the University, to direct the workshop at the School of Architecture when Monsieur René Karman retired.

A decade later, Le Corbusier, who had appointed himself to 'humanize a city without hope', in his always affable tone, called his disciples, Antonio Bonet, Juan Kurchan and Ferrari Hardoy, 'little devils' for trying to work in urban planning in the Municipality of Buenos Aires, reminding them that there they had not heard of urban planning until he, Le Corbusier, had passed by in 1929. This was the new functional version of history as though the nearly 400-year-old city had not existed until 'he' discovered it.[47]

Invited by the *Sociedad de Estímulo de las Bellas Artes* (Society for the Promotion of Fine Arts), Le Corbusier arrived in Buenos Aires in 1929 without any direct relation with the professional sector and without really making an impact on public opinion. The texts from his conferences, basically 'Urban planning in everything, architecture in everything' were collected in the book which gave details on his trips throughout Argentina, Uruguay and Brazil. If Le Corbusier said that he was moved 'by the great affection that I felt for things and people', the city of Buenos Aires seemed to him to be 'the most inhuman that I had ever known'.[48] In a new vision, he would propose the moving of the centre of business and administrative activities, thus modifying the traditional centrality and creating an island with five skyscrapers which would be the 'city of business'. Concerned with the extension of the city, which was double that of Paris, he pointed out the need to revert the process by which the Avenida de Mayo had cut the city into a rich north and poor south.

The proposed concentration would create a city of four million inhabitants located on an area a quarter of the size of what it had in 1880, destroying in this way the entire weave of *barrios* which was already one of the features of the city. A complementary 'rural' vision then inserted woods, nurseries and small farms into those areas where the *barrios* had been; this was a reiteration of the games of urban planning on paper.[49]

These ideas were then developed in the Plan *Director* (Master Plan) which would be carried out by Le Corbusier's Argentinean disciples at the end of the decade, and which would be published in 1947. The plan followed the scheme for urban planning of his '*Ville radieuse*' and of the CIAM, with all the rigidity inherent in zoning, the elevated motorways, the classic buildings on piles, and the reorganization of civic centres differentiated for the Government, Municipality and even a potential 'Centro Panamericano' (Pan-American Centre). Once again the exogenous model did not reflect the reality of the city.[50]

The Vision of Werner Hegemann

As with the invitation to Le Corbusier, the presence of the German urban planner was sponsored by a private institution, *Los Amigos de la Ciudad* (The Friends of the City), which took part in the urban debates of the 1930s. Werner Hegemann came from Berlin in August 1931 and for four months held conferences in Buenos Aires, Rosario and Mar del Plata, leaving publications on these two last cities.[51]

As pointed out by Jorge Tartarini, Hegemann's attitude was substantially different from that of the implementation of the modernist model which motivated the French planners, or the 'shock' strategy proposed by Le Corbusier. His starting point was the city as it was, with both its problems and its good points, and the search for the harmonic integration of the urban planning instruments which controlled its growth: the Urban Plan and the Building Regulations or Building Code.[52]

He clearly perceived that the city should be analysed in conjunction with the area of Gran Buenos Aires (jurisdictionally belonging to the province of Buenos Aires and therefore beyond the frontier of the Federal Capital), as the many urban problems made it essential that the city limits be extended in order to tackle these problems in a unified and coherent manner. Hegemann harshly criticized the fallacy of the *Código de Edificación*, which would allow the location of up to 30 million inhabitants in the city's territory, and applauded the rationality of the typology of popular urban housing.[53]

We know the content of Hegemann's conferences from four articles which he published in the magazine *Wasmuths Monatshefte*, on his return to Germany.[54] Unlike Jaussely, Agache and other French urban planners, Hegemann liked the checkerboard design of the city of Buenos Aires, to which he endorsed the values of democratic conception, flexibility, openness and rationality, although he made some observations on its use in a residential context.

In this context and through his writings in *The American Vitruvius* (1922), we can gain an understanding of his criticism of the Haussmanesque diagonals which had been the *leitmotiv* of urban planning in the building aesthetic half a century earlier, and called on public opinion to support enthusiastically the 'old and venerable system of the grid plan'.

This point of departure coincided with the prediction of the Argentinean planner (educated in Paris), Carlos Della Paolera, with whom Hegemann formed a deep friendship until his death in 1936. He also made an impact on the architect Martín Noel (also educated in Paris) who in 1938 would promote the first *Ley de Urbanismo* (Planning Law) and whose library held works by Hegemann in both German and English.

Hegemann agreed with Forestier on the need to increase the green spaces and stated that Buenos Aires was 'the biggest ocean of buildings with the greatest shortage of green oasis I have known'; however, his park system was a structural element within the urban and regional plan he promoted in order to convert the outskirts into an articulated system of satellite cities.

One of the important themes which Hegemann put forward was the reassessment of the single-family house with garden, as opposed to the proposal for collective and multi-family housing which was being encouraged by European experts, especially the Germans and the Austrians such as Steinhof, who had been in Buenos Aires a few years earlier. Surprised by the quality of the yards and patios typical of the vernacular *porteña* architecture, he agreed with Le Corbusier in the value of this type of residences and lucidly stated: 'I believe that urban planning has really a lot of interest in the architectural traditions that must be kept alive, but I interpret the growth of the traditions as being other than the copy of dead styles. The urban planner is interested in the tradition which has vitality'.

Hegemann supported the proposals made by the Argentinean urban planners and especially encouraged that incentive taken by Della Paolera from 1928 to formulate a *Plano Regulador* (Development Control Plan) as an adequate instrument, due to its flexibility and dynamic development, to adapt itself to the potential changes. His speech, with no arrogance, was supported by evidence which had been taken from the cities of which he spoke. He gave his proposals time and reflection, he valued them and thought deeply on their strengths and weaknesses, offering alternatives which came from that reality without depending on symbolic and exogenous models. This does not mean that Hegemann excluded external references, but he did not use them as a starting point but rather in relation to the real city in which he would work.

His ideas were nevertheless dismissed in an atmosphere where the modern vanguards rejected all that meant the reappraisal of tradition, and proposed the total renovation of the historic city as their goal. Only the local urban planners were able to perceive the deep wisdom of an urban planner who pragmatically assumed the reality for what it was and sought to transform the city to the highest standards which could be reached. Rationality without rationalism and wisdom without simplification seem to have predominated in Hegemann's dissertations.

The Pharaonic Projects for Buenos Aires

In marked contrast are the proposals for urban interventions in Buenos Aires in the 1930s, both from private initiative as well as from the government's architectural and urban planning departments. Perhaps caught up in the great interventions of Mussolini and his 'systematizations', different government offices began remodelling projects in the central areas, demolishing and moving buildings and monuments (even the most symbolic such as the Cathedral, the *Cabildo*, the Government House or the Municipal house), with the view to creating new civic centres in different areas of the city (figure 3.13).[55]

The principles were still drawn from the imagery of the City Beautiful. In 1927, the Uruguayan Jorge Hardoy, educated in Paris, proposed a major intervention in Avenida Alem and Paseo Colón to generate 'an important and grand composition, on a par with an incomparable *"façade de ville"'*. In 1932, the *Exposición Municipal de Urbanismo* (Municipal Exposition in Urban Planning) was held at the same time as the creation of an office for the *Plan Regulador de Urbanización y Extensión*

(Regulating Plan for Urban Planning and Extension), which would be directed by Carlos Della Paolera.[56]

Probably the *Congreso Argentino de Urbanismo* (Argentinean Urban Congress) held in 1935 urged the formulation of projects with major urban impact; but from 1932, Bereterbide and Ernesto Vautier insisted on the moving of some of the administrative activities to a so-called 'Centro Cívico' (Civic Centre), while Julio Oraola presented another project also aimed at diminishing the central value of the district around Plaza de Mayo.[57] All seemed to have been convinced that the centre of the capital was passé and even the *Dirección Nacional de Arquitectura* (National Office of Architecture) studied the idea of the *Ciudad del Gobierno* (Government City) moved to the Costanera Norte.[58] These offices

Figure 3.13 Project by the *Ministerio de Obras Públicas* for the transformation of Plaza de Mayo, 1934. Demolition of the Cathedral, the *Cabildo* and House of State. (*Source*: Archivo del Centro de Documentación de Arquitectura Latinoamericana, CEDODAL)

proposed the construction of two huge buildings for the *Ministerios de Guerra y Marina*
(Ministries of War and Navy), of which only
one – fortunately – was built in the last and
most boring version of French academicism
(figure 3.14).

Perhaps the most important work of the
decade was the opening of the Avenida 9 de
Julio, proposed by Law from 1912, and subject to arduous and slow discussions on its

configuration (figure 3.15). Della Paolera
advocated the demolition of complete blocks
so as to create a parkway, as opposed to the
very minor cutbacks which the other technical offices put forward. From this point of
view, the high-handed gesture by the *Ministerio
de Obras Públicas* (Ministry of Public Works)
in constructing its building (1933) in the middle
of the planned route of the avenue, showed
the latent ideological conflicts between powers.

Figure 3.14 Project by
the National
Government in the
Costanera Norte. It
includes the Cathedral,
Archbishop's Palace,
House of Government,
History Museum,
Library, Public Records
and Embassies. The
historic centre of the
city is being displaced.
Designed by the
architect Federico Laas
in 1934. (*Source*:
Archivo del Centro de
Documentación de
Arquitectura
Latinoamericana,
CEDODAL)

Figure 3.15 9 de Julio (North-South) Avenue project, with the design of the Civic Centre. Designed by the architects Fermín Bereterbide and Ernesto Vautier in 1933. (*Source*: Archivo del Centro de Documentación de Arquitectura Latinoamericana, CEDODAL)

Finally, the avenue was converted into 'the widest in the world', as the city inhabitants like to say, due to a laudable decision taken by the Municipality which marked the beginning of the differentiation of competences between local decisions and the central government's interventions.[59]

The imagery of the new avenue was curious. It combined a landscape which was bucolically French, lacking joy, thought of by Luro in 1909; an exaggerated neo-fascist intervention in a monumental, Mussolini-like style, with wide boulevards proposed by Angel Guido; and the homogeneous illusion which was put forward by Alberto Prebisch, author of the Obelisk, the new symbol of the city in 1936.[60] The harsh reality of the city constructed by real estate speculation allows us today to see the deplorable urban landscape which came with the half century which it took to construct the avenue.[61]

Perhaps one should mention as the last endeavour of urban ideology, also neo-conservative, the task encouraged by Guido in his texts and projects for 'the re-Argentinization of buildings through urban planning'. For the provincial cities of Salta and Tucumán, this ideology led to proposals for major interventions which would alter their urban design and fabric, replacing the French scenery with a neo-colonial one.[62] The change of clothing did not mean a better understanding of the historical city or of the true way of life of its inhabitants.

Balance and Reflections

This survey allows us to understand up to what point the urban planning in Buenos Aires was bound up with the centres of interest of European thought during the last half a century. Building Aesthetic, Hygiene and Transport were the axes along which the discourse of this conservative modernity flowed. Urban embellishment which was held to the fore in discussions, never took into consideration the inhabitants, their lifestyles, nor even the reality which existed.[63]

Lacking historical support, the illusion of the enlightened thought projected its false light on a vanishing model imported from abroad which, in its various forms, always had at root the desire to deny the nation's own identity.[64] However, something was achieved: Buenos Aires shows this scenery – which today forms a privileged part of its patrimony – with the proud certainty that it is the Americas' most European city.

NOTES

1. Clemençeau, G. (1911) *Notes de Voyage dans l'Amérique du Sud. Argentine, Uruguay, Brésil*. Paris: Hachette et Cie.

2. For further information about colonial Buenos Aires, see Molinari, R.L. (1980) *Buenos Aires 4 siglos*. Buenos Aires: Tea; Peña, E. (1910) *Documentos y planos relativos al período edilicio colonial de la ciudad de Buenos Aires*. Buenos Aires: Municipalidad de Buenos Aires; Taullard, A. (1940) *Los planos más antiguos de Buenos Aires*. Buenos Aires: Peuser; Gutiérrez, R. (1992) *Buenos Aires. Evolución histórica*. Bogotá: Escala.

3 Gutiérrez, R. and Nicolini, A. (2000) *La ciudad y sus transformaciones. Apartado de la nueva historia de la Nación Argentina*. Buenos Aires: Academia Nacional de la Historia, Planeta, Vol. IV.

4. Paula, A. de and Gutiérrez, R. (1974) *Santiago Bevans y Carlos Enrique Pellegrini. La encrucijada de la arquitectura argentina*. Resistencia: UNNE, pp. 33, 171.

5. See Balbín, V. (1873) *Mejoras de las vías públicas de la ciudad de Buenos Aires*. Buenos Aires: Imprenta del Mercurio; Sourdeaux, A. (1862) *Apuntes sobre la industria artesiana*. Buenos Aires: Imprenta Berneim y Boneo; Pellegrini, C.E. (1854) Pozos artesianos. *Revista del Plata*, 6, p. 76.

6. The Beare *catastro* (land registry) is kept at the Museo de la Ciudad de Buenos Aires.

7. Senillosa, F. (1875) *Leyes de Espropiación necesarias y embellecimiento de la ciudad de Buenos Aires por medio de las Empresas Particulares*. París: Tipografía Best.

8. Pando, H. and others (1965) *Arquitectura del Estado de Buenos Aires*. Buenos Aires: Instituto de Arte Americano-UBA.

9. Ferrer, A. (1963) *La economía argentina. Las etapas de su desarrollo y problemas*. México: Fondo de Cultura Económica.

10. Gutiérrez, R. (1983) *Arquitectura y urbanismo en Iberoamérica*. Madrid: Cátedra.

11. Santini, S. and others (1997) *La obra de Francisco Tamburini en Argentina. El espacio del poder*. Iesi: Comune di Iesi.

12. Tartarini, J. and Radovanovic, E. (1999) *Agua y saneamiento en Buenos Aires*. Buenos Aires: Aguas Argentinas.

13. Berjman, S. (1998) *Plazas y parques de Buenos Aires. La obra de los paisajistas franceses. André, Courtois, Thays, Bouvard, Forestier, 1860–1930*. Buenos Aires: Gobierno de la Ciudad de Buenos Aires, Fondo de Cultura Económica.

14. On the port of Buenos Aires, see Pinasco, E. (1942) *El puerto de Buenos Aires. Contribución al estudio de su historia (1536–1898)*. Buenos Aires: Talleres Gráficos López; Pellegrini, C.E. (1853) Puerto de Buenos Aires. *Revista del Plata*, 1, 2 and 3, pp. 3–5, 13, 21, 29–30; Huergo, L. (1904) *Historia técnica del puerto de Buenos Aires*. Buenos Aires: Editorial Revista Técnica.

15. Paula, A. de, Gutiérrez, R. and Viñuales, G. (1981) *Influencia alemana en la arquitectura argentina*. Resistencia: UNNE.

16. Jalikis, M. (1925) *Historia de los medios de transporte y de su influencia en el desarrollo urbano de la ciudad de Buenos Aires*. Buenos Aires: Compañía de Tranvías Anglo-Argentina. See also Viglione, L.A. (1878) *Estudios sobre los tranways en la ciudad de Buenos Aires*. Buenos Aires: Imprenta de Pablo Coni.

17. See Iñigo Carreras, H. (1961) *El pueblo de Belgrano. Notas y documentos para su historia*. Buenos Aires: Centro de Estudios Históricos del Pueblo de Belgrano; Cunietti Ferrando, A.J. (1977) *San José de Flores. El pueblo y el partido (1580–1880)*. Buenos Aires: Junta de Estudios Históricos de San José de Flores.

18. Scobie, J.R. (1977) *Buenos Aires. Del centro a los barrios, 1870–1910*. Buenos Aires: Solar-Hachette.

19. Schávelzon, D. (1980) La arquitectura para la educación en el siglo XIX, in *Documentos para una historia de la arquitectura argentina. Período 5*. Buenos Aires: Summa, without pages in the original; Consejo Nacional de Educación (1886) *Planos de las Escuelas Comunes de la Capital construidas bajo la dirección del Consejo Nacional de Educación*. Buenos Aires: Litografía Stiller-Laas.

20. On the railways, see Dirección de Informaciones y publicaciones ferroviarias (1946) *Origen y desarrollo de los ferrocarriles argentinos*. Buenos Aires: El Ateneo; Scalabrini Ortiz, R. (1940) *Historia de los ferrocarriles argentinos*. Buenos Aires: Reconquista; Wright, W. (1980) *Los ferrocarriles ingleses en la Argentina*. Buenos Aires: Emecé.

21. Córdoba, A.O. (1983) *Juan Antonio Buschiazzo, arquitecto y urbanista de Buenos Aires*. Buenos Aires: Asociación Dante Alighieri.

22. Beccar Varela, A. (1926) *Torcuato de Alvear. Primer Intendente Municipal de la ciudad de Buenos Aires. Su acción edilicia*. Buenos Aires: Imp. Guillermo Kraft.

23. On the La Plata and its urban proposals, see Burgos, J.M. (1882) *La nueva Capital de la Provincia*. Buenos Aires: Imp. Pablo Coni; Nicolini, A. (1981) La Plata, la fundación de una capital. *Construcción de la ciudad*, 14, pp. 42–47; Paula, A. de (1986) *La Plata. La ciudad y las tierras*. Buenos Aires: Banco de la Provincia de Buenos Aires.

24. On the Avenida de Mayo, see Comisión Central de la Avenida de Mayo (1890) *Memoria presentada a la Intendencia Municipal*. Buenos Aires, Compañía Sudamericana de Billetes de Banco; Llanes, R. (1955) *La Avenida de Mayo, media centuria entre recuerdos y evocaciones*. Buenos Aires: Kraft.

25. Clemençeau, *op. cit.*, p. 28.

26. The urban ideas by the time of Bouvard's arrival can be seen in Desplats, M. (1906) *Mejoras urbanas*. Buenos Aires: Talleres de la Penitenciaría; Chanourdie, E. (1907) La transformación edilicia de Buenos Aires. *Arquitectura*, 44, pp. 27–30.

27. (1907) *La Prensa* (June 23), p. 5.

28. Berjman, S. (1995) Proyectos de Bouvard para la Buenos Aires del Centenario: Barrio, plazas, hospital y Exposición. *DANA. Documentos de Arquitectura Nacional y Americana*, 37/38, pp. 41–53.

29. Tartarini, J. (1991) La polémica Bouvard-Jaeschke. *DANA Documentos de Arquitectura Nacional y Americana*, 30, pp. 44–52.

30. Bouvard, J. (1910) *El nuevo plano de la ciudad de Buenos Aires*. Buenos Aires: Intendencia Municipal de la Capital.

31. Jaeschke, V.J. (1908) La primera avenida diagonal. Trazado defectuoso y costoso. *Revista Técnica*, 47, pp. 55–58.

32. Tartarini, La polémica Bouvard-Jaeschke, *loc. cit.*; this work can be used as a reference on the subject. On the local reactions to the arrival of the French professionals, see Tartarini, J. (1987) Carlos Altgelt, Arquitecto no Ingeniero. *DANA. Documentos de Arquitectura Nacional y Americana*, 24, pp. 7–14.

33. Bouvard, J. (1907) La futura Plaza del Congreso. *La Prensa* (June 27), p. 6.

34. Jaeschke, V.J. (1927) Urbanismo. Edificación de la Diagonal Presidente Roque Saénz Peña con desprecio a la higiene y a la estética. *Revista de Arquitectura*, 73, pp. 21–24.

35. Luro, P.O. (1911) *Avenida de Norte a Sur. Proyecto y diseño. Cámara de Diputados de la Nación*. Buenos Aires: Imp. Tragant; Municipalidad de la Ciudad de Buenos Aires (1912) *Avenida de Norte a Sur. Ley Nacional 8.855*. Buenos Aires: Imp. G. Kraft.

36. Gutiérrez, R., Tartarini, J. and others (1995) *Sociedad Central de Arquitectos. 100 años de compromiso con el país. (1886–1986)*. Buenos Aires: SCA.

37. Gutiérrez, R., Gutman, M. and Pérez Escolano, V. (1994) *El arquitecto Martín Noel. Su tiempo y su obra*. Sevilla: Junta de Andalucía, Consejería de Cultura.

38. Gutiérrez, R. (ed.) (1998) *Arquitectura latinoamericana del siglo XX*. Barcelona: Lunwerg.

39. Gutiérrez, R. (1979) La búsqueda de lo nacional en la arquitectura. *Revista Nacional de Cultura*, 4, pp. 35–46.

40. Gutiérrez, R. (1995) Buenos Aires, modelo para armar (1910-1927). *DANA. Documentos de Arquitectura Nacional y Americana*, 37/38, pp. 36–40.

41. (1912) La contratación del Arquitecto Chaussemiche. *Revista del Centro de Estudiantes de Arquitectura*, 6, pp. 253–266.

42. Berjman, S. (1992) J.C.N. Forestier y la ciudad de Buenos Aires. *DANA. Documentos de Arquitectura Nacional y Americana*, 31/32, pp. 84–90; this work can be used as a reference on the subject. See also Berjman, *Plazas y parques de Buenos Aires . . ., loc. cit.*

43. (1923) La transformación de Buenos Aires. *La Prensa* (December 12), p. 8.

44. Forestier, J.C.N. (1905) *Grandes villes et systèmes des parcs*. Paris: Hachette.

45. Intendencia Municipal (1925) *Proyecto orgánico para la urbanización del Municipio. El plano regulador y de reforma de la Capital Federal*. Buenos Aires: Talleres Peuser.

46. (1927) Las ideas del Profesor L. Jaussely sobre la urbanización de Buenos Aires. *Revista Arquitectura*, 110, pp. 6–8.

47. Nicolini, A. (1995) Le Corbusier: Utopía y Buenos Aires. *DAN.A Documentos de Arquitectura Nacional y Americana*, 37/38, pp. 106–113.

48. Sendra, R. (1982) Le Corbusier en Buenos Aires

(1929). *DANA. Documentos de Arquitectura Nacional y Americana*, 14, pp. 42–48. See also Le Corbusier (1930) *Précisions sur un état présent de l'architecture et de l'urbanisme*. Paris: C.Grès et Cie.

49. Paula, A. de (1979) Le Corbusier y otros eventos en la arquitectura argentina. *Nuestra Arquitectura*, 509, pp. 46-50. See also Collins, C.C. (1995) Urban Interchange in the Southern Cone: Le Corbusier (1929) and Werner Hegemann (1931) in Argentina. *Journal of the Society of Architectural Historians*, 54(2), pp. 208–227.

50. Le Corbusier and others (1947) Plan Director para Buenos Aires. *La Arquitectura de Hoy*, 4, pp. 4–53. See also Borthagaray, J.M. (1981) El Plan Director de Buenos Aires 1938–1940, in *Le Corbusier y Buenos Aires*. Buenos Aires: CAYC, without pages in the original.

51. Hegemann, W. (1931) *Problemas urbanos de Rosario*. Rosario: Municipalidad de Rosario; Hegemann, W. (1931) *Mar del Plata, el balneario y el urbanismo moderno*. Buenos Aires: Comisión Pro Mar del Plata.

52. Tartarini, J. (1995) La visita de Werner Hegemann a la Argentina en 1931. *DANA. Documentos de Arquitectura Nacional y Americana*, 37/38, pp. 54–63.

53. Jorge Kálnay collaborated with Hegemann in realizing model exercises of the buildings allowed by the actual application of the *Código de Edificación* in force in Buenos Aires at that time.

54. Although they had been avoided in the French urbanists' proposals, Hegemann's articles put before us questions such as housing, that were important in the professional debate by the time other Europeans came to explain the projects of working-class housing in Vienna and Berlin.

55. A detailed list of these projects can be seen in Gutiérrez, R. and Berjman, S. (1995) *La Plaza de Mayo, escenario de la vida del país*. Buenos Aires: Fundación Banco Boston.

56. Della Paolera, C.M. (1933) *Publicación y Decreto aprobatorio del Plan Regulador de Urbanización y Extensión de la Ciudad de Buenos Aires presentado por el Ingeniero Urbanista Carlos M. Della Paolera*. Buenos Aires: Los Amigos de la Ciudad. See also Della Paolera, C.M. (1977) *Buenos Aires y sus problemas urbanos*. Buenos Aires: Oikos, Buenos Aires; Bereterbide, F. (1931) Del Plan Regulador de la ciudad de Buenos Aires y sus alrededores. Buenos Aires: Archivo Cravotto, Montevideo. Typed copy.

57. Otaola, J.V. (1933) *El Centro Cívico de la ciudad de Buenos Aires. Fundamentos de la división funcional*. Buenos Aires: Talleres Gráficos Ferrari. See also Rocca,

G., Bereterbide, F., Palazzo, P. and Vautier, E. (1936) *Ubicación y construcción de los edificios públicos de la ciudad de Buenos Aires*. Buenos Aires: Informe de la Comisión Especial.

58. Municipalidad de la Ciudad de Buenos Aires (1939) *II Exposición Municipal de Urbanismo*. Buenos Aires: Dirección del Plan de Urbanización. See (1937–1938) *Primer Congreso Argentino de Urbanismo*. Buenos Aires: 3 Vols. In this congress, the landscape designer Benito Carrasco presented a project for creating an Instituto de Altos Estudios Urbanos (Institute of High Urban Studies). See Berjman, S. (1991) El pensamiento de Benito Carrasco: Hacia una teoría paisajística argentina. *DANA. Documentos de Arquitectura Nacional y Americana*, 30, pp. 22–30. Having been presented in the congress (Vol. II, p. 130), Architect Laas's project about the decentralization and urbanization of central areas in cities and communes had already been objected to by Della Paolera, C.M. (1934) Opinión de la Municipalidad en el Proyecto relativo a la construcción de 'La Ciudad del Gobierno'. *Boletín Municipal*, 3518 (January 12), without pages in the original.

59. Municipalidad de la ciudad de Buenos Aires (1938) *Avenida 9 de Julio. Leyes, Ordenanzas, Decretos, estudios, datos, informes referentes a su construcción*. Buenos Aires: Municipalidad de la Ciudad de Buenos Aires. See also Della Paolera, C.M. (1937) La Avenida Nueve de Julio. Características y ventajas funcionales y económicas de su apertura en todo lo ancho de la manzana. Separata de *La Ingeniería*, 758.

60. Gutiérrez, R. and others. (1999) *Alberto Prebisch. Una vanguardia con tradición*. Buenos Aires: CEDODAL. See also Guido, A. (1941) Monumentalización funcional de la Avenida 9 de Julio. Conferencia en la ciudad de Rosario del 25 de abril de 1941. Rosario.

61. Gutman, M. and Hardoy, J.E. (1992) *Buenos Aires*. Madrid: Mapfre-América.

62. Guido, A. (1939) *Reargentinización edilicia por el urbanismo. Exposición auspiciada por los Amigos de la Ciudad en ocasión de inaugurarse el Instituto Argentino de Urbanismo*. Buenos Aires: Amigos de la Ciudad.

63. Hardoy, J.E. (1995) Teorías y prácticas urbanísticas en Europa entre 1850 y 1930. Su traslado a América Latina. *DANA. Documentos de Arquitectura Nacional y Americana*, 37/38, pp. 12–30.

64. Gutiérrez, R. (1996) Modelos e imaginarios europeos en el urbanismo americano, *Revista de Arquitectura*, 8, pp. 2–3.

The Time of the Capitals: Rio de Janeiro and São Paulo: Words, Actors and Plans

Margareth da Silva Pereira

Visions of an Imperial Capital in Project: Rio de Janeiro (1822–1840)

With a mixture of curiosity and surprise, in the 1820s, thousands of Parisians and Londoners began to discover Rio de Janeiro almost without leaving home. Brazilian Independence was proclaimed in 1822, and in Paris as early as 1824 the Prévost brothers, the most renowned exhibitors of panoramas in Europe in the early nineteenth century, displayed grand sights of Rio with great success. Through its representation on canvas, Emperor Pedro I introduced the city as the new capital of the Empire of Brazil, thus meeting the expectations that Brazilian America had awakened among European businessmen, intellectuals, artists and naturalists since the country's harbours had opened to free trade in 1808. Similar panoramic sights of the city were shown somewhat later, in 1828, in London this time. In that year, in Leicester Square, Robert Burford also exhibited his grand panoramic images of the city as depicted by William John Burchell.[1]

Regarded by Baudelaire as the 'expression of a new feeling of life', the urban *panoramas* that multiplied in several cities in Europe and America, delimit a time that reaches the end of the nineteenth century, marked by the circulation of city images that celebrated and recognized the urban condition itself from new ideological, epistemological, economic and political perspectives. Exchanging knowledge or trade values, these cities were to engage in a permanent movement of creation and recreation of their interdependent links.

The time of construction of these 'nebulae'[2] of cities was, to use old terminology, a 'bourgeois' one. That is, it was a time in which class values were consolidated; above all, 'living in a city' was established worldwide on a new scale and with a new perspective; and, unlike what still happened in vast areas of Brazil, the older forms of ruling social organization were replaced. Simultaneously, nation states redesigned and consolidated their positions relative to one another, sometimes establishing their significance on the international stage through existing major cities, such as Rio de Janeiro, sometimes through developing new urban centres which, like São Paulo, had until then been of minor importance. The early nineteenth-century exhibit of the panoramic images of the capital of the new Empire of Brazil could be seen as one among the many signs of such alignment of cities that increasingly strengthened their bonds and shared certain of the cultural processes of the progressive world.

In the case of Brazil, this movement rescued the strategic function of the harbour of Rio de Janeiro whose mainstay at the beginning of the eighteenth century had been the export of gold. With the continuous economic activity, promoted by wealth circulation, the city had already achieved, by 1763, the function of political-administrative capital of the Viceroyalty of the State of Brazil.[3]

the transfer of the Court and the opening of Brazilian harbours to free trade in that year, there began a century of social, political and urban 'reforms' which would raise the city to a higher level of both function and activity.

The Court's arrival not only turned Rio de Janeiro into the capital of the Portuguese monarchy in the tropics (1808–1822) but also signalled Brazilian society's irreversible transition to a new place in history. The urban dynamics that were to develop thereafter, although fluctuating, peaked with the proclamation of Independence, placing Rio de Janeiro in the position of capital of the Empire of Brazil, a position that survived until the proclamation of the Republic in 1889.

Thus, Taunay's and Burchell's panoramas of Rio de Janeiro (figure 4.1) captured the moment when the city's new position crystallized as the result of its increasing participation a new – capitalist, urban, merchant and industrial – order, and the city reigned

Figure 4.1 A panoramic view of Rio de Janeiro, by Felix-Émile Taunay, *c.* 1822. Watercolour. Photo: Dominique Delaunay. (*Source*: Private Collection)

In the last decade of the eighteenth century, the centrality already exerted by Rio, together with the emancipation movements which threatened the Portuguese Crown's sovereignty in Latin America, placed the city in an even more privileged position. This was further enhanced by plans to transfer the very capital of the Kingdom of Portugal[4] from Lisbon to Brazil. With Napoleon's expansionism in Europe, the Portuguese Crown was actually to settle in Rio de Janeiro in 1808; thus adding to the city's economically strong role a politically relevant one. With

over the Latin American continent as very few cities did.

In the early nineteenth century, the capital, now of a new Empire, was just one of many cities – among other numerous less important urban nebulae – that were building a closer exchange network (figure 4.2). Hardly exceeding 110,000 inhabitants,[5] its social complexity and economic performance were nevertheless infinitely more significant than in the colonial period.[6] It was depicted in drawings as seemingly among those 'singular' cities that, due to their past history, their current dynamism,

Figure 4.2 A watercolour of Rio de Janeiro by Eduard Hildebrandt, 1844. Photo: Fausto Fleury. (*Source*: Biblioteca Nacional)

or their future promise, began to celebrate or to be celebrated in accordance with the ethos of the panoramas: Constantinople, Rome, Paris, London . . . That is, old and new capital cities which were the badges of history itself and of the advent of the industrial and urban era.

Canvasses depicted the Emperor on the Morro do Castelo (Castelo Hill), which was a belvedere for focusing both the city and, chiefly, the 'untouched' nature in the surroundings. Although the image of Rio de Janeiro would evoke a new Arcadia, the city had nevertheless been the target of numerous criticisms since the late eighteenth century. In fact, the Court settlement and the Independence proclamation not only resulted in the city being more frequently and deeply

analysed, but also began to set up the problem of the symbolic role the capital-city itself should perform in a new political and economic order.[7]

Because of the position Rio de Janeiro occupied, during the century, in the international 'nebulae' of cities, discussions on its shape and role were sometimes heated, and the city's technical elites regularly highlighted its potential *and* its dysfunctions.

In the successive projects that were discussed for the city as the capital of a newly independent territory, two opposing rhetorics are to be seen regarding the image and the function of a capital city. One, the more modern and dynamic, associated the notion of capital with 'circulation', communication, and exchange, thus linking it to the very ability of a capital to attract – human, economic, scientific – 'capital'. It prioritized the efficiency of circulation networks and the flow of – material and immaterial – values and assets that every city, but especially a capital city, should be able to use to advantage and for interaction. This view had been current since the late eighteenth century, and could be said to have caused the emancipation process itself.

Paradoxically, the Court transfer introduced a more archaic, static and symbolic view into the discussions. Bound solely to architecture and the notion of monumentalism, urban 'embellishment' was made the primary instrument for enhancing the city's position and distinguishing it from all others.

During the Imperial period (1822–1889) the focus on Rio de Janeiro's urban form would stand out at least in three instances, which provide evidence of the commitment to this view. The first coincided with the exhibit of panoramas mentioned above and the first stage of the internationalization of the economic space of Brazil, now an emancipated nation. Among the first urban redevelopment projects in the city, the highly original proposals by Grandjean de Montigny

(in 1824–1825, 1827), stand out at the time of the proclamation of Independence.

The second episode is marked by engineer Henrique de Beaurepaire Rohan's projects (in 1843), and peaked with those by Henry Law and the debates on the city's harbour and water front (in 1858–1859), which introduced proposals for the capital's redevelopment of an entirely different magnitude and arising from a more complex set of notions.

Lastly, the projects by the *Comissão de Melhoramentos* (Improvement Commission), by August M.F. Glaziou and by André Rebouças (between 1837 and 1876), after the war against Paraguay, signal that discussion of the capital's reform had been resumed, now on an even greater scale as shown, in the harbour's project by Brunless & McKerrow, around the end of the Imperial period, in 1888 (figure 4.3).[8]

From the point of view of architecture and urbanism, the most important act of modernization undertaken in the short period during which Rio de Janeiro was the Portuguese crown capital, was the hiring of a French Artistic Mission, which in 1816 created the *Escola Real de Ciências Artes e Ofícios* (Royal School of Sciences, Arts and

Figure 4.3 Improvement project for the Harbour of Rio de Janeiro, by Brunless & McKerrow, 1888. (*Source*: Arquivo Nacional)

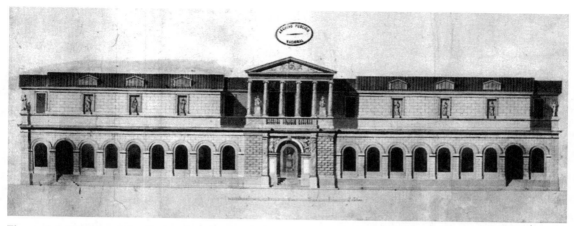

Figure 4.4 Facade of the *Beaux-Arts* Academy, Rio de Janeiro, by Grandjean de Montigny, 1826. Photo: Fausto Fleury. (*Source*: Arquivo Nacional)

Crafts), renamed the *Academia Imperial de Belas Artes* (Imperial Academy of Fine Arts) after the Independence. The *Academia* would be the Americas' first school for the education of architects, directly conceived in accordance to the École des Beaux-Arts in Paris, by Joachim Lebreton – the *Institut de France*'s *Beaux-Arts* secretary, one of the highest authorities in the field of culture during the Napoleonic period.

The Mission also included several artists educated at the *École des Beaux-Arts* and exiled after Napoleon's fall. Among these were Grandjean de Montigny, architect, *prix de Rome*, who had worked in the Court of Jerôme Bonaparte in Cassel; Nicolas-Antoine Taunay, painter and member of the *Institut*; and Felix-Émile Taunay, author already mentioned in the context of the city panorama exhibited by Prévost. From 1816 Grandjean de Montigny made his home in Rio de Janeiro and until his death in 1850 he would be the only teacher of Architecture in the Academy, having created a firm foundation for a new scholarly practice and for the privileged dialogue of the local professionals

with France.[9] Questions of embellishment began to gain ground in the technical and political debates on the capital's reforms around 1824–1827, after de Montigny's first proposals for some areas of the city (figures 4.4 and 4.5). Despite the originality and correctness of the architect's ideas, these would, from an urban and cultural point-of-view, lead in a rather backward direction. Indeed, the 'new' neo-classical image conceived for the city introduced to the local culture an archaic element, until then irrelevant to its tradition. On the other hand, it would shift the local elites' regard not only to the past but also to a perspective external to the country itself, in a more static and mostly architectural and 'monumental' sense. This tendency would become increasingly evident in the second half of the nineteenth century, as a hierarchic, linear and evolutionist view of development and culture became hegemonic in the West.

As in many other cities, hygiene would also be the focus of attention in the debates and projects for Rio de Janeiro. The hygienists' criticism had been condemning since the

Figure 4.5 *Projet d'ouverture de la voie Impériale*, Rio de Janeiro, by Grandjean de Montigny, *c*. 1825. (*Source*: Biblioteca Nacional)

eighteenth century both of the built-up shape of the city, with its compact architecture which had developed in narrow and long lots, and of its harbours, the centre for the spread of epidemics. Medical doctors repeatedly advocated the razing of Castelo Hill, the cradle of the city foundation, alleging it prevented the full 'circulation' of winds in the urban area. In their reports, among other prescriptions, they also strongly encouraged the occupation of the hillsides around the city, intervening on the expansion of the new urbanized areas, causing the surroundings of

Floresta da Tijuca (Tijuca Forest) to be praised as a residential place and a compelling itinerary for the numerous foreign travellers that began to visit the city.

By the 1820s the tripod that would support the urban reforms in many European and Latin American capitals during the nineteenth century – circulation, hygiene, embellishment – had already laid its bases on Rio de Janeiro. In opposition mostly to the European movement, embellishment, as we have seen, would be the last notion to be taken into account in the debates on the capital's functions and roles although the first one to gain visibility after Grandjean de Montigny's projects and one to be often associated with the quest to promote the city's dialogue with its site's exuberant nature.[10]

In spite of those projects and certain technical measures like the updating of the urban cartography, with its successive city maps by J.C. Rivara (1812), J.J. Souza (1818), Steinmann (1831), the political instabilities in this period, which peaked at the abdication of Dom Pedro I in 1831 and dragged themselves until 1840, after Dom Pedro II's acclamation, made the planned reforms unfeasible in those years. However, the internationalisation process of the country's and its capital's economy were in expansion, making itself felt in other locations of the centre-south region, mostly along the Paraíba river valley. From then on the commercialisation of the coffee produced in that region would be the basis of the country's economy, and the commercial dynamism that ensued would gradually pull such cities as São Paulo out of the marginal situation they were in.

Indeed, until Independence, São Paulo was but a distributing centre of goods located on the inland *planalto* (tableland). Like French naturalist Auguste Saint-Hilaire observed when he visited the city in 1819, São Paulo 'would never have flourished . . . more than [the harbour of] Santos . . . had it not become the capital of the Province and seat of all civil and ecclesiastic authorities'.[11] In spite of the growing interest by foreign designers, including Burchell, and of having become a small 'students' burg'[12] after the School of Law was created, the expansion of the coffee culture would begin to turn it, since the 1840s, into a capital-city of another nature and later into a first-magnitude city among the Brazilian urban nuclei.

The Functions of a Capital City: Economy vs. Aesthetics (1840–1860)

Once the political stability was ensured by the proclamation of Dom Pedro II, new re-development projects began to emerge, bringing not only a much more complex view of the capital's role, but also revealing conflicts about the areas to be remodelled and over what should be the focus of a 'progressive' agenda. The first plan to focus on the city overall was that by the engineer Henrique de Beaurepaire Rohan, Director of *Obras Públicas* (Public Works), which was submitted to the City Chamber in 1843. Although they may be deemed imprecise by today's scientific standards, his proposals were a true revolution in the way they sought an objective and systematic vision of the city in order to correct its dysfunctions. A new discourse and new vocabulary for an urbanizing world were his first instruments in the quest for a 'normalization of the social space' and, like those of many other social reformers in the first half of the nineteenth century, Beaurepaire Rohan's plan included no drawings.

With a long argumentation, the engineer disclosed two proposals for the capital. The most radical one required the demolition of one-third of the area so far built up. The second, which centred on circulation, proposed (just as Haussmann would do later in Paris) more than eighteen *percées* (openings in the existing built-up areas), destroying also the Castelo Hill and favouring the improvement of traffic flows in the north-south direction.

Beaurepaire Rohan's Rio de Janeiro had already expanded west of Campo de Santana (Field of Santana), an urban space clearly visible in Taunay's panorama. With around 150,000 inhabitants, the city was active economically, although increasingly socially unequal. The ethnic or socio-professional divisions detailed in the pages of his report tell us of businessmen, slaves and *quitandeiras*,[13] but mostly of foreigners and people from the provinces attracted to the city by the commercial and economic activity. Analysing how these new urban dwellers were suffering in Rio de Janeiro with the housing shortage, Beaurepaire Rohan introduced housing conditions as a matter to be discussed as a state and social problem. In times of competition among cities (and markets), he highlighted the need to undertake 'public works and improvements' for the well-being of citizens. But, he suggested, at such times public bodies should seek to work with private ones in cases where 'philanthropic' ideas could also be 'profitable' ones.[14]

Indeed, the technical debates of this decade were also a consequence of new *Códigos de Posturas* (Posture Codes).[15] The

1840s projects, for instance, responded in part to the new urban norms which, discussed during 1830–1831, were approved in 1838 and published in 1848, becoming examples of codes for other cities in the provinces. The 1840s thus marked a new political and economic era for the country, beginning in the capital Rio de Janeiro and reaching ports such as Recife and urban nuclei located in the expanded area of the coffee culture, such as Campinas and São Paulo.

During the 1840s both in São Paulo and Rio de Janeiro there was the first mention of designating urban expansion areas. '*Subúrbio*' (suburb) is included in a plan for São Paulo dated *circa* 1840,[16] and the expression '*cidade nova*' (new town), which appeared already in Rohan's report in Rio (1843), shaped the new areas in the *Paulista*[17] capital between 1855 and 1863. This was the period when rural properties near these cities were transformed into new urban areas and many great properties were subdivided into lots, beginning with the opening of Rua Formosa (Formosa Street) and of several streets between Praça dos Curros (Curros Square), currently Praça da República (Republic Square) and Vale do Anhangabaú (Valley of Anhangabaú).[18]

How can one discuss the process of development of the city, of opening of new streets, of urban growth or of appearance and circulation of new words, without being aware of the – even unequal – role these cities came to play in a trade system in which coffee was the mainstay of the whole country's economy? As an example, Brazilian exports in the 1840s increased 214 per cent, which created a major change in the inflow of capital to the country. How can one fail to relate these changes with the manifestations that took place in Rio de Janeiro at the same time

although on a larger scale, like the aforementioned project by Henrique de Beaurepaire Rohan, which not only hinted at, but also projected a 'new city' immediately beside the old urban layout inherited from the colonial period?

Although Beaurepaire Rohan's projects were not executed, his ideas continued to be discussed. Altogether, between 1840 and 1850 several social and cultural institutions were created, promoting preservation of certain areas of the city and having a negative effect on others. Therefore, private associations appeared as the *Instituto Histórico e Geográfico Brasileiro* (Historical and Geographical Institute of Brazil) and the *Sociedade Auxiliadora da Indústria Nacional* (Society for the Assistance of National Industry), although there was also relevance in the foundation of governmental institutions for social-life control like the Nova Casa de Correção (New Correction House), the Hospício Dom Pedro II (Pedro II Mental Hospital) and the first indoor markets.

In addition to the new institutions, in 1851 the British Engineer Charles Neate began to manage the modernization of the harbour zone, which had been suggested by Rohan. However, the new works proved to be insufficient in view of the port's growing traffic, fuelled by the incremented production of coffee, which became the country's first product for export.[19]

The prohibition of the slave trade from 1850 freed up capital that could be directly invested in development of the city. At the same time the rapid circulation of ideas, information and goods brought about major changes in the capital, characterized by an intense dynamism. These processes led to the reorganization of *Banco do Brasil* (Bank of Brazil) and *Casa da Moeda* (Royal Mint), as well as to the construction of new buildings for these institutions. Generally, the construction sector expanded and new built-up areas appeared as a result of numerous subdivisions of properties.

These developments, together with special regulations governing economic activity, such as the Commercial Code of 1850, marked a new phase in the life of the country. Several private urban utility companies were set up, such as those for gas lighting and the operation of horse-drawn trams. In 1851 the Royal West India Mail Steam Packet Co. was incorporated to run the first regular steamship service between Rio de Janeiro and Southampton. During the decade, among several other enterprises, twenty new ocean-line companies appeared regularly serving the port of Rio de Janeiro, increasing enormously the postal exchange and the development of urban businesses as a whole.[20]

At the same time the railways underwent major developments. In 1852 Irineu Evangelista de Souza, later Baron of Mauá, who was involved with the reorganization of *Banco do Brasil* and the banking sector, led this movement by his example. Other initiatives in other regions followed, for instance, the organization of the railways of Recife and Água Preta along the banks of São Francisco river (1852), those from Bahia to the São Francisco river (1853), from Rio de Janeiro to São Paulo (1852), and from Santos to Jundiaí (1856), so creating the Brazilian Empire's major communication system.[21]

The government was a key participant in these developments and in 1861 a specific agency to manage such initiatives – the *Ministério da Agricultura, Comércio e Obras Públicas* (Agriculture, Commerce and Public Works Ministry) – was created.

In terms of urban development projects

during this period of internationalization of the economy, as was the case after the 1870s, the city's waterfront gained remarkable importance. Private initiatives also followed this trend. The density of occupation of the bay areas in Glória, Flamengo and Botafogo was greatly increased with the creation of new districts each of which was thereafter called a '*bairro*' – then a new word which began to circulate in the urban vocabulary. In addition to the rapid expansion of public transport from 1850s onwards, the waves of epidemics speeded the expansion of residential developments in those areas and on the hills, giving rise to Santa Teresa, Laranjeiras, and Andaraí as new urban units. In these new *bairros* the contemplation or experience of nature – sea, forest and waterfalls – promoted by new architectural styles contrasting with those of the ancient city, acquired an aesthetic value and expression.

In the 1850s, urban planning initiatives which focused on the waterfront as a source of aesthetic experience, with contemplation of the Baía de Guanabara (Bay of Guanabara) and culminating in the view of Pão de Açúcar (Sugar Loaf), were in continuous conflict with those more directly concerned with the area's functional nature, which focused on the harbour and its connection with the railway.

In fact the building of the Dom Pedro II Railway, linking Rio de Janeiro to São Paulo, created some problems for the effective functioning of the city. Its Central Station, located in the Campo de Santana, was not connected with the harbour, which resulted in disruption of the transfer of goods and passengers. From this period on, the urban tissue began to rend: the older part of the city was now identified as its 'centre', and it concentrated on the projects to raze the hills and the construction of commercial and residential areas. However, most development projects still hesitated regarding expansion of the harbour and the location of the port, sometimes proposing its location on the old harbour front in the downtown, sometimes displaced to the north, consolidating some existing docking sites in the sections of Prainha, Gamboa, and Santo Cristo (figure 4.6).[22]

Words such as physical and moral 'improvement', introduced into the administrative vocabulary from the time of the 1798 medical enquiry – when the viceroy had asked doctors about Rio's sanitary problems – began to add to other notions: 'industrial improvement' (1843, 1873–1876), 'repairs and reform of the city' (1843), 'embellishment', 'street traffic', 'communication', 'rectification'. Together they built Rio de Janeiro's technical lexicon until about the 1870s, in some of the proposals already mentioned.

As happened in several nineteenth-century examples – Barcelona, Marseilles, New York or Chicago – the status of capital began to be associated also with cities that stood out by virtue of their economic vitality or high level of technical and scientific performance, features that sometimes came to be shared by different urban centres in the same country. Such a trend was felt even in distant São Paulo, where local elites began to acquire technology and equipment, or to observe the experiments of a wider range of countries.[23]

War with Paraguay, political instability, and uncertainties of all kinds revealed the unstable position of the country – an ex-colony, now an Empire – and its main cities, and blocked more structural reforms in the urban mesh. However, the worsening of internal conditions such as urban and port circulation, housing shortages, epidemics, the expectations and demands of the new urban population, continued to instigate the imagination of native and foreign engineers and architects, who now worked in the country in increasingly greater numbers.

Figure 4.6 Part of the panorama on the city of Rio de Janeiro, by Victor Frond, 1861. (*Source*: Biblioteca Nacional)

Rio de Janeiro and São Paulo: Times of Disruption (1870–1890)

While the urbanization of Rio de Janeiro between 1870 and 1890 entered an even sharper stage of exchange and criticism of the old structures, in São Paulo it took the form of major changes in the old ways of living in cities. In the early 1870s, Rio de Janeiro, with a population of 235,381 inhabitants, was still the most important city in the country and still waited for the realization of some of the public works demanded during the previous half century. São Paulo, with a little over 30,000 inhabitants, was still a small capital of a province with a role secondary to that of Campinas, the important city in the coffee regions. Around this time, however, São Paulo began to show rapid change. It was not a major increase in population nor an economically strong role that drew attention to the *Paulista* capital, but a series of 'improvements' that showed that the city had begun to tackle urban 'problems' comparable to those of the Empire's capital.[24]

The urbanized areas extended beyond the 'triangle', defined by the monasteries of Carmo, São Francisco and São Bento and delimited by the Tamanduateí and Anhangabaú rivers, which had so much characterized the colonial city. Initiatives by the government and businessmen took shape and succeeded one another, speeding changes in, and technical instruments for, the control of urban expansion. Thus, the first systematic census of the São Paulo's population dated 1874[25] was accompanied by other technical innovations, such as the passing of a new *Código de Posturas* for the city, the lighting

and paving of public roads, the installation of a horse-drawn tramway network. In less than a decade, between 1867 and 1875, the railway connections between the harbours of Santos and Jundiaí in the coffee-expansion regions, and the lines of the Dom Pedro II Railway coming from Rio de Janeiro, were crossing São Paulo. These years also saw such significant gestures towards overcoming the topography limiting urban growth as the proposal by the Frenchman Jules Martin in 1877[26] to build a viaduct-boulevard. The inauguration fifteen years later, in 1892, of the Viaduto do Chá (Viaduct of the Tea) would be a landmark in the city history and a catalyst for the multiplication of subdivisions of numerous properties, named *chácaras*,[27] located on the hills surrounding the 'triangle'. The first among these subdivisions was that giving rise to the Campos Elíseos area, shortly followed that of Vila Buarque, so integrating into the city, ever more intensely, numerous lots of rural and suburban land (figures 4.7 and 4.8).

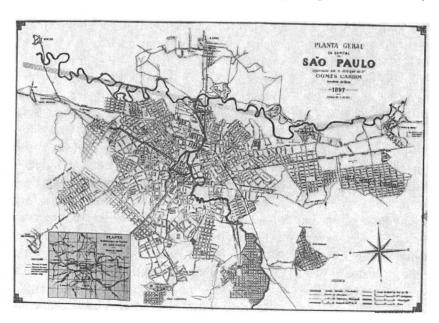

Figure 4.7 General Plan of São Paulo's capital city, org. under the direction of Dr. Gomes Cardim, 1897. (*Source*: *Plantas da cidade*, São Paulo: Comissão do IV Centenário, 1954)

Figure 4.8 Viaduto do Chá, São Paulo, 1892. From *Álbum de vistas da cidade* (1906). (*Source*: Biblioteca Nacional)

As the issue of urban 'embellishment' in Rio de Janeiro gained in influence in the plans presented between 1870 and 1890, Martin's project and the architecture of the new quarters revealed the importance attributed to it by São Paulo's rising bourgeoisie and technical elites.

During this period the development of liberal ideas gained new connotations compared to the 1820s and 1840s.[28] Social degradation, associated with the maintenance of the slave regime, led many to believe that the State should undertake a liberal policy as far as businessmen were concerned, although an interventionist one concerning the *negro* and *mulato* population, which lived 'promiscuously' in various forms of lodgings for low-income people. The State's interventionism would also be fed by the diffusion of the positivistic postulates which gained followers from the 1860s on, mostly among Rio de Janeiro's engineers and medical doctors. A certain political authoritarianism began thus to coincide with a certain prescriptiveness of

urban life which was translated into the multiplication of 'corrective' projects and policies for the city.

In the capital of the Empire, scientific and technical discourse and the desire for great urban projects were increasingly articulated: the opening of new streets and tunnels, the creation of subdivision developments, the levelling of hills were a few of the initiatives approved, although not all implemented, between 1870 and 1875 by a government seeking to renew the capital image. Indeed, during this short time, over ten projects were submitted to, or passed by the government, many with British funding. Among them the following stood out: a high railway between Campo de Santana and Prainha; a waterfront quarter at Calabouço; the organization of the new harbour of Rio de Janeiro from the sea-side at Saúde to the Arsenal de Marinha (Navy Arsenal), encompassing the ground-levelling of São Bento hill and with a subdivision development for commercial purposes; and lastly the ground-levelling of

Castelo and Santo Antônio hills, including the construction of a quay up to Glória, a new Imperial Palace and several administrative buildings.

The surroundings of the Dom Pedro II Railway Station were also the focus of several proposals. In Campo de Santana the French botanist Auguste M. F. Glaziou built a vast public garden during this period and proposed the opening of a great *promenade* tangential east-west to the garden, from Praia dos Mineiros to Andaraí Grande, so as to achieve better circulation in this direction.[29]

Many such initiatives were encouraged by the impact on Brazilian specialists of the completion of Haussmann's *grands travaux* in Paris and, particularly in the case of Glaziou's projects, of Alphand's achievements. The experiments with urban organization developed in the United States, mostly in Chicago and New York, were also followed with interest by *Carioca*[30] specialists, particularly Olmsted's Central Park. These great initiatives contributed to the local elites' will to bring new solutions to conflicts among different logics, rhythms and forms of urban development, that had reached an impasse.

The fever for concession requests led the Ministry of the Empire in 1874 to form an Improvement Commission made up of the engineers Francisco Pereira Passos, Jeronymo Moraes Jardim and Marcellino Ramos. The Commission's goal was to prepare a global plan to articulate the initiatives already approved in order to better the city's sanitary conditions, to improve circulation, and to give enhanced 'beauty and harmony' to the urban constructions.[31]

At this point, the inauguration of the first tramway line in 1868 and the development of numerous lines during the 1870s provided support for strong expansion of the city, as the 1877 *Planta da cidade do Rio de Janeiro e seus subúrbios* (Plan of the City of Rio de Janeiro and Its Suburbs) indicates. In 1874, the *Revista do Instituto Politécnico* (Polytechnic Institute Review) was first published, followed by the *Revista de Engenharia* (Engineering Review). During the 1880s, in addition to a magazine specifically devoted to railways, the *Revista dos Construtores* (Constructors' Review) and the *Revista do Clube de Engenharia* (Review of the Engineering Club) were published in Rio de Janeiro.

In the capital of the Empire the projects for urban and social reform, far from coming to an end, multiplied during the 1880s, showing that utopias, dreams, and desire for change also bore social value. In such a context the proclamation of the Republic late in the decade created a new disruption and opened a new perspective.

In 1885 the population of São Paulo had reached 47,000 inhabitants, and that of Rio de Janeiro more than doubled, reaching 522,651 inhabitants in 1890.[32] During this period the families of coffee farm owners who had come from other cities in the province took up residence in São Paulo. In addition, hundreds of immigrants from regions impoverished by economic depression – Germany, Italy, and even the United States after the War of Secession – were attracted by the increasing development of the coffee culture, and settled not only inland, but also in the city.

In spite of the continuing differences in population size, some parallels may be drawn between the Rio de Janeiro and São Paulo authorities in terms of their ideals; in the process of functional and social division of urban space; and particularly in the quest for government guidelines and policies for the control and the rationalization of urbanization.

At this time, the São Paulo working-class population, mostly immigrant, began to live in different types of accommodation called *cortiços, casas de operários* or *cubículos* (tenement houses, workers' houses, cubicles). In Rio de Janeiro, the poor settled in the old centre which had been abandoned during the 1870s and 1880s by higher-income people who now lived in the new urban areas along the bayside or in the hills. Although the names were different in São Paulo and Rio, and the ethnic and social profiles of the population – of slave origin – also differed, the same phenomenon was observed amongst those crammed into Rio's *estalagens, cortiços, casas de cômodos* (inns, tenement houses, all-rooms-for-rent houses).

In São Paulo the *Código de Posturas* and the *Padrão Municipal* (Municipal Standard), both published in 1886, aimed at controlling urban expansion.[33] The *Padrão Municipal* prohibited the building of low-income public housing in the area known as 'central triangle', and defined areas where poor people should no longer live. In contrast, the *Código de Posturas* designated new upmarket areas by means of legislation separate from that affecting the city as a whole, as shown in the case of the Bouchard I and II subdivisions – which became the district of Higienópolis. The same happened, shortly afterwards, with Avenida Paulista (Paulista Avenue), inaugurated in 1891, the grandest housing neighbourhood of the new urban elites created by the coffee economy and industrialization.[34]

Throughout the Republican era the '*vilas*' (row houses) multiplied: these were subdivisions for the middle classes and workers in the industrial sector. In Rio de Janeiro, despite incentive policies for the construction of lower-income public housing and also of numerous *vilas*, from the 1890s social

segregation took on a new form: the '*favelas*' (slums), which were created by self-building and were to develop further as a consequence, as we will see, of the redevelopment projects for the capital.

In the case of São Paulo, the more effective administrative presence is noteworthy. However, in the *Paulista* capital, until the end of the Empire, employees of the *Câmara* (Municipal Chamber) and members of scientific institutions and professional groups were not the ones to introduce, legitimate or impose urban vocabulary or norms, unlike the situation in Rio de Janeiro. In São Paulo it was businessmen such as Jules Martin who were the instigators of the urban discourse and made the city dwellers familiar with the city's growth.[35]

With the coming of the Republic there were changes in both urban discourse and administration as a result of a new system of government and the influence of worldwide economic and cultural exchange. Between 1902 and 1929 the urban professional debates in the country's two main cities became more in tune with those in major European and North American cities, while urban planning and design thus started to elaborate through long and diverse discourses – both national and international – its new lexicon and practice.

From the end of the nineteenth century onwards, the capital city was no longer only a 'landscape and a spectacle' as in Prévost's panoramas, but became also a symbol and a commodity whose value was measured by its ability to attract investments, tourists, new city dwellers, and a steady flow of capital. Architecture and urbanism became the most efficient instruments for the production and diffusion of an image that evoked the stability and dynamism of the old and new capitals. Now the staging of urban life would put aside the closed spaces of the *passages*, the rotundas in the panoramas, the travel books, the picturesque albums and guides, to decorate the streets. Here, even the harbour, with its lifts, cranes and electrical tramways would be seen, as imbued with a sublime beauty, but different from that of the eclectic palaces.[36]

The Construction of a Capital:
Rio de Janeiro, a Wonderful City (1902–1910)

The nineteenth century might be said to have ended in Rio de Janeiro in 1910, after the completion of great public works undertaken by the Municipality and the federal government, which had begun in 1902 during President Rodrigues Alves's administration. For the President, defeating one more century of uncompleted projects, of waves of epidemics, and of plans piling up in the administrative drawers, was to correct the 'flaws' that 'affect and disturb' not only Rio de Janeiro but also the national development itself. The country ought to be kept in the band of the progressive and developed nations, expanding and better exploring its potentials.

The President had declared in 1903:

The . . . restoration [of the capital] in the world's judgement shall begin a new life, it shall encourage work in the most extensive areas of a country that has land for all cultures, climates for all peoples, rewards for all capital [invested].[37]

Combining the negotiation of large external loans in London and authoritarian procedures such as closing the *Câmara Municipal*, those works brought about a true revolution which began with ending the pile of troublesome concessions still granted by the different Ministries of the Empire, which had not often remained mere bureaucratic documents. Completed in record-breaking time – less than a decade – they crowned the long process that for over a century had been seeking, amidst both progress and setbacks, to turn Rio de Janeiro into a liberal and republican city and to expunge the marks of slavery and its colonial past.

One sees that the city had changed but also that this political project was to be disregarded: the city had been transformed, but the country's 'primitive' dimension sometimes surfaced. On one hand, in that decade the capital of the Republic began to be called 'Cidade Maravilhosa' (Wonderful City); on the other, signs of social exclusion, although distant to the eyes of the central area, piled up.[38]

Although the *Ministro de Viação e Obras Públicas* (Minister of Transit and Public Works), Lauro Müller, and the engineer, Paulo de Frontin, made their mark in the achievements of the Federal Government, it was Mayor Pereira Passos who appeared as the great reformer of the period. Having been involved in the modernization of Rio de Janeiro since 1874–1875, Passos, as we have seen, had extensive knowledge of the city. He began his administration by organizing a major roads plan which anticipated the opening and broadening of numerous streets in the centre, but he was also aware that roads should be opened in the suburb areas. Although he insisted that his plan was both 'modest and necessary enough to be taken into effect and not left lingering in the domain of utopias', the magnitude of the demolitions he undertook – going back to ideas suggested in 1843 by Rohan and in 1874–1875 by the Improvement Commission – resulted in his being considered a 'tropical Haussmann'.

Besides the mass destruction of whole quarters in the central area and the social exclusion promoted by those initiatives, Passos's regularization of the Federal Capital was also a systemic one, just as was that of the *Préfect de la Seine*. Continued by his successors Marshal Souza Aguiar (1906–1909) and General Serzedelo Correia (1909–1910), his plan faced questions concerning salubrity and embellishment and also attacks against the construction of such new institutions as the Teatro Municipal (Municipal Theatre), the Mercado Público (Public Market), and also schools and the first municipal public health centre, among other works.[39]

Side by side with a campaign against the yellow fever commanded by the sanitarian, Oswaldo Cruz, Minister Lauro Müller charged engineer Francisco Bicalho with the expansion and modernization of the harbour zone, definitively setting it in the northern part of the city and linking it to the Central Station of Central do Brasil Railway (the old Pedro II Railway). Warehouses were built, electric cranes were installed to mechanize loading and unloading activities, a wide avenue was opened along the warehouses and the quay (Avenida Rodrigues Alves) and the Mangue canal was expanded, built as it was by Mauá in 1850 to allow the expansion of the *Cidade Nova* (New City).

To complete the set of initiatives by the Ministry, engineer Paulo de Frontin was charged with opening a *percée* – Avenida Central – linking the northern harbour to the new Avenida Beira Mar (Seaside Avenue), which was being constructed southward by the Municipality. Frontin also undertook to

lower Senate Hill in order to open a diagonal between the regions of Lapa and *Cidade Nova*. However the funds coming from the Rothschild Bank arrived a little late: since 1892 the harbour of Rio de Janeiro was no longer the most important in the country, having lost its place to Santos, the ocean port for the São Paulo expansion.[40]

The hallmark of such reforms as a whole was Avenida Central (now Avenida Rio Branco), whose design had been conceived by the Minister himself. Inaugurated in 1905, the Avenue, with its hotels, motion-picture theatres, offices of great companies, shops and governmental buildings such as the Biblioteca Nacional (National Library), the Teatro Municipal, the Senado Federal (Federal Senate), Caixa de Amortização (Amortisation Chamber), encapsulated the very image of modern life with its dynamism and cosmopolitan architecture (figure 4.9). When the Pereira Passos administration ended in 1906, Rio de Janeiro, with its 800,000 inhabitants, was the *Belle-Époque* capital *par excellence* in South America, together with Buenos Aires.

Whether criticizing or justifying them, the *Carioca* press at the time insisted on comparing the works of Pereira Passos with those of Haussmann, a procedure which, taken up by most contemporary historians,[41] pushes to the background a series of initiatives that show some similarity to the planning themes discussed at the turn of the twentieth century. Of particular interest in his plan are, for example, the concern with the perimeter roadways, one of the big issues at the time; the emphasis on the landscape projects, modernization of public parks and the creation of squares, all of which made explicit a new sensitivity to the protection of natural sites and the value of public outdoor areas.[42]

The policies developed in Europe and the

United States in the second half of the nineteenth century regarding outdoor spaces and green areas also arrived in Brazil, where these issues were not new, but were reinforced by the international trend. From the two first decades of the nineteenth century natural spaces had been increasing in value, leading the administration to protect them as a common good and to some extent as natural monuments, as was the case of Floresta da Tijuca.[43] Furthermore, Pereira Passos was one among the first to invest also in the tourist development of such areas, having constructed the Estrada de Ferro Corcovado (Corcovado Railway) (1884) to improve access to the

belvedere on Corcovado and a hotel, all amidst the forest.[44]

Therefore, while Mayor, Pereira Passos's interventions were not limited to great Haus-mannesque surgeries, the works on Avenue Beira-Mar, the succession of gardens and the quay up to Botafogo, the recovery of the gardens in Campo de Santana (today, Praça da República), of the Quinta de São Cristovão[45] and the investments in Floresta da Tijuca show that whole 'landscapes' began to be taken into consideration, with their 'monumental perspectives', as part of the city's technical and financial rationale.

Besides the profusion of buildings con-

Figure 4.9 Avenida Central, Rio de Janeiro, 1902–1906. (*Source*: Biblioteca Nacional)

structed in an old fashioned way certain interventions contemplated the specificity of the place, emphasizing the aesthetic dimension of nature as a place of memory and a monument. As Ferreira da Rosa, chronicler of the period, boastfully wrote:

... The Urbs is hardly outlined ... The time to come is dazzling. Only the first lines have been drawn. The projected improvements ... promise to reconcile this

city with Nature, filling what the man's hand seemingly worked to withdraw from it.[46]

In 1911 the Pão de Açúcar cable railway was inaugurated, marking the apex of this trend. From the top of this mountain the Federal Capital, by now sanitized and embellished, showed its historical form as it dialogued with the ocean and the forest, both having become a part of it as a city.

São Paulo (1900–1910): An Economic Capital without an Image

São Paulo's surprising demographic boom in these years – 61,000 in 1890; 240,000 in 1900; 350,000 in 1910 – together with the new administrative attitude shown in the example of the Federal Capital's reforms, led the urban improvement theme to gain importance also in the *Paulista* capital.

A strong association had been established in São Paulo in these two decades between real estate operations and political or technical decisions, thanks to the strategies of attracting foreign labour to the old province, now the State of São Paulo. Desired from the beginning by the government, participation by private businesses in urban development became a fact,[47] and businessmen began to be seen effectively as partners in government policies that were favoured by different fiscal mechanisms, specially conceived for those who organized low-income public housing development: for example, transfer of municipal properties; years of tax exemption on the housing constructed; interest guarantees; concessions for utilities such as public transportation; and other benefits. The authorities themselves often participated as well in the companies incorporated around such initiatives.

However, the strong participation of private capital in the management of urban

development was no longer limited to the environs of the railways and factories, but instead formed the great patchwork suburb around the *vilas* that multiplied in number.[48]

Two major private companies were involved in this process, associating with real estate operations that were addressed to distinct services and segments of populations: the São Paulo Tramway Light and Power, set up in São Paulo in 1899, backed mostly by Canadian capital, and the City of São Paulo Improvements and Freehold Land Company Limited, created in 1911, in London.[49]

The '*Light*' company had been installed in Rio de Janeiro in 1903 during the Pereira Passos reform. Between 1900, when the first electric tramway line was inaugurated in São Paulo, and 1911, when it was granted the monopoly for the implementation of various urban utilities, the company had become a 'State within the State'[50] in the city and had laid more than 180 km of rails, influencing the occupation and increasing the density of certain areas.

Under the impact of such action by '*Light*' and of the ambiguous interpretation of the limits of liberalism as far as the organization of urban services and management of the city's physical expansion were concerned, between 1911 and 1913 São Paulo discussed – in a very low-key manner in view of its spectacular growth – its most important urban improvement project. This was a set of neighbouring streets in Vale do Anhangabaú, which had become one of the most valuable commercial areas in the centre,[51] near the Teatro Municipal recently constructed by Mayor Antonio Prado.

When Mayor Raymundo Duprat took over in 1911, there were already three existing proposals for the renewal of the area: the plan for 'As grandes avenidas de São Paulo' (The great avenues of São Paulo) by Alexandre de Albuquerque, submitted by a group of businessmen; a project supported by the Câmara Municipal, submitted by the Board of Directors of Municipal Works, designed by Victor da Silva Freire and Eugênio Guilhem; and, lastly, a proposal prepared by the architect Samuel das Neves, hired by the State Government.[52] Facing such conflict of competences and visions of urban development, the Mayor called in Joseph Bouvard, then in Buenos Aires, to arbitrate over the controversies that had arisen during discussion of the projects.

Published since 1905, the Revista Polytechnica dealt tangentially with urban issues, but, with the publication of the bulletin of the Instituto de Engenharia (Institute of Engineering) in 1917 and the journal Architectura e Construções (Architecture and Construction) in the 1920s, technical discussions reached a higher plain. For São Paulo the nineteenth century would end with the debates on those first projects and the city would then enter an irreversibly metropolitan phase.

Bouvard's evaluations not only bore the marks of Camillo Sitte but also certain precepts that the Commission du Vieux Paris (Commission of Old Paris), founded in 1897, had been developing concerning the importance of preserving some groups of buildings providing they formed a homogeneous architecture regardless of their artistic value.[53] As was the case in São Paulo, the French architect prescribed for the

centre . . . respect for the past, uselessness of imaginative flights and exaggerated enlargements, uselessness . . . of making the historical, picturesque, archaeological, interesting nature disappear . . . For the periphery the circulation was adopted by means of new amphitheatre-like distributions as were proper for the picturesque layout of places.[54]

Solutions aimed at untangling the Centro, highlighting its most remarkable sites and providing a suitable frame for the government buildings. The goal was to create in the centre of the Paulista capital 'an aesthetic whole both grandiose and eloquent',[55] thus ensuring at last 'city development under rational conditions'.

And 'the preservation and creation of outdoor spaces, areas of vegetation, reservoirs of fresh air' was not forgotten. In this respect he proposed great parks, squares, gardens and places where dwellers could visit for pleasure, 'islands of health and well-being necessary for both the moral and physical health of the public'.[56] When so speaking, Bouvard did not think only of those sites in the city where the topography was being altered such as the Viaduto de Santa Efigênia (1908–1913), while leaving the bottom of the valley unchanged. He surely also meant other urban spaces – such as the whole area north of Jardim and Estação da Luz, inaugurated in 1908 – for which there was no dedicated plan during the development process (figure 4.10). Here his affinity with the mature discussions in the Musée Social in Paris between 1909 and 1910 became clear, where in a continuation of Georges Risler's lectures and defence

Figure 4.10 Gardens and Light Station, São Paulo, inaugurated in 1908. (*Source*: Arquivo Nacional)

of the plans for *L'aménagement et l'extension des villes* (The Planning and Extension of Towns), W.-F. Willoughby exhibited in detail the achievements that had improved the open areas and urban aesthetic in the United States.[57]

Bouvard summarized:

The moment has come . . . for the city of São Paulo purposefully to follow the way its fast progressive movement has shown. This capital . . . must with a single word foresee, adopt, and judiciously enforce all the measures it claims and are increasingly claimed by its grandeur and importance.

With Bouvard São Paulo gained – in addition to other green spaces and the projects for widening streets Dom José de Barros, Líbero Badaró, São João – particularly the Parque Dom Pedro II and the landscaping of the Vale do Anhangabaú area near the Teatro Municipal (figure 4.11). Seeing also the

Figure 4.11. Valley of Anhangabaú, São Paulo, *c.* 1930. (*Source*: Arquivo Nacional)

advantageous possibilities of investment in the real estate sector, the architect set up the basis for the creation of the City Improvements Company, which started up in 1912 with an estate of over 12,000 hectares[58] of land in the south-west region of the centre.

The company was established with resources from the French banker Edouard Fontaine de Lavelaye; from other foreign partners among whom Lord Balfour, President of Bank of Scotland and of São Paulo Railway Co. stood out; from Victor da Silva Freire, Director of Municipal Works; from Campos Salles, former President of the Republic; and also from directors of other banks, as well as members of the Light company and the economic elite of the city.[59]

In the mid-1910s the company developed its first division of land into lots in the city: a garden suburb conceived by Raymond Unwin and Barry Parker, called Jardim América (figure 4.12). As an expression of the Pan American ideal, which had been developing

since the end of the previous century, the suburb boasted the avenues Estados Unidos and Brasil, crossed by the streets Argentina, Guatemala, Venezuela, Panamá, Peru, Colombia, among others, which picturesquely wound like snakes among gardens and squares. Having lived in São Paulo for two years, Barry Parker contributed directly to the rapid internationalization of the city's urban planning, while working on the conception of a series of subdivision developments: Pacaembu, Alto da Lapa; Bela Aliança.[60] Jardim América's success was remarkable; it attracted members of the rich bourgeoisie who, in the face of a mass of immigrants that did not cease to grow, sought to develop distinguished areas for themselves. Some suburbs in São Paulo thus began to take on a form very similar to those in Anglo-Saxon countries (figure 4.13). Furthermore, the form of the city began to present a configuration very common in certain North American cities where the urban image resulted much more from the green

Figure 4.12 Jardim América, São Paulo. First garden city area by Raymond Unwin and Barry Parker c. 1915. (*Source*: Francisco Prestes Maia, *Estudo de um plano de avenidas para Cidade de São Paulo*, São Paulo, 1930)

Figure 4.13 Jardim Europa, São Paulo, 1924. (*Source*: Francisco Prestes Maia, *Estudo de um plano de avenidas para Cidade de São Paulo*, São Paulo, Melhoramentos, 1930)

suburban residential areas than from the 'historic city'; in other words, that which began to be designated as 'centre', in spite of being perceived as an 'absent' structure.

From this perspective we can understand, as was the case in several North American cities and in São Paulo from the arrival of Bouvard, how urban embellishment, embodied in the City Beautiful movement, had become associated with strategies aimed at shaping in spatial terms the city's identity, as well as with the issue of the creation of a new 'centre'. In terms of building the image of São Paulo as a capital of one state of the Federation, this issue would indeed turn into a problem.

If in Rio de Janeiro the works in the Pereira Passos period had updated the city image, cast its colonial profile with an eclectic and cosmopolitan architecture, creating a new 'historic centre', in São Paulo this was not the trend. Since the end of the Empire, there had been the construction, for instance, of the Museu do Ipiranga (Ipiranga Museum); since the proclamation of Republic, after the inauguration of the Escola Normal (Elementary Teachers' School), Escola Politécnica (Polytechnic School), Estação da Luz, Teatro Municipal, Palácio do Governo (Government Palace) and many other governmental buildings particularly by architect Ramos de Azevedo[61] (figure 4.14), the signs of modernization had increased. However, these landmarks spread over several sites, and so did not constitute either a new or a coherent image of the city.

Figure 4.14 Secretariat of Agriculture and Treasury, Escritório Ramos de Azevedo, São Paulo, 1891. (*Source*: Biblioteca Nacional)

Oscillating between remarkable suburbanization and the absence of a strong image of centrality, different plans were proposed between 1910 and 1930 for São Paulo. The discussion of the image of the 'historic centre' was the one to instigate in São Paulo, even before Rio de Janeiro, movements that began to reassess the colonial past and its image conveyed in architecture. It was also in the *Paulista* capital that the perception of the multifaceted and kaleidoscopic image of the metropolis as the contemporary expression of a capital city would be designed for the first time in Brazil. The starting point would be the awareness by certain groups of intellectuals of the increasing 'Europeanization' of the Brazilian cities not only in demographic, but also in urban-planning terms.

Bouvard's picturesque vision, valuing the old 'historic centre', added to the movement that had been developed from 1914 by the Portuguese engineer Ricardo Severo, which advocated rescuing the history of Portuguese-Brazilian architecture and, consequently, of a 'neo-colonial' image of the city. It ignited in São Paulo debates about the very 'identity' of the country and its cities, and spread them among the *Paulista* elite.

In the early 1920s, in Rio or in São Paulo, although one can talk of surges in urban intervention, of large real estate operations or of the slow diffusion of an American-oriented ideology – and, within it, both of the Pan Americanism and strong support for the neo-colonial movement – perception of such trends was not clear. These themes would gain clarity during the preparations for the International Exhibition which celebrated 100 years of Independence and took place in Rio de Janeiro in 1922. Highlighting the significance and necessity of a debate on the urban form in contemporary terms, at the same time the Exhibition evinced the obsolescence of the achievements of the early century, from Pereira Passos to Bouvard, thus showing the limits of the academic tradition.

Indeed, most pavilions in the Exhibition sought inspiration in the so-called – even at that time – 'traditional' Portuguese-Brazilian style, which had been sharply criticized by the medical doctor José Mariano Filho. Like Severo, he advocated for Rio de Janeiro rescuing the national history, but from a different perspective.

For him, most architects followed only pretentiously the traditional patterns. They focused on decorative details – that is, on superficialities – with no 'understanding of what was characteristic and individual in the problematic of Brazilian architecture'.[62] Synthesizing the characteristics of this national architecture, Filho clarified: it had been brought by the Portuguese colonizer, and as 'the sun's old friend', bearer of a 'secular experience of the race' forged between the West and the East, 'markedly by the Moorish experience'. In the tropical Brazilian environment this architectural practice could confront the environmental factors and adapt to them. In his interpretation the quest for a 'national' plastic expression should break away from both the European historicist eclecticism and the new 'American' historicism as represented by the *'misiones'* (missions) style or the 'decorative' traditional architecture he had seen at the Exhibition.[63]

In this move towards liberalism and nationalism nothing was so culturally striking as the *Semana de Arte Moderna* (Week of Modern Art), which also took place in 1922 in São Paulo, and the works of those who participated, such as Oswald de Andrade's *Poesia Pau Brasil* (1924) (Brazil Wood Poetry) and *Manifesto Antropofágico* (1928)

(Anthropophagy Manifesto). The irreverent and radical cultural movement in São Paulo, together with Mário de Andrade's researches in the history of art, architecture, music and folklore, were the most solid pillar of the nationalist movement, which was building modern Brazil and its institutions.

In the 1920s, the moment seemed to have come for direct confrontation between the intellectual elites and the country's cultural syncretism.

The *Paulista* intellectuals participating in the *Semana* unhesitatingly claimed:

We want the Caraíba Revolution. Greater than the French Revolution. The unification of all effective revolts towards man . . . Only Anthropophagy unites us. The only law in the world . . . only fight – the fight for the way.[64]

That 'anthropophagous' principle meant adopting a universal critical attitude before that which can be regarded as an issue at a given time, regardless of races or dates, since they are linked to the very history of men. Therefore, the 'modern' challenge, unchanged over time, was to rebel against all models, against the moribund ideas, and to act. Brazilians should not forget also their very nature as New World men, who had been the ones to learn from the beginning, due to great undertakings in their history, the need for action.

'Americanism' and 'Brazilian nationalism' thus became synonymous with universality. This was the birth of a cultural revolution:

. . . Against the memory as a perpetuation of tradition; for the memory as a syncretism of geographies, times, races and cultures . . . Only [to be] Brazilians of our epoch . . . Practical ones. Experimental ones. Poets.[65]

So, after the *Semana de Arte Moderna*, and given the traditional scene of the 1922 Exhibition, São Paulo would not allow Rio de Janeiro and the rest of Brazil to forget the present.

The cultural isolation of the *Paulista* elites, separated as they were from the intellectual life of Rio de Janeiro and from their own urban surroundings, limited the movement for change. However, the new approach to the country's history did slowly penetrate the ideological field, generating deep and lasting changes. In fact, this revolutionary interpretation of the local history – more elaborate on indigenous experience and heritage – led to criticism of the idea of the 'national character'. In this sense 'Brazilian Americanism' was understood, above all, as a universal and humanist attitude that, as such, represented the very denial of a notion of nationalism, a point of view still misunderstood today in its complexity.

From this time on São Paulo became a counterbalance to Rio de Janeiro and *vice versa*, and the cultural adjustments of their reciprocal images during the decade supported their rise as metropolises. The recurrent theme of expressing the image of a capital city had thus been put in crisis.

The Capital City Image Adrift: The Birth of Two Metropolises (1922–1930)

The Exhibition's progressive legacy, the open spaces resulting from the razing of the Castelo Hill,[66] the debates on national identity, were all factors that drew attention to the continuity of the urban works that had begun at the turn of the century. These works came to be perceived as inadequate, out of date and formalistic.

As early as 1916, in São Paulo the engineer Victor da Silva Freire, very aware of the contemporary debates, had appropriated the neologism *urbanisme*, translated it into Portuguese and linked urban planning to the national economy.[67] However, if the reformers were linking planning with the housing conditions and trying to control the expansion of slums in Rio or the 'disorderly' low-density extension of *vilas* in São Paulo, architects in both cities were quite removed from these 'problems'. However, by the very nature of their occupation, the architects were most concerned about the appearance of the city and therefore were the strongest advocates of a visual and 'monumentalist' practice of urban planning. One could say that in the 'nebulae' of reformers working in Rio de Janeiro and São Paulo at the beginning of twentieth century, engineers' concerns with traffic and circulation dominated the *Paulista* scene while the symbolic visions of the architects dominated the *Carioca* one.

In Rio, architects trained at the *Escola Nacional de Belas Artes* (National School of Fine Arts) were the key figures in introducing the national 'character' debates and later those of Brazil's anthropophagous Americanism into the technical discourse. In the 1920s the architecture magazines proliferated; to *Architectura e Construções* and the engineering

journals mentioned earlier were added *A Casa* (The House), *Architectura no Brasil* (Architecture of Brazil), *Architectura Mensário da Arte* (Architecture's Art Monthly) and *Forma* (Form).

Influenced by life in a capital city, architects tended to favour a more centralizing model of public management, emphasizing the symbolic relations between the images of the city and the nation. Compared with Rio, in São Paulo, with its cultural mixture, 'Americanism' showed now clearer features, due to the debate fuelled by the Week of 1922, and the joint action by the *Escola Politécnica*'s engineers and the Rotary Club members; all of which intensified the discussions about the federalist administrative structure and North American liberalism.

In 1924–1925 the engineers João Florence de Ulhôa Cintra and Prestes Maia drew up plans for São Paulo's traffic and circulation, in which the ideas of the European planners Joseph Stübben and Eugène Hénard clearly played a role.[68] However, over the next few years, the two engineers' vision of the modern metropolis and guidelines for its growth increasingly began to incorporate the North American example. When in 1930 Prestes Maia prepared the first joint plan for the agglomeration, entitled *Plano de Avenidas* (Plan of Avenues, figures 4.15 and 4.16),

Figure 4.15 São Paulo's *Plano de Avenidas*. (*Source*: Francisco Prestes Maia, *Estudo de um plano de avenidas para Cidade de São Paulo*, São Paulo: Melhoramentos, 1930)

Figure 4.16 São Paulo's *Plano de Avenidas*. (*Source*: Francisco Prestes Maia, *Estudo de um plano de avenidas para Cidade de São Paulo*, São Paulo: Melhoramentos, 1930.

although some of his earlier ideas persisted, the references made, for instance, to Philadelphia's Comprehensive Plan Commission are explicit, as are those made to the American planner Harland Bartholomew's conclusions about vehicle circulation in the central areas.[69]

The work of Prestes Maia clearly demonstrates a rift between 'form and function' at this time. From the circulation point-of-view, his proposals evinced an updated vision, although the formal expression of the buildings in his 'new city' referred to an 'archaic' and historicist monumental image, if we take into account the experiments by architects Gregori Warchavichik and Rino Levi since the mid-1920s in São Paulo.[70]

In less than three years attitudes to urban management, both technical and political, in São Paulo changed, now focusing on North American experiments. The North American view became even clearer in the 1928 lectures by engineer and teacher Luis de Anhaia Mello at the Rotary Club, with a detailed description of the two major problems faced by North American planners – automobiles and skyscrapers.

In that year, North American experiences

of urban planning, the proposals of its planners, the actions of the national or local American associations of overtly urbanism-related aims, all these issues would be expertly disclosed and analysed by Anhaia Mello and compared with what Brazilian planners should do in São Paulo. His lectures combined ingredients from the National League, National Conference on City Planning, American Society for Municipal Improvements, American Society of Landscape Architects – and also by civic or commercial associations – such as the Rotary Clubs, Chambers of Commerce, the Commercial Associations; the European legislation confronting the North-American one, and so on.[71]

Together with the city's elites, the institution in São Paulo that pulled together the reformist proposals that contributed to an accommodation of social forces, ideological currents and technical tendencies, was the Rotary Club, created in the disturbing year of 1924, when a military rebellion shook the country. Focusing on an efficient and economically aware vision of city planning and down playing the artistic dimension favoured by architects, the Rotary Club promoted a union between technical knowledge and political and economic power. In Rio, the club became a pressure body in the advocacy of town planning, together with the new architects' associations, such as the *Instituto Central de Arquitetos* (ICA, Central Institute of Architects), created in 1921 and the *Clube de Engenharia* (Engineering Club). However, the *Carioca* engineers were less articulate and militant than the *Paulista* ones, while the architects, ever motivated by José Mariano and united in ICA, were the ones to represent the strength of the reformist movement.

Having given visibility to the discussions on the need for a global plan for Rio de Janeiro, so as to create for it a metropolitan image, the 1922 International Exhibition ended up reviving the controversies on the capital's transfer to the interior of the country: Planaltina or Brasilia were the two names discussed in 1924 and 1925 both in the *Câmara* and the Federal Senate.

The way the debates evolved between 1926 and 1930, would again place city planning as a political, economic and social question within the public sector, and again the concept of capital entered the agenda. The main actors now were foreigners to the city's intellectual life: two from São Paulo and two Frenchmen.

In years marked by liberalism, the Rotarian Washington Luis's rise to the presidency of Brazil and Antonio Prado Junior's nomination as Mayor of the capital – both from São Paulo – made the *Carioca* professional milieu closer to many themes discussed in the *Paulista* capital. However, conflicting proposals and conflicting professional and economic interests led to a deadlock. Among those considered as possible arbiters of the planning measures to be adopted by the City Hall and the Federal Government – Joseph Stübben, Edward H.

Bennett, Léon Jaussely – Donat-Alfred Agache stood out, probably because of his experience with the plan for Camberra, Australia.[72]

The presence of this planner-architect in Brazil since 1927 and the visit by Le Corbusier in 1929 provoked a confrontation between Europe (France, particularly) and the United States as cultural models through which a new understanding of the notion of 'capital city' could be made explicit.

Agache, supported by the Rotary Club, arrived in Rio to introduce the contemporary trends of urbanism represented by the *Societé Française des Urbanistes*, and soon he was appointed to organize a '*Plano de Remodelação da Cidade*' (Plan for Remodelling the City). Between 1928 and 1930 he co-ordinated the preparation of one of the most detailed studies of Rio's urban evolution, which led to a series of proposals.

At the same time, Le Corbusier's trip to Brazil in late 1929 was on his own initiative, motivated by a desire to disseminate his ideas in South America, and more importantly to design the country's new capital: Planaltina.[73] Welcomed in Rio by leading intellectuals, he gave lectures and, inspired by the sight of the city, wrote essays and prepared planning proposals. He also visited São Paulo and there also lectured and prepared plans. Comparing Le Corbusier's ideas with Agache's Remodelling Plan for Rio de Janeiro, and also with Prestes Maia's Plan of Avenues for São Paulo, it can be seen that an old-fashioned vision of capital cities was replaced.

In the 1920s, changes in urban life brought about the discussion of topics which are still relevant today: 'metropolis' and 'functionalism', 'Americanism' and 'modernity', 'decentralization' and 'control by the State', 'identity' and 'cosmopolitanism'. In the United States the creation of numerous civil associations participating in the discussion of city planning, led urbanism, understood as a Civic Art since the early century, to produce some interesting examples of such discussions, such as Chicago's city planning. We will analyse the proposals by Agache and Le Corbusier regarding two questions that inflamed the debates in Rio: urban expansion and the function of the city as the country's capital.

In mid-1928 the newspaper *O Paiz* promoted an opinion poll on 'the skyscraper and the modern aesthetic'. About ten architectural practices participated, speculating on the form the '*Carioca* skyscraper' would take.

Several professionals recognized the inevitability of the skyscraper and some pointed to Le Corbusier as the one who had best analysed the problem. Interviewed while working in Rio, Agache declared himself in favour of 'verticalization', explaining that he had detailed buildings 60 and 90 metres high for the Castelo Hill area, in a layout of wide streets and large lots 'so as to produce a decorative set'. Contemporary writings show arguments for the construction of tall buildings and increasing urban densities in metropolises were the result of technological

innovations, changes in the society, and new scales of urban growth, associated with the speculation about different ways of occupying a territory. But for Agache, skyscrapers were valued only as a form able to produce a decorative effect, an epitome of his idea of modernity, which centred on style rather than a new perception of mobility, innovation, or change.[74]

Let us focus on Agache's preliminary design for Rio de Janeiro, presented in 1928: the design for the embankment site in the Glória area, called 'Porta do Brasil' (Gate to Brazil), which as a civic centre and symbol of the nation should be the 'mirror of its identity'. His approach to this problem is precisely where his visions of architecture and urbanism are best manifested.

As if in theatrical scenery, two monumental columns and a stairway – opened that Gate to Brazil in front of the Baía de Guanabara (figure 4.17). They defined a square surrounded by the buildings of Belas Artes (Fine Arts) and Palácio das Indústrias (Palace of Industries); opposite the columns, the square was completed by an auditorium and by the *Senado* and *Câmara dos Deputados* (Senate

Figure 4.17 Project for the Porta do Brasil (Gate to Brazil), Donat Alfred Agache, 1927–1930. (*Source*: Donat Alfred Agache, *A Cidade do Rio de Janeiro, remodelação, extensão e embelezamento. 1926–1930.* Paris: Foyer Brésilien, 1930)

and House of Representatives). Two 64-metre wide avenues led out from the square and, showing that the notion of territory was implicit in the project, reached out to the country's heartland: Petrópolis, São Paulo, Belo Horizonte. In that square the nation should begin to recognize its collective identity and values, perform parades and great public ceremonies, receive visitors . . .

Although references to the Chicago plan were obvious, Agache, perhaps afraid of a possible transfer of the capital from Rio to the interior, drafted, but did not detail, the *Senado* and the *Câmara*. Unlike Bennett and Burnham, he did not emphasize buildings that would be the symbol of the civic dimension itself and of the function of Rio as capital, but moved the focus of the composition to the columns at the head of the stairway, which were unable to convey the symbolism of such a theme.

Agache's success with this preliminary project for the Porta do Brasil was ephemeral. His first error was precisely to handle, like a neophyte, the rhetoric character of architecture. Indeed, in a 'new' civilization such as the Brazilian one, where cities had been planned and built on *tabula rasa* since the sixteenth century, the 'voice of architecture' and also the potential of buildings to construct and consolidate 'social bonds' had been made explicit and therefore manipulated since the Jesuit missions. As we have seen previously, even natural landscapes had been invested with the task of 'speaking' and 'recollecting' native myths. Confusing 'monument' with something which was simply 'grandiloquent', and failing to consider the meaning of 'recollecting' rendered impossible the achievement the most visible and pretentiously rhetoric parts of his plan.

During the first half of 1929, criticisms in the *Clube de Engenharia* and the newspapers attacked the project for its technical and financial equivocations and conceptual frailties. Among other things, Agache had disregarded that the debates about Rio's urban expansion and its image as a capital city pressed in order to benefit from certain themes. In short, he had focused short-sightedly on the deep cultural relationship of the *Carioca* (and Brazilian) people with nature (mostly with the Bay of Guanabara), while relying on the debates about their vocation for 'anthropophagy', that is, the fast assimilation of the qualities of the other.

For some journalists Agache 'showed a weak point . . . in directing the capital's reform, a manifest lack of spiritual sympathy with the essential aspects of the city's architectural problem'.[75] The urban planner could not separate himself from ready-made formulae and 'technical theory', thus failing to take into account an 'irreconcilable opposition' between Europe and America. As such, he further disregarded that the American civilizations could '. . . guide the directions of their evolution in compliance with new ideals that are resisted by Europeans'. Thus, the newspapers declared:

. . . [We] American people, and with destinies circumscribed within the orbit of aims of this continent's purposes, we may not forget that . . . New York and Chicago, with their cyclopean skyscrapers, contain inspirations more appropriate to the needs of the new Brazilian spirit than the elegant and delicate lines of the Parisian architecture.

They continued:

New Rio de Janeiro will not be able to be the nationality-representing capital if in its structural aspects the aspirations are not expressed of material progress and intense creative activity . . . A metropolitan city is not only the mirror, but also a school, a core of irradiating currents that stimulate the collective action by the country's populations.[76]

Touched by criticisms by the press and Brazilian technicians, Agache travelled in to see for himself the skyscrapers of Chicago and New York. However, seeking new forms was not the only issue, it was also necessary to evaluate the social and cultural representations associated with them.

One year later Le Corbusier would approach the 'Brazilian identity' question and its visible expression. Arriving in Brazil when such controversies were current and the project of the capital's transfer had been postponed, he soon understood that the 'modern time' was also 'an American time': some sort of an eternal present guided by not only a physical, but also a mental spirit of adventure. Having abandoned the Planaltina dream, he increasingly devoted himself to researching the stored heritage of Latin America and its 'old cities': Buenos Aires, Montevideo, São Paulo, Rio de Janeiro.

Le Corbusier's presence in Rio exposed not so much Agache's limits as a sociologist, statistician, and legislator, but as an architect and planner, this understood as the one professional competent to conceive the city in its physical, constructed, visible form. It further revealed the conceptual differences between the approaches of the two architects when considering the same ideas, sometimes the same theoretical matrices, the same keywords: somewhat literal in the case of Agache; abstract and imaginative in the case of Le Corbusier.[77]

In his sketches for the city, Le Corbusier also addressed the question of Rio as a capital city. In other words, for him Rio should be also conceived as a city that could reflect and recollect its American identity. As such, he carried much further the idea of monument – that is, of a *lieu de mémoire*, a place of some experience of the collective institutions.

To the static nature and fixedness of the monuments constructed from Agache's solution, restricted to the Enseada da Glória (the Senate, the House of Representatives, the columns...), Le Corbusier responded with a project involving the totality of the urban organism: the design of a '(fully) green city'. Its modern capital image was sometimes clear and pure geometry, sometimes expressionist, imprecise, concealed under masses of vegetation. Also ambiguous, but able powerfully to evoke the challenge of the American adventure: the *tabula rasa*, the riddle of the nature and continuous action by men either isolated or in groups, confirming the importance of social life and the need to build cities.

His analysis of Rio de Janeiro's urban structure revealed to him precisely that dialogue between construction and nature, which the *Carioca* people historically preserved as their highest value and as a mirror of their own history, therefore of their identity. However, like Agache, Le Corbusier proposed an experiment. He claimed that his project was inspired by bodies in motion, because he knew that, for those able to recollect a 'pure'-nature situation, to acknowledge themselves as a 'body in motion' was the strongest instrument of memory. Therefore he conceived a long sinuous line with the form of a 'housing-viaduct' indefinitely extended: dynamic, unending as the road of history. Perhaps here is where the Corbusian idea of architecture as a 'promenade' became reality. However, it was surely in this proposal that 'America', more than an idea that was only printed on buildings, could at last be experienced and recollected, along the path of the Corbusian viaduct.

Agache's Porta do Brasil has been forgotten in the pages of the urban planning books, but parts of his proposal were adopted in the great works undertaken by Mayor Henrique Dodsworth between 1937 and 1945, particularly after Presidente Vargas Avenue was opened.[78] Le Corbusier's planning ideas, and particularly his vision of the rhetoric nature of the urban scene, would only be resumed many years later, in the construction of Aterro do Flamengo (Flamingo Embankment).[79] This work, conceived by architect-planner Affonso Eduardo Reidy and landscape designer Roberto Burle Max and carried out in the 1960s, would elaborate on what the Corbusian proposal contained, taking its lessons from the *tabula rasa* teachings of the Brazilian experience, which had been an American one after all.

There, facing the Pão de Açúcar, as Mestre Valentim had suggested when he created his 'doors' to Brazil in the eighteenth century while conceiving the Passeio Público (Public Promenade), the architect and the landscape designer created, more than a *park way*, an urban experience where the *Carioca* people remembered things that were, however, not only theirs. The contemplation of nature, which was preserved and transformed in that place (the Baía de Guanabara, the garden of Aterro itself and the city), was an evocation of the need for action and movement that marks the Americas' history. As Le Corbusier had realized and Agache had ignored, it was that need which generations of architects and urbanists have been trying not to forget.

This was also revealed in São Paulo's unlimited growth, in its continuous rhythm of demolition and construction, not allowing the city to stand still for a moment. '*São Paulo não pode parar*' (São Paulo may not stop) is the slogan the city created for itself in those years.

In the early 1930s the town planning movement set down its foundations. The First Housing Congress was held in 1931,

City Planning Commissions multiplied throughout the country; the *Revista Municipal de Engenharia* (Municipal Review of Engineering) (1932) began publication – the first journal to seek a synthesis between architecture, engineering and the urban issues. Some of the proposals of Prestes Maia's *Plano de Avenidas* were constructed during the Vargas dictatorship (1937–1945), particularly aspects concerning the circulation system. However, even before Prestes Maia – nominated as Mayor – implemented parts of his plan, a new way of

Figure 4.18 São Paulo. Still of the motion picture *São Paulo a: symphonia de uma metrópole* (1928) by Rudolf Rex Lustig. (*Source*: Cinemateca Brasileira Archive)

looking at cities began to be outlined in São Paulo – just as had happened in Rio, with the panoramas. No longer with drawings and watercolours now. Indeed, in 1928, almost coinciding with the first full sound movie, *Lights of New York*, a Brazilian production appeared, the central theme of which was also the city shown in its whole dynamism: *São Paulo, a symphonia de uma metrópole* (São Paulo, a symphony of a metropolis, figure 4.18). Even though the 'urbanism of the plan' would dominate for another quarter of a century, in this film of modest resources, Brazilian architects and urban planners would realize, as the country's long urban tradition had taught, that the image of the capital cities is always ephemeral.

NOTES

1. According to da Silva Pereira, M. (1994) Romantismo e Objetividade: notas sobre um panorama do Rio de Janeiro. *Anais do Museu Paulista*, 2, Jan/Dec, pp. 169–195.

2. The metaphor of 'nebulae' of cities' was inspired by the reading of a recent work by Topalov, C. (2000) *Laboratoires du nouveau, la 'nebuleuse' reformatrice en France – 1880–1914*. Paris: EHES; and by the contributions of different authors, beginning with Sutcliffe, A. (1981) *Towards the Planned City. Germany, Britain, the United States and France, 1780–1914*. Oxford: Blackwell, who have underlined the synchrony of the birth of urban planning in several countries in parallel with a Progressive Era or a *Temps de réformes*. Reading these authors reveals the coherence between the European and North American reformist context and that which is observed in several other countries such as Brazil, when social actors, discourses and strategies are analysed in a comparable perspective. As we understand, this 'Urban Internationale', as expressed by Saunier, P.-Y. (1999) Atlantic crosser: John Nolen and the Urban Internationale. *Planning History*, **14**(1), pp. 23–31, would be not only a 'nebula' formed by urban planning professionals or urban social movements, but also by the very cities in which they emerge as actors or with

which they are in contact and which make them legitimate.

3. Rio de Janeiro was the administrative and political capital of country until 1960, when this function was transferred to Brasilia, the city constructed for this purpose.

4. Marques dos Santos, A. (2000) A cidade do Rio de Janeiro: de laboratório da civilização à cidade símbolo da nacionalidade, in *A visão do Outro. Seminário Brasil-Argentina*. Brasilia: FUNAG, pp. 149–174.

5. All demographic data concerning Rio de Janeiro have been extracted from Laymayer Lobo, E.M. (1978) *História do Rio de Janeiro (do capital comercial ao capital industrail e financeiro)*. Rio de Janeiro: IBMEC, Vol. II.

6. *Ibid.*, particularly Vol. I, chapter II, pp. 75–151.

7. On the criticisms of the function of Rio de Janeiro as a capital city, see da Silva Pereira, M. (1988) Rio de Janeiro, l'éphémère et la perennité. Histoire de la ville au XIXème siècle. Unpublished Thesis Dissertation, EHESS, Paris, pp. 141–164. See also, on the political dimension of these debates, Freire, A. (2000) *Uma capital para a República*. Rio de Janeiro: Revan, chapter I.

8. For a deeper analysis of these projects, see da Silva Pereira, Rio de Janeiro, l'éphémère et la perennité, *loc. cit.*, pp. 238–448.

9. On the 1816 artistic mission see, for instance, Morales de los Rios Filho, A. (1941) *Grandjean de Montgny e a evolução da arte brasileira*. Rio de Janeiro: A Noite; and Rosso del Brenna, G. (org.) (1979) *Grandjean de Montigny e o Rio de Janeiro*. Rio de Janeiro: Puc-Funarte-Fundação Roberto Marinho.

10. *Idem*. On aspects of Grandjean de Montigny's urbanism, da Silva Pereira, Rio de Janeiro, l'éphémère et la perennité, *loc. cit.*, pp. 165–188; and also da Silva Pereira, M. (1995) Paris-Rio: le passé américain et le goût du monument, in Lortie, A. (org.) *Paris s'exporte*. Paris: Picard-Pavillon de l'Arsenal, pp. 141–148.

11. Toledo, B. L. (1989) *Anhangabahú*. São Paulo: FIESP, p .23.

12. This is a Ernani da Silva Bruno's expression in a chapter of his book (1984) *Histórias e tradições da cidade de São Paulo*. São Paulo: Huicitec-Secretaria de Cultura, 1984, Vol. II (Burgo de Estudantes: 1828–1872).

13. Women who mostly sold vegetables in the streets.

14. da Silva Pereira, Rio de Janeiro, l'éphémère et la perennité, *loc. cit.*, pp. 210–236.

15. Code of Postures, Posture Code: a code providing rules for social interaction and safety for all uses and functions that are allowed and exerted in a city.

16. Bresser, C.A. (ca. 1840) Mapa da cidade de São Paulo e seus subúrbios feita por Ordem do Ex. Sr. Presidente Marechal de Campo Manoel da Fonseca Lima e Silva.

17. *Paulista*: attribute designating a native, often a resident, of the State of São Paulo, and anything related to this State.

18. Toledo, *op. cit.*, p. 38.

19. On the economic data of this growth cf. Lobo, *op. cit.*, Vol. I.

20. da Silva Pereira, M. (1999) *A arquitetura dos Correios no Brasil: um patrimônio histórico e arquitetônico*. Rio de Janeiro: MSP-ECT.

21. On the railway expansion in São Paulo see, for instance, Pinto, A.A. (1903) *História da Viação Pública de São Paulo*. São Paulo: Vanorden & Cia.

22. According to da Silva Pereira, A arquitetura dos Correios no Brasil, *loc. cit.*, and De Niemeyer Lamarão, S.T. (1991) *Dos trapiches ao porto*. Rio de Janeiro: Biblioteca Carioca.

23. There are exemplary biographies of F. Paula Souza, one of the future creators of *Escola Politécnica de São Paulo*, who studied in USA, Switzerland and Brazil, as well as of the architect Ramos de Azevedo, who studied in Belgium and would be in charge of the most important of São Paulo's architectural practices from the 1880s. See for instance Wolff de Carvalho, M.C. (2000) *Ramos de Azevedo*. São Paulo: EDUSP.

24. On the notion of 'improvements' in São Paulo, see Bresciani, M.S. (1999) Langage savant et politique urbaine à São Paulo, in Rivière d'Arc, H. (org) *Projet 'Les mots de la ville'*. Paris: MOST-Unesco, document de travail n° 37.

25. Langenbuch, J.R. (1971) *A estruturação da grande São Paulo – estudo de geografia urbana*. Rio de Janeiro: IBGE, p. 77.

26. Toledo, *op. cit.*, p. 48.

27. *chácara*, type of property between urban and rural.

28. Graham, R. (1983) *Grã-Bretanha e o início da modernização no Brasil*. São Paulo: Editora Brasiliense.

29. da Silva Pereira, Rio de Janeiro, l'éphémère et la perennité, *loc. cit.*

30. *Carioca*, attribute designating a native, often a resident, of the city of Rio de Janeiro, and anything related to this city.

31. da Silva Pereira, Rio de Janeiro, l'éphémère et la perennité, *loc. cit.*

32. Data on São Paulo have been extracted from Langenbuch, *op. cit.* and Rolnik, R. (1997) *A cidade e a lei. Legislação, política urbana e território na cidade de São Paulo*. São Paulo: FAPESP-Studio Nobel.

33. (1896, 1921) *Código de Posturas do Município de São Paulo*. São Paulo: Casa Vanorden.

34. Rolnik, *op. cit.*, pp. 35–36.

35. See, for instance, the businessmen that undertook subdivision or other developments, among them Jules Martin, who conceived the Surface Plan of the Capital of the State of São Paulo and its surroundings, 1890.

36. Technology as a new sort of sublime is dealt by Nye, D.E. (1994) *American Technological Sublime*. Cambridge: MIT Press.

37. For a chronicle on the Federal Capital's reform and the ideological vision that presided over it, see Rosso del Brenna, G. (org.) (1985) *O Rio de Janeiro de Pereira Passos*. Rio de Janeiro: Index.

38. *Idem*.

39. De Oliveira Reis, J. (1977) *O Rio de Janeiro e seus Prefeitos*. Rio de Janeiro: Prefeitura Municipal do Rio de Janeiro.

40. da Silva Pereira, M. (1989) The Rio de Janeiro Tramway Light and Power à la naissance de la ville moderne, in *Electricité et électrification dans le monde*. Paris: PUF, pp. 379–399.

41. For the 1902–1906 reforms see, for instance, Rosso del Brenna (org.), *O Rio de Janeiro de Pereira Passos, loc. cit.*; Benchimol, J.L. (1995) *Pereira Passos, um Haussmann tropical*. Rio de Janeiro: Biblioteca Carioca; or Needell, J. (1987) *A Tropical Belle Époque. Elite, Culture and Society in Turn-of-the-century Rio de Janeiro*. Cambridge: Cambridge University Press.

42. Arestizabal, I. (org.) (1994) *A paisagem redesenhada*. Rio de Janeiro: CCBB, catalogue.

43. See Abreu, M. (1992) *Cidade e Natureza*. Rio de Janeiro: Biblioteca Carioca.

44. Ribeiro Lenzi, M.I. (2000) *Pereira Passos: notas de viagem*. Rio de Janeiro: Sextante.

45. *Quinta*: a great estate property in the countryside, with household for living.

46. Arestizabal (org.) *op. cit.*, p. 6.

47. Do Amaral Sampaio, M.R. (1994) O papel da iniciativa privada na formação da periferia paulistana. *Espaço & Debates*, 37, pp. 19–33

48. *Idem*; Rolnik, *op. cit.*, p. 109.

49. See Mc Dowall, D. (1988) *The Light. Brazilian Traction, Light and Power Company Limited 1899–1945*. Toronto/Buffalo/London: University of Toronto Press, pp. 48–79; and Ferreira Santos Wolf, S. (2001) *Jardim América*. São Paulo: EDUSP- FAPESP-Imprensa Oficial.

50. Eletropaulo (1990) *A cidade da Light 1899–1930*. São Paulo: Superintendência de Comunicação/ Depto de Patrimônio Histórico, 2 Vols., p. 13.

51. In Rio, the 'centre' of the city, named and called *Centro*, is still the main site for mostly office-buildings of large and small private companies and governmental agencies.

52. Toledo, *op. cit.*, p. 63.

53. See Gaudin, J.-P. (1991) 'Art-urbain' et sentiment de l'histoire dans la première moitié du XXème siècle en France, in *Atti del XXIV Congresso di Storia dell'Architettura*. Rome. Offprint, pp. 113–124.

54. Toledo, *op. cit.*, p. 64.

55. *Idem.*

56. *Idem.*

57. Risler, G. (1910) Les espaces libres dans les grandes villes et les cités-jardins, in *Le Musée Social. Mémoires et Documents*. Paris: Arthur Rousseau. Offprint, pp. 353–404.

58. 1 hectare = 2,471 acres.

59. Wolff, *op. cit.*

60. Monteiro de Andrade, C.R. (1998) Barry Parker: um arquiteto inglês na cidade de São Paulo. Unpublished Doctoral Dissertation, FAU-USP, São Paulo.

61. Ramos de Azevedo's office was the most important one in this stage of São Paulo's development. See Wolff, *op. cit.*

62. See Filho, J.M. (1992) 'A nossa arquitetura'. *Ilustração brasileira*, 3, March, p. 21.

63. Filho, J.M. (1943) *À margem do problema arquitetônico nacional*. Rio de Janeiro: no editorial

64. See Manifesto Antropofágico, in De Andrade, O. (1996) *Manifesto Pau Brasil, Manifesto Antropofágico, O rei da vela*. São Paulo: Paz e Terra, p. 20.

65. *Idem.*

66. On the razing of Morro do Castelo, see Kessel, C. (2000) Carlos Sampaio and urbanism in Rio de Janeiro (1875-1930). *Planning History*, 22(1), pp. 17–26.

67. Da Silva Freire, V. (1916) A planta de Bello Horizonte. *Revista Polytechnica*, IX(52), pp. 159–174.

68. Leme, M.C (1996) Francisco Prestes Maia – Documento. *AU*, 64, Feb/Mar, pp. 57–67; and Toledo, B.L. (1996) *Prestes Maia e as origens do urbanismo moderno em São Paulo*. São Paulo: no editorial, pp. 119–128.

69. *Idem.*

70. Gregori Warchavchik, of Russian origin, had studied architecture in Rome, and would represent the CIAMs in Brazil. Rino Levi, also graduated in Rome, was as important in the advocacy of the modern architecture in São Paulo.

71. Mello, L.A. (1929) *Problemas de Urbanismo. Bases para a resolução do problema técnico*. São Paulo: Escolas Profissionaes Salesianas.

72. See Silva, L.H. (1996) A trajetória de Donat Alfred Agache no Brasil, and da Silva Pereira, M. (1996) Pensando a metrópole moderna: os planos de Agache e Le Corbusier para o Rio de Janeiro, in (1996) Ribeiro, L.C. and Pechman, R. (org.) *Cidade, povo, nação*. Rio de Janeiro: Civilização Brasileira, pp. 397–410 and 363–376.

73. Rodrigues dos Santos *et al.* (1987) Le Corbusier e o Brasil. São Paulo: Tessela-Projeto.

74. The need to overcome this conceptual equivocation and cope with the mutations of a technological, social and cultural order were being denounced not only by Le Corbusier but even by Eugène Gaillard, vice-president of the most important French association of decorative-artists, one of the organizers of the 1925 *Exposition des Arts-Déco*.

75. (1929) *O Paiz*, January 20, p. 7.

76. *Idem.*

77. See da Silva Pereira, Pensando a metrópole moderna: os planos de Agache e Le Corbusier para o Rio de Janeiro, *loc. cit.*

78. For an analysis of the Dodsworth period cf. Lima, E.F.W. (1990) *Avenida Presidente Vargas: uma drástica cirurgia*. Rio de Janeiro: Biblioteca Carioca.

79. Aterro do Flamengo: a land-filled stretch bordering Guanabara Bay.

Cities within the City:
Urban and Architectural Transfers
in Santiago de Chile, 1840–1940

Fernando Pérez Oyarzun and José Rosas Vera

Cities within the City

Every city has once wanted to be another. In particular moments of their history, cities have tried to copy some admired, and sometimes remote, models. The notion of influence, conceived as a passive one-way movement, is not itself able to describe properly this kind of relationship. In fact, this sort of process of imitation, has sometimes proved to be of a very creative nature. In the attempt to adapt or recreate certain urban models, new interpretations have frequently emerged. In these, even misunderstandings have a role to play. Behind these urban transfers, a web of connections travels in both directions, and the way individuals came to be in contact is usually hidden from official history, all of which are factors in a complex and delicate cultural network. Far from being exclusive of our contemporary and – so-called – globalized world, this kind of process seems to have taken place very early in the history of our cities.

Recognizing the cultural status of travel, means to be conscious of the fact that along with goods and people, ideas, images and values are exchanged as a result of travel. In this context, travel appears as something intimately linked to the process building up an urban culture. The encounter with new and even alien models, with existing territories or settlements, is something that cities in the Americas have experienced from their very beginnings. The attempts to recreate the European environments in new territories is well expressed in the process of naming both countries and cities, with European names very often recurring. However, something completely new would emerge from places such as New York or Nueva Granada.

After Independence, most Latin American cities, which had developed within strict colonial patterns, turned their eyes towards new sources of inspiration. These came mainly from Europe and North America. That meant not only importing ideas and images, but also new professionals, who were able to embody those new ideals and needs. Travel opportunities, development of international relationships, and the presence of qualified immigrants, would produce a significant cultural change in Latin American countries.

Located in one of the southern borders of the Spanish Empire, Santiago de Chile was not immune to that process. Its rather marginal geographic position gave to it at once modesty and freedom. In spite of this, the period from the establishment of the republican government to the introduction of modern urban planning was particularly rich in these kinds of transfer and interaction. They happened, and therefore can be described, at many different levels from urban representation to urban plans, and from particular projects to the whole city.

Following Pedro de Valdivia's foundation of the city in 1541, the development of Santiago de Chile had been mainly the result of local builders' work, occasionally with the addition of more formally trained professionals, generally connected with religious orders.[1] For more than two hundred years the city developed as a result of this rather local and provincial culture.

A major exception to this was the presence of the architect Joaquin Toesca, during the last two decades of the eighteenth century. Educated in Italy, Toesca would be responsible for some of the most outstanding buildings in Santiago during that period. Among them, the Casa de Moneda (The Mint), currently Presidential Palace, and the Cathedral's east façade. Toesca, who tackled works of a new scale and complexity, brought with him both the experience of large-scale masonry and classical language, being responsible for training builders and disciples, who would continue producing buildings following his style and technique, until the mid-nineteenth century.[2]

Testimonies of travellers and visitors should also be considered in connection to those kinds of interchange. They have provided us with valuable representations of the city in plans, sketches and paintings. Far from being neutral, they express particular interpretations which remind us of the extent to which representing a city is thinking and even dreaming about it. Among them, Amédée-François Frezier produced the first reasonably accurate plan of the city in 1712. Sketches by Mary Graham, Moritz Rugendas and Claudio Gay, and a series of panoramic views produced during the nineteenth century, are worthy of mention.[3]

During the early years of republican government there was little room for urban transformation. Designing and planting the Alameda (Poplars Promenade), was one of the first concerns of Bernardo O'Higgins, Supreme Director of the State (1818–1823). But beyond that first attempt, many political problems had to be addressed, before planning or embellishing the city would be possible. It was only during the mid-nineteenth century, after the end of the war against Peru and Bolivia, that some changes in the city became visible.

Building the Republican City 1840–1870

Manuel Bulnes's presidency (1842–1852) was culturally dynamic. During that period, a significant number of intellectuals, from both Europe and Latin America, came to live in Chile, promoting a great deal of intellectual activity which would place the country in an outstanding cultural position among its Latin American counterparts.[4] The government, conscious of the need of intellectual and professional support, hired architects, artists and scientists to encourage education and cultural development. This tendency was to continue during the following governments of Manuel Montt and José Pérez.[5]

During that time, it is not yet possible to speak about general plans for the city. However, a series of specific interventions, most of them due to the presence of foreign architects, would change the face, and in part, the structure of the city. They would introduce a new scale and formality to the capital, allowing republican institutions and social life to be housed and represented. Thanks to them, the entire city fabric registered a certain change. Scarcely perceived in colonial buildings, the systematic use of classical language, and the adoption of new materials and techniques, would play an important role in that change.[6]

Foreign architects were invited either by the government or by the Church to tackle significant commissions. Among the former, Claude François Brunet de Baines[7] arrived as government architect in 1848, followed by Lucien Ambroise Henault[8] in 1857. A strong connection with France, and therefore to the *Beaux-Arts* tradition, can be perceived in government architects,[9] whereas most of those working for the Church, such as Chelli and Provasoli, came from Italy.[10]

The presence of foreign professionals also had further implications in the country. Part of a wider cultural movement, including the foundation of the Academy of Arts by the Italian Alessandro Cicarelli in 1848,[11] the aim was to promote local education in that field. Brunet de Baines and Henault were in charge of the first architectural courses organized in the country. It was for them that Brunet published his *Curso de arquitectura*[12] (Architecture course), the first of its kind in Latin America,

in 1853. Thanks to these teaching activities, a first generation of Chilean architects emerged, after Toesca's disciples, among whom Fermín Vivaceta and Manuel Aldunate should be mentioned.

A plan drawn between 1834 and 1836 and included in a book by Fr. José Javier de Guzmán[13] (figure 5.1) gives us an idea of the state of the city before the foreign architects were hired by Bulnes. The colonial grid appears as a very homogenous pattern. The Plaza de Armas is the only clearly perceivable urban space. A few tiny plazas, generally associated with churches, introduce some exceptional episodes into the neutral grid. The wide course of the Mapocho river appears not yet to have been canalized and the incipient plantation of the Alameda is seen as little more than a dried-up branch of the river. Significant points listed in the plan are mostly churches and convents.

In contrast, the plan designed by the Italian Mostardi Fioretti (figure 5.2), dated 1864, registers a series of changes that have happened in the city, mostly during Montt's government (1852–1862). The plan is drawn west side up, underlining the south and west expansion, and two different types of urban textures are clearly distinguishable. The first one corresponds to the remains of the colonial grid: a series of continuous façade blocks, with central patios. The second, a number of significant buildings, plays the role of a set of figures against the background of the grid. Among them, those of the Parliament, the Municipal Theatre, new commercial buildings around the Plaza de Armas and others, are not only recognizable, but also explicitly listed in the plan. Finally the extension of the Alameda, and the apparition of many other tree-lined avenues such as Matucana, Recoleta and Cañadilla, speak

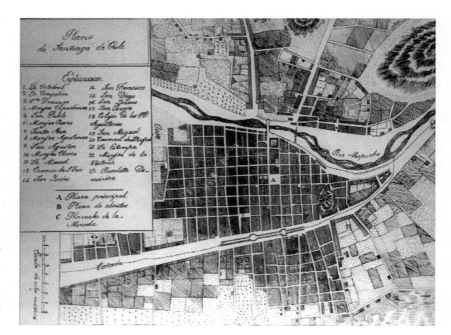

Figure 5.1 Santiago by 1830. Plan published by Fr. José Javier de Guzmán, *c*.1835. (*Source*: Archivo Fotográfico Universidad de Chile)

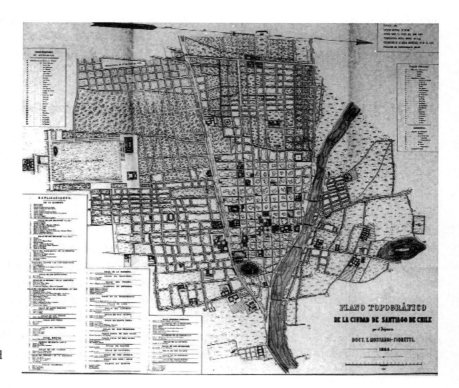

Figure 5.2 Plan of Santiago by Tomás Mostardi Fioretti, 1864. (*Source*: Archivo Fotográfico Universidad de Chile)

Figure 5.3 Parliament Building, by the early twentieth century. (*Source: Nueva Geografía Ilustrada*. Barcelona: Montaner and Simon, 1917)

about a new sensibility, which sees the street as a promenade. Public spaces such as Quinta Normal (a botanic garden) and Campo de Marte (the military parade ground) would play a similar role.

The Parliament Building (figure 5.3), one of the most significant of its time, was designed and built during a long span of time and many architects were involved in the process.[14] Representing one of the main institutions of the young republic, and clearly inspired by the ideals of the French Revolution, it took over the original location of the Jesuits' convent and church. Its neoclassical language, even rather conventional and schematic, shows the traces of Brunet de Baines's and Henault's professional mastery. The south–west location of the building mass, liberating space for public gardens, sought new possibilities of build-

ing in the colonial grid.[15] Gardens themselves were quite a new addition to the city, providing the possibility of public promenade. Halls for the Deputy Chamber, the Senate and the General Assembly of the Parliament, the main institutional elements of the building, refer to different sources of inspiration. The two first two were conceived in the semicircular pattern of French parliament, whereas the third followed the English pattern, organized in two facing groups.

The Municipal Theatre (figure 5.4) is the equivalent to the Parliament, in the realm of social and cultural life. Since colonial times there had been attempts to provide the city with an adequate theatre. However, all of them seemed to have been rather precarious and improvised. It was only in 1847, that a serious initiative to build an Opera Theatre

Figure 5.4 Municipal Theatre in Santiago, against the background of colonial houses and the Santa Lucía hill, a few years after they have been refurbished and planted, *c*.1880. (*Source*: Archivo Fotográfico Universidad de Chile)

was launched. This was accomplished only years later, when after several attempts, the commission was given to Brunet de Baines, requiring the intervention of several other architects, most of them foreigners, in subsequent years.[16] The amazing scale of the building, against that of the colonial houses in the surroundings, is readily perceivable in some of the nineteenth-century pictures, making clear the new urban quality of those institutional buildings constructed at the time. Following a French model, the theatre was considered the centre of social and cultural life, which it would continue to be until the mid-twentieth century.

The list of significant buildings added to the city at this time, would certainly be very long. Some of them implied the adoption of new building techniques. The Central Market

(1869–1872), built in prefabricated iron structures, by Manuel Aldunate and Fermín Vivaceta, is one such example. The structures were imported from Great Britain and, together with the metal bridges built over the Mapocho river in subsequent years, would represent an important addition to the quality of the city fabric.

Perhaps it is not by chance that many of those significant architectural creations which changed the face of the city in the third quarter of the nineteenth century were named as '*palacios*' (palaces),[17] a word completely alien to the rather humble colonial city. The idea of building 'palaces', despite being modest by international standards, reflects the increased prosperity of local families during a time of economic growth. Some, like the Pereira Palace, by Henault, speak an aristocratic classical language. Others, like the Alhambra Palace, by Manuel Aldunate, refer to Moorish buildings in southern Spain.[18] The emergence of a new social sensibility not afraid to show

wealth, international aspirations, and enjoyment of life, would not only include exotic iconographies, but would also envisage the city under a new light.

The Vicuña Mackenna Era, 1870–1900

The idea of transforming the city as a whole, perhaps for the first time in its history, originated with Vicuña Mackenna's intervention on Santiago. Different from later concepts of planning, Vicuña Mackenna's idea of urban transformation, consisted of approaching the whole city through a series of projects, including infrastructure, public spaces and buildings.

Born in 1831, Benjamín Vicuña Mackenna revealed from his early youth a passionate and charismatic character. His participation in politics forced him to leave the country in 1851. Those circumstances, as well as his own curiosity, led him to a long period of travel including Paris, London, New York and Vienna. When he returned to Chile, he was designated Intendente[19] of Santiago, by President Federico Errázuriz Zañartu (1871–1876), in order to distract him from the political scene.[20] Paradoxically, having undertaken his task with enormous talent and success, Vicuña Mackenna became a candidate to the presidency of the country in 1875. Dealing with the city and its transformation seems to have been particularly well suited to a man who had publicly expressed his ideas on the subject.[21] Being a skilled politician, he was at the same time an intellectual, a writer, journalist, and historian.[22] But above all, he was an inspired man of action.

Following his designation as Intendente in April 1872, Vicuña Mackenna launched an initiative aiming to generate and put into

action a new urban plan. Both the process and the content of the plan are described well in his book La transformacion de Santiago[23] (The transformation of Santiago), one of the fundamental documents in Chilean and even Latin American urban history. The book is, in fact, a political report addressed to the Municipality, the Parliament and the Government. It was produced in the brief space of three months, and makes clear the strategy that Vicuña Mackenna had envisaged to carry out his plan.

The aims of the plan are outlined in a brief dedication written at the beginning of the book:

. . . in the hope of a supreme cooperation which definitely redeems the capital of the republic of those evils that periodically affect it; and positions the diverse classes of its population in those conditions of cultivated and Christian societies; giving it all the hygienic improvements allowed by the most healthy and beautiful weather in the world, and lastly, allowing it to enjoy all the possible amenities and embellishments, which still today are possible . . .[24]

This idea of cooperation which pervaded Vicuña Mackenna's political operation is well reflected in the organization given to his plan. He identified a series of twenty key projects which were meant to respond to the most urgent needs of the city.[25] Having done so, he was able to get together a complete team, reaching three hundred people, to work on the plan preparation. They were organized in commissions, reporting to him on each of the projects. This organization allowed Vicuña

Mackenna to produce a coherent plan in a very short time, and to involve many people who supported it from its very beginning.

An epitome of Vicuña Mackenna's urban ideas,[26] the transformation of Santa Lucía hill (figure 5.5), represents, better than other projects, both his efforts to incorporate health and beauty into the city and the contradictions of his romantic sensibility. As one of the few projects actually completed during his period as *Intendente*, the park would become his burial place as a homage to his passion for the city he had dreamt to transform.

Already under construction when the book, which included the chapter '*Apertura de nuevas plazas*' (Opening of new squares), was published, the Santa Lucía project is not exhaustively described in *La transformación de Santiago*.[27] Eighteen new squares were proposed by Vicuña Mackenna to tackle the lack of public spaces, which at the time comprised

only the colonial Plaza Principal and the unused land along the river banks. They were seen as connected to the citizens' health and to that new urban dimension of social life that Vicuña Mackenna had admired in London and Paris. Therefore, they are not presented as a luxury, but as urgently needed by the city.[28] Designated as *paseo* (promenade), Santa Lucía appeared a valuable addition to social life, hitherto confined to the domestic realm or to religious processions. Starting with the existing platforms, originally conceived as the bases of fortifications, the project aimed to plant the hill, to create roads and paths, and so make it enjoyable as a promenade, with new facilities such as a theatre and a restaurant. To work out his project, Vicuña Mackenna asked for the help of the most qualified professionals in the country. In a first stage, Lucien Henault had some part, and after his resignation as government

Figure 5.5 Paseo del Santa Lucía, once completed and with new entrance from Alameda, *c.*1915. (*Source*: Archivo Fotográfico Universidad de Chile)

Figure 5.6 Watercolour by Manuel Aldunate showing a series of proposals for the Paseo del Santa Lucía, 1872. (*Source*: Biblioteca Nacional de Chile)

architect, his disciple Manuel Aldunate took over from him. However, the technical complexities of the project asked for the participation of an engineer, and the Frenchman Ernest Ansart played a significant part in this respect.

A watercolour presented by Manuel Aldunate to the *Intendencia* (Council) on 10 September 1872 (figure 5.6), synthesizes the complexities of the project. Sometimes considered 'historicist and vulgar',[29] this painting expresses not exactly Aldunate's personal preferences, but his synthetic view of a series of proposals for the hill coming from different sources. A neo-gothic church and an electric lighthouse, which is meant to illuminate the city, preside the composition. This contrast between a new technological device and a religious symbol embodied in a neo-mediaeval iconography, reflects both the tensions between European culture and Vicuña Mackenna's own sensibility, split between his attraction for technological and social progress

and his romantic feelings. Completing the composition, the ancient fortresses, once again treated in a neo-mediaeval manner, make clear a pragmatic attitude, taking advantage of the existing military remains, and a picturesque taste.

The building works were carried out by prisoners and it is said that Vicuña Mackenna had to invest his own money to finish the building and to pay for the many works of art purchased in Europe. Several reports on the progress of the work were published between 1872 and 1874, including an Album (1874) containing the main views of the new promenade. All of them, but particularly the Album – one of the first systematic attempts at a photographic survey of the city – give account of the importance acquired by this project within Vicuña Mackenna's plan.

A city plan produced by Ernest Ansart in 1875 (figure 5.7) reflects the condition of the city after Vicuña Mackenna's influence, re-

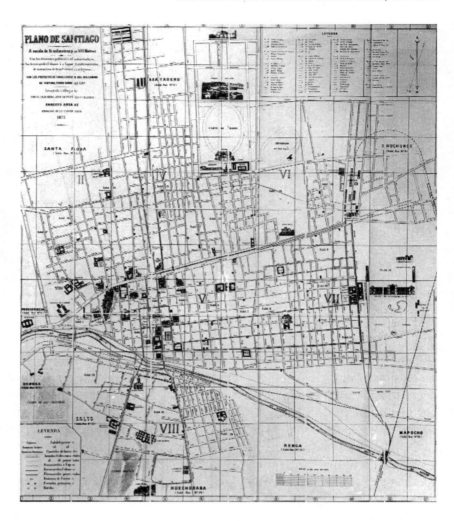

Figure 5.7 Plan of Santiago by Ernest Ansart, 1875. (*Source*: Archivo Fotográfico Universidad de Chile)

vealing, at the same time, the modesty of the achievements and the ambitions of the projects. Ansart's presence is a key one, both in the cultural environment of the country and in the actual building of the city. Having participated in Paris's transformation under Napoleon III, he acted as Professor of Engineering at *Universidad de Chile* (University of Chile). Several of Vicuña Mackenna's urban projects were under his responsibility.

In contrast to Mostardi Fioretti's plan which was drawn west up, Ansart's plan is presented

south up, giving importance to one of the areas most transformed following Vicuña Mackenna's intervention. The predominance assumed by agriculture and farms surrounding the city in Mostardi's plan, is replaced here by infrastructure elements. The *Camino de Cintura* (Ring Road), one of the most ambitious proposals by the *Intendente*,[30] is represented in a partially completed and partially proposed version. Acting simultaneously as an urban limit and as a promenade, as a road and as a symbolic boundary, that ring road was meant to guarantee a true urban condition to the city. Links to the contemporary transformations of peripheral boulevards in Paris have been frequently mentioned. However, beyond the worldwide influence of Parisian transformation, Santiago's Ring Road exhibits particular conditions. Firstly, it needed to be adapted to the grid pattern, which led to its being conceived as four perpendicular avenues surrounding the city. Second, and different from Paris or Barcelona, Vicuña Mackenna's Ring Road is less connected to the expansion of the city than to the intention of establishing a strict limit to it.

Several other engineering projects are represented in Ansart's plan. The canalization of the river and a series of urban railways are the most significant of them. Despite its bias towards infrastructure, the plan is quite a figurative one, including some of the most outstanding urban façades and views of the transformed city. Santa Lucía hill, Cousiño Park,[31] the old Central Railway Station and the Exhibition Palace in Quinta Normal, designed by Paul Lathoud (figure 5.8), are among the most visible of them. The presence of the Hippodrome, located by the *Camino de Cintura* in the southern area, speaks of the influence of British culture in spite of the fact that its first building was designed by the Frenchman Henault.[32] As a whole, the city which Ansart had represented and to whose transformation he had contributed, by that time boasting 150,000 inhabitants, looked quite different from the colonial town of half a century before.

Being the paradigmatic capital of the late nineteenth century, Paris was, obviously, a permanent and yet remote model for all these transformations. But Vicuña Mackenna's

Figure 5.8 1875 Exhibition Palace by Paul Lathoud, *c*.1885. (*Source*: Archivo Fotográfico Universidad de Chile)

references went far beyond the French one. Many other cities, including London, New York, Chicago and Buenos Aires, are mentioned in *La transformación de Santiago*, particularly in connection with infrastructure and roads, showing an amazingly precise knowledge of them.[33] Equally, it would be wrong to think that there was only admiration towards foreign capitals in Vicuña Mackenna's mind. A series of criticisms of foreign cities as well as enthusiastic praise of local values, especially those connected with geography and climate, can be found in his writings. His main intention was to make Santiago an international capital, equivalent but not necessarily equal to others. Having involved the participation of twenty-eight countries, the International Exhibition of 1875 was a clear proof of that attitude and one of the best illustrations of the urban achievements of the period.

Only a small part of Vicuña Mackenna's proposals were fulfilled during his administration. But many of them remained in Santiago's urban agenda which he, so powerfully, contributed to establish. They were developed during subsequent administrations.[34]

Contradictions and Tensions: The Centennial Celebration 1900–1925

A victim of his own success and political naïveté, Vicuña Mackenna lost his battle for the presidency in 1876. The economic crises at the end of President Errázuriz's period made it difficult to maintain the same rhythm in public works. He died in 1886 at fifty-five. In the meantime, the country would be involved in difficult international affairs: border problems with Argentina, and mainly, the Pacific War against Peru and Bolivia, would consume the energies and resources of the country until the mid-1880s.

During Balmaceda's presidency (1886–1891) participation of the country in international events continued. Chile was present at world exhibitions, both in Paris and Barcelona, in 1889. For the Parisian exhibition, on the occasion of the French Revolution centennial, Chile built a small pavilion which was located near the Eiffel Tower. Designed by Henry Picq, in prefabricated cast iron, the cubic pavilion, crowned by five crystal domes, combined both technological and classical references. Sent back to Chile, the pavilion was rebuilt in Quinta Normal Park, not far from the Exhibition Palace of 1875, where it housed an international mining exhibition in 1894. Following the same technological trend, a series of bridges over the Mapocho river would contribute to establish iron structures as characteristic urban elements in the city (figure 5.9).[35]

It was the proximity of the centennial of Independence which, as in other Latin American countries, put the urban issue once again on the public agenda, and with renewed strength. As Adrián Gorelik[36] has pointed out for Buenos Aires, the Centennial was an opportunity both to make a assessment of the first republican century and to exhibit its achievements to the world. The publication of a *Baedecker* guide, dedicated to Santiago, in 1910, is a clear indication of the international dimension given to the celebration. The festive side of the event included new monuments, buildings and public spaces. But digging deeper, the celebration concealed a tension between nineteenth-century aesthetic ideals and twentieth-century social and political demands. Public claims about the

Figure 5.9 Iron bridges over the Mapocho river. In the background to the right hand side, the Fine Arts School, still under construction, *c*.1909. (*Source*: Archivo Fotográfico Universidad de Chile)

quality of workers' housing had led to the creation of the *Consejo Superior de la Habitación Obrera* (High Council of Workers Housing) in 1906.[37] The lack of proper sanitary conditions was an important component of those preoccupations. Thus a certain tension between urban embellishment and infrastructure needs coloured the whole centennial celebration.

Many of the monuments built around the centennial are, strictly considered, infrastructure. Namely, three railway stations: Mapocho, Central and Pirque. Furthermore, although less frequently mentioned, the building of a sewerage system should be considered a major achievement in the urban renewal of those years. The aim of embellishing the city, being more explicitly declared than in Vicuña Mackenna's time, had to be negotiated with the social claim about poor health and housing conditions. In 1910 the city had already reached around a quarter of a million inhabitants. Attempts to study a new drainage

system had been made, at least, since 1888, and a law on the subject promulgated in 1906.[38]

Santiago had been historically dependent on its water supply and sewage systems. During colonial times, a system of irrigation ditches, going east-west across the blocks, fulfilled both water supply and sewage roles. Building a new sewerage network meant not only the incorporation of the internationally available technology but also redundancy of the old irrigation pattern. Moving the sewerage to an underground network below the streets, involved a major structural change, since from then on, both the traffic and service networks would be concentrated in one system.

Carried out following the plan of the Batignoles-Fould company around the time of the centennial, the sewage works had a significant urban influence (figure 5.10). Reinforcing the process of the widening and new alignment of the streets, they confirmed the validity of the colonial grid, making difficult any further attempt to change it. This ground and underground structure was at once complementary and supportive of other centennial interventions.[39]

Published precisely at this time, *La higiene aplicada a las construcciones* (Hygiene applied to buildings)[40] – a monumental book by Ricardo Larraín Bravo, a Chilean architect educated in France – shows both the intellectual level which the subject had reached,

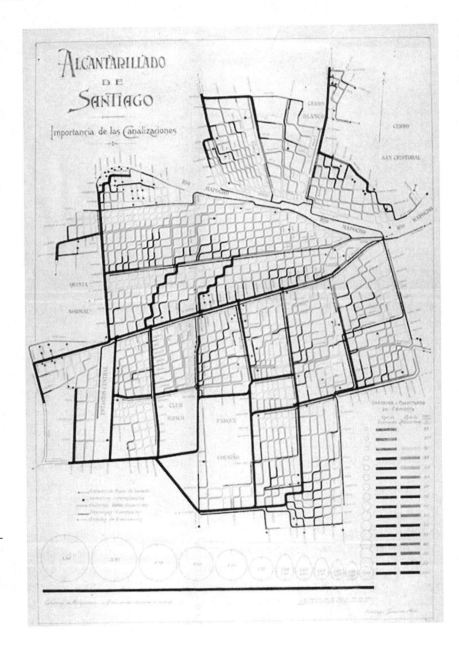

Figure 5.10 Sewer system plan in Santiago. (*Source*: R. Larraín Bravo. *La higiene aplicada a las construcciones*. 1909–1910)

and the very wide and up-to-date knowledge which supported the author's teaching in Schools of Architecture.

If social criticism found a partial answer through the building of a new sewerage network, the intellectual and aesthetic one about the colonial grid was less successful. A small book published by Ismael Valdés Valdés in 1917, curiously titled the same as Vicuña Mackenna's one – *La transformación de Santiago*[41] – sums up the urban design discussion in those centennial and post-centennial years. The enormous difficulties found in transforming the city is the first concern expressed by Valdés. Not without a certain nostalgia, he refers to new cities built, from scratch, according to strict planning criteria, without the limitations imposed by a pre-existing urban fabric. Washington, La Plata and Canberra, making profuse use of diagonals or even curvilinear streets – both considered paradigmatic by Valdés – are among those mentioned.

In spite of these circumstances, Valdés did not relinquish the possibility of transforming existing cities. He mentions Paris, Rio de Janeiro and Guayaquil as examples of this kind of transformation, and claims that a new discipline, *urbanism*, was responsible. Haussmann, Stüben and Buls[42] were, according to Valdés, the most outstanding exponents of that discipline. Paris continued as a dominant paradigm, but a wider set of references are mentioned in the book, showing again a very complete knowledge of the international state of the art.[43]

The colonial grid is one of the main targets of Valdés's attacks, being necessary to 'avoid homogeneity and monotony of that colonial building system, when all houses were the same both from inside and outside'.[44] Instead of this, the idea of variety appears as the driving force to reform the city. All exemplary places

mentioned in the book are particular and highly identifiable moments in the urban fabric. Diagonal streets appear as signs of urban quality, both in technical and aesthetic terms. This attitude represents a certain peak in the criticism of the colonial grid, reached at the beginning of the twentieth century.

A series of utopian plans produced in those years exhibit a similar attitude.[45] Among them, those by the *Sociedad Central de Arquitectos* (Central Society of Architects) (figure 5.11) and Ernest Coxhead (figure 5.12) are especially remarkable. They radically modified the existing grid by creating a series of centres from which diagonals radiate in all directions. Almost nothing of that was actually fulfilled. The small intervention with diagonals in the Stock Exchange block (figure 5.13), quoted by Valdés as a remarkable one, remained an isolated example of what the city could have been if these changes had been accomplished. But behind these utopian proposals, a deeper

Figure 5.11 Urban renewal plan for Santiago, by the *Sociedad Central de Arquitectos, c.* 1910. (*Source*: Biblioteca Nacional de Chile)

Figure 5.12 Urban renewal plan for Santiago by Ernest Coxhead, 1913. (*Source*: Biblioteca Nacional de Chile)

Figure 5.13 Hotel Mundial, by Alberto Schade and Rodulfo Oyarzun Philippi, one of the new buildings of the stock exchange block development, following the fashionable diagonal pattern, *c*.1923.

discussion about a new centrality for the city, which was to emerge in the following years, was hidden.

Other significant attempts to modify the urban structure of the city at this time must be mentioned. Among them those by Carlos Carvajal Miranda are especially relevant because they reflect the new ideas of the linear city. Partially incorporated as a ring road in the *Sociedad Central de Arquitectos* plan, his ideas continued being influential through his participation in the *Comisión de Transformación de Santiago* (Santiago's Transformation Committee) of 1915, as well as through many other publications in subsequent years.[46]

The presence of a new generation of foreign architects hired either by the government or by the Church, is another indication of the international connections existing in the country during the centennial years. Two Frenchmen, Emilio Jecquier and Emilio Doyére, and one Italian, Ignazio Cremonesi,

are among the most significant. The government's connection to France and the Church's connection to Italy continued to be important, in spite of the presence of other foreign architects in the country at that time.[47]

The role of official foreign architects would continue to be similar to those of the mid-nineteenth century, combining professional practice and academic activities. Thus, they not only produced significant pieces of architecture but were involved in the education of future professionals, through their teaching at the recently founded Schools of Architecture.

Born in Chile and son of a French engineer working for the Chilean railways, Emilio Jecquier was educated in France and is the author of significant architectural monuments, such as the Mapocho and Pirque railway stations, the Fine Arts School and Museum, and the second phase of the Catholic University building.

During a period associated with Jecquier, Doyére was responsible for the outstanding Palacio de los Tribunales (Court Palace), consisting of two masonry blocks with a glass and iron arcade in between them, which reminds us of the work of Henri Labrouste. Associated with Patricio Irarrázaval, a Chilean architect, he also produced a highly imaginative drawing for a new southern façade of the presidential palace, transforming Toesca's building into a neo-baroque monument from which a series of diagonals spread in all directions. Even though totally utopian, this project is quite expressive of the search for a new monumental centrality, to be addressed in the following years.

Arriving in 1889 to work on several church commissions, Ignazio Cremonesi remained in the country until 1903. His most important and at the same time polemical intervention was the refurbishment of the Cathedral, covering with stucco part of the colonial stone fabric. Violent reactions against this project, even at that time and within the Church, are one of the first signs of criticism against imported iconography and recognition of the value of local and colonial buildings.

No other building expresses better both centennial aesthetic and urban paradigms than the Fine Arts Museum and School (figure 5.14), designed by Emilio Jecquier. With clear references to French design, the building is conceived as a mixed miniature of both the Petit and Grand Palais built in Paris for the Great Exhibition of 1900.[48] Alberto

Figure 5.14 Fine Arts Palace, by Emile Jecquier, west façade (Fine Arts School), *c.* 1910. (*Source*: Archivo Fotográfico Universidad de Chile)

Figure 5.15 Fine Arts Museum, original interior arrangement including gardens by Georges Dubois.

Mackenna, responsible for the museum project and later its Director, visited the Paris exhibition and bought there a series of works of art for the new museum. It is highly probable that the glamorous image of both pavilions remained in his memory as a model. Jecquier, for his part, often inspired by explicit precedents, seemed to have no difficulties in starting from those references, even in the interior arrangement, including gardens designed by the French George Dubois (figure 5.15).[49] Beyond those explicit quotations, the design was quite creative in responding to the brief requirements of combining a school and a museum. Its glass and iron domed hall, fabricated in Belgium, according to Jecquier's design, is one of the most outstanding public spaces in Latin America.

The discussions about the urban location of the museum also raised some interesting problems. The museum was originally to have been located on the Alameda, by Santa Lucía hill. As that avenue was an institutional

spine of the city, this was a rather conventional location for such a building. But Enrique Cousiño, *Intendente* at that time, suggested another one: it should be moved to land gained following the canalization of the river. Placed in the recently planted Forestal Park (figure 5.16), close to Loreto bridge, the new Museum and School of Fine Arts' location was not only, in many respects, reminiscent of the French models, but also became

Figure 5.16 Fine Arts Museum aerial view showing urban location, 1999. (Photograph by Catalina Griffin)

part of a wider strategy for developing the north-eastern downtown area, running from Mapocho station to Plaza Italia.

Already proposed by Vicuña Mackenna, and having involved Ernesto Ansart in its first steps, the successful urban development generated by the canalization of the river would concentrate, and not by chance, the great majority of the monuments connected with the centennial celebration. In a kind of processional arrangement, beginning with Mapocho station and the Fine Arts School and Museum, it continued eastbound. The monument given by France was coherently located opposite to the museum façade. Further away, in the eastern extreme of the park, was the amazing fountain given by Germany.[50] All this effort ended up in Plaza Italia, including the monument given by Italy and the beautiful Pirque station designed by Jecquier.

Once completed,[51] Plaza Italia became a landmark which epitomized the entire Centennial operation (figure 5.17). Following loosely the *rond-point* iconography, and being one of the key points where the new sewerage system connected to the river, it was able to sum up both the monumental and infrastructure sides of the centennial. At the same time, it manifested a new orientation in the development of the city. Vicuña Mackenna's interventions had tended to structure the city towards the south. The sections of the Ring Road already built, the Cousiño Park and the Club Hípico (hippodrome) were standing there to witness a certain success. Following the same direction of the monumental procession, the city, mainly through its social elites, was about to move towards the east, where dreams of new cities would try to be realized.

Figure 5.17 Plaza Italia *c.* 1960. Looking towards the east, the Mapocho River, riverside avenues and the Parque Japonés. (*Source*: Centro de Informaciones Sergio Larraín García Moreno, Facultad de Arquitectura, Diseño y Estudios Urbanos, Pontificia Universidad Católica de Chile)

Doubts and Expectations: Modernity and the Plan, 1925–1940

Ideas of transforming the whole city to escape the monotonous colonial grid were never realized. However, smaller and localized attempts were successful during the late 1920s. This time, the driving force was not that monumentality associated with diagonals, but the picturesque, following consciously or unconsciously, Camilo Sitte's ideas. Both Paris-Londres and Concha y Toro districts were the result of successful urban renewal in the border of the downtown area. They were made possible thanks to the subdivision of large properties,[52] and the subsequent building of middle- or upper-class houses, following the eclectic patterns of the day. Curvilinear streets, intentionally breaking visual continuity, created the picturesque fantasy of a mediaeval village.

Almost at the same time, that is, on the verge of the 1929 economic crisis, new ideas, associated with modern urban design and planning began to influence the city. No one could embody better those ideas than Karl Heinrich Brunner von Lehenstein, invited to Chile in 1929, thanks to the contacts of Rodulfo Oyarzun Phillipi.[53] Born in Vienna in 1887 and educated there, his ideas represented a shift of paradigm both in professional and cultural terms. After working in Chile, Brunner would extend his influence to Bogotá, Colombia and Panama City.[54] Following his long lasting Latin American experience, he would practise back in Vienna after World War II.

The same year that Brunner arrived in Chile, the Frenchman Jacques Lambert visited the country and Le Corbusier made his first trip to Latin America, including Buenos Aires, Asunción, Montevideo, São Paulo and Rio de Janeiro.[55] The Frenchman Jean Claude Forestier had been working in Buenos Aires and La Habana, and Alfred Agache was doing the same in Rio de Janeiro. Werner Hegemann would visit Argentina during this period, and a few years later, Maurice Rotival together with Jacques Lambert would be working in Caracas. Representing different cultural backgrounds and also different disciplinary positions, the presence of so many distinguished foreign visitors led to the reproduction of some of the European tensions around the urban issues in the Latin American scenario.[56]

The way in which Brunner operated in Chile resembles very much that of other foreign professionals during the nineteenth century. Hired by the Chilean government as a technical adviser, he would produce a plan for the city within the Ministry of Public Works.[57] In addition to that, an academic connection with Universidad de Chile would lead him not only to organize the first seminar on urbanism in Latin America, and later a Department of Urbanism, but also to gather a group of disciples who would embody and spread his ideas. Exhibiting a well balanced set of intellectual and pragmatically-oriented skills, Karl Brunner inaugurated a new era of professional urbanism in the country, and was a key character in associating the government, the municipalities and the university in tackling the complexities of urban problems.[58] His more holistic and systematic idea of planning, which starting from sociological and economical facts, would never neglect the morphological dimension, and would prevail until the North American influences became dominant in the late 1950s.

Brunner's ideas on Santiago are well summed up in the book published after his first mission to the country: *Santiago de Chile. Su estado actual y su futura formación* (Santiago de Chile. Its current state and future formation).[59] Following a scientific methodology, Brunner started studying the social conditions of the city, paying special attention to the population's growth problem (figure 5.18). Addressing both the historical and the contemporary conditions of the city, the book represents very accurately the complexities of Brunner's attitude. On the one hand, he was oriented towards scientific or, at least, systematic knowledge. On the other, he displayed a pragmatic and even conservative approach, relying on the possibility both of reinterpreting the existing urban tissue and using traditional design tools such as axes, continuous façades and public spaces such as plazas and parks.

Organized in two main sections, the book tackles both the transformation of the central district, that is Santiago Municipality, and the Great Santiago, including the whole set of metropolitan municipalities (figure 5.19). Quite evident in the book, Karl Brunner's knowledge of the international state of the art, allows him to make detailed references to European, North and South American cases. However, some of the illustrations in the book make clear the nature of Brunner's cultural background. It is not by chance that the chapter 'La formación de la ciudad' (The city formation) is headed by a picture of a street crossing in Berlin. Giving a great deal of attention to the housing problem, references to new Siedlungen in Vienna and Hanover made a big contrast against the working-class districts in Santiago. The inclusion of Alexander Klein's housing plans must be

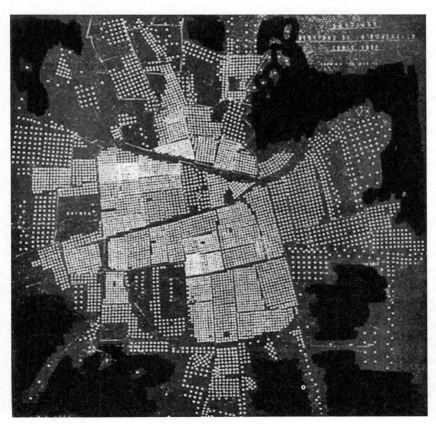

Figure 5.18 Density of population in 1930, according to a plan published by Karl Brunner, Santiago de Chile, su estado actual y futura formación.

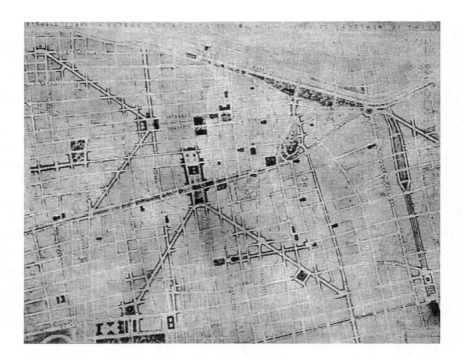

Figure 5.19 Karl Brunner's urban renewal proposal for the Central Area including diagonals. *Santiago de Chile, su estado actual y futura formación.*

specially underlined, both to explain the origin of Brunner's own housing schemes, included in the book, and his connection to the most pragmatic wing of the modern movement.

His most ambitious proposals, like a metropolitan railway, remained only on paper, except for a few traces here and there. That is the case with the partially built Diagonal Oriente (East Diagonal avenue), which shows Brunner still engaged with diagonals, as technical and aesthetic devices.[60] However, it is in the development of the downtown area where Brunner's influence is most visible. Firstly, in the direction imposed on the development of the area as a whole, and then, in the creation of the Barrio Cívico (Civic District).

Referring to the central area as a *city* (in English in the book), Brunner pointed to its emerging metropolitan role, focusing on business and public affairs, whereas the periphery was intended to be dedicated to housing and industry.[61] Brunner's proposal for the central district was at the same time representative of his pragmatic approach and his positive vision of the historical heritage of the city. On the one hand, the old colonial grid was there, and for various reasons was difficult to modify; but on the other hand, he was convinced that it was possible to regenerate it, providing a sense of order to the city which would prevent it from the dangers of indiscriminate modernization.[62]

Following those ideas, the urban regulations which would guide the development of the central area during the 1940s and 1950s, would produce a very homogeneous urban fabric, twelve floors high, perforated at the ground floor level by an amazing grid of arcades and galleries.[63] Announced by the construction of Oberpauer building[64] (figure 5.20), actually included in the book, this attitude supposed the capability of the traditional block to receive the figurative impact of modern architecture. Although producing rather sad inner courts, downtown renewal as a whole can be seen as a quite valuable urban episode. One in which a rather anonymous but very qualified architecture is able to generate a compact and wisely modern city fabric.

Conscious of the practical difficulties of dealing with the old square block of 120 by 120 metres, Brunner suggested various forms of dividing, modifying and enriching it,[65] proposing different forms and sizes when applied to new developments. However, the block continued being for him the basic urban unit. Multiplying the commercial front and providing private space for public activities, the arcades were quite a successful urban addition.[66]

Figure 5.20 Oberpauer building, built *c.*1930, first modern addition to the central district. (*Source*: E.H. Moreno, *Arquitectura y modernidad en Chile*. Santiago: ARQ, 1989)

The project for the Barrio Cívico was the most ambitious of Brunner's urban operations. As a public counterpart to the private renewal of the central area it had to overcome all kind of difficulties: the economic Depression of the 1930s, the big earthquake of 1939, and long public discussions. Begun during Carlos Ibáñez's first presidency (1927–1931), it was carried on during the second one of Arturo Alessandri (1932–1938), and even during that of Aguirre Cerda's (1938–1941).[67]

Interpreting old urban aspirations, actually rooted in some of the centennial proposals, the Civic District was able to take advantage of a favourable political moment in which the state grew and developed. The idea of a new civic centre, different from the traditional Plaza de Armas, had been gaining public and political support for some time.[68] Precipitated by the move of the Presidential Palace to the formerly peripheral position of the old Mint (La Moneda) during the nineteenth century, the Barrio Cívico project reveals a deeper discussion about a new centrality for the city.[69] Geometrically located in a more central position, by the Alameda, it embodied the idea of a specialized civic area, revealing how far the idea of zoning had permeated both traditional and *avant-garde* urbanism.

The operation was obviously a complex one. As the seat of the government, La Moneda required a new façade towards Alameda and its central condition needed to be highlighted by means of monumental axes, while expanding the central civic district towards the south. Finally, public spaces were required for both practical reasons and to express the new role and size of the state.[70]

Following Brunner's second proposal, the scheme finally developed by Carlos Vera, included two new plazas: a north one, Plaza de la Constitución (Constitution Plaza), which would involve the demolition of a complete block, and a south one, Plaza Bulnes, on both sides of the Alameda. Only one monumental axis, Avenida Bulnes, was finally opened towards the south, abandoning Brunner's initial idea of two diagonals. A series of buildings of a neoclassical design, destined for ministries, around the presidential palace, and for commerce, offices and housing along Avenida Bulnes, would provide the proper façade to the urban operation.[71]

A complementary figure to those of Brunner and Vera provides additional clues about the Civic District. Josué Smith Solar, born in Chile, and son of a North American engineer, had studied architecture in the United States. After travelling through Europe and practising in North America, he returned to Chile to run a successful office in the country.

As an amazingly gifted architect, his technical and artistic skills were clearly perceivable behind his rather eclectic approach to architecture, including the neo-mediaeval iconography that he had experienced in the United States.

The idea of opening a monumental public space in front of La Moneda's northern façade, seems to have been proposed by Smith Solar years before it was formally planned and built. In fact, a series of tall buildings were built on the edges of the plaza, before the area was actually renewed; among them, the *Ministerio de Hacienda* (Ministry of Finances) by Smith Solar himself, and the *Edificio del Seguro Obrero* (Workers' Insurance Building) by Gonzalez Cortés (figure 5.21). Furthermore, Smith Solar obtained the commission for the refurbishment of the Presidential Palace. In con-

Figure 5.21 Urban transformations in the Civic District: southern façade of the Presidential Palace and new plaza towards the Alameda. Beyond the palace to the north, tall buildings on the edges of the future Plaza de la Constitución still unbuilt.

trast to the neo-baroque fantasies of Doyére and Irarrázaval, Smith kept the same neo-classical language imposed by Toesca, creating an elegant and intelligent southern façade. In some of its details a neo-colonial sensibility can be perceived, revealing his North American education. An official competition for the Plaza de la Constitución scheme was actually won by Freitag in 1935. The same sort of neoclassical sensibility, prevailing in the Barrio Cívico, dominated his scheme which was only partially built.[72]

The presence of a landscape architect such as Oskar Prager, active in the country during the 1940s and 1950s, is another testimony of the significant influence of a German and Central European sensibility visible in Chile during the mid-twentieth century. Assuming a role which can be equated to that of Dubois in the beginning of the century, Prager would share with Brunner the same attraction for classical modern aesthetics, nurtured in his case by an intensive use of local flora. His participation in the Parque Japonés (Japanese Park) design, prolonging Parque Forestal towards the east and along the river, announced a new expansion of the city, in which he was about to play an outstanding role. Once again looking for healthier environmental conditions, a peculiar interpretation of the Garden City would play the main role[73] in that eastwards expansion. Dominated by the imposing presence of the Andes, and free from those difficulties and constraints which made expansion difficult to the north, south and west,[74] places such as Providencia or Las Condes were ideal settings for a new urban utopia. Social elites following the path opened by foreigners, among them many Germans, would move in large numbers to that area.

Alberto Mackenna can be seen, once again, as the political figure behind a great part of the urban changes taking place during the first four decades of the twentieth century. *Intendente* between 1920 and 1927, he represented a continuity between the Centennial projects and the foundation of the *Instituto Nacional de Urbanismo* in 1935.[75] Through the refurbishment of the San Cristóbal hill and the opening of riverside avenues such as Santa María and Andrés Bello, he would play an important role in the expansion of the city towards the east.

In 1939 Le Corbusier made a curious attempt to obtain a commission in Chile. Through Roberto Dávila Carson, who had worked in his Atelier by the early 1930s, he offered a plan for Santiago and, after the big earthquake of 1939, for other Chilean cities. The very mention of that visit and proposed commission, provoked one of the most stormy controversies on urban issues that happened in the country. Brunner's disciples strongly opposed the visit, which finally failed to succeed. As in many others Latin American cities, a more pragmatic and conservative approach to modern urbanism, and in this case with strong Central European connections, would overcome the bright and utopian Parisian *avant-garde*.

In 1941, on the occasion of the fourth centennial of the city, a series of cultural initiatives were promoted. Among them, and not by chance, the two main commemorative publications showed a distinctive historical character. Both *Santiago de siglo en siglo* (Santiago from Century to Century)[76] by Carlos Peña Otaegui and *Arquitectura en Santiago* (Architecture in Santiago)[77] by Eduardo Secchi, sought to recover the historical roots of the city, paying special attention to colonial times.[78] One historical cycle seems to end with them. The city, until then apparently obsessed by enacting the roles of other cities, probably responding to a latent trend accompanying all its historical development, would reveal a hidden intention of that masquerade, announcing the emergence of a new obsession: the search of its own identity.

During the early 1940s, a new generation of young architects, strongly committed to both the values and the iconography of modern architecture, would graduate from both *Universidad Católica* (Catholic University) and *Universidad de Chile*. The figure of Le Corbusier and the pedagogical model of the Bauhaus would become the most visible references for that generation. Nevertheless, a broader and more eclectic set of influences, including Richard Neutra's activities in the United States, and later, Brazilian architecture, would affect Chilean architects. The North American influence would extend to the field of urbanism and planning, bringing along a new conception of the city, more attached to social and political sciences. The foundation of the CIDU (Interdisciplinary Centre of Urban Development) at *Universidad Católica*, in the early 1960s, is a clear sign of this shift in Chilean urban thinking towards a more North American position.

Meanwhile, professional organizations had developed and settled. The *Sociedad Central de Arquitectos* (Central Society of Architects), which had initially grouped foreign professionals and the first generation of Chilean architects, made way to the *Asociación de Arquitectura de Chile* (Chilean Architecture Association) during the 1920s. Finally in 1942, by law No.7211, the *Colegio de Arquitectos de Chile* (Chilean College of Architects) was created.

A series of journals published during that period reflect these changes in the professional culture. Some of their names are, in themselves, expressive of that phenomenon as is seen in the cases of *Arquitectura y Decoración* (Architecture and Decoration), published between 1929 and 1930, *Urbanismo y Arquitectura* (Urbanism and Architecture), published between 1936 and 1941, and *Arquitectura y Construcción* (Architecture and Construction), published between 1945 and 1950.[79]

To sum up, one could maintain that, after fifty years, Vicuña Mackenna's notion of urban transformation, conceived as a series of articulated projects, would acquire a new and more comprehensive meaning, when used by Brunner and his disciples. Closer to the idea of urbanism, mentioned by Ismael Valdés Valdés, Brunner's eclectic but realistic approach gave to social and historical issues the same importance that he gave to physical and morphological ones. In his own, and also in his disciples' view, the great public works were still considered as the most effective planning tool. Juan Parrochia, a key character in the Chilean urban scene, acting from the 1960s to the 1980s, is the last representative of this way of thinking.[80]

The shift from European towards North American references occurred when Brunner's influence began to decline, and this involved a deep change in the conception of the urban phenomenon. Within this new idea of planning, which became increasingly significant during the 1960s and 1970s, the built environment of the city would no longer be considered the main focus of interest. Seeing the physical environment as the result of social and economical processes, the new planners would focus on more global strategies, finally conceived as political ones. The more abstract zoning proposal of the *Plan Intercomunal de Santiago* (Inter-municipal Plan of Santiago), conceived during the mid-1960s, would reflect these new criteria. Later on, and as in a pendulum movement, these ideas would be the target of strong criticism, when the physical fabric of the city again attracted the attention of architects and planners and the possibility of a systematic planning process again became a goal.

NOTES

1. See Guarda, G. (1997) *El arquitecto de La Moneda, Joaquín Toesca 1752-1799; una imagen del imperio español en América.* Santiago: Universidad Católica de Chile.

2. Juan José de Goycolea is the best known of those disciples. He carried out the project for the *Real Audiencia* (High Court) building.

3. Among panoramic views of Santiago de Chile, those by Smith (1855), Harvey (1860) and Dejean (1867), must be mentioned.

4. To the active presence in Chile of the Venezuelan Andrés Bello and the Spaniard José Joaquín de Mora, it should be added that of Argentine immigrants, such as Sarmiento, Mitre and López. The French painter Monvoisin remained in Chile until 1840, and the Italian Cicarelli received from the government a commission to create a new Art Academy. Scientists such as Ignacio Domeyko and Claudio Gay contributed to the enrichment of one of the most remarkable moments in the intellectual history of the country.

5. Before being elected President of the Republic, Pérez had been secretary of the Chilean Legacy in Washington and Consul in Paris.

6. The Cathedral building completed in the eighteenth century by Joaquí Toesca, just as other works by him and his disciples, are the exceptions. Even in those cases, the use of classical language is retained and simplified.

7. Claude François Brunet de Baines (1799–1855) studied in the *École des Beaux-Arts* in Paris. He was contacted by Francisco de Rosales, Chile's *chargé d'affaires* in Paris. Rosales played a fundamental role as a cultural contact for Chileans in Paris.

8. Lucien Ambroise Henault (1823) studied architecture at the *École des Beaux-Arts* in Paris, where he was hired by Manuel Blanco Encalada in 1856, remaining in Chile until 1872.

9. Both architects also did work for the Church, which at the time was attached to the government.

10. Chelli was involved in important Church commissions, among them the Buen Pastor, Agustinas and Recoleta Dominica churches. Provasoli designed Nuestra Señora de la Divina Providencia.

11. A series of other foreign painters were brought to the country in connection with the academy. In spite of their academic training they were immediately attracted by local subjects.

12. Brunet de Baines, C. F. (1853) *Curso de arquitectura, traducido al castellano por Francisco Solano Pérez.* Santiago de Chile: Imprenta de Julio Belén y Compañía.

13. Guzmán, J.J. (1834–1836) *El chileno instruido en la historia topográfica civil y política de su país.* Santiago: Imprenta Nacional de Santiago.

14. The Parliament was one of the first commissions given to Brunet de Baines (1848). Begun in 1858, after Brunet's death in 1855, Henault took over from him. Manuel Aldunate and Eusebio Chelli also played a part in the building process.

15. It had been originally planned to replace only the ancient Jesuit convent. A big fire in 1863, destroyed the old Jesuit church making it possible to use the complete block.

16. In addition to that of Brunet de Baines, several other projects were considered for the Municipal Theatre. Among them one by two English architects, another by the painter Alejandro Cicarelli, and one sent from France by Francisco Javier Rosales. The contractor for the theatre was the Frenchman Emilio Lafourcade, and its building process lasted from 1853 to 1856. After a big fire in 1870, the commission for its reconstruction went to Lucien Henault. The Frenchman Paul Lathoud and the Italian Eusebio Chelli took over from him.

17. Parliament and court buildings such as the Fine Arts Museum were called palaces as was the Archbishop's residence and some private residences. Vicuña Mackenna referred to the Central Market as a palace of glass and iron.

18. The interest in exotic cultures and exotic iconography was an important cultural feature of the late nineteenth century. In Santiago people enriched by mining activities spent a great deal of money on travelling and introduced new social activities such as fancy dress parties. See Aguirre, F.(2000) La apariencia de lo exótico en el Santiago del siglo XIX., and Domínguez, T. (2000) Mausoleos exóticos en el Cementerio General, in Pérez F. and. Hecht, R. (2000) *Transferencias urbanas, arquitectos, ideas y modelos*, collected papers available in the library. Seminario de Investigación. Santiago: Escuela de Arquitectura Pontificia Universidad Católica de Chile, without page numbers in the original.

19. 'Intendente' is the President's representative in a province.

20. See Encina, F. A.(1964) Resumen de la historia de Chile, redacción iconografía y apéndices de Leopoldo Castedo. Santiago de Chile: Zig-Zag. 5th ed, p.1323.

21. Vicuña Mackenna's ideas on the transformation of Santiago had been anticipated in his articles for El Mensajero de la Agricultura as early as 1856–1857.

22. Vicuña Mackenna had an amazing production as a writer, including the history of both Santiago and Valparaíso. He has been considered one of the main contributors to Chilean historiography, due to the invaluable set of documents he collected during his life.

23. Vicuña Mackenna, B. (1872) La transformacion de Santiago. Notas e indicaciones respetuasamente sometidas a la Ilustre Municipalidad, al Supremo Gobierno y al Congreso Nacional. Santiago: Imprenta de la Librería del Mercurio de Orestes L. Tornero.

24. Ibid., p. 5 (translation F. Pérez Oyarzun).

25. The projects included in the plan were the following: canalization of the Mapocho river; the Ring Road; transformation of southern neighbourhood; expansion of running water; creation of new squares (Santa Lucía promenade); completion of the new market; creation of new food markets; centralization and building of new schools; opening of closed streets; building of double channel of Negrete; building of the vaulted course of San Miguel channel; building a new slaughterhouse in the north of the city; suppression of the public chinganas (cheap dance halls) and the creation of four big houses dedicated to public entertainment; building a new City Hall; replacement of street pavings; project for widening pavements; completion of Ejército Libertador and Cementerio Avenues; radical amendment of the slaughterhouse; amendment and completion of the city prison; new clothes and armaments for the police.

26. See. Guevara S. (2000) Espacio público en la ciudad de Vicuña Mackenna: El Cerro Santa Lucía, presencia de lo artístico y sublime en un plan urbano, in Pérez and Hecht, op. cit., without page numbers in the original.

27. Vicuña Mackenna, op. cit., pp. 45–51.

28. Ibid., pp.127–128: 'We have exposed nothing, neither formulated nor discussed, anything not related to the most essential works in the city . . . Nothing superfluous, nothing of embellishment . . .' (translation F. Pérez Oyarzun).

29. Pérez de Arce, R. (1993) La montaña mágica. Santiago de Chile: ARQ, p. 153.

30. A complete series of appended documents, relative to the Camino de Cintura, are included in Vicuña Mackenna, op. cit., pp. 131–176, giving account of the complexities of the project, which asked for a series of expropriations and significant investments.

31. Cousiño Park had replaced the old Campo de Marte, a military parade ground. It was a public park which in addition to imitating the Bois de Boulogne, even in its connection to the hippodrome, was a kind of anchor in a successful urban development.

32. The first Sociedad Hípica de Chile (Chilean Horse Society) organized 'carreras a la inglesa' (English races) to differentiate them from the traditional 'carreras a la chilena' (Chilean races). See Letamendi, F. La arquitectura del Club Hípico de Santiago y la contribución de Josué Smith Solar, in Pérez and Hecht, op. cit., without page numbers in the original.

33. The references to France, England and the United States are enormously precise in terms of the width and section of the Camino de Cintura as well as of the types and technical conditions of pavements. See Vicuña Mackenna, op. cit., pp 99–112 and 134–135. In the competition for which kind of pavement to use, two foreign shops settled in Valparaíso, a French one (Thomas La Chambre i Ca.) and an English one (Cross i Ca) donated to the government two thousand paving stones each, from Cherbourg and Edinburgh respectively, to serve as samples for future pavements.

34. Many of the urban projects undertaken in the last three decades of the nineteenth century as well as some others during the Centennial and even later, in Brunner's times, were contained in Vicuña Mackenna's proposal.

35. See Palmer, M (1970) 50 años de arquitectura metálica en Chile. Santiago: Facultad de Arquitectura y Urbanismo, Universidad de Chile.

36. See Gorelik, A. (1998) La grilla y el parque. Espacio público y cultura urbana en Buenos Aires. 1887–1936. Buenos Aires: Universidad Nacional de Quilmes, pp. 181–234.

37. Law No.1838, 1906.

38. Vicuña Mackenna explicitly mentioned the 'cloaca máxima' (major sewer) as following in importance to the canalization of the river project. In 1890 the Belgian engineer Rafael Pothier carried out a project for the sewage of the central area. In 1906, the law No.1835 on drainage system and running waters was promulgated.

39. A similar situation in Caracas can be seen in Almandoz, A. (1997) Urbanismo europeo en Caracas (1870–1940). Caracas: Fundarte, Equinoccio, Ediciones de la Universidad Simón Bolívar, p. 323.

40. Larraín Bravo, R. (1909–1910). *La higiene aplicada a las construcciones*. Santiago: Cervantes.

41. Valdés Valdés, I. (1917) *La transformación de Santiago*. Santiago: Soc. Imprenta-Litografía Barcelona.

42. *Ibid.*, pp. 7–8.

43. Buenos Aires and Barcelona appear as good examples of well-planned urban expansions. Rome, Montecarlo, Prince Rupert and Playas Blancas, a never-built curvilinear urban plan, by Josué Smith Solar in Chile, are mentioned as well.

44. *Ibid.*, pp. 19–20.

45. See Gross, P. (1995) Utopías haussmanianas y planes de transformación de Santiago, in Bannen, P. (ed.) *Santiago de Chile, quince escritos y cien imágenes*. Santiago de Chile: ARQ, pp. 95–105.

46. A friend of Arturo Soria y Mata, Carvajal was a convinced follower of his ideas about the linear city. He defended the possibility of a new ring road around Santiago, following a linear city pattern, to order the city expansion. Until the late 1930s Carvajal carried on proposing other linear city proposals, in the country, including some at a territory scale: linear city Santiago-San Bernardo (1928); Santiago-Maipú (1929); Santiago-Puerto Montt(1929) and Santiago-Concepción (1939). His ideas were widely known in the country and also received attention in Spain, through his publications in the journal *Ciudad Lineal*.

47. Names like Burchard and Fortezza tell about other foreign connections, which would grow in importance during the following decades.

48. See Arrasate, M. I. (2000) Interiores urbanos, nuevos espacios del centenario: 1890–1920. El Museo de Bellas Artes y sus precedentes extranjeros, in Pérez and Hecht, *op. cit.*, without page numbers in the original. The main façade refers to the Petit Palais, the iron and glass domed interior space, to the Grand Palais.

49. George Dubois had also designed the Forestal Park, where the building is located.

50. An inspiringly similar case is described for Buenos Aires. See Gorelik, *op. cit.*, pp. 206–234.

51. Plaza Italia's present scheme centred around General Baquedano's statue was designed by Carlos Swinburn and Alberto Velez in 1928. Before that, the Plaza exhibited a rather rectangular form dominated by the Italian monument.

52. Paris-Londres district was developed on a piece of land originally belonging to San Francisco convent. Concha y Toro was built on what had been Concha Cazotte palace, including a big residence and park.

53. Rodulfo Oyarzun had a strong German family connection, and had met Brunner while studying in Europe. This indicates the prominence that the German speaking colony had reached in Chile.

54. Brunner (1887–1960) had studied in the Technische Hochschule in Vienna. His first mission in Chile was in 1929, a second in 1934. In 1933 he organized the Municipal Department of Urbanism in Bogotá, Colombia. There he designed a university city, was urban adviser of the government and published an urban manual in 1939. He extended his influence to Panama City. Once back in Vienna, he was hired by the Municipality as urban adviser (1948–1951), participating in the reconstruction of the city. Avoiding every *avant-garde* attitude, Brunner's eclecticism followed both the European tradition of Sitte and Hegemann, and that of Olmstead and Burnham in North America.

55. See Pérez Oyarzun, F. (ed.) (1991) *Le Corbusier y Sudamérica, viajes y proyectos*. Santiago de Chile: ARQ.

56. See Almandoz, *op. cit.*, pp. 280–292.

57. Within the Ministry of Public Works, Brunner was attached to the Department of Architecture and its Urbanism Section. There, he worked with Hermógenes del Canto, José Luis Mosquera and Luis Muñoz Maluska.

58. Brunner's participation in the Conference of Mayors held in 1931 is good evidence of that.

59. Brunner, K. (1932) *Santiago de Chile. Su estado actual y su futura formación*. Santiago de Chile: Imprenta 'La Tracción'. Before arriving in Chile, and perhaps influenced by his experience as a pilot during World War I, he had published *Weissungen der Vogelschau; Flugbilder aus Deutschland und Österreich und ihre Lehren für Kultur, Siedlung und Städtebau* (München, 1928) containing a series of aerial views of Germany and Austria. Aerial views are, in fact, included in his book on Santiago and in his *Manual de Urbanismo* (Bogotá, 1939).

60. Brunner had trusted the traditional device of diagonal connections, although justifying them more in technical than in aesthetic terms. First proposals by Brunner relied very much upon diagonals.

61. Brunner's ideas on the metropolitan condition and subsequent specialization of certain urban areas, shows a clear and more systematic use of the concept of zoning than was usual in previous plans.

62. Brunner's criticism of New York skyscrapers is reminiscent of some of those by Le Corbusier, *op. cit.*, pp. 74–79.

63. This development of the central area was a very long and complex one. It was the result of general and specific regulations, in most of which Brunner played an outstanding role. During the 1930s, in between two devastating earthquakes (Talca, 1928 and Chillán, 1939), a series of planning legal instruments were developed. In 1929, the law No.4563, referring to a-seismic constructions is promulgated. In May 1931 a new regulation on urban planning and construction (D.F.L. 345) was dictated, but it was only gradually applied during the following five to ten years. Hired by the university and the Ministry of Public Works, Brunner developed different approaches to a planning scheme for the central district. Specifically hired by the Municipality to do that in 1934, the scheme would be developed by Roberto Humeres. It was approved in 1939, along with its specific regulations and applied thereafter until 1957.

64. Oberpauer department store was housed in a building designed by Sergio Larraín García Moreno and Jorge Arteaga. Larraín had spent his childhood in Germany and France. The Oberpauer project followed a journey to Europe by Larraín in 1928.

65. In certain areas, Brunner had suggested to plant public gardens or parking areas in the centres of the blocks. *Op. cit.*, pp. 52, 67.

66. The attention paid by Brunner to financial problems in the urban renewal field could have helped to generate the legal and economic instruments to reinterpret the colonial block and its particular pattern of land subdivision.

67. See Cáceres, G. (1995) Santiago de Chile: antes durante y después de la modernización autoritaria (1927–1945), in Bannen, P. (ed.) *Santiago de Chile quince escritos y cien imágenes*. Santiago de Chile: ARQ, pp. 115–122.

68. Brunner quotes and publishes a project for a Plaza de la República (Plaza of the Republic) by José Luis Mosquera (1918), one of those *Beaux-Arts* fantasies around La Moneda, to justify his own project for Plaza Bulnes. Brunner, *op. cit.*, p. 31.

69. Although not involving the Presidential Palace, the same debate about a new centrality seems to have taken place in Buenos Aires. See Gorelik, *op cit.*, pp. 318–337.

70. Before that, only a small longitudinal square had underlined the importance of the main façade of the building towards Moneda street.

71. Both in language and spirit, the iconography of Barrio Cívico is reminiscent of Alberto Prebisch's proposals around the obelisk in Buenos Aires.

72. Freitag's missing colonnades in Plaza de la Constitución are quite reminiscent of some German and Italian architecture of the thirties.

73. See Palmer, M. (1984) *La comuna de Providencia y la Ciudad Jardín*. Santiago: Universidad Católica de Chile, Facultad de Arquitectura y Bellas Artes; Palmer, M. (1987) *La Ciudad Jardín como modelo de crecimiento urbano: Santiago 1935–1960*. Santiago: Universidad Católica de Chile Facultad de Arquitectura y Bellas Artes.

74. The cemeteries to the north, the open sewerage of Zanjón de la Aguada, plus a slaughterhouse to the south, and finally, the railway system to the west, imposed serious difficulties to urban expansion.

75. Alberto Mackenna, together with Rodulfo Oyarzun, Luis Muñoz Maluska y Alfredo Prat, were tightly linked with several of Brunner's projects.

76. Peña Otaegui, C.(1944) *Santiago de siglo en siglo: comentario histórico e iconográfico de su formación, evolución en sus cuatro siglos de existencia*. Santiago: Zig-Zag.

77. Secchi, E. (1941) *Arquitectura en Santiago, siglo XVII a siglo XIX*. Santiago: Comisión del IV Centenario de la Ciudad.

78. The preoccupation of preserving the remains of the past, paying attention to colonial times, had been already expressed in the historic exhibition organized in 1873 by Vicuña Mackenna. A law (No. 651) on the preservation of historic buildings had been already promulgated in 1925.

79. Among other journals, must be mentioned *Revista de Arquitectura*, a first attempt by *Asociación de Arquitectos* in 1923; the *Boletín del Colegio de Arquitectos de Chile* which began to be published in 1944; and *Pro-Arte*, published from 1948 to 1956. Interesting examples of the penetration of new modern ideas both in the profession and in the Schools of Architecture are the six issues of *Arquitectura* published in 1935–1936 (Jorge Aguirre being the editor) and the issue No.1 of *Plinto*, published by the students of the Catholic University in 1947.

80. Born in 1930 and educated in the *Universidad de Chile*, Parrochia is known, among other achievements, for the planning and building of the underground railway in the city. See Parrochia, J. (1979) *Santiago en el tercer cuarto de siglo*. Santiago: Universidad de Chile, Departamento de Planificación Urbano-Regional.

The Urban Development of Mexico City, 1850–1930

Carol McMichael Reese

The eminent Argentine urban historian Jorge Enrique Hardoy wrote in 1992 of the lack of a 'general history of urban planning in Latin America [and] of any urban history of any individual country during the decades of the great transformation of the cities'. The central hypothesis of Hardoy's essay, which appeared shortly before his untimely death in 1993, was that those who led the dramatic development of Latin American cities between about 1850 and 1930 adopted 'changing attitude[s] . . . toward the city and its needs', which cannot be separated from the cultural shift that accompanied Latin America's increasing involvement in international finance and trade. Hardoy analysed the broad contours of European urban theory and practice in the late nineteenth and early twentieth centuries that appear to have influenced Latin American urbanization as connections with Europe proliferated and promoted unprecedented flows of imports, exports, migrants, and capital. Hardoy identified the 'transfers' of European urban ideas, and he argued that they were 'not imposed voluntarily' but, rather, were adopted selectively. He suggested that

the analysis of historically specific circumstances would yield differing assessments of urban pasts, which might promote more beneficial approaches to contemporary urban problems.[1]

This chapter takes the urban development of Mexico City between about 1850 and 1930 as its subject and responds to Hardoy's challenge regarding not only the lacuna of Latin American urban histories but also his argument regarding European influence. Elsewhere I have written about the burgeoning international profile of the capital during its first period of significant expansion, the *Porfiriato* or the Presidency of Porfirio Díaz (1830–1915), who served as Mexico's head of state for more than thirty years, from 1876 to 1880 and from 1884 to 1911.[2] I have argued that those who were most influential in the development of Porfirian Mexico City sought to create a modern capital whose character would be both international *and* Mexican. This desired city would provide a comfortable, healthy, and even familiar base of operations for foreign capitalists whose investment in Mexico's industrialization was crucial for the nation's entry into the international market economy. However, Porfirian politicians, municipal administrators, architects, engineers, capitalists and other citizens who directed the capital's modernization also desired that the progressive city would be an emblem of the nation – of its particular historical circumstance as the complex product of the Spanish colonization of indigenous peoples, or of its cultural 'hybridity', to refer to the concept borrowed from contemporary cultural studies.[3]

Historians and analysts of Mexico City's development during the Porfiriato have often written that the model that guided the capital's growth was 'French'.[4] Their arguments have depended, in part, on the cultural embrace of the Porfirian elite – the '*científicos*' – of all things French, whether education, manners, clothing, food, and styles of residences and furnishings.[5] Such descriptions neglect not only the persistence of Mexican tradition in guiding urban growth but also the role of other sources of influence in Mexico City's modernization and expansion, especially after 1900, when capitalists from England, Germany, and, prominently, the United States lived, worked, and invested in the capital.[6]

The interplay of tradition and innovation in Mexico City's new urban patterns comes into relief, however, when the fabric of its new late nineteenth- and early twentieth-century neighbourhoods or *colonias* is the focus of inquiry. Therefore, I emphasize the histories of neighbourhoods as the basis for writing the capital's urban history. I establish a set of typologies based on the clientele to whom districts were marketed, and I analyse not only their two-dimensional forms, as established in their plot plans, but also their profiles as developed in their housing. In addition, I trace the crucial delivery of municipal services, such as potable water, street paving and lighting, and drainage and sewer systems that were responsible for sanitary and safe living conditions, following Hardoy's recommendation for 'solid research . . . into working-class housing and the evolution of the urban infrastructure [as well as] the history of the building and administration of cities'.[7]

Mexico City was undoubtedly the crucible in which modern, industrial Mexico was forged. From its founding as a Spanish colonial city in 1521 on the rubble of the Aztec capital Tenochtitlan, after Hernan Cortés's defeat of the last Aztec general Cuauhtémoc, Mexico City was the largest urban centre in New Spain and the Viceroyalty's administrative hub – its religious, commercial, and political capital. With the Independence of Mexico from Spain in 1821, the capital of the new republic maintained that primacy within the nation throughout the nineteenth century. Although the growth rates of other Mexican cities sometimes exceeded that of the capital's during the twentieth century, as regional industrial centres developed, these rapidly urbanizing cities never challenged Mexico City's size or function as the country's political and economic nerve centre. Indeed, Mexico City's staggering expansion after 1940 made it a global megalopolis, attaining the status of the world's largest city.[8]

This study examines the physical formation of early modern Mexico City during an initial period of industrialization, in which an urban real estate market was developed and the physical and social characteristics of the colonial city changed dramatically. Historians of Mexican and Latin American urbanism commonly parse this historical era as two periods: the first beginning after the War of Independence, in the 1820s, and the second beginning about 1900, by which time a growing bourgeoisie comprised of commercial and industrial elites had superseded the landed aristocracy as national power brokers. For Mexico City, this periodization has yielded consideration of the 'city of independence' and the 'republican or nationalist city'. Moreover, scholars often identify the latter period chronologically with the *Porfiriato*.[9] For the purposes of this chapter, however, we will consider as contiguous the period from the mid-1850s, when petitions were first filed for initial subdivisions, to the late 1920s, when suburban plans exhibited distinctively different formal characteristics and professional urban planners began to consider how to shape an automobile-oriented city.

At the beginning of this period, in the 1850s, Mexico City resembled many other Latin American capitals, with a Plaza Mayor and towered, domed sixteenth-century cathedral at its heart. The whole was organized spatially by the rectilinear colonial grid that emanated from the cathedral square or Zócalo, as it came to be called in the mid-nineteenth century. The city's geography as well as its Pre-Columbian and colonial history were significant determinants of its nineteenth-century development. The Aztec capital included two urban centres, Tenochtitlan and Tlatelolco, which were founded in the early fourteenth century (1325 and 1327, respectively) on islands in the vast Lake Texcoco.[10] The Spaniards began to drain the lake almost immediately after taking possession of the territory, but the process of the *desagüe* (drainage) was not completed until 1903.[11] The less desirable low and swampy land to the east and south-east of the colonial centre traditionally attracted the capital's poor, while the higher and drier terrain to the west and south-west – where the air circulated well and plants flour-

ished – supported the city's highest real estate values and, in the late nineteenth century, residential enclaves of the middle and upper classes. Colonial governmental structures also established spatial segregation of class and race beyond the city centre. The two indigenous districts – Santiago Tlatelolco on the north and San Juan Tenochtitlán on the south – which answered to Spanish authorities but maintained jurisdiction over Indian lands outside the city limits, developed as nodes of poverty. While social heterogeneity had largely characterized the colonial capital, increasing urban social homogeneity accompanied nineteenth-century speculation in land.[12]

Before 1850, colonial and republican Mexico City increased only minimally in territory beyond the four sections framing the Plaza Mayor that were established in 1521. As early as 1782, however, observers noted with dismay the irregular, disordered development of districts outside the city. In response the Viceroy, the second Count of Revillagigedo, commissioned architect Ignacio Castera to draw one of the earliest ambitious plans for the expansion of the city (1794, figure 6.1). This plan was equitable in its response to the unequal topographical conditions of the city, suggesting the extension of the city limits towards the four cardinal points and the development of four new square plazas with sides of 550 m each. Unexecuted, Castera's plan did predict the incorporation of two traditional pleasure grounds that significantly became important magnets for later nineteenth- and early twentieth-century development – the Alameda and Viga *paseos* (promenade routes) on the west and south, respectively.[13]

Internal and external political strife, as well as the development of national and international railroads were key factors that

Figure 6.1 *Plano ichnographico de la ciudad de México. . .* (Iconographic plan of Mexico city . . .), by I. Castera, 1794. East is at the top of Castera's map. The Plaza Mayor forms the centre of his diagram to regulate the city's expansion, and the newly enlarged Alameda appears at the bottom centre of the map with the Paseo de la Viga at the top right. (*Source:* Geography and Map Division, Library of Congress, Washington, DC)

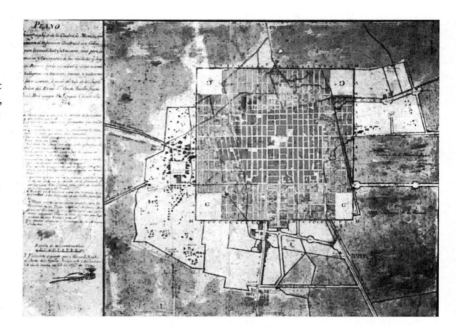

set in motion the capital's nineteenth-century expansion after 1856 (figure 6.2). The city remained stagnant in size in the middle decades of the nineteenth century, between about 1820 and 1870, for two primary reasons, according to Alejandra Moreno Toscano: (1) the expulsion of Spaniards in 1827, which left a 'vacuum' of commercial leadership that was not filled until later in the century (and then by English, French, and North American

Figure 6.2 Panorama of Mexico City taken from balloon, by C. Castro, 1856. Castro's bird's eye view looks from the northwest in the lower left to the south-east in the upper right. It was conceived before the state appropriation of church properties that began in the 1850s and before the building of Mexico's inter- and extra-urban railroads that promoted the accelerated urban development of the capital in the later nineteenth century. (*Source:* Mapoteca Orozco y Berra, México)

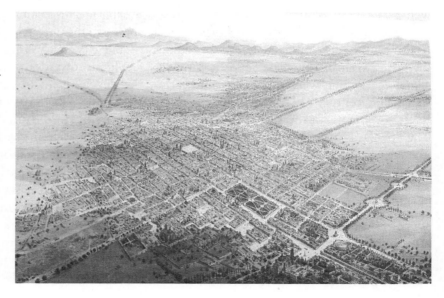

businessmen); and (2) the rise of regional cities that served as ports (San Blas and Tampico), border gateways (Piedras Negras and Matamoros), and distribution centres (San Luis Potosí and Monterrey) within an expanding network instigated when the new republic opened to international trade. Civil war in the United States also benefited the rise of Mexico's regional cities, stimulating the country's northern Gulf ports when U.S. ports ceased operation and encouraging the immigration of agricultural workers to produce cotton in Sinaloa and the Yucatán for European markets. However, with the completion of the inter-oceanic rail line across Mexico in 1881, as well as with the completion of the line between Mexico City and Ciudad Juárez on the Texas border in 1884, the capital reasserted its dominance at the hub of the newly unified Mexican rail network, as it had dominated the colonial system of highways. In sum, the strengthening and completion of long-distance rail lines, which promoted rapid transit of goods, benefited large-scale exporters in Mexico City and contributed to the doubling of the population of the capital from approximately 200,000 in 1858 to 367,446 in 1900, and the increase of the city's area from 450 to 850 hectares.[14]

Also contributing to the initial physical expansion of Mexico City was the entailment of religious and civil properties, which resulted in their availability for sale, altering completely the structure of the colonial urban fabric.[15] Mexico's anti-clerical reform movement of 1855, adoption of a federal constitution in 1857, and adoption in 1858 of laws providing for the separation of Church and State, established a legal basis for both the municipality and the federal district to institute selling mortgages on Church property. Moreover, Porfirio Díaz applied the ban on corporate land holdings not only to Church properties but also to Indian lands, opening even more territory to speculation. In 1894, the government decreed that unused land – terrenos baldíos – could also be appropriated.[16] As real estate proved to be a viable commodity, it became an important source of income, and the government often sold it expediently in large blocks, rather than strategically in smaller parcels.[17] Among the most notable fortunes made as republican Mexico embraced capitalistic enterprise on an international scale were those of speculators in land, who helped to define Mexico City as a modern, urbane environment in which international entrepreneurs and investors could operate in comfort and even luxury.[18] Realization of profits on the sale of land, however, depended on a stable political situation, which the 'order and progress' regime of Porfirio Díaz provided.[19]

Indeed, according to Luis Unikel, 'social agitation' during and immediately following the Revolution resulted in migration from rural sectors to the capital, since it was perceived to be safer. Thus, Mexico City's population increased steadily between 1910 and 1921, despite the fact that the population growth rate actually slowed. The capital's area enlarged in this period as well, increasing from 962 hectares in 1910 to 2,154 hectares in 1918, when the urbanized metropolitan area (including the Municipality of Mexico and 12 outlying municipalities) reached 3,250 hectares. The first census taken after the Revolution, that of 1921, counted a population of 615,367 in Mexico City and 906,063 in the Federal District; the subsequent census of 1930 reported a population in the former of 1,029,068 and in the latter of 1,229,576. By 1929, when the Ayuntamiento (Council) of the city of Mexico was dissolved and the surrounding municipal districts were reconfigured as eleven 'delega-tions' under the Department of the Federal District, the urbanized area covered 6,262 hectares. Thus, after 1929 and the expansion of the limits of the capital to encompass almost the entire metropolitan area, the city of Mexico became very nearly coterminous with the Federal District. From 1921 to 1930 – the 'constructive' post-Revolutionary stage – the foundations for the explosive demo-graphic, economic, and urban growth that occurred after 1940 were laid in Mexico City: communication networks were improved, and highways and rail lines were expanded, which facilitated external trade relations and con-centration of commercial activities. During the 1930s, however, the country and the capital suffered the effects of worldwide eco-

nomic depression, and Mexico City saw its lowest growth rate of the century. In the late 1930s, migration to Mexico City, as well as to other large cities in Mexico including Monterrey and Guadalajara, increased in the wake of the expropriation of the Mexican petroleum industry and in relation to various economic effects of the World War II. Although Unikel characterized Mexico City's growth in the first four decades of the twen-tieth century as 'slow' in comparison to that of the period after 1940, the capital – together with São Paulo and Los Angeles – exhibited one of the fastest rates of urban expansion within the Western Hemisphere between 1920 and 1940, achieving a popula-tion within the Federal District of 1,757,530 in 1940.[20]

The Paseo de la Reforma, French Structure and Mexican Imagery

Urban historians of Mexico City commonly cite the planning and building of the Paseo de la Reforma (Reform Avenue) as an initial undertaking that brought early modern con-cepts of urban development to Mexico from Europe and established the city's profile as an international capital (figure 6.3). Designed by Mexican architects Juan Agea (b. 1825) and Ramón Agea (b. 1827) in 1864 under the patronage of Emperor Maximilian (and, reputedly, the inspiration of Belgian-born Empress Carlota), this broad thoroughfare followed the path of an ancient causeway. It connected the central city with Chapultepec Park (figure 6.9), the site of Maximilian's castle and a public pleasure ground, some 3.5 km west of the Zócalo.[21] Designed as a diago-nal boulevard in relation to the colonial grid and embellished by landscape plantings and *glorietas* (roundabouts), the Reforma responded

to the inspiration of the Parisian boulevards and parks that Georges Eugène Haussmann, Prefect of the Seine (1853–1870), improved and designed in Napoleon III's capital.

Originally named the Paseo del Emperador (Emperor Avenue), the Reforma was renamed after the triumph of liberal forces under Benito Juárez and Maximilian's execution in 1867. It developed slowly but by 1910 had attained fully functional and symbolic form. With the patronage of President Sebastián Lerdo de Tejada between 1872 and 1876, *glorietas* were enlarged and trees – including black poplars, eucalyptuses, cypresses, and willows – were planted to create shady pedestrian *allées* (paths) that bordered the 70 m wide, paved roadway. As the Reforma evolved after its inauguration in 1877, it played a key role in attracting investors to plan elite residential subdivisions along its path. This development of the

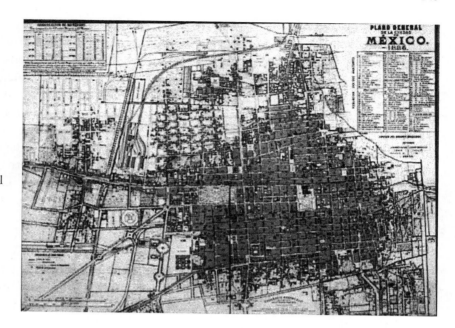

Figure 6.3 General plan of Mexico City, 1886. Mexico: Debray. The Debray map illustrates the relationship of the Paseo de la Reforma to the older Paseo Bucareli, which it eclipsed, the still undeveloped land through which the Reforma passed, and the first three *glorietas* to be planned. (*Source*: Geography and Map Division, Library of Congress, Washington, DC)

capital's most expensive suburbs resulted in the addition of service roads to either side of the Reforma, which opened newly subdivided districts to traffic on the boulevard (see figure 6.4). Thus, when fully built, the Reforma consisted of five sections and closely followed the engineer and garden designer Jean-Alphonse Alphand's plans for Haussmann's Parisian boulevards.[22]

If the Paseo de la Reforma symbolized

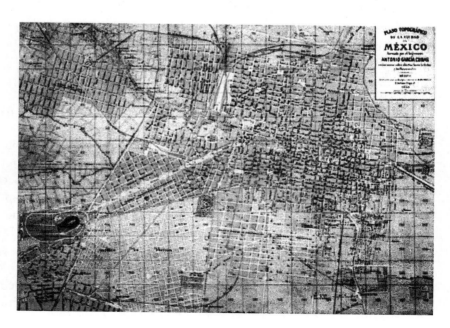

Figure 6.4 Topographic plan of Mexico City with the new streets opened up to date and the trails, by A.G. Cubas, 1903. Geography and Map Division, Mexico: Murguia. (*Source*: Library of Congress, Washington, DC)

modern European urbanity, the sculptures that it boasted not only proclaimed a narrative of national identity but also positioned the capital as the nation's first city.[23] Manuel Tolsá's bronze equestrian statue of Carlos IV of Spain (1796–1802) stood in the *glorieta* where the Reforma began its south-westward sweep toward Chapultepec Park – at the intersection with the Paseo de Bucareli, a north-south boulevard, and the Avenida Juárez, an east-west street that marked the southern edge of the Alameda (Poplar Avenue). During Díaz's presidency three more statues were added to the *glorietas* that Lerda's government had expanded. From east to west they were Henri Joseph Cordier's monument to Christopher Columbus, which was produced in Paris in 1873 and unveiled in 1887; Francisco M. Jiménez's monument to the last Aztec prince Cuauhtémoc, which was begun in 1876 and completed after Jiménez's death in 1884; and Antonio Rivas Mercado's Independence monument, which was designed from 1902 to 1910 with the engineer Gonzalo Garita.[24] In 1889, the historian Francisco Sosa initiated a project to contribute two statues from each of the eighteen states of the republic to be placed on both sides of the Reforma in the pedestrian *allées*; there they alternated with bronze vases designed by Gabriel Guerra.[25] The importance of the iconographical scheme of sculpture along the Reforma to an evolving 'text' of national and urban identity can hardly be overstated.

The compositions in the four *glorietas* symbolized historic stages in the triumphant development of modern Mexico, from Columbus's 'discovery' to Cuauhtémoc's 'noble' Indian resistance, and from Carlos's Spanish rule to Independence. The honorific portrait statues from the provinces paid tribute to the capital's hegemony. When the Independence Monument was inaugurated with great fanfare as one of the key events of the Porfirian Centennial Celebrations of 1910, which celebrated 100 years of Mexican independence from Spain, a new and improved Mexico City took its place on the worldwide stage for an invited international audience.[26] While the form of the Paseo de la Reforma may have recommended Mexico City as 'French' to citizens and foreign visitors alike, revealing Mexico's aspirations for global stature, its sculptural embellishments related to national references that gave it immediate, local currency.

Mexico City's First Subdivisions, a Mexican Model for Growth?

The capital's first subdivisions, or *colonias*, were all envisaged before 1860, and they established a horizon of choices not only for investors with varying resources but also for potential residents of different social strata and income levels. Thus, a rationale for conceiving the development of the city would already seem to have been implicitly operational in the projects of early subdividers. With the hindsight of historical distance, the contours of that rationale can be sketched in terms of individual, but complementary decisions to market properties to distinct groups with varied needs: Santa María de la Ribera, which offered to the middle-class a quiet zone to the north and west of the central city that had been largely agricultural; Guerrero, which offered to workers the possibility of residence close to their workplaces north of the central city; and Arquitectos, which offered to the upper class a district to the south-west that was already identified with leisure and the promenade of the *paseo*.[27] These three initial projects are instructive not only for their creators' visions of an expanding city but also for the role of the Municipal government in the establishment of regulations aimed at promoting and ensuring the public good.

Santa María de Ribera: a Suburban District for the Middle-class

Santa María de la Ribera was the first of the three to take shape and was the project of large landholders, the brothers Estanislao and Joaquín Flores, who requested permission to subdivide for sale their Rancho Santa María de la Ribera de San Cosme in 1856.[28] Although the architectural profile of Santa María developed over time, the rural ambience and verdant history of its site recommended this district as ideal for the construction of *casas de campo* or country villas, in the Anglo-American terminology developed by mid-century writers on landscape, such as John Claudius Loudon and Alexander Jackson Downing.[29] The planning of the district was inspired by Mexican colonial tradition, with a plaza sited at the centre of a rectilinear grid and a church to one side, creating one and one-half blocks of open, public space (figure 6.4). However, the single-family houses that were built in Santa María were more consistent with contemporary North American and European trends. Many residences were set back from the street with front gardens. In their eclectic variety, they corresponded to richly evocative, associational styles prevalent in domestic architecture internationally, with the distinction that Spanish colonial architecture was a strong stylistic referent. Neo-colonial decorative motifs associated with the Latin American 'ultra-baroque' – lobed arches, tiled façades, complex mouldings – gave the district a distinct Latin American, indeed Mexican, flavour. The first homebuilders in Santa María were middle-class merchants and professionals, but with the inauguration on the district's eastern edge of the capital's major Buenavista Railroad Station in 1873 and the development of Guerrero immediately east of the station, property owners constructed *vecindades* or apartment buildings to rent to working-class tenants. In contrast to the decorative exuberance of the middle-class single-family houses, these multi-family buildings of three or four storeys were simply detailed.[30]

Guerrero: Working-class Residences near Sites of Labour

The urban identity of Guerrero developed quite differently from, although simultaneously with, that of Santa María de la Ribera.[31] Lawyer, industrialist and prominent landholder Rafael Martínez de la Torre founded Guerrero in the area directly north of the Alameda (figure 6.4). While Santa María de la Ribera depended on the designation of land for a church and a plaza to establish its new urban identity, Guerrero took advantage of the location of the Convent of San Fernando (1755) in its south-west corner. Here in the churchyard were buried not only the district's namesake, Vicente Guerrero

(1782–1831), a leader in the Independence movement and later president, but also Benito Juárez (1806–1872), the hero of the restoration of the republic and president. Additionally, in the northern zone of Guerrero, the existing plaza of the Indian village at Santa María de los Ángeles created a second civic node. Martínez de la Torre commissioned architect Manuel Rincón y Miranda to produce a subdivision plan for Guerrero in 1874 that comprised three sections of land: one purchased from the Indian corporation of the village of Los Angeles, a second from the Hacienda de Buenavista, and a third from the Convent of San Fernando.[32] Beyond Los Angeles, Guerrero stretched north towards the pre-Columbian village of Tlatelolco, so that its relationship with the indigenous past was strong.

Indeed, it seems that labourers were the clientele whom Martínez de la Torre and the government had in mind, for President Lerdo de Tejada inaugurated Guerrero as a workers' district in 1874. Undoubtedly the 1873 opening of the Buenavista Railroad Station between Santa María de la Ribera and Guerrero indicated that a new subdivision could be profitably developed to house those who worked not only in the rail yard, but also in the transport, storage, commercial, and industrial ventures that were associated with movement of people and goods through the capital's most important station and the national Aduana (Customs House), which was sited just north of Guerrero. For the labourers whom the government expected to settle in Guerrero – among them indigenous workers and migrants to the capital – the tombs of Guerrero and Juárez at San Fernando could serve to inspire ideals of national fealty and instruct in national history. María Dolores Morales proposed that the government might have promoted the

sale of land in Guerrero to those of low economic status as effective political propaganda and as a political means of controlling worker unrest. She calculated, however, that between 1874 and 1876, 68 per cent of the subdivision was sold to only ten buyers, who invested in properties for resale, although some lots were sold to workers and artisans.[33] These purchasers were in the minority, since most labourers could not even afford to rent houses, and they rented rooms in *vecindades* instead.[34] Because the government did not establish regulations for the delivery of municipal services such as potable water and street lighting in the capital's newly opened subdivisions until after 1900, it is curious that Guerrero was proclaimed as a model workers' district when no provisions were made for insuring the health and safety of its residents.

Guerrero grew rapidly, gaining 10,000 inhabitants and 800 houses by 1877. However, Rincón y Miranda's plan did not establish regular lot sizes on the district's blocks, and buyers defined the shapes of properties according to their desires. This gave the district an irregular profile that was at odds with both colonial tradition and modern planning practice. The district included predominantly working-class and lower middle-class residences. The former ranged from *corrales de jacales* – groups of huts or sheds made from discarded materials – to *vecindades* – a traditional building type that had evolved in Mexico since the eighteenth century. Guerrero's *vecindades* were often constructed as two-storey buildings with narrow interior patios running their length. Rooms (often without windows) opened from these patios or, above, from overhanging passageways. Most *vecindades* included an area of common toilets on the ground floor. Street façades masked the commonly crowded and unsanitary living conditions; rooms at the front and back of the buildings could be higher or larger and let for more expensive rents, and those who lived on the upper floors were often also considered to be of a higher social class. Multi-family buildings with higher rents than the *vecindades* were two-storey, simple stucco-covered buildings, which housed several families in apartments of more than one room. These buildings also often accommodated shops and businesses on the ground floors.

Guerrero's middle-class, single-family residences were generally of a vernacular, popular type that had evolved from houses built during the viceroyalty. These were one- or two-storey dwellings with narrow doors and two or three windows on the street. They met the district's sidewalks with no setbacks and filled their lots laterally at the street. Their side walls were usually unadorned, but their street façades could be lavishly decorated with

brick, channelled stucco, or even masonry facing, as well as elaborate window surrounds and balustrades. Indeed, the degree of ornament often identified the economic status of owners or residents – skilled workers, artisans, or small shopkeepers. Interior, linear patios provided light and air on lots as narrow as 7 m. In style, these houses followed the colonial Spanish traditional mode or adopted French townhouse motifs, namely mansard roofs. At the southern edge of Guerrero, near the Plaza of San Fernando and the intersection of Reforma and Bucareli, some impressively scaled single-family houses were built, which were set back from the street within landscaped gardens. Also built in this comparatively luxurious section were apartment buildings with façades inspired by late baroque European palaces, which were designed to be rented to upper middle-class residents.[35]

Arquitectos: Elite Residences for Professionals

In 1858, the same year that the Flores brothers filed plans for Santa María de la Ribera, Francisco Somera (1828–1889) established the Colonia de los Arquitectos on land to the south-west of the central city that the Spanish crown had given to the city as early as 1529, for use as common grazing pastures. The wealthy son of a Spanish wine merchant who had immigrated to Mexico, Somera played powerful roles in the capital's government at the time that he created the Arquitectos project. Through the offices that he held, he was well placed to assess current land values and to predict future ones. He served on the City Council during the 1850s and early 1860s as chief administrator and controller of the office that oversaw roads and canals. In 1862

he organized the *Dirección General de Obras Públicas* (General Directorate of Public Works) as the first modern municipal office to direct the city's development, in which professionally trained civil engineers and architects replaced administrators without technical expertise. During Maximilian's regime, Somera served as Municipal Prefect and as controller of the city's Treasury Department.[36] Somera represents, then, the wealthy Mexican businessman who invested in real estate and contributed to the modernization of the capital through the business acumen that he brought to the discharge of public offices. Although not a planner *per se*, Somera contributed importantly to the professionalization of governmental offices charged with overseeing the physical expansion of the city, and his own investment activities enabled others to imagine new possibilities for the capital's growth.

Somera worked for years to gain possession of the tract of land that included the Arquitectos project and, finally, using his politically privileged position, took title in 1855. The name of the subdivision encapsulated the clientele whom Somera hoped to attract – architects, engineers, artists, and others associated with the Academy of San Carlos.[37] Somera offered 60 lots for sale in 1858 (figure 6.4), and in the first year of sales, 65 per cent of the lots were sold, acquired for the most part by distinguished architects. However, few of the original purchasers built on their lots, reselling them to others. In 1865, Somera initiated the critical step of petitioning the city to provide potable water to the district, although it was sparsely populated. Architect Francisco de Garay undertook the project, which was notable since the provision of potable water to many areas of the city was still lacking and was undertaken comprehensively only in the 1880s. When Somera returned to the capital in 1870 from a four-year sojourn in Europe, gas lighting was installed in the district, and, in the following year, crews employed by the *Ayuntamiento* levelled land and paved the streets, perhaps through his political influence. Arquitectos prospered with the continued improvement

of the Paseo de la Reforma during the 1870s under Lerdo's and Díaz's administrations. Thus, the stage was set for Arquitectos to become the capital's premier subdivision, not only through its access and proximity to the civic amenities of the city's most prominent boulevard, but also through its internal provision of urban necessities such as potable water and street paving and lighting.

Somera did not live to see the full profile of his idea take shape, but his conception of a modern extension of the city demonstrated to residents and administrators alike how the city might guide and implement development policy. Today Somera's Arquitectos has no real presence in the modern city, as do Santa María and Guerrero, which persist as neighbourhoods with strong identities. Nevertheless, the memory of Arquitectos figures significantly in the capital's urban development, since it became the node of a district in which Porfirian and foreign elite built residences and created a showcase of Mexico's ascendance, not only as a site for lucrative capital investment but also as a participant in international markets. Indeed, it was the success of Arquitectos, and the neighbouring subdivisions that were designed and developed around the district after Somera's death, that prompted the Municipality to institute regulations and restrictions insuring healthy conditions in its burgeoning territory.

The Progeny of Guerrero, Arquitectos, and Santa María

Thus, by 1880, the prototypical subdivisions Santa María (1858), Arquitectos (1858), and Guerrero (1874), had established models of sorts for urban residential expansion. Each prepared the way for districts planned with residents of distinct economic sectors in

mind, and each of these types occasioned attendant problems, challenges, and accomplishments. Until 1903 and the passage of revised and expanded legislation governing contractual agreements between developers and the Municipality, subdividers faced few requirements. Before 1903, laws regulating subdivisions provided that developers cede to the Municipality not only streets but also land for a plaza, a market, and a church; the Municipality provided tax exemptions in return. Principal streets were required to be 20 m in width, but others could be narrower. The provision of services generally followed rather than preceded the construction of dwellings, but the law required neither the city nor the developer to provide them. To residents generally fell the responsibility of levelling their properties and constructing sidewalks. The Ayuntamiento exercised wide latitude in approving petitions for concessions to develop *colonias*. The government sometimes attached stipulations to developers' petitions, but ensuing contracts were often vague and responsibilities were not emphatically assigned to participating parties. Moreover, in some cases developers chose to ignore the government's demands after the contracts were written, while in others, they subdivided without filing petitions at all. *Colonias* developed to attract working-class clientele suffered most significantly under the laxity of the Mexico City's subdivision laws in the latter half of the nineteenth century.[38]

Porfirian Residential Spaces of Labour

Working-class districts, which were comparable to Guerrero in the residents whom they attracted and in the housing types that characterized them, developed in significant clusters around industrial zones in the north and north-east and also in the wetter and more marshy zones of the south-east, although they proliferated across the city as the population swelled during the *Porfiriato*. By the turn of the nineteenth century, Mexico City was the third largest city in Latin America (Buenos Aires, the first, and Rio de Janeiro, the second). In 1900, migrants accounted for half the population of the capital, which John Lear described as a 'city of workers'. These citizens predominantly earned their livelihoods in the sectors of commerce, delivery of services, production of consumer goods, and, after 1900, in heavy industry, following the widespread electrification of factories, for which foreign companies were primarily responsible. Mexico City's labouring population included a high percentage of indigenous workers, which marked a significant difference between the Mexican capital and Latin American port cities that attracted large flows of immigrants from Europe. The majority of workers, however, were unskilled, and more than a quarter found employment in domestic service. Lear calculated that between about 1895 and 1921, perhaps 20 to 25 per cent of the city's population was comprised of workers living in *vecindades* either in the city's oldest districts – around the Zócalo, for example – or in new *colonias*.[39] Because the city could not provide services at a rate to keep pace with the opening of the new subdivisions and because the government did not enforce regulations related to the activities of developers, unsafe and unhealthy slums arose in many of these new districts. Rather than emphasizing reform of the physical environments affordable to the city's poor, the government regulated social behaviour (clothing, street vending, begging, drunkenness, sleeping in public parks or on the streets). This state of affairs worsened steadily during the *Porfiriato* until the *Departamento de Obras*

Públicas was strengthened and more stringent laws regulating subdivision practices were passed in 1903.[40]

Urban public transportation developed in Mexico City, as in other large cities, first with streetcars pulled by horses and mules or powered by steam. These types of lines were established in Mexico City beginning in 1857. Electrified trolleys began operation in 1896 through a system that utilized overhead cables, which were necessitated by the moisture in the soil. Standard-gauge track was imported from England, and cars (J. G. Brill, Philadelphia) and generators (General Electric) were imported from the United States. English and, later, Canadian companies won the earliest concessions to operate the capital's trolleys (figure 6.5).[41] While the capital's expanding network of streetcars potentially allowed workers to commute to the sites of their employment, most could not afford to pay for public transportation. Thus, subdividers developed working-class districts in proximity to urban zones where likely residents could be em-ployed. The north/north-eastern sector of the capital expanded as the most prominent of these zones during the Porfiriato. This urban zone was the ambit of pre-Columbian Tlatelolco, marking its association not only with the capital's indigenous population but also with the labouring class. In addition, the municipality and the federal government built key nineteenth-century institutions here, which included the penitentiary, the Aduana Nacional or Customs House of Santiago, the Rastro General or Municipal Slaughterhouse, the machine shops of the rail line to Guadalupe, and the (northern) Hidalgo Railway Station (1874). One of the capital's first racetracks, the Hipódromo of Peralvillo (Peralvillo Racecourse), was built in the northern sector of the city, so that this zone also became identified with leisure activities. However, as the character of the sector consolidated around working-class residence, the elite Jockey Club moved its operation of the Hipódromo to the south in proximity to land with higher real estate values and middle- and upper-class clienteles.[42]

Figure 6.5 Mexico Tramways Company, Lines and Properties in Mexico City, 1910. New York: Rand, McNally. (*Source*: Geography and Map Division, Library of Congress, Washington, DC)

Thus the institutional spaces of transportation, control, industry, and provision to the north and north-east of the central city functioned as magnets that drew speculators in land development to these districts, where they hoped to attract workers to settle in proximity to sites of labour.[43] Among the subdivisions laid out here were Violante (or Tepito, 1882), Morales (1886), Díaz de Léon (1893), Rastro (1897), Vallejo (1898), and Valle Gómez (1899), Peralvillo (1899), la Bolsa (unauthorized by the *Ayuntamiento*), Chopo (or Industrial, 1904), and Maza (1909). Valle Gómez was exemplary of the deplorable living conditions that existed in some of these working-class subdivisions. Here crime flourished with the lack of police presence, and residents, who lived with flooded, trash-filled streets and open sewage ditches that even contained dead, decomposing animals, were forced to petition the city for services.

Developers also contemporaneously established 'popular,' working-class subdivisions in other geographic sectors of the capital as well, seizing opportunities for investment along rapidly expanding inter- and intra-urban rail lines. To the north-west were Tlaxpana (1884), Santa Julia (1884), Santo Tomás (1900), and San Alvaro (1900), all of which developed around the streetcar lines that extended to Tacuba, Azcapotzalco, and Tlanepantla. In the south, working-class subdivisions, which included Del Valle (1895) and Cuartelito (1899), developed around the railroad line that served the villages of Tacubaya, Mixcoac, San Angel, and Tlalpam. In the eastern zones, subdivisions such as Scheibe (unauthorized) and Manuel Romero Rubio (1908) were developed around the nodes of the San Lázaro Railway Station and the new penitentiary (1900). Indeed, the capital's burgeoning network of rail lines was not alone responsi-

ble for the multiplication of working-class districts at greater and greater distances from the historic centre, since workers could not usually afford to pay for public transportation. The government's decision to build key public institutions on the periphery of the city, therefore, played an important role in shaping the emerging social and labour geography of Porfirian Mexico City. Those institutions particularly identified with the capital's poor and needy became centrifugal forces for opening new residential districts. While the north/north-east sector had been the locus in the later nineteenth century of social service establishments, in the early twentieth century the government judiciously built hospitals, sanitariums, asylums, and schools on the edges of the city in the north-west, south-west, and east in advance of urban development.[44]

Despite the heavy Porfirian investment in institutional construction, however, the first model workers' colony in Mexico City appeared only in 1908. It was the Manuel Romero Rubio subdivision – east of the new penitentiary – and here the political rhetoric concerning the establishment of a singular community for workers, which had accompanied the inauguration of Guerrero in 1874, finally became manifest. Founded by Rafael B. Gómez, who had developed the reviled subdivision Valle Gómez, Romero Rubio followed new regulations decreed by the *Ayuntamiento* in 1903 and 1905 for the opening of subdivisions.[45] These stipulated the supervision of the Department of Public Works during the development phase and prohibited purchasers' from taking up residence until the improvements required of subdividers – paved streets, potable water, drainage systems – were in place. They also regulated planning with the intent of creating an image of civic propriety and encouraging the development of civic amenities. As required, the square blocks of Romero Rubio were organized around a central plaza, and diagonal boulevards intersected the rectilinear grid. Embellishing Romero Rubio's plan were *chaflanes* or chamfered corners of blocks that facilitated traffic flows and provided regular sites for commercial establishments.[46] In following the new planning regulations, and, indeed, in surpassing them, Romero Rubio was atypical of working-class subdivisions. Only in the wake of Mexico City's post-Revolution recovery would the initial efforts of Porfirian municipal administrators and engineers have comprehensive material effect on the living conditions of the capital's labourers.

Porfirian Municipal Administration and Urban Planning

In Porfirian Mexico City and before 1930, there was no sustained urban discourse *per se*, although architects and engineers published prolifically in professional organs such as the *Revista de Ingeniería* of the *Sociedad Escuela Nacional de Ingenieros* (National School of Engineers Society) (1908–1909), the *Boletín de Ingenieros* of the *Secretaría de Guerra y Marina* (Secretariat of War and Navy) (1910–1914), the *Memorias* of the *Asociación de Ingenieros y Arquitectos de México* (Mexican Association of Engineers and Architects) (1915–1919), and the *Revista Mexicana de Ingeniería y Arquitectura*, which began publication in 1923. In such publications as *Ateneo, Repertorio Ilustrado de Arte, Ciencia y Literatura* (1874–1877) and *Arte y la Ciencia* (1899–1911), which addressed more general audiences, they discussed new, highly visible building projects and expounded on issues that included modern building materials and techniques, such as reinforced concrete; the search for an appropriate national style, and the relationships among art, archaeology, and architecture. The periodical *Planeación*, however, began publication only in 1927 (to 1935), and not until 1939 was an international congress dealing specifically with urbanism held in Mexico City. If urban planning theory and practice were not widely debated in print, the quotidian achievements of those government officials charged with urban improvement were routinely reported in such federal publications of the *Secretaría de Commuicaciones y Obras Públicas* (Secretariat of Communications and Public Works) as the *Memorias* (1891–1958), the *Anales* (1902–1924), and the *Boletín* (1920–1928), and in such summaries of the activities of the *Ayuntamiento* as the *Actas de Cabildo*.[47] In the last, the activities of various professionals working among the overlapping jurisdictions of federal and municipal offices that oversaw urban development in the capital come into high relief. Two of the most highly trained and influential of these were the engineers Roberto Gayol y Soto (1857–1936) and Miguel Angel de Quevedo (1862–1946), and Quevedo emerges as the progenitor of modern urban planning in Mexico City.

Gayol, Quevedo's senior, studied in Mexico City and directed the city's great water and sewer sanitation projects in the 1890s. In 1903, with the reorganization of the governments of the *Distrito Federal* and *Ayuntamiento*, he became the director of *Obras Públicas* for the Federal District. Under Gayol's supervision, Quevedo's role in professionalizing the federal and municipal offices charged with sanitation and beautification projects in Mexico

City was fundamental, and he can be considered the capital's first planner, whose public career coincided with the birth of urban planning in Europe and the United States. Trained as a civil engineer in France, he returned to Mexico in 1888 to participate in the federal drainage projects and the remodelling of the Veracruz port. In 1901, he entered municipal service in the capital, where he was appointed director of the city's Public Works Department. In 1903, Quevedo assumed responsibility for public spaces (open areas) within the federal district and continued to oversee the Department of Public Works within the municipal government, as well as to head city government's Commissions of *Embellecimiento* (Embellishment) and *Construcción y Mejoras en los Mercados* (Building and Improvements of the Markets). Named head of the forestry section in the federal *Secretaría de Agricultura y Fomento* (Secretariat of Agriculture and Patronage) in 1909, he mounted a remarkable campaign to reforest and replant Mexico City, which he continued as his primary activity after the Revolution. Known as '*el Apóstol del Arbol*' (Apostle of the Tree), he instigated the establishment of more than forty urban gardens and plazas and created tree nurseries and forest reserves in the larger metropolitan district (Coyoacán and Xochimilco). As a private practitioner, Quevedo contributed to the modernization of the capital's pre-Revolutionary architecture, designing functionally progressive buildings and employing the latest ferro-concrete structural systems to increase the safety of tall buildings on Mexico City's seismically active soil.[48]

Two of Quevedo's projects illustrate the key contributions that he made to the introduction of modern urban planning concepts in Mexico City – one in the arena of park planning and the other in multi-family housing design. Quevedo's Balbuena Park (1910) was the first important public space in the capital planned to address the needs of the city's working class. Quevedo conceived Balbuena Park, located in the south-eastern sector, as an active park that accommodated sports, such as tennis, and provided playground spaces for children. In this way, Quevedo implemented in Mexico City the concept of governmental responsibility for providing opportunities for physical recreation within the urban environment. He brought notable examples established in Europe and the United States – particularly in the Chicago and Boston parks and playgrounds of Frederick Law Olmsted and his successors – to bear on Porfirian municipal planning.[49] Indeed, during the presidency of Plutarco Elías Calles (1924–1928), when the municipal government undertook sanitary operations on a grand scale in order to combat typhoid, Balbuena became the site of the first of the city's great sports fields. Thus, a quarter century after the opening of Balbuena, Quevedo's far-sighted planning accommodated the goals of a distinctly liberal regime whose projects included the creation of '*colonias proletarias*' (working-class suburbs).[50]

Quevedo's impressive contribution to the concept of modern housing in Mexico City was his Buen Tono apartment complex (1912), which he designed as company housing for workers in Ernesto Pugibet's Buen Tono tobacco factory. This complex marked a striking example of design practice devoted to ameliorating the living conditions of Mexico City's workers. Quevedo transformed the traditional *vecindad* (neighbourhood) plan to incorporate interior 'streets' that recapitulated the customary Mexican internal patio arrangement but gave families their own private apartments with indoor plumbing and abundant natural light. The Buen Tono apartments were all the more important as a demonstration project in the capital's development because of their location. They were sited south-west of the city centre near Pugibet's factory at the end of Paseo de Bucareli in the small *Colonia* Bucareli (1890) and in the vicinity of the late eighteenth-century Viceroyal tobacco factory (today the Ciudadela housing the National Library). Here the Buen Tono apartments mediated between the

Colonia del Paseo (1897, later Juárez) – which became the most elite residential district of the Porfirian capital – and the *Colonia* Roma (1902) – which evolved as one of the city's most modern and well-appointed upper middle-class districts. Quevedo's complex demonstrated unequivocally that urban planning could achieve a humane transition between districts in which residents of widely varying economic status clustered.

The Elite Reforma Subdivisions and Mexico City's Cosmopolitan Image

Buen Tono's outstanding design set a standard for economical multi-family dwellings that was unsurpassed in Porfirian Mexico City. Indeed, the successful projects of enlightened investors such as Ernesto Pugibet – and Francisco Somera before him – urged the government, in turn, to strengthen and enforce design guidelines and regulations. Francisco Somera's vision for Arquitectos had provided an exemplary strategy, and those who subsequently developed land after Somera's death (1888) tangential to his holdings, and even further south, improved upon the model that Arquitectos established. Along both sides of the Paseo de la Reforma (figure 6.6), they built the most spectacular and opulent of Porfirian *colonias* – Teja (1882, devel-

oped after 1904 as Cuauhtémoc) and Juárez (including *colonias* Limantour, 1890; Paseo, 1897; and Nueva del Paseo, 1903). Embassies, consulates, and diplomatic residences were established here, making the Reforma subdivisions the centre of the capital's foreign 'colonies'.[51] It is well known that between 1895 and 1910, the population of foreigners in Mexico City increased from approximately 9,000 to 26,000, a rate of increase that was twice that of the population growth within the city during the same period.[52]

While Mexico City's working-class suburbs were almost exclusively the production of Mexican investors, the elite suburbs – the most prominent of which were chartered in New Jersey – were the joint ventures of

Figure 6.6 Perspective plan of the city and valley of Mexico D. F., 1906. Milwaukee, Wisconsin: Wellge. (*Source*: Geography and Map Division, Library of Congress, Washington, DC)

Mexican and foreign capitalists, who formed partnerships and served on interlocking directorships of banks, railroads, newspapers, and companies involved in real estate development such as construction, paving, plumbing, electrification, and public transportation.[53] Jorge Jiménez Muñoz has written of the foreign investors who took up residence in Mexico, and, according to the mentality of 'carpetbaggers' proceeded to remake Mexico in the image of the United States. Yet, the image of the city was more complexly cosmopolitan than simply 'yanqui' (Yankee) – the product not purely of North American urban ideas, but a mixture with a significant component of Mexican urban traditions and ideas of civic propriety.[54] Undoubtedly, however, businessmen from the United States played a larger role in the expansion of Porfirian Mexico City than historians have previously emphasized. Key among the North American participants in the development of the capital's elite suburbs were R. Frederic Guernsey and his partner Charles L. Seeger, who published the *Mexican Herald* (established in 1896) and the *Mexican Financier*.[55] Nevertheless, Mexican investors in the Reforma subdivisions were prominent; they included José Yves Limantour, who became Minister of the Treasury and Public Credit in 1893; Joaquín Casasús, lawyer and businessman, who served as President of the Congress in 1895 and 1903; and Fernando Pimentel y Fagoaga, President of the *Banco Central Mexicano*. In 1906, Pimentel y Fagoaga merged his bank with the American Bank and the Condesa and Nueva del Paseo Extensions Company to form the *Compañía Bancaria de Obras y Bienes Raíces* (Banking Company of Works and Real State) with a dual-national board of directors, solidifying the types of multi-national business relationships that gave the Reforma *colo-*

nias their sophisticated, international appeal.

Street nomenclature in the Reforma subdivisions of Teja and Paseo bespoke internationalism, as streets in the former were named after the world's rivers, and in the latter, after the world's capitals or largest cities. Indeed, in 1903 the Municipal *Comisión de Embellecimiento* (Commission of Embellishment) debated the image of modern Mexico City that street nomenclature declared, placing a nominal and a numerical system in opposition. Legibility and simplicity were key concerns, but also at issue were the place of tradition and history in the modern city, and such philosophical oppositions as the rational versus the romantic, elite versus popular, religious versus secular. In 1904, the Commission voted for the nominal system, which two of the three Commissioners – Quevedo and architect Nicolás Mariscal – supported.[56]

The original designs of the Reforma *colonias* advanced some of the characteristics that the *Ayuntamiento* regulated in the municipal laws of 1903 and 1905, which were intended to reform subdivision practice in Porfirian Mexico City. Hence these elite subdivisions played an influential role in recommending design guidelines for the city on a broad scale. Paseo was organized around a *glorieta* at its centre, with street trees planted throughout the district by the developer. Rather than planning, however, impressive architecture and gardens established identity and coherence in the Reforma *colonias*. Several types of residences gave this urban zone its unique character. The first to be built here were (1) palatial houses set in the midst of ample gardens with detached stables and service quarters and (2) single-family detached houses lacking broad lawns and multiple service buildings but set back from the street with plantings. As the Reforma subdivisions developed after the Revolution, semi-detached houses – generally of two storeys, but some of a single storey – appeared and filled out the blocks. Although the early mansions were grandiosely scaled, they were largely built close to the lot lines, with projecting porches or *portes cocheres*, giving the Reforma subdivisions the tightly 'packed' look of metropolitan development and distinguishing them from the truly suburban districts further south, such as Tlalpam, with their *quintas* or *casas de campo* (villas or country houses). The stylistic iconography of residential architecture in the Reforma subdivisions was broadly associative and romantically picturesque. Plans of the houses in the Reforma subdivisions also drew upon various international traditions of domestic interior arrangements, from American plans with side entrances under *portes cocheres* and central circulation spaces, to French plans with clearly differentiated functional zones, and to Mexican plans with long side halls and rear patios.[57] If the new, elite Reforma subdivisions represented an image of cosmopolitan urbanity that signified the desire for displays of the wealth and progress of Porfirian government officials and capitalists, whether Mexican or foreign, the new middle-class *colonias* of Roma (1902) and Condesa (1902) to the south perpetuated a stronger sentiment of Mexican urban traditions, even as they embraced modern necessities.

Roma and Condesa: Middle-class Subdivisions and the Persistence of Mexican Urban Traditions

Roma and Condesa were the twentieth-century progeny of the capital's first nineteenth-century middle-class subdivision Santa María de la Ribera (figure 6.7). Established immediately south of the Reforma subdivisions, Roma and Condesa boasted some of the finest urban embellishments of the capital's new *colonias*. They illustrated the city government's increased control of development and planning through the involvement of Quevedo's Department of Public Works, as well as that of the municipal *Consejo de Salubridad* (Board of Health). The development group, *Companía de Terrenos de la Calzada de Chapultepec*, which included North American investors Cassius Clay Lamm and Edward Walter Orrin, as well as Mexican Pedro Lascurain, followed all the restrictions that the Municipality legislated in 1903, which specified the filing and approval of plans prior to construction, minimum street width, the granting of title of streets to the city, the paving of streets and sidewalks, the construction of sewage and potable water systems, the planting of street trees, and the ceding of land for public amenities such as parks, markets, and schools. The city, in turn, agreed to reimburse construction costs within specified budgetary limits and to provide for street cleaning and lighting when a specified minimum number of dwellings had been built. The grand Plaza Rio de Janeiro created a formal centre in Roma, while two fountains on *glorietas* provided elegant nodes in Condesa. Water from artesian springs in the area supplied the fountains and was pure enough to provide drinking water for the residents. Streetcar lines connecting Roma and Condesa to the central city were in full operation by 1913.[58]

Figure 6.7 Advertisement for Colonia Roma. *Mexican Herald,* 22 February 1902.

Roma and Condesa accommodated many types of dwellings, from the mansions of the wealthy and ample houses of the upper-middle class that stood in garden settings, to row and party-wall single-family residences, and to multi-family apartment buildings composed of self-contained units with kitchens and bathrooms. Many houses and buildings in Roma/Condesa were decorated with Art Nouveau ornamentation, and the district was known as the site of architecturally innovative structures, such as Manuel Gorozpe's and Miguel Rebolledo's eclectic Iglesia de la Sagrada Familia (1910–1912), which was an important early example of a reinforced concrete structure. Alberto Robles Gil's and Óscar Braniff's elegant Condesa bullring (1907) utilized a

modern steel structure. Indeed, Adamo Boari (1863–1928), the Italian architect of the famed Art Nouveau Teatro Nacional or Palacio de Bellas Artes (begun 1904) – perhaps the most celebrated of Porfiran institutional buildings – built his house in the centre of Roma/Condesa. Many of the capital's intellectuals, politicians, artists and other Porfirian cultural leaders made their homes in Roma/Condesa, drawing attention to this zone as an incubator of national achievement and pride.

The image of these subdivisions as that of the most advanced in the capital also confronted local history. The pre-Columbian village of Aztacalco and its colonial successor, the *pueblo* (village) of Romita, lay in the northeast corner of Roma. Here at Santa María de la Natividad (1530), Fr. Pedro de Gante baptized the first indigenous converts in the Valley of Mexico. Romita had developed an unsavoury reputation, however, because Santa María was known as the church where criminals sentenced to death prayed for their souls. In the 1920s, old buildings were demolished in conjunction with urban improvement efforts.[59] Modernization, therefore, eventually overcame historical legacy in this area, where Art Deco, Moderne, and International Style buildings and Anglo-American-inspired garden-city planning was undertaken, begin-

ning in the late 1920s. The centrepiece of this new approach to urban design was an interior park, José Luis Cuevas's and Carlos Contreras's Parque General San Martín (1926, or Parque México), designed for the southerly extension of Condesa – the Condesa Hipódromo subdivision (compare figures 6.5 and 6.8).[60] During the 1920s, Roma/Condesa/Hipódromo supplied an image of modernity, prosperity, and a renewed sense of nationalism for the middle class in Mexico City, who found growing affluence in a consolidating post-Revolutionary economy.[61]

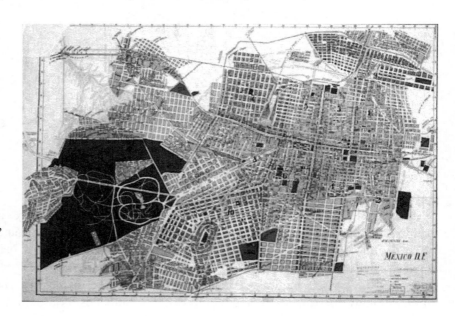

Figure 6.8 Plan of Mexico, by D. F. Cluerg, *c.* 1925. (*Source*: Geography and Map Division, Library of Congress, Washington, D. C.)

Suburban Developments and Post-Revolutionary Nationalism

The growth of outlying towns around the capital during the Porfiriato is beyond the scope of this chapter, but in post-Revolutionary Mexico, those in the high and dry southwesterly reaches of the Federal District became both strongholds of traditional Mexican urban imagery and seedbeds of modern art,

architecture, and urban planning. Exemplary of this trend are the towns of San Ángel, where muralist Diego Rivera built his remarkable studio/house (1928) designed by Juan O'Gorman in a Corbusian style, and Coyoacán, where the painter Frida Kahlo – Rivera's wife – maintained her family's typical, patio-style house, and where Rivera built his spectacular Anahuacalli (1945), the brooding stone evocation of an ancient Mexican temple, in which he housed his collection of pre-Columbian artifacts.[62]

In both San Ángel and Coyoacán, the survivals of indigenous and Spanish colonial historical memories played fundamental roles in establishing an environmental ambience from which the early twentieth-century nationalists could project visions of a new Mexico. The land on which San Ángel was built was given by Charles V to Hernán Cortés, and in the early twentieth century, two sixteenth-century convents and the eighteenth-century house of the Bishop of Madrid survived. In the vicinity of Coyoacán had been an important Aztec temple dedicated to Huitzilopochtli, and Cortés and his soldiers settled in Coyoacán between 1521 and 1524. The houses of Cortés, Diego de Ordaz (one of his generals), and La Malinche were local landmarks, as was the Dominican convent of San Juan Bautista (1590). At the end of the nineteenth century, a plan for a *Colonia* Hernan Cortés in Coyoacán was filed with the *Ayuntamiento*. To the east of San Ángel on the outskirts of the Indian town of Tlalpam, where Porfirio Díaz and other powerful Porfirians owned *casas de campo*,

Mexican and foreign shareholders built the Mexico Country Club, and developers laid out adjacent Country Club subdivisions.[63] All these suburban developments took advantage of the connections to historical landscapes and monuments. The southern suburbs – in which developers built *around* the past rather than obliterating it – were the soil in which Mexicans and foreigners alike planted the roots of nationalistic sentiment during Mexico's post-Revolutionary economic recovery.

During the 1920s, at the same time that the Mexico City's southerly streetcar suburbs grew around the nodes of outlying colonial villages, developers planned new subdivisions closer to the centre in a manner distinctly related to North American practice.[64] Prominent among these was Lomas de Chapultepec (Chapultepec Heights, figures 6.9 and 6.10), west of Chapultepec Park. A new boulevard, the Calzada de la Exposición (Exhibition Road), led through the park to the subdivision's entrance, emphasizing the link between park and district by an automobile promenade. The curving streets of Chapultepec Heights (José Luis Cuevas, 1921), which followed the hilly contours of the terrain, gave the sub division a dramatically different character from that of the capital's earlier, regularly

Figure 6.9 Panorama of Chapultepec Gardens, *c.* 1925. This view shows the Casa del Lago at the centre, which was the headquarters of the capital's automobile club in the early twentieth century. (*Source*: Prints and Photographs Division. Library of Congress, Washington, DC)

Figure 6.10 A gasoline service station at Chapultepec Heights, *c.* 1925. The prominent entrance from the city to the Lomas de Chapultepec (Chapultepec Heights) sub-division, designed in 1921 by José Luis Cuevas, was through Chapultepec Park along the Calzada de la Exposición (see figure 6.9, today an extension of the Paseo de la Reforma). (*Source*: Prints and Photographs Division. Library of Congress, Washington, DC)

gridded *colonias*. Not only the emphasis on the automobile in Chapultepec Heights, but also the relationship between house styles there and in contemporary Los Angeles signalled the growing presence of North American sub-urban residential imagery in Mexico City – a presence that commentators ascribed to the increasing influence of Hollywood films. Indeed, the fanciful Spanish Baroque revival style of the upper middle- and upper-class houses of Chapultepec Heights, Polanco, and other new elite subdivisions in the 1920s, 1930s, and 1940s is locally known by the playful, ironic appellation '*Hollywoodiana*'.[65]

Mexico City's Central Core and 'La Ciudad Latina'

Government officials who led Mexico City's urban development in the early twentieth century produced no comprehensive plans for a formal civic centre that correspond to City Beautiful planning efforts in the United States. They chose, instead, to improve the buildings immediately surrounding the Zócalo, to add new public buildings on available properties nearby, and to cluster additional new public buildings in the district between the Zócalo and the Alameda.[66] Had the Palacio del Poder Legislativo (Palace of Legislative Power) been completed on the site where it was begun in 1904 – approximately as far to the west from the Alameda as was the Zócalo on the east – the capital might have devel-oped very differently in terms of the spatial dispersion of its official architecture. How-ever, the magnificent neo-classical domed build-ing was essentially still born. Following a hard fought competition held in 1897, its design was given to the French architect Emile Henri Bénard. He undertook construction, but the building fell prey to the economic uncertain-ties of the Revolution. Between 1933 and 1938, Carlos Obregón Santacilia created the Monu-ment to the Revolution out of its shell, using the arches that had been constructed as a base for his copper-sheathed cupola.

The Porfirian government's failure to achieve the construction of the Palacio del Poder Legislativo was uncharacteristic, however, and its legacy of new public buildings transformed the capital. On the eastern edge of the Zócalo, Manuel Torres Torija remodelled the sixteenth-century, Spanish Renaissance style Palacio Nacional, maintaining the essence of its original aspect (1904). On the southeast corner of the Zócalo, Manuel Gorozpe remodelled the Edificio del Ayuntamiento (City Hall) (1906), which had been built between 1720 and 1724 in a late Renaissance style with a plaza level arcade and square corner towers. Following the dissolution of the *Ayuntamiento* in 1929, the offices of the Federal

District were housed here, and in 1932, Federico Mariscal and Fernando Beltrán y Puga designed a second, western building for Municipal district offices as its twin. Directly west of the Zócalo on Calle Tacuba, Silvio Contri designed the Italianate Renaissance style Palacio de Comunicaciones (1911) facing one of the capital's most magnificent late colonial public buildings, Manuel Tolsá's neo-classical Colegio de Minería (1797–1813, figure 6.11). At the next corner to the west, Adamo Boari and Gonzalo Garita built the new general post office (1907, figure 6.11). The

Figure 6.11 Palaces of Minería and Correos, J. López, 1926. México. El Paso, Texas: J. R. Díaz. This photograph illustrates an impressive streetscape of Mexico City's early twentieth-century central business district in a view looking south and west along Calle Tacuba (west of the Zócalo). It demonstrates the way in which Porfirian architects charged with modernizing the capital (Adamo Boari's neo-Plateresque Central Post Office, 1903–1910, is at the right) responded to the scale and grandeur of late colonial monuments (Manuel Tolsá's neo-classical College of Mining,1797–1813, is in the foreground). (*Source*: Prints and Photographs Division. Library of Congress, Washington, DC)

Correos façade related to Italianate late Gothic and Spanish Plateresque designs for corner-towered urban palaces – with Spanish Isabeline-style ornament around the window – which enriched the eclectic mix of styles of Porfiran public buildings. Sited for maximum urban effect, Correos fronted the site at the eastern edge of the Alameda Park designated for the new National Theatre (Palacio de Bellas Artes), a commission that Boari also won (1904). Boari designed the building in an ebullient Art Nouveau style with ornament based on neo-indigenous motifs, and Federico Mariscal completed it after the Revolution (1934) with Art Deco detailing. Also in this central zone rose Mauricio Campos's *Beaux-Arts* Cámara de Diputados (Chamber of Deputies) (1910) and Samuel Chávez's addition to the Escuela Nacional Preparatoria (National Pre-university School) (1908–1911), where José Vasconcelos's nationalistic mural programme was initiated after the Revolution.

Porfirian public buildings were modishly cosmopolitan in their stylistic references and, in many cases, thoroughly modern in their construction techniques, using reinforced concrete and fire-proofed iron and steel structural methods. These qualities marked their commercial counterparts, as well. Notable examples in the central business district were Eleuterio Méndez's *Joyería La Esmeralda* (1893), Daniel Garza's *El Centro Mercantil* (1897), Emilio González del Campo's *Casino Español* (1903), De Lemos & Cordes's *Compañía de Seguros la Mutua* (1905), and Genaro Alcorta's *Compañía de Seguros la Mexicana* (1906). Mexico City's height ordinances meant that skyscrapers, which signified modern urbanity, were not built until after 1930 – Manuel Ortiz Monasterio's ten-storey *La Nacional Compañia de Seguros*

(1930–1932) was one of the first. A prominent proponent of height limitations was Miguel Angel de Quevedo, who argued for a maximum limit of five storeys in order to protect what he described as the '*carácter de la ciudad latina*' (character of the Latin city)[67] Athough Quevedo himself applied technical innovations in his buildings, which made it possible to erect ever taller structures on Mexico City's earthquake-prone land, his critiques and those of his younger contemporaries, such as Jesús T. Acevedo (1882–1918), bespoke an emerging *nacionalismo* movement that would take hold in post-Revolutionary Mexico.[68] Energetic Porfirian public debates concerning the search for an appropriate national approach to architectural and urban design that would communicate the sweep and complexity of Mexico's history, as well as the country's embrace of modernity, contest eloquently assessments of Mexico City's early modern development as more 'French' or 'North American' than 'Mexican'.

Histories of early modern cities often focus on the design of monumental public buildings and the production of densely built commercial centres and transportation networks as expressions of progress and urban identity. In contrast, this chapter emphasizes the character of Mexico City's expanding residential fabric during the Porfiriato, against which the capital's monuments were displayed. Attempting to reweave an image of this fabric, which was both Mexican and 'other' and which is rapidly disappearing, gives a sense of the vital texture of the whole city and of the often historically anonymous residential landscape, which existed as the complement of the impressive new banks, department stores, theatres, hospitals, governmental buildings, and cultural institutions that were the glories of Porfirian capital.

Postscript

By 1930, Mexico City was well on the way to post-Revolutionary recovery, and with the dissolution of the *Ayuntamiento* in 1929, the Federal District assumed full control of planning for the capital's development. The government put forward the first project for a comprehensive urban plan in 1930, the hallmarks of which were measures to increase sanitary and health conditions in Mexico City. Unbuilt acreage was to be converted into parks and gardens, and a number of municipal markets were to be built, in order to remove street vendors to centralized locations and to clean up the streets. In 1933, however, new ordinances maintained the traditional duality of separate departments that divided planning into two areas: (1) the authorization of street plans, overseen by the Dirección de Obras Públicas which dealt with such physical qualities of the city as opening and aligning streets, dimensioning lots, and placing services; and (2) the issuing of construction permits, overseen by the *Consejo de Salubridad* (Council of Health), which dealt with zoning regulations including use, height, volume, and methods of construction. Between 1929 and 1933, the government also passed property-tax measures that, above all, had the effect of increasing the number of single-family houses. During Lázaro Cárdenas's presidency (1934–1940), the government took the first truly holistic approach to urban planning in a law of 1936, which established a coherent system of circulation and educational institutions, addressed the problem of housing, and took control of those areas in which private interests threatened to overwhelm those of the public. Responses to this more enlightened planning of the 1930s began to take shape in the 1940s, when a ring boulevard circling the central city was begun, and the capital's first modern multi-family, government-sponsored public housing was constructed.

Even as the government made significant progress in improving urban sanitary conditions, promoting the smooth flow of traffic, and providing housing for low-income residents, the population of the capital spiraled in the 1940s, almost doubling from 1,757,530 to 3,050,442 in the Federal District. In 1941, changes in urban planning laws were made, declaring residents' associations that did not register with the Federal District illegal and setting in motion what Alejandra Moreno Toscano has termed 'anarchic' processes, which the government could not effectively contain.[69] Whether Mexico City's development is considered anarchic or 'informal', as José Castillo has recently written, the origins of those processes and their insinuation in the evolution of the capital undoubtedly date from the first period of its growth, from about 1850 to 1930, the preamble to its current status, which Peter Hall compelling described as 'the ultimate world city: ultimate in size, ultimate in population, ultimate in threat of paralysis and disintegration, ultimate in the problems it presents'.[70]

NOTES

1. Hardoy, J.E. (1992) Theory and practice of urban planning in Europe, 1850–1930, in Morse, R.M. and Hardoy, J.E. (eds.) *Rethinking the Latin American City.* Washington, D.C.: Woodrow Wilson Center, pp. 20–49.

2. McMichael Reese, C. (in press) Nationalism, progress, and modernity in the architectural culture of Mexico City 1900, in Widdifield, S.G. (ed.) *La amplitud del Modernismo, 1861–1920.* Mexico City: CONACULTA.

3. Klor de Alva, J.J. (1993) Mestizaje as Myth and Metaphor in the New World. Typescript of a lecture delivered at the University of California, Los Angeles, 23 January. García Canclini, N. (1995) The hybrid: a conversation with Margarita Zires, Raymundo Mier, and Mabel Piccini, in Beverley, J., Aronna, M. and Oviedo, J. (eds.) *The Postmodernism Debate in Latin America*. Durham, North Carolina: Duke University Press, pp. 77–92.

4. Hayner, N.S. (1945) Mexico City: its growth and configuration. *The American Journal of Sociology*, 1, pp. 295–304. Medel Martínez, V. (1987) Desarrollo moderno de la ciudad colonial en México, in *La ciudad iberoamericana: Actas del Seminario Buenos Aires 1985*. Madrid: Centro de Estudios y experimentación de Obras Públicas, pp. 333–350.

5. Tenorio-Trillo, M. (1996) 1910 Mexico City, space and nation in the city of the centenario. *Journal of Latin American Studies*, 28, pp. 75–104.

6. Schell, Jr., W. (2001) *Integral Outsiders, The American Colony in Mexico City, 1876–1911*. Wilmington, Delaware: Scholarly Resources.

7. Hardoy, *op. cit.*, p. 23.

8. Unikel, L. (1976) *El desarrollo urbano de México: Diagnóstico e implicaciones futuras*. Mexico: Colegio de México. Davis, D.E. (1994) *Urban Leviathan, Mexico City in the Twentieth Century*. Philadelphia: Temple University Press.

9. Segre, R., et al. (1986) *Historia de la Arquitectura y del Urbanismo: América Latina y Cuba*. Habana: Pueblo y Educación. Vargas Salguero, R. (coord.) (1998) Vol. III, *El México independiente*, tomo II *Afirmación del Nacionalismo y la Modernidad*, in the series Chanfón Olmos, C. (general coord.) *Historia de la Arquitectura y el Urbanismo mexicanos*. México: Fondo de Cultura Económica.

10. Hardoy, J.E. (1975) Two thousand years of Latin American urbanization, in Hardoy, J.E. (ed.) *Urbanization in Latin America, Approaches and Issues*. Garden City, New York: Anchor, pp. 11–13.

11. Perló Cohen, M. (1999) *El paradigma porfiriano: historia de desagüe de valle de México*. Mexico: Programa Universitario de Estudios sobre la Ciudad, Instituto de Investigaciones Sociales.

12. Morales, M.D. (1976) La expansión de la ciudad de México en el siglo XIX, el caso de los fraccionamientos, in Moreno Toscano, A. (ed.) *Investigaciones sobre la historia de la Ciudad de México II*. Mexico: Instituto Nacional de Antropología e Historia, typescript publication, pp. 71–96+. Republished with revi-

sions in Moreno Toscano, A. (coord.) (1978) *Ciudad de México: Ensayo de construcción de una historia*. Mexico: Instituto Nacional de Antropología e Historia, pp. 189–200. Morales, M.D. (1975) Concentration of urban property ownership, sources and analytical perspectives, 1813–1900, pp. 125–127, in Moreno Toscano, A. et al. Research progress on urban history, Mexico. *Latin American Research Review*, 10, pp.117–131.

13. Lombardo de Ruiz, S. (1978) Ideas y proyectos urbanísticos de la Ciudad de México, 1788–1850, in Moreno Toscano, *Ciudad de México, loc. cit.*, pp. 169–188. For a discussion of 'communicentric' readings of images of the Plaza Mayor and Alameda, see Kagan, J. and Marías, F. (2000) *Urban Images of the Hispanic World, 1493–1793*. New Haven, Connecticut: Yale University Press.

14. Moreno Toscano, A. (1972) Cambios en los patrones de urbanización en México, 1810–1910. *Historia Mexicana, Revista Trimestral Publicada por el Colegio de México*, 32, pp.160–187. Espinosa López, E. (1991) *Ciudad de México, Compendio cronológico de su desarrollo urbano, 1521–1980*. Mexico: E. Espinosa López. (1986) México, Ciudad de [Siglos XVII–XX (1910)] and (1910–1970), in *Diccionario Porrua de historia, biografía y geografía de México*. Mexico: Porrua, 3 Vols., pp. 1859–1866.

15. Tovar de Teresa, G. (1991) *La Ciudad de los Palacios: crónica de un patrimonio perdido*. Mexico: Vuelta. 2 Vols.

16. Medel Martínez, Desarrollo moderno . . ., *loc. cit.*, p. 339. Skidmore, T.E. and Smith, P.H. (1984, 2001) *Modern Latin America*. New York: Oxford University Press, p. 224.

17. Morales, Concentration of urban property ownership . . ., *loc. cit.*, p. 126.

18. Morales, M.D. (1978) Francisco Somera y el primer Fraccionamiento de la ciudad de México, 1840–1889, in Cardoso, C.F.S. (coord.) *Formación y desarrollo de la burguesía en México, siglo XIX*. México: Siglo Veintiuno, pp. 188–230.

19. Creel, E.C. (1930) Discurso, in Martínez, R. (comp.) *La celebración en México del primer centenario del natalicio del Gral. Porfirio Díaz*. México: no editorial, pp. 13–40.

20. Unikel, L. (1975) Urbanism and urbanization in Mexico: situation and prospects, in Hardoy, J.E. (ed.) *Urbanization in Latin America . . ., loc. cit.*, pp. 391–433. Scobie, J.R. (1986) The Growth of Latin American Cities, 1870–1930, in Bethell, L. (ed.) *The Cambridge History of Latin America, Volume IV, c.*

1870 to 1930. Cambridge: Cambridge University Press, pp. 233–266.

21. Katzman, I. (1973) *Arquitectura del siglo XIX en México.* Mexico: Universidad Nacional Autónoma de México-Centro de Investigaciones Arquitectónicas, p. 266.

22. Alphand, J.A. and Hochereau, E. (1867) *Les promenades de Paris, histoire–description des embellisements – Dépenses de création et d'entretien des Bois de Boulogne et de Vincennes, Champs-Élysées– Parcs – Squares – Boulevards – Places plantées, étude sur l'art des jardins et arboretum.* Paris: J. Rothschild.

23. McMichael Reese, Nationalism, progress, and modernity . . ., *loc. cit.*

24. Schávelzon, D. (comp.) (1988) *La polémica del arte nacional en México, 1850–1910.* Mexico: Fondo de Cultura Económica, pp. 113–135.

25. Tenenbaum, B.A. (1992) Murals in stone, the Paseo de la Reforma and Porfirian Mexico, 1873–1910, in *La ciudad y el campo en la historia de México, Memoria de la VII Reunión de Historiadores Mexicanos y Norteamericanos, Oaxaca, 1985.* Mexico: Universidad Nacional Autónoma de México, Vol. 1, pp. 369–379.

26. Reese, T.F. and McMichael Reese, C. (1994) Revolutionary urban legacies, Porfirio Díaz's celebrations of the centennial of Mexican Independence, in *Arte, historia e indentidad en América: Visiones comparativas.* Mexico: Universidad Nacional Autónoma de México-Instituto de Investigaciones Estéticas, Vol. II, pp. 361–373. McMichael Reese, C. and Reese, T.F. (1999) The euphoria of the centennial and the future of the metropolis: Celebrations and exhibitions, in Gutman, M. (ed.) *Buenos Aires 1910: Memoria del porvenir.* Buenos Aires: Gobierno de la Ciudad de Buenos Aires, pp. 320–341. This catalogue accompanied an exhibition with venues in Buenos Aires, New York, and Washington, D.C.

27. Morales, M.D. (1974) Rafael Martínez de la Torre y la creación de Fraccionamientos, el caso de la Colonia Guerrero, in Moreno Toscano, A. (ed.) *Investigaciones sobre la historia de la Ciudad de México I.* Mexico: Instituto Nacional de Antropología e Historia, typescript publication, pp. 1–63+. Morales, Francisco Somera . . ., *loc. cit.* And Morales, La expansión de la ciudad de México . . ., *loc. cit.*

28. See (1982) *500 planos de la Ciudad de México.* Mexico: Secretaría de Asentamientos Humanos y Obras Públicas, p. 180, fig. 243, for a plan drawn in 1858, from the Mapoteca Orozco y Berra, which shows the proposed 'Cuartel Mayor de Santa María de la Rivera' as regularly subdivided into rectangular blocks of equal size (as boundaries permitted), with the Calzada Ribera de San Cosme forming its southern boundary.

29. John Claudius Loudon (1783–1843): see (1835) *An Encyclopaedia of Cottage, Farm and Villa Architecture and Furniture.* London: Longman *et al.* Alexander Jackson Downing (1815–1852): see (1844) *Cottage Residences, Rural Architecture and Landscape Gardening.* New York: Wiley and Putnam, and (1850) *The Architecture of Country Houses.* New York: Appleton.

30. Hernández, V.M. (1981) *Arquitectura doméstica de la ciudad de México (1890–1925).* Mexico: Universidad Nacional Autónoma de México.

31. Johns, M. (1997) *The City of Mexico in the Age of Díaz.* Austin, Texas: University of Texas Press.

32. Morales, Rafael Martínez de la Torre . . ., *loc. cit.* Martínez de la Torre was one of Mexico's wealthiest nineteenth-century capitalists, accumulating his fortune through investments in *haciendas,* ranches, factories, agricultural concerns, and mines.

33. Morales, Rafael Martínez de la Torre . . ., *loc. cit.* The most important of these was Félix Carvajal, who founded the cooperative society of the colony.

34. The majority of working-class immigrants to the capital before 1910 came from the nation's central states, and almost one-third of those were from the state of Mexico; Gortari Rabiela, H. d. (1987) 'Un modelo de urbanización.' La ciudad de México de finales del siglo XIX. *Secuencia, Revista Americana de Ciencias Sociales,* 8, pp. 42–52. Lear, J. (1996) Mexico City: Space and class in the Porfirian capital (1844–1910). *Journal of Urban History,* 22, pp. 454–492. Titles to houses and lots were not granted until final payments were made, so that 'only the most skilled worker with stable employment could aspire to own or even rent his own house', pp. 481–482.

35. Hernández, *op. cit.,* pp. 37–41.

36. Morales, Francisco Somera . . ., *loc. cit.*

37. See Katzman, *op. cit.,* pp. 45–61.

38. Morales, La expansión de la ciudad de México . . ., *loc. cit.,* pp. 84–85.

39. Lear, J. (1998). Mexico City: popular classes and revolutionary politics, in Pineo, R. and Baer, J. A. (eds.) *Cities of Hope: Politics, Protests, and Progress in Urbanizing Latin America, 1870–1930.* Boulder, Colorado: Westview, pp. 53–87.

40. Lear, Mexico City: Space and Class . . ., *loc. cit.,* pp. 479–480. Morales, La expansión de la ciudad de México . . ., *loc. cit.,* p. 85.

41. Vidrio, M. Sistemas de transporte y expansión urbana: los tranvías, in Moreno Toscano, *Ciudad de México, loc. cit.*, pp. 201–216.

42. Beezley, W. (1987). *Judas at the Jockey Club and Other Episodes of Porfirian Mexico*. Lincoln, Nebraska: Nebraska University Press.

43. Although Lear writes of the 'apparent attempt to physically displace elements that detracted from the Porfirian vision of progress – namely prisons, tenements, hospitals, and orphanages' from the city centre, this phenomenon of functional clustering was an international one and can be observed on the peripheries of industrializing cities in Europe and the United States as well; Lear, Mexico City, Space and Class . . ., *loc. cit.*, pp. 474–475.

44. The best recent survey of Porfirian architecture is to be found in Vargas Salguero, *op. cit.* But see also the impressive commemorative centenary album in which new government buildings were lavishly illustrated: García, G. (1991). *Crónica oficial de las fiestas del Primer Centenario de la Independencia de México*. Mexico: Centro de Estudios de Historia de México. Cortina Portilla, M. (intro.); facsimile edition of the 1910 publication.

45. On Gómez, see Jiménez Muñoz, J. H. (1993) *La traza del poder, historia de la política y los negocios urbanos en el distrito federal de sus orígenes a la desaparición del ayuntamiento, 1824–1928*. Mexico: CODEX, p. 38. Jiménez Muñoz accomplished stellar work through painstaking archival research in identifying those individuals who plannned, paved, plumbed, and electrified Mexico City's *colonias*. His book lacks an index, however, making it difficult to assemble composite biographical images of investors and their activities.

46. Morales, La expansión de la ciudad de México . . ., *loc. cit.*, pp. 85–88. The planning of Romero Rubio would seem to have been influenced by the well-known example of Barcelona's nineteenth-century extension, which proceeded according to the 1859 plan of Catalan engineer Ildefonso Cerdá (1816–1876). Here I take issue with Hardoy who wrote that Cerdá's 'concept of an open city . . . had no influence on the thinking of the mayors of Latin American cities or their experts', see Hardoy, Theory and Practice of Urban Planning in Europe . . ., *loc. cit.*, p. 23.

47. Eguiarte Sakar, M.E. (1996) *Urbanismo y arquitectura en México, catálogo de referencias hemerografías: 1861–1877*. México: Instituto Nacional de Antropología e Historia. Sigal, I. (1985) *Catalogo de publicaciones periódicas mexicanas de arquitectura,* *urbanismo y conexos*. México: Secretaría de Educación Pública, Instituto Nacional de Bellas Artes. Schávelzon, *op. cit.* Mendoza Lopez, M. (1972) Catálogo general del Archivo del Ayuntamiento de la ciudad de México. Mexico: Departmento de Investigaciones Historicas Publicaciones del seminario de Historia Urbana (typescript). See also García Barragán, E. (ed.) (1982) *Manuel F. Álvarez, Algunos escritos*. México: Secretaría de Educación Publica, Instituto Nacional de Bellas Artes.

48. On Quevedo's leadership in instituting modern urban planning and architectural design practices in Mexico City, see my Nationalism, Progress, and Modernity . . ., *loc. cit.* A celebratory biography published before his death is Prado, J. (1936) *El apóstol del árbol, biografía del Señor Ingeniero Don Miguel Angel de Quevedo*. Mexico: Pardo e Hijos. Quevedo published an autobiography, *Relato de mi vida*, in 1943, three years before his death.

49. Zaitzevsky, C. (1982) *Frederick Law Olmsted and the Boston Park System*. Cambridge, Massachusetts: Belknap. See also, Beveridge, C. E. and Rocheleau, P. (1998, rev. ed.) *Frederick Law Olmsted, Designing the American Landscape*. New York: Universe.

50. México, Ciudad de (1910–1970), *loc. cit.*, pp. 1863–1866.

51. A map published in Hernández, *op. cit.*, fig. 4, p. 59, shows 10 official residences in Juárez in 1910. Juárez includes the district well known today to tourists as the Zona Rosa. See Segurajauregui, E. (1990) *Arquitectura porfirista: La Colonia Juárez*. México: Universidad Autónoma Metropolitana Azcapotzalco.

52. Gortari Rabiela, 'Un modelo de urbanización' . . ., *loc. cit.*

53. Interestingly, investors in the model working-class subdivision Romero Rubio included the Mexico City Banking Company, which was organized by A. A. Robinson, former president Mexican Central Railroad, and other U. S. citizens, as well as the Building and Loan Company, which was founded by E. N. Brown, General Manager of the Mexican National Railway, with W. O. Staples, John R. Davis, and Julio Limantour; see Schell, *op. cit.*, p. 97.

54. On the Mexico City Improvement Company, the Chapultepec Land Company, and the Paseo Development Company, all chartered in the United States, see Jiménez Muñoz, *op. cit.*, pp. 70–72, writing of the 'audaces capitalistas de portafolios . . . los portafolieros' (audacious capitalists of portfolios or *portafolieros*) whose intent was 'hacer la América' (to make the Americas).

55. Schell, *op. cit.*

56. In the Archivo del Ex-Ayuntamiento de la Ciudad de México, see Calles. Estudio de la nueva nomenclatura definitiva, 1904–1906, tomo 478.

57. Hernández, *op. cit.*, p. 160.

58. Tavares López, E. (1995) *Colonia Roma*. Mexico: Clío. Morales, La expansión de la ciudad de México . . ., *loc. cit.*, pp. 85–88.

59. Tavares López *op. cit.*, pp. 28, 34.

60. See the exemplary guide: Martínez, E. A. (coord.) (1999) *Ciudad de México, guía de arquitectura*. Mexico: Colegio de Arquitectos, pp. 203–204. See also Anda Alanís, E. X. de (1990) *La arquitectura de la Revolución Mexicana, corrientes y estilos de la década de los veintes*. México: Universidad Nacional Autónoma de México, and Burian, E. R. (ed.) (1997) *Modernity and the Architecture of Mexico*. Austin, Texas: University of Texas. Fraser, V. (2000) *Building the New World, Studies in the Modern Architecture of Latin America, 1930–1960*. London: Verso, pp. 22–86.

61. Ward, P. (1998) (2nd ed.) *Mexico City*. Chichester: Wiley.

62. Fraser, *op. cit.*

63. *500 Planos de la Ciudad de México, op. cit.*, fig. 374, Colonia Hernán Cortés en Coyoacán (n.d., *c.* 1890); fig. 389, Coyoacán, Zona Urbana (1929); fig. 453, Plan of the Mexico Country Club and Adjacent Subdivisions (1907); figs. 487, 488, San Angel, Zona Urbana (1929); figs. 491, 492, Xochimilco, Zona Urbana (1929); figs. 485, 486, Tlalpan, Zona Urbana (1929).

64. Gortari Rabiela, 'Un modelo de urbanización' . . ., *loc. cit.*

65. See Cuevas's advertisement for Chapultepec Heights in *500 Planos de la Ciudad de México, loc. cit.*, fig. 474. The growth of the Mexican movie industry paralleled that of Hollywood. The Pan-American Highway was completed in 1937, further strengthening the connections between Mexico and the United States; Hayner, Mexico City: its growth . . ., *loc. cit.*, p. 300.

66. Alvarez, M.F. (1916) La Plaza de la Constitución, Memoria histórica y artística, y Proyecto de reformas, in García Barragán, *op. cit.*, pp. 39–60.

67. Quevedo, *Espacios libres* . . ., *loc. cit.*, p. 12. In 1903, height regulations limited tall buildings to five storeys (22 m); Espinosa López, *op. cit.*

68. See Acevedo's theoretical tract published posthumously: Mariscal, F. E. (prologue) (1920) *Disertaciones de un arquitecto*. México: Ediciones México Moderno.

69. Moreno Toscano. A. (1984) Análisis histórico del desarrollo urbano en México, in García Salgado, T. (recopilador*) Conferencias del bicentenario de la fundación de la Escuela de Pintura, Escultura y Arquitectura*. México: Universidad Nacional Autónoma de México, pp. 161–167, who lamented anarchy in the capital's urban development, not as a proponent of totalizing modern planning, but rather as a passionate defender of the government's responsibility to insure healthy and humane urban living conditions.

70. Hall, P. (1984), quoted in Castillo, J. (2001) Urbanisms of the informal, in *Praxis, Mexico City, Projects from the Megacity*, 2, pp. 102–111.

The Script of Urban Surgery: Lima, 1850–1940

Gabriel Ramón

Setting and Circumstance

Teddy Crownchield speeds towards the centre of the city. His route takes him along the new Leguía Avenue which, from the air, appears as a line connecting the new southern end of Lima to the old intramural space, which he enters after crossing the Moorish Arch donated by the Spanish community for the centennial celebration to mark Peru's Independence (1921) (figure 7.1). The narrator does not need to specify where the main character lives, as the above description is sufficient to deduce his social class and therefore his place of residence. This simple association – between place of residence and social class – is already a historic indicator: a few decades earlier it would have been unheard of.[1] Set in 1928, and published in 1934, *Duque,* written by José Diez Canseco, reveals a specific social topography, strung together through a number of urban details which makes it realistic as a story and places it squarely in the early part of twentieth-century Lima.[2]

Like other capitals on the continent, Peru's was going through a decisive (and typical) period for the modern Latin American cities:

the abandonment of the centre of the city as the upper-class residential area, the so-called 'flight to the south' of Lima.[3] Nevertheless, even in the novel, the move was still taking place: Carlos Suárez, Teddy's well-off friend, was living – with his grandfather – in a large old house on the central street of San Ildefonso.[4] The new segregation meant the specialization of the centre as commercial space and the appearance of crowded residential areas where the most diverse seedy establishments could be found. Among the latter were the famous opium smokers in the Chinese sector of the city, or the brothels on Patos and Huevo streets often visited by the characters in the novel and their contemporaries. It is precisely on this theme that the author tries to build on the documentary nature of *Duque.* A footnote is included: through a Prefect's decree – issued after the writing of the novel – the various brothels were moved to the newly founded popular district of La Victoria to the south-east of Lima. In a city where all activities were being duly zoned, prostitution could not be left out. The paradox which came from this reform did not escape Diez Canseco: in the move which was made in an attempt to clean up the area which had been abandoned by the upper classes, the bawdy houses ended up occupying 'all the streets which bore the names of the country's leaders or saints'. Contrary to the Municipal Council's aim to isolate 'seedy activities', the antitheses – virtue and sin – were symbolically united in the urban framework.[5]

Unlike the scant urban historiography of the period and that following it, *Duque* is a social reflection of the spaces and – more importantly – it makes them speak. Teddy goes from the south to the centre, from the pastoral Country Club to the Palais Concert in the centre of the city, from Leguía Avenue to the bathing resort of La Punta, from the lawn tennis courts to the beds on Patos street, making use of the various activities of the different parts of Lima. For the first time within the novel, the unusual speed of the car allows the city as a whole to be embraced. In spite of its detailed descriptions, the spatial limits of the most outstanding among its narrative forerunners – *Tradiciones peruanas* (1872) by Ricardo Palma – were always much more modest.[6] This makes *Duque* a special point of departure from which to question the func-

Figure 7.1 Aerial view of the Avenida Leguía, 1924, by Jochamowitz *et al.*, *Mi vida profesional* (1931) in the album given to the President A. B. Leguía by the Ministry of Patronage, showing the publics works done between 1919 and 1930.

tioning of the city at that time – the context of the novel helps us to understand the adoption of foreign urban models which were the essential ingredients for the surgery in Lima.[7]

At the beginning of the twentieth century, Lima's perimeter went well beyond the limits of the former colonial city, with the most outstanding public places at the time being in the centre of the route described above with the Parque de la Exposición (Park of the Exhibition) as the epicentre. It is in one such place, the renowned restaurant in the Parque Zoológico, that the main character and Suárez meet a couple of Hungarian actresses! – an indication of the fledgling cosmopolitanism of the area. The Peruvian capital was beginning to break out of its Viceroyal borders. On the one hand, the flow of information from the big cities of Europe and the United States allowed a faster acceptance by the public of the cultural models in vogue at that time; and on the other, in urban terms, the city exceeded by far the area within the walls which was intrinsically colonial. The

time for planning another centre had arrived. With a traditional centre which was largely regular and tight-packed (in which intervention was difficult), a southern border which was definitely residential and the rest of the incipient outskirts, poverty-stricken, the official interest – to judge from the emphasis placed on construction and the orientation of the projects – pointed to the well-known park and its surroundings. Originally prepared for the huge Exposición Nacional (National Exhibition) (1872), this complex contained a Botanic Garden, a Zoo and several pavilions to which monuments, fountains and other installations were slowly being added. The high point of this urban area came in 1898 when it was divided by the majestic 9 de Diciembre Avenue (9th December Avenue) (figure 7.2) Adorned with marble sculptures and bordered by elegant residential buildings, the road began to function as a Creole boulevard par excellence overshadowing the central Jirón de la Unión (Unión Avenue). On a lesser scale, but as in Rio de Janeiro and

Figure 7.2 Avenida 9 de Diciembre or Paseo Colón, 1906. (*Source*: *Memoria de la Municipalidad de Lima*, 1906)

México City, the stylistic coordinates of the city planning projects in Lima were explicit and constant. Under the influence of the great international exhibitions, the general design – and even the components – of the Palacio de la Exposición (Palace of the Exhibition) (1872) followed the European models, especially the Italian and the French. Three decades later, at the height of the interest in public health, the Institute of Hygiene would be constructed opposite. Use was made of the materials and the form of the Peruvian pavilion, constructed by the French architect Fernand Guillard, which had just been a part of the Great Exhibition in Paris (1900) (figure 7.3).[8]

The description of the city found in *Duque* and the space which the Parque de la Exposición occupied are at the centre of the process we are to discuss. They are the corollary and prelude to a path which must be outlined, by visiting areas of a city waiting to be described.

Figure 7.3 Paseo 9 de Diciembre and the Instituto de Higiene, during building, 1902. (*Source: Memoria de la Municipalidad de Lima*, 1902)

The Bourbon Background

The reforms introduced during the Bourbon regime can be considered the first project of urban modernity in Spanish America. Under these guidelines, from the second half of the eighteenth century, a number of buildings marked Lima's horizon. The buildings belonging to this period were characterized by the concentration of the activities carried out, which consequently led to an increase in their size. Due to the grid layout which imposed limits on the space, as well as the incipient adoption of ideas on public health and safety in the city, a large number of these buildings were removed to the outskirts. This occurred, for example, with the Gallos (Cockfighting) Coliseum (1762), a building for the control of this sport, which had previously taken place anywhere in the city. The Coliseum, located near the walls, became an exclusive space for this activity and was supplied with ample installations. Something similar occurred with the Plaza de Toros (Bullring) (1780) or the Santa Catalina Barracks (1806), which were deliberately moved due to their size and the activities carried out within. This process was accompanied by the slow introduction of neo-classicism reflected in buildings such as in the renovated gates of Callao (1800) and Maravillas (1807) and the austere Santo Cristo church (1780). In this construction period,

which included at least twenty large works between new buildings and reconstructed ones, the most representative building was the General Cemetery (1808). Although the dead had traditionally been buried in the churchyards, from the middle of the eighteenth century – in step with the Enlightenment – the metropolitan authorities decided that, for public health reasons, they should be relocated on the outskirts. Therefore, an adequate site for the unification of this funerary function was needed, and so the cemetery was located to the leeward on the east of the city, beyond the walls. This building, constructed by the Spaniard Matías Maestro, was one of the first of its kind in the capitals of Latin America and symbolized a reform and an era. As with the rest of the buildings, it reflected the change in colonial architectural orientation under the auspices of an empire subordinate to the French aesthetic canon.[9]

The Guano City, 1847–1875

When the Bourbon period ended, the Peruvian capital underwent a construction hiatus, which lasted for several decades. The decomposition of the Spanish colonial system caused the authorities in Lima to abandon the renovation projects in the city in order to dedicate themselves exclusively to the defence of the Empire. The uneasiness and anxiety experienced in the first decades of the new regime confirmed the so-called 'ruralization' of the capital. As indicated in testimonies at that time, Lima looked like a devastated city.[10] Around the middle of the nineteenth century, thanks to the economic bonanza from the export of guano (a fertilizer made from bird excrement), financial aid could be given to

projects undertaken by the Peruvian state. For the neglected capital, this led to a new cycle of construction (table 7.1). A series of buildings were built with a common trait, revealing traces of the city-planning programme at that time.

Firstly, these buildings reveal the influence of specialists who, with new information obtained from the industrialized countries, proceeded to implement these trends in Lima. Physicians such as José Casimiro Ulloa, who after travelling to France to learn about the new techniques in psychiatry, proposed the construction of the mental asylum.[11] The versatile lawyer Mariano Felipe Paz Soldán travelled extensively throughout the United

Table 7.1 Main buildings and avenues, 1850–1930.[12]

Guano period

Plazuela 7 de Setiembre	1847
Terminal del ferrocarril	1851
Mercado Central	1852
Matadero General	1855
Escuela Normal Central	1857
Monumento a Bolívar	1858
Manicomio	1859
Penitenciaría	1860
Fábrica de Gas	1862
Hospicio Manrique	1866
Escuela de Artes y Oficios	1870
Plaza 2 de Mayo	1872
Puente Balta	1872
Palacio de la Exposición Nacional	1872
Hospital 2 de Mayo	1875

Aristocratic Republic period

Quinta Heeren	1890
Barrio Obrero La Victoria	1896
Casa de Correos	1897
Avenida 9 de Diciembre	1898
Avenida Brasil	1898
Avenida La Colmena	1899
Renovación Plaza Mayor	1901
Hipódromo de Santa Beatriz	1903
Facultad de Medicina	1903
Instituto de Higiene	1904
Casa Barragán	1904
Banco del Perú y Londres	1905
Monumento a Bolognesi	1905
Casa Courret	1906
Cripta de los Héroes	1908
Avenida del Sol	1908
Teatro Segura	1909
Quinta Alania	1909
Estación Ferroviaria Desamparados	1912
Teatro Colón	1913
Casa Fernandini	1913
Casa de Depósitos y Consignaciones	1915
Almacenes Oechsle	1917
Palacio Arzobispal	1917

Oncenio Leguiísta period

Teatro Forero (Municipal)	1920
Colegio Guadalupe	1920
Avenida Leguía	1921
Arco Morisco	1921
Monumento a San Martín	1921
Monumento a Washington	1922
Parque Universitario	1923
Avenida del Progreso	1924
Edificio Rímac	1924
Sociedad de Ingenieros	1924
Monumento a Petit Thouars	1924
Edificios Plaza 2 de Mayo	1924
Museo de Arqueología Peruana	1924
Hospital Loayza	1924
Museo de Arte Italiano	1924
Hotel Bolívar	1924
Fuente China	1924
Fuente Norte Americana	1924
Monumento a Sucre	1924
Edificio Minería	1924
Monumento al Obrero	1926
Monumento a Manco Capac	1926
Country Club	1927
Avenida Alfonso Ugarte	1928
Parque de la Reserva	1929
Banco Italiano	1929
Club Nacional	1929
Palacio Legislativo	end of the 1920s
Edificios de portales de Plaza San Martín	1930
Orfanatorio Pérez Araníbar	1930
Reconstrucción del Palacio de Gobierno	1926–1938
Palacio de Justicia	1926–1938

States collecting information on new advances in the area of prison systems and then later proposed and directed the construction of a prison following the panoptic model. The opportunities resulting from the break with the Spanish colonial system, led to the arrival of professionals from other European countries, mainly Italy and France. Of the six large works constructed during this period, at least three were in the hands of the Italians which is not surprising considering the predominant role that these immigrants had acquired in Peru.[13] During the government of J. Echenique (1851–1854), the French engineers Emilio Chevalier and Charles Farraguet, and the Pole Ernesto Malinowski were hired to supervise great engineering works. Immediately, the *Comisión Central de Ingenieros Civiles* (Central Commission of Civil Engineers) (1852) was formed and in 1860 the *Reglamento para el servicio de ingenieros y arquitectos del Estado* (Regulations for the service of the State's engineers and architects) was passed. The first professional architects, Maximiliano Mimey, José Tiravanti, Miguel Trefogli, Domingo García and Manuel San Martín began working. The *Escuela de Ingenieros del Perú* (School of Engineers of Peru) was founded in 1876, under the direction of the Pole, Eduardo de Habich. The bases for the formation of the main technical institution in the country from which the first local architects would graduate were thus laid down. Due in part to the importation of foreign specialists, as well as the training received by local artisans, the country began to rely on personnel capable of constructing new types of buildings.[14]

Secondly, the large buildings which were constructed broke with the architectural pattern by proposing unknown forms, intimately linked to the renewed institutional content. Until then, the architecture in Lima had been typified by its regional character, the result of the slow change from the traditional forms. In spite of the presence of elements of an industrial nature, it was a type of architecture which was empirical and artisan, carried out by master builders and carpenters often under the guidance of the owner. Due to their size and the special function for which they had been constructed, works such as the Penitentiary called for a more technical and rational approach to design and construction. Leaving this in the hands of traditional artisans was out of the question.[15] It was a matter of ingredients and contents. The panoptic disposition of the Penitentiary building and the Dos de Mayo Hospital, the straight lines and the

majestic façades were not isolated aspects but rather were associated with the disciplined proposal undertaken by the State. The façade of the Penitentiary building reflected a severe style in keeping with its purpose as an impregnable prison while the interior included rooms where the inmates would be trained to work during the day and individual cells for sleeping at night. On the other hand, the hospital, which had been constructed after a yellow fever epidemic, would combat future massive diseases. As a result, the design of its operating rooms was completely different from that of its colonial predecessors.

Thirdly, each one of these buildings replaced a number of small establishments from the colonial era: a large slaughterhouse instead of the many small places for cattle, a mental asylum instead of several mad houses, among others. This would result in a break with the previous scale of structures, as in the case of the Penitentiary, which occupied almost three hectares, unheard of even for the great colonial churches that were in harmony with the architectural panorama at that time.

Fourthly, for motives similar to those argued during the previous construction period (space, public health and safety), many of the buildings of this period were situated far from the centre of the city with the notable exception of the Mercado Central (Central Market) which made use of the extensive land expropriated from the nuns of the Concepción order. The Manicomio (Mental Asylum) was moved to the outskirts, to the east of the city; the Penitentiary to the far south; the Hospital Dos de Mayo, next to the Portada de Cocharcas (Cocharcas Gateway). The General Slaughterhouse, the Palacio de la Exposición, the Paper Factory, the Gas Factory and the Plaza Dos de Mayo could be found outside the walls.

In spite of being different from their Bourbon predecessors, these buildings shared some basic features. For example, the construction of the Central Market in 1852 achieved one of the most important goals from the end of the colonial period: the reorganization of the sale of goods within the city walls. Another common characteristic, which has already been pointed out, was the removal of buildings to the outskirts, although the most important difference lay in the change of the area of projection. Although during the second half of the eighteenth century the northern (the right bank of the Rímac river) and the eastern (linked to the Maravillas Gateway and the Cemetery) areas were prominent, during the *Guano* period, the shift was to the south.[16]

Added to the list of constructions already mentioned, was an urban undertaking of great importance: the demolition of the walls and the subsequent re-utilization of the outlying areas. The large area of clay soil which surrounded the city was totally undeveloped. Among the many projects of the North American Henry Meiggs was his dream of demolishing the walls and making use of the cleared lands. In order to measure and evaluate the area, the government commissioned an engineer, Luis Sada di Carlos who had come from Chile, to manage the *Instituto Modelo de Agricultura* (Model Agricultural Institute). Meiggs later bought the area and planned – with Sada's advice – a number of circular *alamedas* (poplar avenues), 50 metres wide with five parallel avenues each. From this great avenue, there would be branches which would lead down town as well as 'squares' or gardens which, according to one of the engineers involved in the project, 'besides being a centre of attraction or meeting place, would also be extremely useful for

the health of the city'. As a complement, a very wide avenue was planned with six rows of trees which would run from the Callao port to the 2 de Mayo plaza (Second of May plaza), thereby linking the port to the capital, which in turn would have all its sections connected.[17]

This undertaking which would be an epilogue to the *Guano* period was possible due to the economic bonanza and the increasing value of the land found on the outskirts, resulting from the growth of the city. The size of the project which was in tune with the European panorama – that is, tendencies towards the reforms which Baron Haussmann had implemented in Paris – are explained by the attraction that Lima held among investors such as Meiggs and the help received from the government of José Balta.[18] This not only permitted the renewal of professional groups but also the implementation of projects using advanced technology. The vanguard character of this undertaking explains why – in spite of interruptions – it would become a kind of prologue for the future Lima. Sadá's *Plano Topográfico* (Topographical Plan) (1872), drawn up under these circumstances, summarizes the basic guidelines for the city planning script of the following construction periods (figure 7.4).[19] So radical were the series of reforms envisaged that there even were (unsuccessful) plans to move the vital city centre (in other words, the group of the main institutional buildings) southwards to the future area of La Victoria.[20]

The stylistic tendency in the *Guano* construction period was mentioned by different Europeans at that time, among which the testimony of the French traveller Charles Wiener, who visited Peru and Bolivia in the mid-1870s, is worth mentioning. After his journey, he would consult the work of

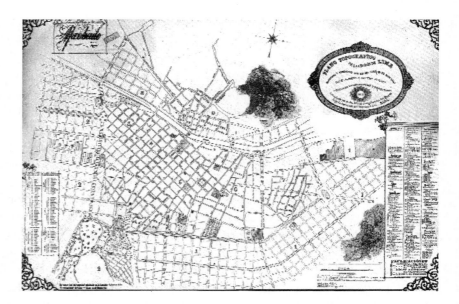

Figure 7.4 Luis Sada's Plan, 1872. (*Source*: J. Bromley and J. Barbagelata, *Evolución urbana de la ciudad de Lima*. Lima: Concejo Provincial de Lima, 1945)

Leonce Angrand, a diplomat who had been in the Peruvian capital a few decades earlier (1847). After criticizing the changes found in Lima and the loss of the 'traditional values' (alluding to the sketches made by his predecessor), Wiener recognized with nostalgia that

these sketches . . . seemed to me to send out a note that . . . now cannot be found. I later understood that this delicate nuance had unfortunately been erased by time. Lima is progressing and in doing so the adorable colonial city is becoming Europeanized. The new houses seem similar to the prosaic residences of our little shareholders.[21]

Later on, visitors would be even more emphatic, comparing – on an urban scale – the changes in Lima to those carried out in Paris. This was the case of André Besson (1886), who would refer to the 'Haussmanization' of Lima, or his fellow countryman Émile Carrey, who pointed out that

for several years a complete change like that carried out on our walls by Mr. Haussmann, of a questionable reputation, has made Lima a new city . . . Its fortifications have been converted into boulevards.[22]

Orchestrating the Great City, 1895–1930

Like the major setback suffered during the colonial period, the War of the Pacific (1879–1883) meant a new interruption to urban projects in Lima. The images of the destruction caused by the Chilean army in the aristocratic bathing area of Chorrillos highlight the damage suffered: elegant houses were burnt and in the centre a square with marble sculptures was completely destroyed.

After the military occupation of the city and the end of the conflict, a period of national reconstruction began which, apart from the restoration of the city exteriors, would also touch the private spaces.

Although new trends had previously been principally restricted to the huge public buildings, in the two construction periods which followed, the Aristocratic Republic (1895–

1919) and the *Oncenio* (eleven-year period) of Augusto B. Leguía (1919–1930), the emphasis would be laid on relieving the congestion of the layout. During the first period, political power lay directly in the hands of the oligarch, while during the government of Leguía there was an attempt to modernize Peruvian society and redefine its relationship with imperialism. The strong presence of the United States led to an increase in the number and scope of public works in the area. The Foundation Company, a North American construction company in charge of the main avenues, stood out.[23] Both periods had a decisive influence in the urban panorama in Lima and – beyond the nuances – shared two traits. With regard to the great city stage, enormous avenues were planned and constructed (ring roads, cross-streets and inter-urban connections); and in so far as the internal structure was concerned, attention was placed on mass housing. The official concern for the location, form and disposition of popular residential areas became an imperative on an agenda which acknowledged the lack of mere 'strategic embellishment'.

A contradictory equation seems to have summarized the preceding residential situation in Lima. During the end of the colonial period, the city had grown very little, a trait which it held throughout the nineteenth century. Meanwhile, the number of inhabitants had been continually increasing. The (housing) palliative for this demographic increase had been the popular residences, both those which had been expressly planned for such a purpose (*callejones* or alleys), as well as those which came about due to the subdivision of the wealthy houses (houses with rooms for rent). In 1839, the number of *callejones* was 247, with this figure doubling in the following two decades. But this was not the only type of residence which increased as in the same interval the number of dwellings went from 10,605 to 13,093, and only two years later to 14,002, in what a commentator from the period described as a 'prodigious growth'. While maintaining its fabric and practically without changing its surface area, the city had to divide itself in order to accommodate the growing population.[24]

At the beginning of the twentieth century, the situation changed and the city overflowed its colonial borders from 456 hectares at the close of the eighteenth century, to 1,292 in 1908. The demographic rates were also alarming: between 1891 and 1908 the population had increased from 103,956 to 140,884. Lima now had some 671 *callejones* and 755 tenement houses which gave home to almost half of the population. In a city characterized by slow growth – compared with the other Latin American capitals – between 1903 and 1908, the number of buildings had gone from 12,311 to 14,230, with an annual average of 384 constructions, divided between public buildings, residences, factories and workshops.[25] To this, one should add the aforementioned flight to the south by the upper classes which contributed to the densification of the large residential buildings as well as the centre as a whole.

Added to the general deterioration in the public services (*tugurización*), another contradictory trait was found: the main institutional buildings and business places remained downtown. The dilemma was how to establish a business district in the middle of the poor quarter. It was precisely in this period of growth and overcrowding that the concern for public health peaked. From the end of the nineteenth century, after a deadly spate of epidemics, the branch of medicine dealing with city health had acquired special relevance.

Since its founding, the *Sección de Salubridad Pública del Ministerio de Fomento* (Public Health Section of the Ministry of Trade and Industry) (1907) had become an essential tool in urban planning. Coming even before the architects themselves, the public health doctors worked hand in hand with the engineers who established the guidelines for the construction of popular housing.[26]

It is within this context that Lima's urban renewal at the end of the nineteenth and the beginning of the twentieth century should be seen. At this point one may ask: how did the arrival of the new architectural patterns make themselves known? Although the transition to the new century was marked by the most varied kind of events, the meaning of novelty can be clearly perceived from the moment at which certain spaces were subject to successive changes. In this respect, three elements: working-class housing, avenues, and plazas should be considered.

Housing the Working-Classes

To move the poor population, residential areas were built, such as La Victoria (1896) where 'prohibited' activities in places such as the brothels mentioned in *Duque* were, in fact, regulated. At the same time, the central area was also worked upon. A planned campaign of official criticism of the congested popular residences preceded the intervention and construction activity. Thought of as seedy establishments from which various types of diseases could be spread, the houses of the poor, especially the *callejones*, lived up to their disastrous fame when the bubonic plague broke out in 1903. The first building experiments were the houses for the workers who took part in the construction of the railways, planned by the North American Henry Meiggs (1875); the plans drawn up by Ricardo Monti (1871) to create credit unions which would

pay for the construction of the houses for the 'proletarian and middle classes', and the projects for groups of houses drawn up by Glicerio Joya (1896). At the end of the century, the *Sociedad de Beneficencia Pública* (Society of Public Charity) began an orchestrated construction campaign. This institution, which owned a large part of the real estate patrimony in Lima, carried out projects in which the engineer, Felipe Arancivia (1894–1895), the French architect Claudio Sahut (1912, 1916), and especially Rafael Marquina participated. This prolific Peruvian architect who had studied at Cornell University in the United States carried out – from the end of the 1920s – more than twenty projects for building houses for workers, mainly in Barrios Altos (to the east side of the centre of the city) and the area of Rímac.[27]

Connecting the City

The grid has been a characteristic feature of Hispanic American cities. The colonial maps of Lima show a regularly formed centre and outlying areas marked by curved lines, a spatially and chronologically relevant fact as it reveals the manner in which the urban plan of the viceregal era was slowly being forgotten. This fabric survived the colonial period and it is only towards the middle of the nineteenth century that slight changes can be seen. There was for instance the pioneer Plazuela del 7 de Setiembre (7th of September Square) (1847) – which will be touched upon later. There was also the Mercado Central (1852), whose construction caused a conflict between the government and the nuns from the convent whose land was to be expropriated and severed. To justify the intervention, the Minister in charge indicated that the lands belonging to the convent occupied two blocks and thus interrupted the traffic between the residential areas in the upper and lower sections of the city. Initiating an era of opening up the urban fabric, the street was laid out.

The next stage began with the demolition of the walls and the project associated with it. Sadá's already-mentioned *Plano Topográfico* included a great circular avenue with a number of plazas and avenues which would penetrate into the grid. The coordination between the old city and the new would take place in the eastern area, where two great avenues formed a cross that would traverse the old fabric. In spite of it being a relatively poor area, without important buildings – and therefore ripe for redevelopment – the project was not successful.

At the end of the nineteenth century, three basic avenues began to be laid out. In 1898, the 9 de Diciembre, afterwards known as Paseo Colón due to its predominant use by pedestrians, was inaugurated. This avenue connected the area to the future Plaza Bolognesi (1905) and Grau Avenue, cutting the Parque de la Exposición in two sections. A year later, work began on the Interior Avenue or La Colmena which would run from the Plaza 2 de Mayo to Grau Avenue, crossing Lima from west to east. Although in the 1940s the project had still not been completed, the main

section of the road – up to the projected Plaza San Martín – was ready in 1911. The third avenue, Brasil (1899) was much longer, starting from the site which Plaza Bolognesi would occupy to the sea coast, approximately five kilometres. Another project can be added to this group, the Central Avenue (1899) which would cross the entire centre of Lima perpendicularly to the Interior Avenue. It would run from Plaza Bolognesi to the Alameda de los Descalzos (on the other side of the river), passing through Jirón de la Unión. Only small sections of this avenue were constructed.

In view of the above, three types of avenues can be identified. The great circular avenue which, like the Viennese Ringstrasse, separated the centre from the outskirts but at the same time connected them. In Lima, this was done through the Grau Avenue to which Paseo Colón and Alfonso Ugarte (1928) avenues were added. In so doing, an avenue was constructed surrounding the old city beginning on the far east and passing through the new centre until it arrived at Plaza 2 de Mayo.

The other type was the cross avenue like La Colmena and the projected Central Avenue, which would be the most complicated but the most longed for. The great project of that period was the 28 de Julio Avenue (1906) which would give a majestic view from the Plaza Mayor to the future Plaza San Martín (figure 7.5). In spite of the steps taken by the Mayor, Federico Elguera (1901–1909) and an expropriation law which was specifically passed, not a section of the road was built.

The third type was the avenue which made contact with other urban centres. Apart from Brasil, there were the Leguía Avenue (1921) and Progreso (1924), both undertaken by the Foundation Company. The former followed and brought about a turn in the course of the

Figure 7.5 Perspective of the project of Avenida 28 de Julio, 1901. (*Source*: *Memoria de la Municipalidad de Lima*, 1901)

upper classes in Lima, linking the central area to Miraflores and the intermediate residential areas. The latter permitted a faster flow between the centre and the port of Callao.

Plazas in the Parisian Style

The colonial tradition was characterized by the rectangular plazas situated opposite the ecclesiastic sites. The *Guano* period began to break this pattern with the construction of the Plazuela del 7 de Setiembre (1847). This levelled area was rare because of its location, as it was built in front of a theatre, as well as because of its shape, which was semicircular.[28] The next urban landmark of this type was the Plaza 2 de Mayo (1874), erected in honour of those who had fought in the battle in which Spanish and Peruvian forces had come face to face in the port of Callao (1866). The area this monument would occupy had been especially favoured by the Bourbons who had erected a neo-classical gateway that led to a walkway with a number of roundabouts. Due to its strategic location

as the gateway to the city for those who arrived through the port, and a supposed spatial link with the Independence campaign, President Manuel Prado chose the spot to install a memorial. An international contest was held for the implementation of the work and the winners were two French artists, the sculptor León Gugnot and the architect Edmond Guillaume. Before being installed in Lima, the piece was exhibited in the Palace of Industry opposite the Champs Elysées in Paris (1872). Photographs of the period show the conflict between the style and the magnitude of this artefact and its surroundings, old single-storey houses (figure 7.6). As in the case of Plazuela 7 de Setiembre, the break was in form and location, but on a greater scale. It was a huge circular plaza located on the outskirts and was also the first of a number of levelled areas which would shape the immediate peripheral areas of the city.[29]

Fifty years later (1924), Víctor Larco Herrera, a magnate from Trujillo, a Peruvian city and province, who was of Italian descent, would decide to regularize the surrounding scenery and financed the construction of a number of elegant houses several storeys high in an attempt to obtain a complex similar to la Place de l'Étoile in Paris. The original plans were given to the architect Claudio Sahut and the construction – slightly different – to the Polish architect Ricardo Malachowsky. The

decayed area would be thus changed, the surroundings of the plaza would be combined to the style of the central monument, as well as to the fashionable buildings on the new Colmena Avenue, on whose opposite end the Plaza San Martín (1924) would be built.[30] This grouping had a formal appearance similar to that of Paseo Colón, in disposition (an avenue which led to a circular plaza), style and magnitude. However, the Plaza 2 de Mayo did not come about as a result of a specific project but rather as a slow process which would span half a century.

Beyond the thematic divisions discussed in

Figure 7.6 2 de Mayo monument, 1874. (*Source*: Archivo Histórico Riva Agüero)

this section, it should be pointed out that the notable elements became part of the layout of the great avenues like La Colmena, which epitomized novelty in urban planning. Apart from serving as a communication route, this work implied the construction of houses and the display of the city's renewed scenery (figure 7.7). The testimony of Pedro Dávalos (1907) – who returned to Lima after more than five years abroad – is illustrative. On describing La Colmena he says:

all the buildings are of a modern style and enjoy a comfortable disposition unseen in Lima. They belong to the type of residences, thus being the cost and the stately air, which could only be inhabited by the rich . . . Nothing has been taken from the old colonial house model.

However, the innovation was not limited to this avenue but had become a trait in the urban arteries:

Paseo Colón is the most significant test of progress and general well being, of the spirit of greatness and hygiene which floats above the pessimistic and conservative masses. A break has been made with all that was old. Nothing has been copied from the old Lima which was located within walls.[31]

During the two construction periods discussed, the European presence continued to play a decisive role in the elaboration of the urban script. After the Haussmannesque experiment, the Parisian model acquired universal prestige and became the compulsory point of reference in Latin America. Beyond the multiple nationalities from which the Poles (Malachowsky), Spaniards (Agustín Querol, Mariano Benlliure) and Italians (Gaetano Moretti, Julio Lattini) stand out, there is the French influence: three of the most prolific architects of that time, Émile Robert, Claudio Sahut and the aforementioned Malachowsky, had studied at the École des Beaux Arts in Paris.[32] The details in the Plaza 2 de Mayo, Frenchified from beginning to end, was proof of the mark, which would last well into the twentieth century.

Figure 7.7 Avenida La Colmena, 1906. (*Source*: *Memoria de la Municipalidad de Lima*, 1906)

The (Foreign) Management of What is Peruvian

Accepting the novelty stemming from the different periods of construction linked to the República Aristocrática and the *Oncenio* of Augusto B. Leguía, it is worth considering an ephemeral yet precise feature that lets us characterize, against this background, the process of assimilation of foreign trends of urban culture: namely, the search for an architectural expression which would express national sentiment.[33]

The well-known debate on 'national character', which attracted the intellectual circle in Lima at the start of the twentieth century, had repercussions in diverse areas, including architecture.[34] Although neither the socialist José Carlos Mariátegui, nor the ultra-conservative José de la Riva Agüero proposed specific formulae for success, their urban preferences were associated with their respective political views. The latter emphasized the Spanish tradition while the former proposed an integration which would highlight the indigenous culture.[35] However, it was the incipient group of architectural professionals who took charge of transforming words into actions. From the start of the Republican regime, attempts had been made to incorporate some qualities of the 'imagined Peruvian community' into the urban scenery.[36] It is meaningful to note that the first series of public sculptures associated with the *Guano* period had been exclusively dedicated to characters from classical mythology, for example those in Alameda de los Descalzos and Plaza del Cercado. A partial exception might be the sculpture of Christopher Columbus (1860), donated by the Italian community, which included an indigenous woman, a Carib. Nevertheless, the 'presence' of the pre-Hispanic past – as in Mexico – was permanent whether it be through the multiple archeological discoveries (abundant in the valley of Lima) or through their descendants (the indigenous population).[37]

It was only toward the second decade of the twentieth century that references to the pre-Hispanic past became evident in the urban context. Significantly, these were linked to the high-spirited construction period, the *Oncenio* of Leguía, which reached its peak during the Independence celebrations (1921, 1924).[38] The monument dedicated to Manco Capac (1926), donated by the Japanese community and which would occupy centre stage in the main La Victoria square, is worth mentioning. A piece of greater importance was the Parque de la Reserva (1929), designed by the Peruvian engineer Alberto Jochamowitz, in collaboration with Sahut. Located to the immediate south of Parque de la Exposición, this unusual urban project attempted to give Lima an intra-urban green space and was clearly inspired by similar examples in Europe. Besides its typically Western elements (the loggia, pergola and fountain), this space also incorporated vernacular innovations: indigenous scenes in relief, individual sculptures of indigenous people, a Fuente Incaica (Inca fountain) and an ornamental *Huaca*.[39] The latter particularly stood out as its form and ornaments made up a small pre-Hispanic structure. It is not by chance that this pioneering experience in plastic arts was in the hands of the renowned painter of indigenous motifs, José Sabogal, who was linked to the group of intellectuals concerned with the 'national problem'.[40]

At the same time, the Museo de Arqueología (Archaeological Museum) (1924), the first and only public building which was radically pre-Hispanic within the city landscape in Lima, was built on the Alfonso Ugarte Avenue.

It was located a few metres from the Plaza 2 de Mayo and was financed by the magnate Víctor Larco, referred to earlier. There was a contest for the construction of this museum which was won by Malachowsky's project, whose façade with Inca ornaments was completed by unusual pre-Inca elements (a pair of Tiahuanaco monoliths made of concrete).[41]

National identity as a cultural synthesis was even seen in the large-scale urban projects like Plaza Perú (second half of the 1930s), based on the proposal made by the Polish architect Bruno Paprocki. This levelled area would connect the eastern side of the Palacio de Gobierno and the façade of the Congress building following the demolition of the blocks between them. Each one of the four sections would bear the names of historic periods (the Inca empire, Viceroyalty, Independence, Republic) and would include groups of sculpture related to each of the departments which made up the country.[42]

The works mentioned above were concrete reflections of an instability that ran through the city and whose architectural corollaries were the so-called neo-colonial and specifically neo-Peruvian styles. In both cases, they were stylistic synthesis but with radically different nuances: the first emphasized the recovery of the colonial Spanish element while the second attempted to bring back the indigenous element (pre-Hispanic and colonial) as the basis for national identity. Of significant importance in the creation of a neo-Peruvian movement was a Spanish sculptor and architect: Manuel Piqueras Cotolí (1886–1937). In his work on the façade of the *Escuela de Bellas Artes* (Fine Arts School) (1919) and a salon of the Palacio de Gobierno (1919), he experimented with indigenous decoration on European, Creole and Spanish forms. However, his search went further as he attempted to go beyond the mere decoration. Piqueras would later identify a '*ritmo escalonado*' (rhythm in steps) which he considered to be characteristic of Andean plastic art and would incorporate it into his most outstanding creation: the Peruvian pavilion for the *Exposición Ibero-Americana* (Latin American Exhibition) of Seville (1929). He supported his choice by pointing out that 'the Nation should appear before others . . . with something of its own, of its very own, which would stand it apart from the others, which would assert its artistic personality'.[43]

Coordinates of the New City Planning: Between Hovels and Slums

While the neo-Peruvian movement was being abandoned, the neo-colonial was acquiring official recognition. Adopting this style made its use compulsory in the construction of buildings in the centre of Lima and it was also seen in some homes on the elegant outskirts.[44] The areas surrounding the new Plaza San Martín underwent a neo-colonial regularisation (1925). Moreover, the buildings which surrounded the most representative square in the city – the Plaza Mayor – were subject to a conmpositional experiment in this respect, which ended in 1944.

A paradoxical situation arose: while this 'national' style (neo-colonial) was invented and extended officially, the traditional domestic forms of construction which were unique to the architecture in Lima, were in crisis. Although the construction periods of the past had been characterized by the introduction of new trends, the situation had now deteriorated. The trademark of the artisan workmanship found in the detailing, disposition and ornament of buildings, form and ornaments which had served as a foundation of Peruvian architecture, began to crumble. An eyewitness critically defined the elements of this transitional period:

'Tradition' does not mean for me Arequipa-like portals, ornaments from Tiahuanaco and conic-shaped adobe cross sections. I understand tradition to mean bright and colourful streets, plenty of open spaces and fields of crops; the tradition of interior gardens and flat façades; illumination from above, flat roofs, low constructions and specially chosen materials, worked with refinement.[45]

This style of construction which coordinated the specific work with its context – a sort of micro-plan – was weakened by the proliferation of new materials and techniques. To evaluate this crisis, George Kubler referred to three points: the replacement of adobes by bricks, the new use of windows and the relationship between the set and space. These details showed the way the traditional, hand-crafted and harmonious way of conceiving construction would disappear while elements were superimposed in a disorderly fashion in the name of a pretended functionality.[46]

To this crisis, which could be thought of as qualitative, another with a wider scope would be added and which would make the first seem like mere detail. From the 1920s, immigration to Lima from the rest of the country became more and more intense: the centre of the city could no longer act as the reception area for those arriving from the countryside and the little working-class housing that existed could no longer meet the increasing demands for dwellings. Soon, the empty spaces of little value, on the outskirts or near to the city, began to be used for urbanization or rather adapted, in a primitive fashion, for housing. It is from this period that the typical phenomenon found in the metropolitan cities of Third World countries arose, and was known in Lima as the *barriadas* (shanty towns), examples of which are Armatambo (1924), Puerto Nuevo (1928) and Mendocita (1931) among others. In the face of the development of these poverty-stricken townships, which would mark the future of the city, all previous architectural display and splendour began to fade.[47]

After the earthquake of 1940, the situation was so grave – due in part to the destruction as well as to the number of destitute – that the new urban planning officials like the architect Emilio Harth-Terré, had to give in to this popular innovation, using it as a solution for this emergency.[48] Urban planning had to give way to migratory impetus. Anxiety over the *barriadas* seemed to surpass the fear of the *callejones*. If previously one of the most important points had been the clearing of the centre, now the growing number of slum areas on the outskirts was a priority. Construction was massive, self-conducted and precarious in nature and this pushed any official construction plan out of the way. New borders appeared between the great city, which had been formally erected, and these housing manifestations. An official reply would be the creation of massive residential blocks using new urban planning models, the theme of another chapter in history.

Epilogue

The distinction between the different periods of construction (Bourbon, *Guano*, Aristocratic Republic, Leguía's *Oncenio*) allows the urban development of Lima to be separated into sections. Although each one could have been the result of diverse urban planning projects, *a posteriori* their patterns can be specifically characterized. It was not only the construction of a number of buildings but rather their coordination according to a set pattern. In terms of space and style, the Bourbons broke the traditional colonial pattern and placed it on the threshold of urban modernity. The peak of the *Guano* period, in the early part of the Republican era, allowed many of the hopes of the previous period to become concrete, such as the concentration of activities and the move toward the outskirts, with an architecture which placed emphasis on public buildings. By sharing the same urban fabric, different regimes at different times carried out projects in the same areas, creating in effect a series of palimpsests and evincing the strategic importance of those areas. This occurred, for example, with the area around Plaza 2 de Mayo, which was worked on during the four construction periods discussed.

The case of the plaza was not unique as other spaces were constantly reworked. It is precisely this reworking of the same spaces which shows that there was an agreement with regard to objectives. A point in question occurred towards the end of the *Guano* period when the central themes of the following cycles – Aristocratic Republic and Leguía's *Oncenio* – were proposed: the clearing of the intramural space and the two planning strategies associated with this: the creation of great avenues and the construction of popular housing. Significantly, the pioneering works on both fronts were in the hands of the same businessman, Henry Meiggs. The later construction periods faced a similar challenge but on a larger scale both demographically and spatially. The former limits in Lima began to disappear with a marked difference emerging between the old intramural space and the outskirts. The new urban system led to the reutilization of the existing structure. Although the centre maintained its primary function and reinforced its symbolic value, other important places emerged. From the end of the nineteenth century, this alternative role was taken over by the southern peripheral area (the Palacio de la Exposición and its surroundings). Witnesses predicted, with some degree of certainty, that the immediate future would be found in this area, especially 'around the cardinal points of the Bolognesi Circle' (figure 7.8).[49]

The appropriation of foreign models, a characteristic of a colonial and neo-colonial society such as Peru's, had some features which should be stressed. The adoption of the neo-classical norms from the French during the Bourbon period would be the start of a long relationship. The political separation from Spain would allow a greater flow of foreign schools and professionals. During the *Guano* period, as a result of migration, there would be a marked presence of a number of specialists, commercial intermediaries, and even material from Italy. On a second level, the French presence would increase as the Parisian model acquired a greater prestige especially from the Haussmannic experiment. The local adoption of this model would be especially important during the decade of the 1870s, coinciding with the layout of the basic lines for the new city, epitomized in the famous plan of Sada. Summarizing this tendency, an engineer of the time stated that Lima had to be made into 'the Paris of the Hispanic American Republics'.[50]

The following two construction periods (Aristocratic Republic and Leguía's *Oncenio*) reconfirmed the French influence, although during the second the North American impe-

Figure 7.8 Plaza Bolognesi, 1906. (*Source*: *Memoria de la Municipalidad de Lima*, 1906)

rialist presence was felt through important undertakings. However, the prestige of the French architectural school explains its paradoxical permanence even when politically France was relegated to the background. The style adopted for the great avenues confirms this inertia. At the beginning of the twentieth century an unforeseen situation would occur. In occupying a markedly backward position in Latin America, Lima would adopt intermediate continental models such as those of Buenos Aires or Santiago de Chile. Intermediate, as they served as an example for the implementation of projects based on the European experience, as in the case of the great avenues. To encourage the implementation of the 28 de Julio Avenue project, the mayor, Federico Elguera, would refer to the experiences carried out in these capitals.[51]

Although reference can be found to Europe's twentieth-century architectural schools among the Peruvian specialists of the time, the former did not leave any mark. Until World War II, the urban structure continued to be dominated by a combination of the traditional colonial fabric and some great cross streets from Haussmannic association lineage. For diverse reasons, Lima was not the centre of attraction for the spokesmen of this new architecture who visited and carried out projects in other cities of Latin America.[52] On the other hand, the national trend which had received most exposure (the neo-colonial), had a short life span. In 1947, a group of local architects, along with other specialists, published a renowned manifesto in which they harshly condemned the 'neo-colonial' and 'neo-Peruvian' styles, referring to them as 'falsification and copies of the past', and calling on their colleagues to follow the steps of the new European masters.[53]

NOTES

1. In colonial Lima, as well as during a great deal of the Republican period (nineteenth century), social status was not defined by the residential area, but by the address. There was a social heterogeneity within the city that combined two tendencies: prices were lower the further a property was from the Plaza Mayor. However, a luxurious house could be found next to the poorest one; in fact, some popular residences were located near the centre. This situation at the beginning

of the twentieth century is confirmed by Burga, M. and Flores Galindo, A. (1987) *Apogeo y crisis de la República Aristocrática*. Lima: Rikchay Perú, p. 13; Parker, D. (1998) Civilizing the city of kings: hygiene and housing in Lima, Peru, in Pineo, R. and Baer, J. (eds.) *Cities of Hope. People, Protests, and Progress in Urbanizing Latin America, 1870–1930*. Boulder: Westview Press, pp.166–167.

2. Diez-Canseco, J. (1934) *Duque*. Santiago de Chile: Ercilla. More about *Duque* and its relation with the city (as a literary phenomena), is found in the illustrative essays of Ortega, J. (1986) *Cultura y modernización en la Lima del 900*. Lima: CEDEP and Elmore, P. (1993) *Los muros invisibles. Lima y la modernidad en la novela del siglo XX*. Lima: Mosca Azul, Caballo Rojo.

3. For references to this trait of the urban continental history see Gutiérrez, R. (1983) *Arquitectura y urbanismo en Iberoamérica*. Madrid: Cátedra, p. 479; Scobie, J. (1984) The growth of Latin American cities, 1870–1930, in Bethell L. (ed.) *The Cambridge History of Latin America*. Cambridge: Cambridge University Press, Vol. IV, pp. 256–258, which refer to similar situations in Buenos Aires, Rio de Janeiro, Quito, Mexico, Santiago and São Paulo.

4. J. Basadre highlights the prestige that the traditional zone maintained among wealthy families, pointing out the case of the millionaire Eulogio Fernadini, who decided to build his mansion in the very centre of the city, during the second decade of the new century. See Basadre, J. (1983) *Historia de la República del Perú*. Lima: Universitaria, Vol. IX, 7th ed., pp.375–378

5. Diez-Canseco, *op. cit.*, p. 28.

6. It is symptomatic in the distance between *Duque* and *Julia, o escenas de la vida de Lima* (1861) by Luis Benjamín Cisneros. In this early novel of Lima, the scarce allusions to urban spaces are brief. Descriptions or perceptions of the city are almost absent; it all happens in the houses or when passing by them. And to show this fact clearly, maybe to avoid urban descriptions, the main characters live in nearby streets.

7. Besides the general work of Romero, J. (1976) *Latinoamérica, las ciudades y las ideas*. Buenos Aires: Siglo XXI; Rama, A.(1985) *A cidade das letras*. São Paulo: Brasiliense; Gutiérrez, *op. cit.*; methodological observations are considered, drawn from Latin American specific comparisons. When dealing with Belo Horizonte, Agnoti Salgueiro, H. (1995) Revisando Haussmann. Os limites da comparação. A cidade, a arquitetura e os espaços verdes (o caso de Belo Horizonte). *Revista U.S.P.*, 26, pp. 195–205, has emphasized the necessity

of setting the distances the way they did in Paris and identifying elements (like avenues) in order to compare. In the case of Caracas, Almandoz, A. (1997) *Urbanismo europeo en Caracas (1870–1940)*. Caracas: Fundarte, Equinoccio, Ediciones de la Universidad Simón Bolívar, pp. 25–26, shows the need of for putting in context the urban ideas in the midst of cultural importations, and therefore not reducing the search to 'impossible monuments or avenues'. In an analogous way, for the case of Lima, the importance of considering edifications in close relation with the projects has been stressed by Ramón, G. (1999) *La muralla y los callejones. Intervención urbana y proyecto político en Lima durante la segunda mitad del siglo XIX*. Lima: Promperú-Sidea. The pioneer article written by Hardoy, J. (1987) Teorías y prácticas urbanísticas en Europa entre 1850 y 1930. Su traslado a América Latina. *Revista de Indias*, 47(179), pp.187–224, strictly speaking the only specific approximation to the subject of this book from a continental perspective, includes very little information about the 'rear of the process': the capitals of the Pacific, especially the Andean republics.

8. Bromley J. and Barbagelata J. (1945) *Evolución urbana de la ciudad de Lima*. Lima: Concejo Provincial de Lima, p. 96.

9. On Bourbon constructions in Lima, see Ramon G. (1999) Urbe y orden. Evidencias del reformismo borbónico en el tejido limeño, in O'Phelan, S. (ed.) *El Perú en el siglo XVIII. La era borbónica*. Lima: Instituto Riva Agüero, pp.295–324. And on the emergence of the hygiene policies, see Clement, J. (1983) El nacimiento de la higiene urbana en la América española del siglo XVII. *Revista de Indias*, 23(171), pp. 77–95.

10. The English functionary, McGregor, J., Bosquejo general del Perú (1847), in Bonilla H. (1987) (ed.) *Informes de los cónsules británicos*. Lima: I.E.P./F.L.B.I.P., Vol I., pp. 111–172, p. 163, summarized the situation in Lima: 'Now everything gives the impression of poverty and decline, a shameful change from its rich past. This appearance could be seen not only in the city but also among the citizens. Entire families had been swept away and the ancient servants, or foreigners, had become owners of their houses and properties'.

11. Ruiz, A. (1994) *Psiquiatras y locos. Entre la modernización contra los Andes y el nuevo proyecto de modernidad. Perú: 1850–1930*. Lima: Instituto Pasado y Presente.

12. This list – necessarily incomplete – has been made on the basis of the information from Bromley and

Barbagelata, *op. cit.*; García Bryce, La arquitectura en el virreinato y la república, *loc. cit.* The dates are from inaugurations, therefore, in some cases – specifically in the case of avenues – one must assume that they were finished long after that date.

13. Migration to Peru was less important than that experienced on the Atlantic shores of Latin America. Nevertheless it was significant in the leading groups. In 1896, foreigners controlled 103 out of the 113 importing companies in Lima, 161 of the 196 commercial houses and 74 out of the 92 industries. Ten per cent of the population living in Lima was European and half of that was Italian, after Morse, R (1973) La Lima de Joaquín Capelo: un arquetipo latinoamericano, in Capelo, J. *Lima en 1900.* Lima: I.E.P., pp. 9–45. The statue of Simón Bolívar was sculpted by Adán Tandolini, the Manrique Hospice by M. Trefogli, the Palacio de la Exposición by Antonio Leonardi and the Hospital Dos de Mayo by Mateo Graziani and Miguel Trefogli. On the Italian presence, see Velarde, H. (1978) *Arquitectura peruana.* Lima: Editorial Studium, 3rd ed., p. 409.

14. Bromley and Barbagelata, *op. cit.*, pp. 89–90; García Bryce, J. (1980) La arquitectura en el virreinato y la república, in *Historia del Perú (Procesos e instituciones).* Lima-Barcelona: Editorial Juan Mejía Baca, Vol. IX, pp. 102–103; López Soria, J. (1999) *Historia de la Universidad Nacional de Ingeniería,* Vol I. *Los años fundacionales (1876-1909).* Lima: U.N.I., introduction (without pages in the original) and first chapter.

15. García Bryce, J. (1967) Arquitectura en Lima 1800-1900. *Amaru,* 3, pp. 51–52.

16. Besides a series of buildings (Penitenciaria, Palacio de la Exposición, Hospital 2 de Mayo, Escuela de Artes y Oficios, among others) the first project of land subdivision and development of the Republic, which remained unfinished, was located to the south (1860).

17. In Bresson, A. (1874) Las alamedas. Estudio sobre los trabajos de embellecimiento y de salubridad de Lima. *La Patria,* April 28, without page numbers. Information from Stewart, W. (1946) *Henry Meiggs. Yankee Pizarro.* Durham: Duke University Press, pp. 225–227, is included.

18. On this relationship, compare the plan of Sada (1872) with the one of the reconstruction of Paris (1873). See Benevolo, L. (1995) *A cidade na história da Europa.* Lisboa: Presença pp. 190–191.

19. It is necessary to point out the remarkable – and unexplored – formal correspondence between Sada's plan and Ildefonso Cerdá's project for the expansion of Barcelona (1858) (see Frampton, K. (1980) *Modern Architecture. A Critical History.* London: Thames and Hudson, p. 25) and the plan of Ciudad de La Plata in 1882 (see Gutiérrez, *op. cit.*, p. 508).

20. Bromley and Barbagelata, *op. cit.*, p. 86–87, 88–89.

21. Wiener, Ch. (1880) *Pérou et Bolivie.* Paris: Hachette, p. 14.

22. On Besson, see Macera, P. (1976) *La imagen francesa del Perú (siglos XVI-XIX).* Lima: I.N.C., p. 141; Émile Carrey (1875) *Le Pérou. Tableau descriptif, historique et analitique des êtres et des choses de ce pays.* Paris: Garnier Frères, Librairies-éditeurs, p. 362.

23. Burga and Flores Galindo, *op. cit.*, and Thorp, R. and Bertram, G. (1985) *Perú: 1890–1977. Crecimiento y política en una economía abierta.* Lima: Mosca Azul, p. 181.

24. Ramón, *op. cit.*, pp. 137–138.

25. All this statistical information is from Bromley and Barbagelata, *op. cit.*, pp. 100, 92, 100, 101, respectively.

26. Ramón, *La muralla y los callejones, loc. cit.*, pp. 144–183.

27. Ruiz, M. (1993) Las casas para obreros de Rafael Marquina. *Huaca,* 3, pp. 33–41.

28. Brescia, R. (1968) Obras públicas del siglo XIX en Lima. Unpublished bachelor thesis, Facultad de Arquitectura, Universidad Nacional de Ingeniería, Lima.

29. Information about the monument of 2 de Mayo is to be found in Majluf, N. (1994) *Escultura y espacio público (Lima 1850–1879).* Lima: I.E.P., pp. 14–16.

30. On the project of the residences surrounding the square, see the anonymous article (1921) Los bellos proyectos que tenía don Victor Larco Herrera to Lima's ornamentation, *Mundial,* 80 (November 25), without pages in the original.

31. Dávalos y Lissón, P. (1908) *Lima en 1907.* Lima: Gil, pp. 29, 61.

32. Robert led the building of the Palacio Legislativo and the Cripta de los Héroes; among other projects, Sahut did the Salón dorado (Golden Salon) of the Palacio de Gobierno (Government Palace), the Teatro Colón (Colón Theatre) as well as other projects; and Malachowsky built the Club Nacional (National Club), the façade of the Palacio Arzobispal (Archbishop's Palace), the Banco Italiano (Italian Bank), the Palacio de Gobierno, among others.

33. In relation to this subject, from a continental perspective, see Gutiérrez, *op. cit.*, pp. 550–567. There is not enough secondary information to evaluate of neo-

colonial and neo-Peruvian. In this sense, the reference still is García Bryce, La arquitectura en el virreinato y la republica, *loc. cit.* It is necessary to confront the information and arguments from Salazar, S. (1974*) Lima la horrible.* Lima: Peisa, pp. 95–106; Velarde, H. (1946) *Arquitectura peruana.* México: Fondo de Cultura Económica and *op. cit.* An article dedicated specially to this subject is the one by Rodríguez, L. (1980) El estilo neocolonial en la arquitectura peruana, in Matos R. (ed.) *III Congreso Peruano. El hombre y la cultura andina.* Lima: Lasontay, pp.879–892, that unfortunately did not have further development.

34. In relation to the 'national problem', see the chapters of Burga and Flores Galindo, *op.cit.*, III.2, III.3.

35. Without being the main topic, *Amauta*, the emblematic magazine led by Mariátegui, included some photos of Peruvian buildings with some comments. When presenting the façade of a house in Arequipa, it stated: 'The Indian technique of the ornamentation, robust and naive, integrates naturally with the Spanish structure. The *mestizaje* (mixture of races) was achieved'. (1928) XII, p. 10. As a comment that mirrors a tendency, beside the photography of a church it was pointed out: 'This example was completely made of *mestiza* Peruvian architecture. *Even in the whole there is an indigenous influence'.* (1928), XII, p. 9 (author's emphasis).

36. Information on this subject can be found in Ramón, *La muralla y los callejones, loc. cit.*, pp. 92–100.

37. A clue to the progressively imperative character of this presence was the exhibition of the archaeological material at the Exposición Nacional (1872). See Middendorf, E. (1973). *El Perú.* Lima: U.N.M.S.M., Vol. I, p. 443.

38. See Table number 1, especially between 1921 and 1924. Frequency of monuments and buildings is related to the official interest in celebrations, and to the presents given by many foreign colonies. In 1921 a century of the formal Declaration of Independence was celebrated, and in 1924, the century of the Ayacucho Battle.

39. *Huaca*, quechua word to name – in general – any archeological pre-Hispanic site.

40. On this park, see the personal testimony of Jochamowitz, A. (1931) *Mi vida profesional.* Lima: Torres Aguirre. Information about the inauguration in

(1929) *Mundial*, 453 (February 22), without pages in the original. On Sabogal, there is an illustrative article by Mariátegui, J. C. (1928, 1980) La obra de José Sabogal. *El artista y la época*, pp. 90–93.

41. See the anonymous article Los bellos proyectos que tenía . . ., *loc cit.* The alternative design by Sahut, who also participated, can be seen in Morales, C. (1940) Claudio Sahut y su obra. *Arquitecto Peruano*, 37 (August) without pages in the original.

42. (1938) *Arquitecto Peruano*, 14 (September 15), without pages in the original.

43. Piqueras, M. (1930, 1993) Las bellas artes y arquitectura peruanas. *Huaca,* 3, pp. 61–62. See Basadre, *op. cit.,* p. 344, for more information on the pavilion. As a coincidence, at the IV Congreso Panamericano de Arquitectos held in Brazil, they recommended that 'each nation tried to live its national architectural tradition'. Gutiérrez, *op. cit.,* p.565.

44. García Bryce, La arquitectura en el virreinato y la república, *loc. cit.*, p. 47.

45. Kubler, G. (1948) Sobre arquitectura actual en Lima. *Las Moradas,* II (6), pp.263–269.

46. *Ibid.*, pp. 264, 269.

47. A synthesis on this subject is Driant, J.C. (1991) *Las barriadas de Lima. Historia e interpretación.* Lima: IFEA/DESCO.

48. This was proposed by the directors of the Junta Urbana (Urban Board) of Lima and Callao, the engineer Roque Vargas Prada and the architect Emilio Harth-Terré in a newspaper article (*La Prensa*, 2 June 1940). Quoted by Crupi, T. (Ms) Nation Divided, City Divided: Urbanism and its Relation to the State 1920–1940. Unpublished manuscript, p. 25.

49. Dávalos y Lissón, *op. cit.,* p. 73.

50. Bresson, *op. cit.,* no pages in the original.

51. (1906) *Memoria de la Municipalidad de Lima*, VII-IX. Lima: Gil.

52. On the impact and presence of Le Corbusier, members of the CIAM and their followers in Latin America, see Hardoy, *op. cit.,* pp. 212–215.

53. On the declaration of the 'Agrupación Espacio', see García Bryce, La arquitectura en el virreinato y la república, *loc. cit.* p. 154; Rodríguez, El estilo neocolonial . . ., *loc. cit.*, pp. 884–885.

Havana, from Tacón to Forestier

Roberto Segre

To Sergio Baroni in memoriam
(Mantua 1930, Havana 2001)

The 'Modern' Colony of the Nineteenth Century

Is there a significant representation of the 'classical' Havana which is different from the preceding colonial and later modern one? If we were to take a ride through the city today, apart from the architectural value of the work carried out until the eighteenth century with its corresponding urban spaces and the accelerated modernization which began to take place from the 1940s with the layout of fast roadways, new residential areas and the collection of 'modern' buildings from the 1950s and later the 'revolutionary' period, the strongest and most pervading image that the visitor has, is still that of the academic surroundings. The importance of the castles, the beauty of the parks and colonial monuments, not even the elaborate layout of the highways and residential areas are questioned. But one cannot easily forget the impact produced by the monumentality, the elegance, the quality of the design of the green spaces and the urban furnishings of Parque Central (Central Park) and Parque de la Fraternidad (Fraternity Park) with the surrounding buildings – Capitolio (Capitol

building), the Centros Gallego and Asturiano (Asturian and Galician Centres), (figure 8.1) the García Lorca Theatre, the Inglaterra and Plaza Hotels or the unforgettable trip through Paseo del Prado (Prado Promenade), the most beautiful urban 'salon' in the city, and then the experience of the residential area of Vedado, with its mansions and majestic avenues framed by royal palms. It is from this that one can see the importance of the classical cycle which began with the neo-classical expansion in the avenues and arcades in the nineteenth century, and finished with Forestier's Master Plan at the end of the 1920s. The landscape, the cultural, symbolic, urban and architectural values created in this stage came together to define the 'identity' of Havana, the images of space and form whose expression and significance have not been surpassed even to this day.[1]

The nineteenth century, full of violent political and social conflict – which ended in the war of 1895 between peninsular Spaniards and the Cubans – while characterized by complex economic contradictions and dissimilar

Figure 8.1 Parque Central, Havana. In the foreground, Paul Belau's Centro Gallego (1915). In the background, Manuel del Busto's Centro Asturiano (1927). Photo: Roberto Segre. (*Source*: Archivo Roberto Segre)

cultural influences, was a period of splendour in Havana.[2] The city was alive, in spite of the antagonism and radical tensions, in the early stages of modernity. At this time, the basic productive structures of the Cuban economy were formed, and survived to the present day in the *'contrapunteo'* (counterpoint) between tobacco and sugar.[3] Both establish a double antithesis: the first is essentially urban, controlled by the Spanish financial and commercial system; the second is rural, related to the push for expansion by the Creole landowners. Thick with the aroma of tobacco and honey, the city consolidated itself through the antithesis which arose from these two dynamic and radically

changing forces. In spite of the entry of almost a million slaves between the eighteenth and nineteenth centuries,[4] the steam engine, introduced in Cuba in 1796,[5] was the main technological factor that accelerated production and demographic changes. It was accepted without any prejudice and was the first 'Spanish' railroad (1837) – prior to that of Peninsular Spain – and connected Havana to the sugar cane fields in the interior of the island, up to Matanzas.[6]

Although the military action of the three Wars of Independence, fought between 1868 and 1895, took place mainly in the interior of the country,[7] the divergences between the Spaniards and the Creoles found its epicentre in the capital. The formation of a local 'sugar aristocracy' was evident from the ideas of the rich, highly intellectual elite, the embryo of the political and cultural Cuban personality created and formed by lucid thinkers, among whom were Domingo del Monte, Francisco de Arango y Parreño, Presbítero Félix Varela, José de la Luz y Caballero, Gaspar Cisneros Betancourt and others.[8] Attracted by the growing prosperity of the island, more than 100,000 Peninsular Spaniards arrived in Cuba between 1760 and 1860 in search of work. Then, between 1864 and 1894, in spite of the successive wars, another 400,000 arrived. There was also a group of wealthy individuals who left the continent after the Battle of Ayacucho (1824) – the last in Latin America to be fought by Spain against Simon Bolívar's army – and who settled mainly in Havana. The social composition of the previous centuries, dominated by people from Andalucía, Extremadura and Castilla, was now complemented by the new immigrants from Galicia, Asturias and the Canary Islands.[9]

The demographic growth of the city – 80,000 at the beginning of the century; 200,000 in 1861 and 250,000 in 1898[10] –

brought about the high density of buildings within the limits of the primitive colonial *'lenteja'* (lentil), while there was a frenzy for construction in the outlying districts, beyond the useless city walls.[11] Although the stone ring represented a radical interruption between the two urban areas, the Royal Ordinances of 1819 regulated the plan for the straightening and *ensanche* (widening) of the new residential areas carried out by the engineer Antonio María de La Torre.[12] Within this space, the seed of the 'modern' Havana, with its tropical character, was sown – it was the neo-classical 'city of columns' described by Alejo Carpentier[13] (figure 8.2), extending from the centre to the immediate outskirts with shady roadways and arcaded avenues – in a series of public and private initiatives: (*a*) the urban reforms carried out by Captain General Miguel Tacón; (*b*) the demolition of the *Murallas* (city walls) and the emergence of the residential area with the same name; (*c*) the presence of tobacco factories in the central area; (*d*) the roads, technical infrastructure and new social functions; (*e*) the distant residential areas of the wealthy classes in El Cerro and El Vedado.

Figure 8.2 Cienfuegos Street, El Cerro, Havana. Neo-classical galleries in front of dwellings, late nineteenth century, beginning of the twentieth. Photo: Roberto Segre. (*Source*: Archivo Roberto Segre)

Tacón's Urban Changes

While the majority of Latin American capitals were stuck in time and space until the end of the nineteenth century – with the exception of Mexico City, vibrant under the brief stay of Emperor Maximilian – in Havana, multiple and dissimilar influences combined in the paradoxical category of 'Creole Hispanic'. In urban terms, this conjunction meant that the initiative of the Peninsular Governors, who were repressive and autonomous with regard to the community in most aspects of colonial life – the 'absolute power' of the Crown's emissary[14] – as well as foreign-oriented interests of the rich shopkeepers and businessmen, did not come into conflict with the building projects of the Creole landowners. At the same time, urban and technological innovations from the United States were assimilated and put into practice.

During his period in office (1834–1838), the Captain General Miguel Tacón, inspired by information received from Spanish diplomats in Washington, the most developed city at that time, provided Havana with a road system, technical infrastructure and the services of a modern city. The layout of two perpendicular arteries meeting at Campo de Marte – San Luis Gonzaga Road and Tacón or Carlos III Avenue, joining Isabel II and Prado Avenues – formed the regular design which would influence later urban growth outside the city walls. Despite the construction of numerous public buildings which accompanied this initiative – the Tacón Theatre, the markets, fishmongers and slaughter house, and the embellishment of some older buildings and components of street furntiture – the local population still felt itself controlled by the very authoritarian character of the government. The arteries joined the new jail – ostensibly situated in the entrance to the bay, at the end of the Paseo del Prado, and the biggest building in the city in terms of volume – the Campo de Marte (Military field), the Captain General's summer house – situated in the Quinta de los Molinos (Manor Mill House) – and the Prince's castle. In other words, the promenades and recreation areas of Havana's aristocracy on the tree-lined avenues were protected or watched over by the menacing signs of power.

The architectural staging of political antagonisms meant that within small areas there was a battle between different symbolisms. In Plaza de Armas (Military Square), the sombre and monumental palace of the Captain General faced the light neo-classical temple built by the Bishop de Espada y Landa (1828) in hypothetical homage to Fernando VII, where the

design clearly refers to the Communal Rights monument in Guernica.[15] In the extension of the tree-lined Paseo de Extramuros (Promenade Outside the Walls) – the Paseo de Isabel II (Queen Isabel II Promenade) – Tacón placed the Los Leones fountain, reaffirming Spanish power on the island; while the Quarter Master General, Claudio Martínez de Pinillos, Count of Villanueva, having contact with the Creole landowners, installed the Indian or Noble Havana fountain (1837), a clear indication of the city's cultural roots.[16] The most luxurious neo-classical palace in the city was constructed in the Campo de Marte: the landowner Domingo Aldama, who would support the freedom movement and later be forced into exile in the United States, built his residence there in 1844, designed by the engineer Manuel Carrerá. Finally, the wealthy classes refused to support Tacón's desire that they build their luxury and monumental mansions along the new parkway. Paseo Militar (Military Promenade), also called Paseo de Tacón (Tacón's Promenade), remained undeveloped until the end of the century; only the Reina Road was partially occupied, and the dream of a new and luxurious boulevard for Havana was thus abandoned. The residential initiative undertaken by Conde de Pozos Dulces and Don José Domingo Trigo, owners of farms which had been converted into the residential areas of Vedado and Carmelo, was the Creole sector's alternative in the creation of the future settlements for the rich Cuban bourgeoisie.[17]

The City Walls Neighbourhood: First Monumental Layout

The Plano Pintoresco de La Habana (Picturesque Plan of Havana) (1849), drawn by the engineer José María de La Torre (fig-

ure 8.3), shows a city where the areas beyond the city walls are greater than the original *lenteja* within the walls which had been laid

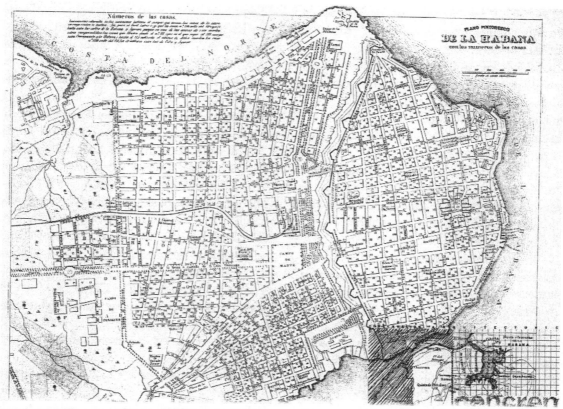

Figure 8.3 Picturesque Plan of Havana, by José María de la Torre, 1849. Reproduction by CENCREM. (*Source*: Archivo Roberto Segre)

out three hundred years ago.[18] Although the roads which would define the shape of the new urban development, parallel to Prado, Galiano, Belascoaín and Infanta Streets, had already been laid out, drawn up by Mariano Carrillo de Albornoz,[19] urban monuments predominate over the general ensemble, as seen in the vignette drawn around the plan. A decade later, under the population pressures in the area – 122,730 inhabitants living outside the city walls compared to 46,445 in its interior[20] – accelerated changes began which would shape the nature and character of the 'modern' Havana. Two important events are the Construction Ordinances of 1862, drawn up

by the military engineer Antonio Mantilla and Vidal D'Ors,[21] followed by the demolition of the city walls in 1863 and the start of the 'Reparto' (Neighbourhood) in 1865, which was the idea of the military engineers, Juan Bautista Orduña and Manuel Portilla y Portilla.[22]

The 476 articles of the First Ordinances, which were in force until well into the nineteenth century, led to the creation of the principles of urban design which established hierarchies and categories of roads, urban areas and urban functions, and which were certainly influenced by the norms and regulations of Cerdá's *Ensanche* of Barcelona and Carlos María Castro's Master Plan of Madrid.

With these, the arcade was established as a distinguishing feature of parks, roads and avenues, thereby imposing the continuity of the blocks and a protective and pleasant environment for pedestrians along the main roadways. The 'Reparto de las Murallas' (Walls neighbourhood) – an area of 26 hectares, 1700 metres long and defined as the 'ring' of Havana[23] – paved the way for the diversity of social functions, which would be identified with the highly animated urban life of Havana and was the key to linking the scale of the colonial city and the new proportions demanded by modern architecture. The high columns of the arcades along the streets – reminiscent of Galicia and Asturias – gave this urban space an air which harked back to the city's traditional European heritage.

It is surprising to note the dynamics of construction and the developments in Havana in the three decades between the beginning of the First War of Liberation (1868) and the end of Spanish rule (1898). This was accelerated by the North American intervention in the fight by the Cuban patriots. In fact, there was no optimistic outlook to justify the construction of luxurious palaces, highly decorated theatres, modern hotels at a time of social and political tension, whereas the economic relationship between local landowners and United States businesses began to increase.

Meanwhile, Spanish importers and businessmen living in the capital continued to hold sway as they controlled 70 per cent of the trade in the country.[24]

Apart from the resources available, the amount of construction carried out during this period, was also due to the presence of master builders and quality surveyors of either Catalan or local origin, who had studied in the new *Escuela Profesional* (Professional School) (1856).[25] Another factor which shows the ambiguity of the relationship between the Spaniards and the Creoles is their coming together in this confined area of the city. If the central power lay in the area of the Plaza de Armas and the members of the 'sugar aristocracy' moved their residences to Cerro and then to Vedado, the Murallas neighbourhood (eighteen blocks long and four wide) marked the preferred venue for political, economic and cultural confrontations. At the same time, tobacco factories – the productive mainstay of the city – were also found in the same area. Galicians, Asturians, Catalans, Creoles, North Americans, blacks, mulattoes, businessmen, financiers, speculators, landed gentry, landowners, artists, incipient tourists from the North and humble workers from the tobacco factories, crossed paths daily in a clear expression of the Caribbean environmental 'syncretism' which was forged in Havana.

The New Functions of Centrality

The crisis which was approaching was manifest in the lack of new urban development and buildings by the colonial state, which supported such projects providing they brought quick economic benefits – as in the Murallas neighbourhood – but opposed unproductive investments. The high cost of expropriation made it impossible to lay out Serrano Avenue (1862), designed by the architect Saturnino Martínez, and which would have joined Plaza de Armas with tree-lined Isabel II, demolishing all the blocks located between Obispo and O'Reilly Streets. The different interests are seen in the 'ring' project. In the new space, ideal for the location of public buildings (the City Council suggested locating the University, a new Cathedral and the tax offices in an area which was the green heart of the block and followed Cerdá's Master Plan for Barcelona), the majority of the land was sold to private parties, triggering the race in urban speculation.

Some of the main monumental palaces were built there, an example of which was the Aldama residence, looted by Spanish militia of 'volunteers' on verifying his link to the patriotic cause and converted into a tobacco factory; Balboa palace (1871), by the Madrid architect Pedro Tomé, the only example set away from the street, thus interrupting the alignment of the urban design; and the palace of the Marquesa de Villalba (1879), designed by the Cuban Eugenio Rayneri Sorrentino, who had studied in the School of Architecture in Madrid (figure 8.4). It is a unique phenomenon in Latin American urban development that a few metres from these luxurious residencies, there emerged the majestic and classical presence of tobacco factories, built in their interior with metallic structures, and owned by Galicians and Catalans. Pedro Murias's 'La Meridiana', José Gener's 'La Excepción' and Miguel Jané's 'La Majagua' were some of the most important of the 134 factories in existence in 1880.[26] Aristocrats and proletarians did not remain segregated in different areas as can be seen in the proximity of the local popular residential areas, some in the direction of the Arsenal (Jesús María), others in the gaps between the roads and avenues: Monte, Reina, Galiano, Belascoaín, Infanta.[27]

Finally, the Murallas neighbourhood (figure 8.5) brought together the life and noise from the theatres, hotels, business places, regional cultural centres, cafes and restaurants. Here, too, the social and political groups were polarized. According to Emma Álvarez-Tabío, '. . . this would be the first time that Havana would personalize a confrontation, an ideology, strong sentiments and passions which were clearly human and not urban . . .'[28] While the Creole sector met in the 'Acera del Louvre', in the lower regions of the Inglaterra Hotel, the Spaniards met in the Escauriza Room. The shows at the Tacón and de Villanueva Theatres had a content that was clearly critical and led to reprisals from the militia of 'Volunteers', while the Spanish colony attended shows at the Albizu, Payret and Irijoa Theatres and the Jané Circus Theatre, constructed by rich Catalan businessmen. The

Figure 8.4 View of the palaces of the 'Ring', Havana. In the foreground, the palace of the Marquesa de Villalba, by architect Eugenio Rayneri Sorrentino, 1879. Photo: R. Segre. (*Source*: Archivo Roberto Segre)

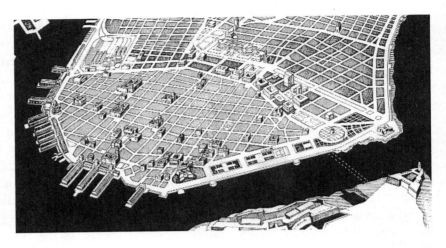

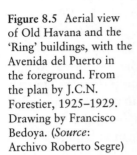

Figure 8.5 Aerial view of Old Havana and the 'Ring' buildings, with the Avenida del Puerto in the foreground. From the plan by J.C.N. Forestier, 1925–1929. Drawing by Francisco Bedoya. (*Source*: Archivo Roberto Segre)

popular genre was being promoted in the Politeama and La Alhambra, closed in 1895. In the same area the first branches of the *Beneficencia Catalana* (Catalan Charity) and the Asturian and Galician centres were set up, along with a commercial centre (1890) which occupied an entire block. This was the initiative of Juan de Zulueta and was later continued by Andrés Gómez Mena and today is known as 'Manzana de Gómez' (Gómez's block) (figure 8.6).

The presence of countless hotels in this area indicates the beginning of North American influence in the city. In the wake of the increase in commercial exchange and the growth of tourism, along the Alameda and in the

blocks of Las Murallas, the Zequeira family constructed the Pasaje Hotel (1876) with a crystal gallery which joined two streets, following the Parisian *passages* (passageways).[29] Nearby, the Roma and Telégrafo Hotels (1880), Plaza and Quinta Avenida (1879), built by the Catalan Bartolomé Junqué were to be found. Before the end of the nineteenth century, there would be twenty-five hotels in the urban area, an expression of a hedonistic cosmopolitanism. The social life along the arcades caused a traveller to remark:

In contrast to Madrid, which slips between the shadows and the half light, Havana is the other side of the coin. Here everything is diaphanous, light, like the atmosphere which surrounds it . . .[30]

Vedado: the First Caribbean 'Garden City'

The residential area of Vedado, the first residential district in Havana designed as an urban unit, was developed at the same time as new ideas were being put into practice by Ildefonso Cerdá in the *Ensanche* of Barcelona. While in Ponce, San Juan de Puerto Rico or in the expansion of Havana Centre as far as Infanta Street, the blocks retained their square, com-

pact nature, in Vedado, the articulation between full and empty, free spaces and buildings, acquired a new dimension which was identified with the open weave conceived of by Cerdá. Both the theories on hygiene and the imminent changes in the transport system, with the appearance of the steam and electric locomotion, established the new rules in sub-

Figure 8.6 'Gómez's block', Parque Central, Havana's Centre. First multifunctional building of the city, including offices and commercial galleries. Designed by architects Pedro Tomé and F. Ramírez Ovando, 1894–1917.
Photo:Roberto Segre.
(*Source*: Archivo Roberto Segre)

urban layouts: tree-lined roadways, empty spaces in the interior of regular blocks which kept the square pattern of the grid away so different from the picturesqueness associated with the sinuosity of the Garden City. In this way, the different options available in residential living, characterized by the proposals made at the end of the century in Europe and the United States – from the meaning of nature in the designs of Frederick Law Olmsted, to the open fabric of the Garden City by Ebenezer Howard, and to the proposals for multifunctional organization in the interior of the habitat put forward by Cerdá[31]– were brought together in Vedado. The appropriate use of urban space to the climatic conditions in the tropics was also found reflected there.

The creation of Vedado as a residential area began in 1858 when the City Council approved the parcelling of the El Carmelo estate. This was made up of 105 blocks along the coast in a direction of the west of the historic city. In 1859, Vedado farm was sold and the large expanse of land which extended from the Almendares river to Infanta Street was incorporated into the project. The design was made in 1860 by the engineer, José Yboleón Bosque, creator of the first 'Garden City in Latin America'.[32] In spite of the undulating urban land, its extension was basically flat, with a slight decline towards the coast thereby aiding the checkerboard structure.[33] The blocks were drawn in squares with sides of 100 metres and there was a strict rule with regard to the occupation of the lands. A density of 160 inhabitants per hectare was planned which would leave 30 to 55 per cent of the surface area of the parcel free. A number of public parks were also planned and a

hierarchy of roadways for vehicular circulation. The streets were 16 metres wide and the avenues up to 50 metres with a *parterre* centre. The pavements were tree-lined and each house was to leave a green space of 5 metres to the front and construct a 4-metre high arcade to maintain the transparency of the block. There was easy communication with the centre by means of the tramway, first drawn by horses and then powered by steam. Areas for sport and recreational activities were developed and the first wooden bungalows were constructed. In 1883, the Trotcha Hotel was built, which became famous in the city because of the high social status of its guests.[34]

The roads were intelligently oriented to aid the path of the day and night breezes. The main avenues – Paseo and Presidentes – worked as hierarchical arteries perpendicular to the coast, where their *parterres* generated shade and,

Figure 8.7 Avenida de los Presidentes, Vedado, Havana. 1920s mansions. Photo: Roberto Segre. (*Source*: Archivo Roberto Segre)

along with the breeze, constituted the micro-climate in the area which was completely different from the compact central areas. Although the area was to be predominately residential, the corners were conceived to receive both the most luxurious mansions as well as local business, surrounded by arcades. The secluded setting of the mansions was balanced by the quality of the public space which, from the 1930s, attracted the construction of tourist installations, luxurious hotels and recreational facilities.[35] At the beginning of the Republican period, when construction was reinitiated, the availability of free space made Vedado the ideal site for the construction of the luxurious residences of the bourgeois Creole class (figure 8.7). In two decades, the residential area was completed along with monumental palaces, emulating those found in Paris and New York, the majority of which were designed within the norms of the tradition of the *Beaux-Arts* tradition.[36]

In the same way that Barcelona managed to maintain the dynamism and spirit of Cerdá's *Ensanche* throughout the twentieth century by adapting to the changes in function, technology, needs and architectural expressions and cultures, in Havana, Vedado represented a flexible, urban modernity which substituted and continued with the colonial square and which knew how to adapt itself to the radical changes which were taking place throughout the same period. It was precisely its open form and its mixed uses which constituted its vitality;[37] absorbing both the majesty of the great eclectic residences, the foliage of the centenarian trees as well as the multiple versions of the Miami kitsch spread by hotels and apartment buildings.

The Transition towards a Republican City

In spite of the negative vision of Havana in terms of health and social life to be created by generals and photographers from the North American government prior to its intervention[38] – not so true in the light of the large number of *quintas de salud* (suburban health centres) and the Mercedes Hospital inaugurated in 1879 in Vedado – the architectural and urban development achieved towards the end of the nineteenth century reveals the interest engineers and architects showed in innovations which were occurring in Europe and the United States. The Cuban engineer, Francisco de Albear y Lara (1816–1887), whose work still awaits detailed study, had a strong influence on the dynamics of the city. With knowledge of the Cerdá experience during his stay in Barcelona, he carried out the project of the Havana aqueduct (1858–1873), which is still in operation today, in keeping with the latest developments in this specialized area. He received the Gold Medal at the World Fairs held in Philadelphia (1876) and Paris (1878).[39] As head of the Office of Public Works, he supported the demolition of the city walls and drew up the most detailed plan of the city in the nineteenth century (1874). He put forward proposals for new neighbourhood developments and the creation of a maritime boulevard along the Caribbean sea coast.[40] Added to these initiatives was the project and the construction of Columbus cemetery (1870) by his collaborator, the architect Calixto de Loira, later supported by Eugenio Rayneri. Like those found in Europe, its monumentality made it a symbol of Havana's social history.[41]

The early presence of the railway linked the nearby rural settlements with the city, not only in terms of production but also in the possibilities made available to inhabitants willing to leave the overcrowded central area. Although some settlements were strengthened – Regla, Casablanca, Guanabacoa, San José de las Lajas, Marianao – there was no marked tendency towards suburban living. The peripheral location of the *quintas de salud* belonging to the regional centres set up for immigrants from the different regions of Spain such as Catalonia and Galicia was more important. The Galician Centre established 'La Benéfica' in the residential area of Concha neighbourhood. Summer residences for the well-off sprang up in Cerro, *casa-quintas* (suburban villas) later converted into permanent residences, with clear neo-classical configuration, different from the Anglo-Saxon model.

However, the dark storm clouds of the war of 1895 progressively stopped the construction initiatives.[42] Considered the Vietnam of the nineteenth century, the violence of these bloody wars in the wake of Spain's persistent desire to keep the island at all costs, turned Havana into a military camp. Some 220,000 soldiers arrived to fight in the swamps. The cruel Captain General Valeriano Weyler, remembered for his fierce repression against the anarchists in Barcelona,[43] had the merit of being the founder of the first shanty towns in Latin America. These were located along the city boundaries, and appeared around the same time as the *favelas* sprang up in Rio de Janeiro, paradigms of the living places for the poor of the region.[44] With the Liberating Army approaching, the Governor decided to empty the Cuban fields to remove any opportunity for help and food to be given to the patriotic fighters. The so-called process of 'Reconcentration' of the country folk was carried out in Havana, Matanzas and Pinar del Río. One hundred thousand people survived in the capital in precarious health conditions. According to the United States Consul, 57,000 died from poverty and epidemics in 1897.[45] At the end of the war, ragged, dirty-looking beings wandered the streets of the city dimming the architectural brilliance, the noise and street joy which had existed for decades.

Contradictory Influences: Spain versus United States

The North American intervention (1898–1902) created an *interregnum* in the evolution of the city, awaiting political solutions and stable economic programmes. The uncertainty and insecurity with regard to the future of the country were left behind with the proclamation of the Republic, while construction in Havana was aggressively reactivated by the Creole sector as well as the peninsular Spaniards. If in economic and political terms it would be reasonable to state that Cuba passed from the Spanish colonial regime to the neo-colonial North American one,[46] the influence of 'Big Brother' on urban and architectural development was not significant until the 1940s. Spain and France were hegemonic in bringing forth models and typologies. Le Reverend maintains that the Spanish cultural dominance ended with the fall of the Dictator Machado (1933),[47] but the continuity of the traditional urban structures ended, paradoxically, with the presence of the Catalan architect José Luis Sert in Havana (1939). At this time, while on his way to the United States in flight from the Franco Dictatorship, Sert visited the island and came into contact with the professional elite. This link would culminate with the drawing of the Director Plan in 1956, a proposal which disowned four centuries of urban homogenity.[48]

In spite of the bloody nature of the war, hate and rancour quickly disappeared. The North American authorities were extremely interested in filing away the contradictions as they trusted the conservative nature of the rich Spanish business class more than that of the libertarian aspirations of the Cubans, who were resentful for being pushed aside after years of fighting for independence. In the Republic, the accelerated economic growth of the sugar industry held until the crisis of the 1920s opened the way for investors from different origins. The American enterprises took over the urban services and channelled their investments in agricultural property as did the local landowners, while the Spanish concentrated on business and small-scale production in the city. A climate of prosperity led to the arrival in Cuba, between 1902 and 1925, of almost a million immigrants, the majority being Spanish.[49] The population of Havana rose from 250,000 at the start of the century to 500, 000 in 1925.[50] Paraphrasing the metaphor used by Blas de Otero, 'Spain the mother country has become Spain the stepmother'.[51]

The intervening North American government concentrated its efforts on the modernization of the urban infrastructure: paving the streets, hygiene, public lighting, health, and the start of the construction of the Havana 'Malecón' (Seafront). Although few public buildings were constructed – the Science Academy and the School of Arts and Crafts – the main initiative related to the architectural profession was the early creation of the School of Engineers and Architects. Although

from that time on the importance of master builders and surveyors – the majority of whom were Spanish – diminished and the academic ties with Madrid weakened, the privilege being given to North American universities, a radical change in orientation cannot be said to have occurred in terms of the style. The Paris *École des Beaux-Arts* (Fine Arts School) continued to be a universal model for architectural and aesthetic choices. The contradictions which existed came from the symbolic association of the different social groups and the limitations imposed on building craftsmen by the new professionals from the university. While the nouveau riche Cubans adopted academic canons from France or the United States, the emerging and needy Peninsular Spaniards identified with the decorative variety of Art Nouveau (or Catalan Modernism) employed by the building contractors and master builders in the narrow and crowded houses in the centre of Havana.[52]

The growth of the city was determined by two basic mechanisms: the spontaneous, speculative urbanization under private initiative and the official or theoretical proposals of the Master Plans. In both cases, the Peninsular and European inheritance remained until the 1940s. Both in Havana's 'Centre' as well as in the immediate surrounding areas of the middle classes – the neighbourhoods of Luyanó, Lawton, Santos Suárez, La Víbora – the layout kept the model of flat-roofed semidetached houses, with or without a porch, forming a dense and compact screen along the block. In contrast to what happened in Santo Domingo or San Juan de Puerto Rico, the curved and meandering pattern of circulation with emphasis on green spaces, in the style of Olmsted, was rare in Havana. This was far removed from the isolated cottage or chalet, rare examples of which appeared in

Vedado.[53] Only a wealthy elite chose part of this model as seen in the residential areas of Kohly and the Country Club Park (1918) in Marianao, and this is linked to the architects form the United States – Bertram Goodhue, Thomas Hastings, Schultze & Weawer, and George Duncan.[54] The Cuban bourgeoisie, on the other hand, accepted the regular pattern of Miramar, an area laid down in 1908 by the Compañía Urbanizadora de la Playa de Marianao (Marianao Beach Urban Development Company). The cultural and architectural references are still nearer to those of Paris than New York.[55] This identification is seen reflected in the state initiatives: the Dictator Gerardo Machado looked toward France; a quarter of a century later, the new tyrant of the hour, Fulgencio Batista, found his paradigms in the United States.[56]

Jean-Claude Nicholas Forestier: the Maturity of Academic Urbanism

The proposals put forward for the new monumental centre in the city from the beginning of the nineteenth century showed clear references to Haussmannesque models and, to a lesser degree, to the 'City Beautiful' of Daniel Burnham. In the projects for the modernization of the urban structure carried out by Enrique J. Montoulieu y de la Torre (1879–1951) and Pedro Martínez Inclán (1883–1957), the importance given to the avenues, diagonal arteries and green areas over the concentration in height of a business city is predominant. Quotes from North American authors – Mulford Robinson, Cowper, Lewis, Mawson, Lay – refer to the technical and sanitary aspects while the images come from Rue de Rivoli in Paris and the proposals made by Soria y Mata, Werner Hegemann, Camillo Sitte and Karl Brunner. There was still belief in the cultural dimension of the city, created by the articulation of the street pattern, the generosity of the green spaces, the symbolic value of the monuments and the homogeneity of the residential areas.

When the Dictator Gerardo Machado and his Minister of Public Works, Carlos Miguel de Céspedes, decided that Havana would be transformed into the Paris of the Caribbean, two decades after similar aspirations in Buenos Aires on the Río de la Plata, confirming its role as the West Indian metropolis, they invited a team of urban planners and French architects headed by J.C.N. Forestier (1861–1930) (figure 8.8).[57] Forestier, who was renowned in Spanish and Latin American circles for work carried out in Seville (María Luisa Park), in Barcelona (Montjuich Park) and the coast of Buenos Aires,[58] was asked to carry out an integral project for the city, foreseeing future peripheral expansion. His urban vision joins the harsh academic arterial layout, the monumental scale of the *boulevards,* the intimate dimension of the Barcelona promenades and the vision of the 'landscaper' which assimilates the local context and its natural attributes. Paseo del Prado (figure 8.9), the urban 'salon' designated for its use by the local bourgeoisie, was redesigned during his visits to Havana and was marked by sober street furniture of bronze and stone, conserving the green roof formed by leafy laurels. Today, in spite of its prolonged neglect, it is one of the most beautiful public places in the Havana 'ring'.[59]

If the majority of the proposals did not materialize due to the fall of the Dictatorship

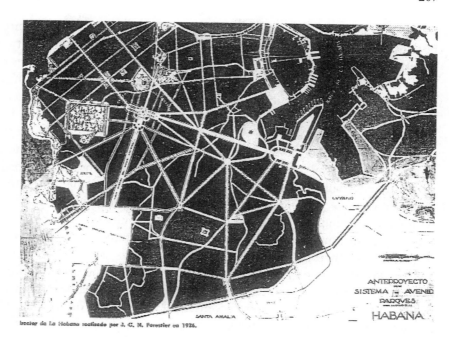

Figure 8.8 Director Plan of Havana, by J.C.N. Forestier, 1926. (*Source*: Archivo Roberto Segre)

in 1933 and the unexpected economic difficulties of the World Depression of 1929, the personality of the capital was closer to the classical structures which sprang up in that period than to the stale image of colonial ancestry. In fact, despite an advanced state of deterioration, the consistency of the residential areas from the beginning of the twentieth century that made up the Municipality of Havana Centre, form an urban landscape which is more consistent and unified than that of the original historic nucleus. In contrast to the dryness and abstraction of the colonial urban and neo-classical spaces, Forestier's skill lay in expanding the periphery of the road layouts so that the new centre – the proposed 'Plaza Cívica' (Civic Square), which was supposed to be equidistant from

Figure 8.9 Havana's Centre. View of the Paseo del Prado, after its reform by Forestier, 1929. Photo: Roberto Segre. (*Source*: Archivo Roberto Segre)

the main residential areas in the city – would be closer to the areas of tourist movement generated by the renovated port and associated with the new train station which would permit access to the beaches in other regions of the country. At the same time, he improved the quality of the landscape of the areas where the bourgeoisie had their own lifestyle – especially the coastal area from the centre to the Miramar residential area, conceived as a continuous *malecón* of social activities – without neglecting the design at the pedestrian scale, making use of the subtle variations of the natural and topographical accidents of the territory.

The open green spaces in the city were veiled with shadows which were accentuated aesthetically by the choice of the street furniture. One could travel along the new roads, shaded by the abundant foliage of the trees, rest on the indestructible benches, looking towards the heights of the gentle hills or towards the horizon of the infinite sea. From the Parque de la Fraternidad, one could descend to Parque Central, slowly, like a *flâneur,* progress through the urban 'salon' of the Paseo del Prado to the *Malecón,* and then follow Port Avenue with its parks, theatres and gardens, ending in Old Havana. Or one could go in the opposite direction, along the moulded façade formed by successive porticoes, which accompanied the winding coast up to the monument commemorating the 1898 sinking of the American warship Maine by the Spanish (the trigger of the Hispanic-American War) which was opposite the National Hotel, the symbol of the presence of North American tourism in Cuba. In another interior journey, one could go up along the Reina and Carlos III Avenues, in the direction of the Prince's Palace on the top of which a museum was to be installed and a system of gardens from

where one could admire the city from above and then cross over to Vedado towards the sea, along the *parterres* of Presidents' Avenue or Paseo Street, with alternating luxurious small palaces, monuments, fountains and gardens. The 'Pearl of the Antilles' has transformed the bleak classicism, changing it to something bright, pastoral and natural.

Until the 1940s North American influence did not come into conflict with the architectural codes imposed by the Peninsular community. During the expansion of the American empire in the Caribbean region, the importance achieved by the south of the United States – between California and Florida, which were Hispanic in their tastes – brought about a revival of the neo-Hispanic architectural elements and their adaptation to the public and private buildings. In other words, 'neocolonial' was, at the same time, the restoration of local traditions and camouflage for the presence of foreign economic interests.[60] Although in the historic centre orthodox classicism replaced the colonial style of the countless banks and office buildings found in the area, recreating a small Wall Street, the architectural exponents of the dependency were 'nationalized', in terms of style, outside of the *lenteja*. A clear example is the *Compañía Cubana de Teléfonos* (Cuban Telephone Company) (1927) by Leonardo Morales, decorated in the Spanish Plateresque,[61] very similar to that of the *La Telefónica* in Madrid (1925) by Ignacio de Cárdenas Pastor, both subsidiaries of ITT of New York. The series of public buildings designed by professional North Americans – the Central Railway Station (1912), the Customs House (1914), the Seville Biltmore Hotel (1921) and the National Hotel (1930) – were perfectly integrated into the symbols of the regional Spanish communities in Parque Central: the Centro Gallego (1915) by Paul Belau, and the Centro Asturiano (1927) by the architect Manuel del Busto.

The epigones of classic urban planning lasted until the beginning of the 1950s in the series of projects for the configuring of the Civic Centre proposed by Forestier in the Loma de Los Catalanes. With the creation of the *Comisión Central Pro-Monumento a José Martí* (Central Committee for José Martí's Monument) in 1937, a competition was organized for the design of a monument in honour of the national hero. After a number of ups and downs, this was finalized in 1953 during the Dictatorship of Fulgencio Batista. All the solutions put forward by the local architects – Govantes y Cabarrocas, Manuel de Tapia Ruano, Manuel Copado, Aquiles Maza, Enrique Luis Varela, Raúl Otero, Víctor Morales and others – maintained the academic structure of architectural composition, which were complemented by the first public buildings in the square: the National Library and the Palace of Justice. The removal of the classical orders gave way to the assimilation of the Deco codes within the parameters of Modern Movement which had begun to spread throughout Europe with the advent of totalitarian regimes as well as democratic governments. In the 1940s, as World War II brought about the end of the economic bonanza, the State built countless offices, schools and hospitals scattered throughout the city, within the 'PWA' (Public Works Authority) building style. This had been borrowed from the works undertaken by the Roosevelt government in the United States. The layout of rapid-transit roads for the growing number of cars replaced the tree-lined avenues proposed by Forestier, still conceived with the urban pedestrian in mind. The new roads aided communication between the centre and the different suburban residential districts, designed from the 'Garden City'

model which was quickly breaking up the compact city. As stated earlier, the brief visit by José Luis Sert to Cuba in 1939, on his way to North America, marked the definite break with the academic tradition and the start of the spread of the Modern Movement among the young architects and local urban planners, who became progressively closer to Harvard and the well-known figure of Walter Gropius.

With the creation of the *Junta Nacional de Planificación* (National Planning Board) during the Dictatorship of Fulgencio Batista in the 1950s, José Luis Sert and his partnership (Wiener and Schulz) were invited to carry out the Master Plan for Havana, within the parameters laid down by the Athens Charter. The urban proposals orthodoxly followed the CIAM thesis on the separation of functions (*zoning*) and the predominance of empty spaces in the central areas.[62] The opposition to the survival of traditional structures was shown in the radical intervention proposed for 'Old Havana', where the colonial fabric had been stripped of its original layout. Roads for rapid transit, 'modern' blocks disguised as old ones and a main centre made up of hotels, business places and offices, would reduce the memory of the colonial architecture to a handful of historic monuments.[63] The hope of achieving a metropolis with three million inhabitants – in a country of six million in the 1950s – was a utopia which was totally removed from the reality of an island characterized by underdevelopment and prevailing poverty in the greater part of its territory. It was the illusion of forming a city destined for North American tourism, integrated with the Miami-Las Vegas axis, where the structure would facilitate exterior and interior links generated by the specialized functions of tourism. The social, political and economic contradictions led to a crisis, and the advent of the revolutionary

Figure 8.10 Outline of Havana's urban development during the 1950s. The towers in Vedado, and the expansion of eastern Havana, at the other side of the bay can be seen. Drawing elaborated at the FAU, ISPJAE. (*Source*: Archivo Roberto Segre)

government in 1959 dashed both projects and implementation once and for all, as work carried out in the compact area of the capital was stopped for decades (figure 8.10).

The exceptional fact about Havana is that it has conserved almost all its classical inheritance intact, due to the movement of its centre from where it was during the Colonial period to where it is today, as well as to the minimal construction work carried out within the city in the last 40 years. In other words, from the 1950s, when the massive demolitions were to begin to produce the 'modern' city, the social, economic and political changes created the frozen 'socialist' capital which remained fixed in its physical evolution, unlike the developments in the other Latin American cities. While in Mexico City, little remains of the colonial Roma or Condesa, and only the isolated small palaces from the northern residential area have survived in Buenos Aires, and in Rio de Janeiro there have been great changes to the original characteristics of the Central Avenue which emulated the Avenida de Mayo, which miraculously remains. In the 'Pearl of the Antilles' the academic structures of the monuments conserve their original homogeneity.

In spite of little conservation and maintenance of the buildings during the last forty years, a fact which has also affected entire residential areas like Havana Centre,[64] Vedado is almost unscathed. As a result, national and international campaigns have recently been intensified to avoid the possible penetration of foreign capital spurred on by the need for hotels, offices and apartment buildings, which could destroy the heritage of Vedado and Havana Centre.[65] At least, the start of the twenty-first century has seen significant restoration of the historic centre.[66] It is hoped that the national awareness of urban and architectural heritage will come to encompass wider urban and spatial values, giving coherence to the classic environmental design of the main metropolis in the Indies.

NOTES

1. Recently two books were published which, for the first time, integrate evolution of architecture and urbanism in Havana in the last two centuries. Rodríguez, L.E. (1998) *La Habana. Arquitectura del siglo XX.* Barcelona: Blume; Lobo Montalvo, M.L. (2000) *Havana: History and Architecture of a Romantic City.* New York: Monacelli Press.

2. Portuondo, F. (1965) *Historia de Cuba 1492–1898*. La Habana: Editorial Pueblo y Educación.

3. Guerra y Sánchez, R. (1970) *Azúcar y población en las Antillas*. La Habana: Editorial de Ciencias Sociales; Ortiz, F. (1963) *Contrapunteo cubano del tabaco y el azúcar*. La Habana: Consejo Nacional de Cultura, p. 61.

4. Rallo, J. and Segre, R. (1978) *Evolución histórica de las estructuras territoriales y urbanas de Cuba (1519–1959)*. La Habana: Facultad de Arquitectura, ISPJAE.

5. Moreno Fraginals, M. (1964) *El Ingenio. El complejo económico social cubano del azúcar (1760–1860)*. La Habana: Comisión Nacional Cubana en la UNESCO, Vol. I, p. 30; Le Reverend Brusone, J. (1992) *La Habana. Espacio y vida*. Madrid: MAPFRE.

6. Alfonso Ballol, B. *et al.* (1987) *El camino de hierro de La Habana a Güines. Primer ferrocarril de Iberoamérica*. Madrid: Fundación de los Ferrocarriles Españoles; Zanetti Lecuona, O. and García Alvarez, A. (1987) *Caminos para el azúcar*. La Habana: Editorial de Ciencias Sociales.

7. Moreno Fraginals, M. (1995) *Cuba/España. España/Cuba. Historia común*. Barcelona: Grijalbo Mondadori.

8. López Segrera, F. (1989) *Cuba: cultura y sociedad (1510–1985)*. La Habana: Editorial Letras Cubanas.

9. Segre, R., Coyula, M. and Scarpaci, J. (1997) *Havana. Two Faces of the Antillean Metropolis*. Chichester: John Wiley & Sons, p. 43.

10. Roig De Leuchsenring, E. (1963) *La Habana. Apuntes históricos*. La Habana: Consejo Nacional de Cultura, 3 vols; Pérez de La Riva (1965) Desarrollo de la población habanera. *Bohemia* (November, 12), pp. 100–102.

11. Segre, R. (1971) La dimensión espacio-tiempo de la ciudad. *Arquitectura/Cuba*, 340, in Segre R. (ed.). Número monográfico, Habana 1, p. 35; Segre, R., Instituto de Planificación Física (1974) *Transformación urbana en Cuba: La Habana*. Barcelona: Gustavo Gili.

12. Bens Arrarte, J. M. (1960) La evolución de la ciudad de La Habana desde mediados del siglo XIX hasta las primeras décadas del XX. *Arquitectura/Cuba*, 327/328/329, p. 437; Le Reverend Brusone, J. (1960) *La Habana. Biografía de una provincia*. La Habana: Academia de la Historia.

13. Carpentier, A. (1982) *La ciudad de las columnas. Fotografías de Grandal*. La Habana: Editorial Letras Cubanas.

14. Chateloin, F. (1989) *La Habana de Tacón*. La Habana: Editorial Letras Cubanas.

15. Segre, R. (1995) *La Plaza de Armas de La Habana.*

Sinfonía urbana inconclusa. La Habana: Editorial Arte y Literatura.

16. Pereira, M. de los A. (1994) La producción monumentaria conmemorativa en Cuba. Unpublished PhD Thesis. Facultad de Artes y Letras, Universidad de La Habana, La Habana.

17. Bens Arrarte, J. M. (1954) Urbanismo y Arquitectura: La Habana colonial durante el siglo XIX y principios del siglo XX. *Arquitectura*, 260, pp. 486–504. Bens Arrarte, J. M. (1995) Urbanismo y Arquitectura. Siglos XIX y XX, in Préstamo y Hernández, F. J. (ed.), *Cuba. Arquitectura y urbanismo*. Miami: Ediciones Universal, pp. 199–220.

18. Pezuela, J. de la (1863) *Diccionario geográfico, estadístico, histórico de la isla de Cuba*. Madrid: Libería extranjera y nacional, científica y literaria; Torre, J. M. de la (1863) *Compendio de geografía física, política, estadística y comparada de la isla de Cuba*. La Habana: Spencer y Cía.; Weiss, J. E. (1996) *La arquitectura colonial cubana. Siglos XVI al XIX*. La Habana/Sevilla: Instituto Cubano del Libro, Junta de Andalucía.

19. Weiss, J. E. (1967) Un urbanista olvidado. *Arquitectura Cuba*, 337, pp. 69–71.

20. Venegas Fornias, C. (1990) *La urbanización de las Murallas. Dependencia y modernidad*. La Habana: Editorial Letras Cubanas.

21. Rigau, J. (1994) No longer Islands: Dissemination of Architecture Ideas in the Hispanic Caribbean, 1890-1930. *The Journal of Decorative and Propaganda Arts*, 20, pp. 237–251.

22. Bens Arrarte, J. M. (1948) La urbanización de Extramuros. *Revista de la Propiedad Urbana*, XV (176), p. 12.

23. Fernández y Simón, A. (1956, 1995) Los distintos tipos de urbanizaciones que fueron establecidos en la ciudad de La Habana durante su época colonial, in Préstamo y Hernández, *op. cit.*, pp. 163–196.

24. García Álvarez, A. (1990) *La gran burguesía comercial en Cuba, 1988–1920*. La Habana: Editorial de Ciencias Sociales.

25. Llanes, L. (1985) *Apuntes para una historia sobre los constructores cubanos*. La Habana: Editorial Letras Cubanas; Tejeira-Davis, E. (1987) *Roots of Modern Latin American Architecture. The Hispano-Caribbean Region from the late 19th. Century to the Recent Past*. Heidelberg: Heidelberg University.

26. Venegas Fornias, C. (1989) Las fábricas de tabaco habaneras. *AU/Arquitectura/Urbanismo*, X(3), pp. 14–22.

27. Zardoya, M.V. (1998) Estudio histórico-tipológico

de las viviendas eclécticas en las calzadas de La Habana. Unpublished PhD Thesis, FAU/ISPJAE, La Habana.

28. Álvarez-Tabío Albo, E. (2000) *Invención de La Habana*. Barcelona: Casiopea, p. 64.

29. Benjamin, W. (1993) *Paris capitale du XIXe siécle. Le livre des Passages*. Paris: Les Éditions du Cerf.

30. Fernández Miranda, M. (1985) La Habana, ciudad de América, in *La Habana Vieja. Mapas y planos en los Archivos de España*. Exposición en el Castillo de la Fuerza. La Habana: Ministerio de Asuntos Exteriores de España, Ministerio de Cultura de España, Ministerio de Cultura de Cuba, Madrid, p. 13.

31. Segre R. and Baroni, S. (1998) Cuba y La Habana. Historia, población y territorio. *Ciudad y Territorio. Estudios Territoriales*, **XXX** (116), pp. 351–379.

32. Maribona, A. (1957) El fantástico crecimiento de la propiedad urbana en la Gran Habana. *Revista de la Propiedad Urbana*, **XXIV** (284), p. 13.

33. Marrero, L. (1981) *Geografía de Cuba*. Miami: La Moderna Poesía.

34. Llanes, L. (1996) Arquitectura y poder. La vivienda en La Habana (1898-1921). La Habana: Unpublished essay.

35. Coyula, M. (1999) En defensa del Vedado. *Revolución y Cultura*, 41(5), Época IV, pp. 21–25.

36. Álvarez-Tabío Albo, E. (1989) *Vida, mansión y muerte de la burguesía cubana*. La Habana: Letras Cubanas. Llanes, L. (1999) *The Houses of Old Cuba*. New York: Thames & Hudson.

37. Martín Zequeira, M. E. and Rodríguez Fernández, E. L. (1998) *La Habana, Guía de Arquitectura*. Sevilla, La Habana: Junta de Andalucía, Ciudad de La Habana.

38. Bretos, M. A. (1996) Imaging Cuba under the American flag: Charles Edward Doty in Havana, 1899–1902. *The Journal of Decorative and Propaganda Arts*, 22, Cuba Theme Issue, pp. 83–103.

39. Fernández y Simón, A. (1950) *Memoria histórico-técnica de los acueductos de la ciudad de La Habana* (Primera Parte). La Habana: Edición del Autor. Impresores Ucar García.

40. Venegas Fornias, C. (1994) El malecón habanero. *Revolución y Cultura*, 33(4), Época 4, pp. 46–50; Carley, R. (1997) *Cuba. 400 Years of Architectural Heritage*, photos by Andrea Brizzi. New York: Whitney Library of Design.

41. Martínez y Martínez, E. (1995) El Cementerio Cristóbal Colón, in Préstamo y Hernández, *op. cit.*, pp. 407–415; Aruca, L. (1996) The Cristóbal Colón Cemetery

in Havana. *The Journal of Decorative and Propaganda Arts*, 22, Cuba Theme Issue, pp. 37-55.

42. Pino Santos, O. (1983) *Cuba: historia y economía*. La Habana: Editorial de Ciencias Sociales.

43. Hughes, R. (1995) *Barcelona*. São Paulo: Companhia das Letras, p. 453.

44. Segre, R. (2000) Rio de Janeiro: 'Favela-Bairro'. Il riscatto della cittá informale, in Gutiérrez, R. (ed.), *L'altra architettura. Città, abitazone e patrimonio*. Milano: Jaca Book, pp. 125–129.

45. Poumier, M. (1975) *Apuntes sobre la vida cotidiana en Cuba en 1898*. La Habana: Editorial de Ciencias Sociales, p. 235.

46. Llanes, L. (1993) *1898–1921: La transformación de La Habana a través de la arquitectura*. La Habana: Editorial Letras Cubanas.

47. Le Reverend, *La Habana . . ., loc cit*.

48. Segre, R. (1995) La Habana de Sert: CIAM, ron y cha-cha-chá. *DANA. Documentos de Arquitectura Nacional y Americana*, 37/38, pp. 120–124.

49. Pérez de La Riva, J. (1975) *El Barracón y otros ensayos*. La Habana: Editorial de Ciencias Sociales; Álvarez Estévez, R. (1988) *Azúcar e inmigración. 1900–1940*. La Habana: Editorial de Ciencias Sociales.

50. Le Reverend Brusone, J. (1974) *Historia económica de Cuba*. La Habana: Editora del Ministerio de Educación.

51. Arrom, J. J. (1980) *Certidumbre de América*. La Habana: Editorial Letras Cubanas, p. 165.

52. Bay Sevilla, L. (1941) La evolución de la arquitectura en Cuba. *Arquitectura,* **X**(101), pp. 412–426; Weiss, J. E. (1950) *Medio siglo de arquitectura cubana*. La Habana: Universidad de La Habana; Venegas Fornias, C. (1996) Havana, between two centuries. *The Journal of Decorative and Propaganda Arts*, 22, Cuba Theme Issue, pp. 13–34.

53. De Soto, L. (1929) The Main Currents in Cuban Architecture. Unpublished PhD Thesis, Faculty of Philosophy, Columbia University, Nueva York.

54. Gelabert-Navia, P. (1996) American architects in Cuba: 1900–1930. *The Journal of Decorative and Propaganda Arts*, 22, Cuba Theme Issue, pp. 133–149.

55. Duverger, H. (1994) El maestro francés del urbanismo criollo para La Habana, in Leclerc, D. (ed.), *Jean Claude Nicolas Forestier (1861–1930). Du jardin au paysage urbain*. Actes du Colloque International sur J. C. N. Forestier. Paris: Picard Éditeur, pp. 221–290.

56. Segre, R. and Sambricio, C. (2000) *Arquitectura en la ciudad de La Habana. Primera Modernidad*. Madrid: Electa España.

57. Segre, R. (1990) El sistema monumental de la ciudad de La Habana 1900/1930, in Segre, R. (ed.), *Lectura crítica del entorno cubano*. La Habana: Editorial Letras Cubanas, pp. 89–113.

58. Lejeune, J.-F. (1996) The city as landscape: Jean Claude Nicolas Forestier and the great urban works of Havana, 1925–1930. *The Journal of Decorative and Propaganda Arts*, 22, Cuba Theme Issue, pp. 151–185.

59. Stout, N. and Rigau, J. (1994) *Havana/La Habana*. New York: Rizzoli.

60. Segre, R. (1994) Preludio a la modernidad: convergencias y divergencias en el contexto caribeño (1900–1950), in Amaral, A. (ed.), *Arquitectura Neocolonial. América Latina, Caribe, Estados Unidos*. México/San Pablo: Memorial de América Latina, Fondo de Cultura Económica, pp. 95–112.

61. 'Intricate highly decorative style of early sixteenth-century Spain, supposedly resembling fine silversmith's work, with enrichments derived from Classical, Gothic, Moorish and Renaissance sources, extravagantly applied to the walls of late-Gothic buildings and generally unrelated to any expression of construction.' Stevens Curl, J. (ed.) (2000) *Dictionary of Architecture*. Oxford: Oxford University Press, p. 505.

62. Rogers, E.N.; Sert, J.L.; Tyrwhitt, J. T. (1961) *El corazón de la ciudad: para una vida más humana de la comunidad (CIAM)*. Barcelona: Editora Científico-Médica.

63. Segre, R. (1996) La Habana siglo XX: espacio dilatado y tiempo contraído. *Ciudad y Territorio. Estudios Territoriales*, **XXVIII**(110), Tercera Época, pp. 713-731. Coyula; M. (1992) Dándole taller al barrio. *AU/Arquitectura/Urbanismo*, **XIII**(1), pp. 49–54.

64. Gutiérrez, P.J. (1998) *Trilogía sucia de La Habana*. Barcelona: Anagrama.

65. Duany, A. (1999) Una ciudad con vista al mar, entrevista de María E. Martín Zequeira. *La Gaceta de Cuba*, 3–4, pp. 10–13; Coyula, M. (2000) Havana Forever, *Cuba Update*, **XXIV**(2–3), pp. 2–4.

66. Leal Spengler, E. (1999) *Desafío de una utopía. Una estrategia integral para la gestión de salvaguarda de La Habana Vieja*. La Habana: Oficina del Historiador de la Ciudad de La Habana; Coyula, M. (1991) Al reencuentro de la ciudad perdida. *AU/Arquitectura & Urbanismo*, **XII**(1), p. 50.

Chapter 9

Caracas: Territory, Architecture and Urban Space

Lorenzo González Casas

Introduction: Strata and Games in the Modernity of Caracas

The urban structure of Caracas is the result of a struggle between imported models and disciplines and the specific conditions of the place. Given that the source of inspiration in urban modernization comes from abroad, one can distinguish a characteristic set of foreign influences, accompanied by local reactions, at each phase in the development of the city. In this way, the city was transformed through the gradual build up of superimposed layers. In the case of Caracas, this is evident by the consecutive import and implantation of urban ideas and plans coming from Spain, France, Britain and North America.

Together with the concept of the stratification of the ideas of modernization, the notion of 'game' will be used in this chapter as a key to interpret the influences from abroad and the complex process of negotiation between the existing and the new cultural spheres. Thus, we will analyse how the original grid in Caracas became the centre of the city and the great scenario for the dialectics between continuity and change, in which the dynamics of urban growth, the hierarchical placement of its uses and the representation of power, took place. The word 'game' will be understood, not in the light-hearted sense, but as a strategic and experimental operation of negotiation used by social agents or key players to make decisions in which every move conditions or anticipates the next.

This chapter has two major emphases: on the 'stratum' or period between centuries or, as it was called by Jose Luis Romero,[1] the period corresponding to the so-called 'bourgeois' city at the end of the nineteenth and the beginning of the twentieth centuries; and a spatial emphasis on the territorial, architectural and public space dimensions of Caracas's urban design and development.

Historical Background: The Colonial City and the Beginnings of the Republic

In 1578, in compliance with a royal mandate, Juan de Pimentel, Governor and Captain

General of the province of Venezuela between 1576 and 1583, sent his report on Santiago de León de Caracas to the court of Felipe II (Phillip II), which included the first known map of the city (figure 9.1). Nevertheless, far from being an accurate description of the new settlement in America, Pimentel's map was more a representation of the Crown's wishes than reality. Therefore, as some recent archaeological work seems to show,[2] it was more a plan than a map, more a landscape of symbols, than facts.

On this board – I want to express the form of the city as the board in the so-called 'science game' – consecutive moves or trials, to use a laboratory[3] metaphor, of Venezuelan urban culture would take place. The first attempt at modernization, under Spanish rule and co-

inciding with Renaissance ideals, meant the creation of a completely new city in the valley of Caracas and the establishment of an urban structure base, the fundamentals of which were almost constant between the sixteenth and nineteenth centuries.[4]

Like the distinction made by Aldo Rossi[5] between the primary and secondary elements of the urban structure, the original grid of Caracas had basically two kinds of pieces, placed on similarly sized squares: churches and convents (as the main elements) and houses (as pawns). Pimentel's map – a sort of letter in the literal and figurative sense – provided a timely opportunity to inform – or ratify – those who were on the other side of the ocean, the status of this royal hallmark in American territory whose urbanization, it must not be

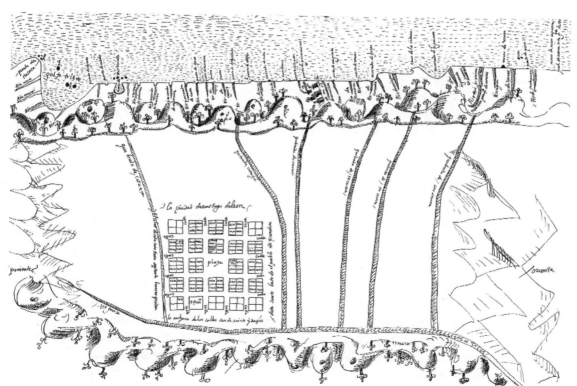

Figure 9.1 Detail from the Plan of Caracas, by Governor Pimentel, 1578. (*Source*: Irma de Sola Ricardo. *Contribución al estudio de los planos de Caracas.* Caracas: Ediciones del Cuatricentenario de Caracas, 1967)

forgotten, was the result of the cooperation between the Catholic Church and the Spanish crown, the main players in the process of conquest and colonization.

As the product of that commitment, the main church, which would later be converted into the Cathedral, was placed on the most important site: across from the Plaza Mayor (Main Square). Besides the church, four other ecclesiastic properties appear on the map, including the site where the San Francisco Convent, which would occupy an entire block of the new city, was to be built. In contrast to the multiple religious areas, there was just one on the plan designated for governmental activities. Sixty-five lots occupied by houses, twenty-three empty lots, a main central space and other minor public places made up Pimentel's city, a finite modular object immersed in vast surroundings. The scale of the plan was altered to combine the interest in the details of the lots with the most complete reference to the natural environment possible. In so doing, the plan tried to put together two different spatial realities: that of the ocean-like immensity and omnipresent nature, generous and gigantic – which had led a dazzled Christopher Columbus to remark that he was in the earthly paradise or Land of Grace when he saw the Venezuelan coasts during his third voyage to the New World – and that of everyday life. The regular form of the city was perhaps one of the few ways to record the human presence in such a huge territory.[6]

Caracas was founded in 1567, six years before the publication of the *Leyes de Indias* (Law of the Indies), by a group of 136 Spaniards under the command of Diego de Losada. It was the most eastern settlement on Venezuelan soil at that time and occurred after several prior attempts at settlement had met strong opposition from the native inhabitants. After the defeat of the Indian chief, Guaicaipuro, by Diego de Losada, the town was located in the far west of the long and narrow valley, about 920 m above sea level, near the route to the Caribbean sea. The site chosen was located between hills and streams: to the north, the Avila – the highest mountain – to the east, the Catuche stream, to the south the Guaire river and to the west, the Caroata stream and El Calvario hill. Pimentel's map paid special attention to these hydrographical and orographical landmarks with the rivers marking the distance and the mountains representing the walls surrounding the board.

Caracas grew slowly during the sixteenth and seventeenth centuries restrained by poverty, widespread throughout the province, earthquakes and epidemics that highlighted the fact that Caracas was a small city which could not be compared in size and wealth to the vice-regal capitals. On the other hand, the notion of a unified territory was absent during a large part of the colonial period. The seven provinces of the Captaincy General (Caracas, Barcelona, Cumaná, Margarita, Mérida, Trujillo and Barinas), functioned as almost completely independent city-harbour systems.

The growth of the city of Caracas was controlled with the new population being settled within the same urban perimeter.[7] As a result, there was a growing subdivision and break up of the city fabric due to the division of blocks into progressively smaller units. Thus, in 1772, the urban area of Venezuela's capital was almost the same as in 1806 while, during that period, the population rose from 19,000 to more than 40,000 inhabitants.

Although Caracas had not been originally planned as the formal capital, it had, however, been gradually assuming the role of the capital city of the province both politically as well as religiously speaking. After the move by the governor (1576), the royal public servants (1570), the bishop (1613) and finally the seat of the Cathedral (1637), a Royal decree in 1777 declared it the capital of the Captaincy General of Venezuela, while the main institutions would be established there: the Royal Audience (1786) – a level of colonial administration, inferior to that of Viceroyalty – the Royal Consulate (1793) and the seat of the Archbishop (1803); as well as the houses of the most wealthy agricultural landowners, the University, the offices of the legal advisors, religious orders and the most outstanding titles and donations awarded by the Spanish crown.

From the end of the seventeenth to the beginning of the nineteenth centuries, Caracas enjoyed a period of relative prosperity. The economy, based on the export of coffee and cocoa, improved under the Guipuzcoana Company (founded in 1728) and the later liberalization of commerce, which contributed to the economic growth of the province and its capital and led to a boom from 1780. Late-eighteen-century Caracas is represented on another plan known as '*exacto*' (exact) and drawn by Juan Vicente Bolívar, Simón Bolívar's father (figure 9.2) in 1772, almost two hundred years after the Pimentel Plan. With limited accuracy, the plan highlights the hydrography of the land (the base of the economy and the means of support of the isolated town), the military check points and the churches. The rural-urban continuum is seen in the use of colours to distinguish the figures and the background.[8]

By 1810, on the eve of the War of Independence, the city had more than 42,000 inhabitants and was divided into five religious parishes: Catedral, San Pablo, Candelaria, Altagracia, and Santa Rosalía (the last being

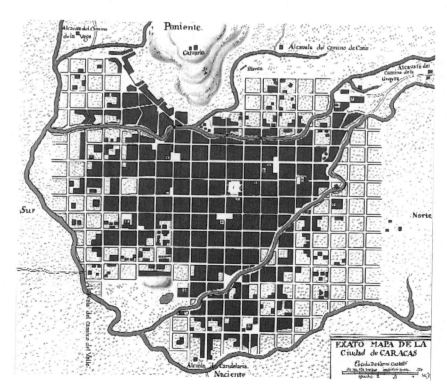

Figure 9.2 Plan of Caracas by Juan Vicente Bolivar, 1772. (*Source*: Irma de Sola Ricardo. *Contribución al estudio de los planos de Caracas*. Caracas: Ediciones del Cuatricentenario de Caracas, 1967)

added in 1777). The religious edifices continued being the landmarks in a city with low buildings. The Plaza Mayor was the open space where all public functions took place: religious, political and social meetings; military parades; the market; the administration of justice; and games and recreational activities in general. Some public buildings were found around the Plaza Mayor but the Cathedral continued to be the most important one. Other open spaces or sub-centres were created on the parish–religious base. Nevertheless, these spaces never managed to occupy the entire block and held second place to the Plaza Mayor.

In typological terms, the buildings were generally organized around a courtyard. In this way, the concentric layout of the city – solid blocks around an open space – was repeated on a domestic scale. This concentric urban layout was of a diagrammatic quality: among other things, it expressed the hierarchical order in the city through the arrangement of the open spaces: from the central courtyards in the buildings to the local spaces (parish squares), to the city centres (main squares). This arrangement, with city life organized around open spaces, is a fundamental feature in understanding both the urban planning as well as the sense of housing in the colonial city.

Some civil institutions began slowly to acquire a certain amount of pre-eminence on the board. In 1751, the Spanish Governor, Felipe Nicolás Ricardos, introduced the Bourbon reforms, a reflection of the enlightened despotism of this Royal House, which were intended to 'make Caracas modern, conscious of itself and loyal'.[9] Caracas was once more an arena of colonial reforms undertaken by the Spanish crown; new ordinances were proclaimed, public offices were created and some urban spaces were reconstructed. Between 1753 and 1755, the Plaza Mayor was remodelled when porticos were constructed on the south and east sides, diagonal to the Cathedral. The square's function as a public market for the city was strengthened, small shops were constructed on the inside of the wall and these were rented (with the city gaining control over tax payments). Robert Ferry has argued that 'the reformed square was an effective expression both functionally as well as symbolically, of the King's authority'.[10]

Colonial rule came to an end when the fight between the Creole families and the Peninsular businessmen and authorities led to the War of Independence and the extremely costly search for a new order. After Independence and with Venezuela's separation from Gran Colombia – which included modern Colombia and Ecuador – Caracas became the capital of an independent country. This did not mean huge urban changes, for although Independence had broken the stability of Spanish order in many aspects, in many others, the colonial structure continued being the base for the social and economic organization of the country. The formation of a free state and the creation of a new Republic encountered many enormous obstacles due to the fight for power among the old leaders of the Wars of Independence and the Balkanization of the country. The Captaincy General's centralistic model remained intact and was attacked by the rural regional leadership. This caused struggles between regional *caudillos* (political or military leaders) and led to bloody civil wars which held the country in a state of permanent strife, and the capital in a state of slow growth. Nature, in its savage form, seemed to hold reign as reflected in the pictorial works of Ferdinand Bellerman, Camille Pissarro and Sir Robert Ker Porter.

More than fifty years after the devastating earthquake of 1812, which had destroyed two-thirds of the buildings in Caracas and caused the death of 10,000 to 12,000 of its inhabi-tants,[11] the ruins still remained throughout the city, evidence that something in the colonial order had been broken, for which there was no clear replacement.

Guzmán Blanco and the Re-creation of a Republican City

In April 1876, Roberto García, an engineer who until March of that year had been the Minister of Public Works in the Venezuelan government, dedicated an album to the 'Illustrious American, Reformer and President of the United States of Venezuela', Antonio Guzmán Blanco (figure 9.3). On the back page of the album was an oval drawing with Guzmán Blanco, dressed with the solemnity and distinction which the occasion required, in a three-quarter pose and surrounded by symbols which reflected national sentiment and instruments of power. At the top, was the national coat of arms hanging as a kind of republican crown over the head of the ruler, a sort of genealogical coat of arms for the historic justification of the character. In the middle, symmetrically placed and coming from the centre of the oval like numerous rays, were the national flags and pieces of weaponery – cannons, swords and bayonets – the latter being the instruments which had taken Guzmán Blanco into power and the symbols of the monopoly of 'the State's legitimate violence' which would frequently have to be used to confront opposition to the regime. In the lower section, and of greatest interest to us, hidden behind the illustrations of vegetation decorating the borders, was a group of plans and drawing instruments (compass and ruler) acting as the basis of the composition. If one looks carefully, the plans contain the plan and façade of the Federal Palace, the new building set diagonally to the central square, for which García had been the construction engineer. This was destined to house a Congress which, at least in name, made reference to the division in power found in the modern parliamentary regimes. It is not by chance that the plans for the Federal Palace make up the vertex of a pyramidal composition which ends in the national coat of arms and are the figures which give stability to the oval where Guzmán Blanco is placed.

Figure 9.3 Back cover of an album devoted to Antonio Guzmán Blanco, by Roberto García, 1876. (*Source*: Leszek Zawisa. *Arquitectura y obras públicas en Venezuela, Siglo XIX*. Caracas: Ediciones de la Presidencia de la República, 1988)

The iconography, full of symbolic meaning so costly for the Masonic leaders, such as the giver as well as the receiver, is useful to illustrate some of the keys to understanding the effort made at the end of the nineteenth century aimed at breaking the inertia and creating a new stratum of a modern city. This process envisaged, among other things, the partial fragmentation of the environmental unity and consistency in the colonial city. Towards the end of the nineteenth century, under the aegis of Guzmán Blanco, an unprecedented boom in construction began in Caracas. Simultaneously, the country opened its doors to foreign investment and European migration, with Great Britain and France the dominant centres in the economic and cultural scene.

Guzmán, a prominent member of the Masonic lodges of that time, had travelled as a diplomat to Philadelphia, New York, Washington, London, Madrid and Paris. He fought in the Federal War as General Falcón's right-hand man and had visited Europe as plenipotentiary. He met Napoleon III in Paris and was acquainted with the work of Baron Hauss-mann. He was interim President of the Republic and came to power in 1870, governing, with some interruptions, until 1888. The attempts made by Guzmán Blanco to transform the small settlement into a modern city were clearly inspired by the new ideas obtained from the enlightened rhetoric of Napoleon III. The liberal *caudillo* wanted to control the forces which would change the city and to introduce a novel form through which the city could express its representational role as the capital, at the same time obtaining lucrative personal benefits from the financial and business arrangements tied to the construction. New philosophical and political principles, as well as social processes, were underway: among which were the belief in the rationality of scientific criteria, liberalism, free and compulsory education, journalism, accurate accounting and budgeting techniques, the organization of public administration, a systematic national census, and public statistics.

Domesticating the Territory

The modernization processes encouraged by Guzmán Blanco envisaged new ways of looking at the territory. A permanent source of concern for the rulers was defining the country's limits with neighbouring countries, Colombia and British Guyana. The discussion of the border issue with the latter, led to a break in relations with England. The clear marking of territory and the spreading of a common history would be the bases for building notions and imageries of nationality, sovereignty and citizenship needed to unify the fragmented country.

Within the national boundaries, statistics and cartography would play a dominant role in rationalizing and calculating the activities in the territory. Regional differences (with dozens of revolutions and uprisings which converted every estate into a barracks, each landowner into a general and each peasant into a soldier), the economic crisis and natural disasters made the territory, apart from being unknown, look like an emerging danger zone. To counteract this hostile atmosphere and to articulate the movement and flow of production – giving incentives to national and foreign businesses, the majority of which were linked to the boom in coffee production – a rational assessment of the country and its conditions was needed.

The image made in 1877 by the painter and engraver Ramón Bolet to illustrate the cover of the *Album de Caracas y Venezuela* (figure 9.4) was a step in this direction. A solemn neo-classical figure – victoriously crowned with laurels and holding a palette and paint brushes – dominates what is supposed to be the landscape of the Orinoco river, on which a steam boat sails and on whose banks are diagonally cultivated lots with pyramid-shaped mountains in the background. Among a stock of tropical plants – a concession to romanticism and a desire for the exotic and picturesque – one finds the main figure at whose feet lie several objects which point to a domesticated landscape: a horn overflowing with fruits, pictures of landscapes already framed, a roll of paper and a jar on a pedestal, all bordering a rising staircase. The moral was clear: the land should be put into production; nature, seen as a source of opportunity, would be changed into a 'civilized land', in the kingdom of calculation and abstraction whose pinnacle would be the metropolis. To achieve these ends, an agenda for the organization of the territory would first have to be developed, followed by another for urban design.

The main focus of this first agenda was the large-scale implementation of the old wish to improve communication between Caracas and the rest of the country, which had begun decades earlier, with the highways to La Guaira (1845) and Los Teques (1858). Under the aegis of the modernizing *caudillo*, the road to Charallave was built in 1872 and extended the following year to several towns in the centre of the country (Ocumare, Cúa and San Casimiro). In 1875, the road to the east was built up to Guatire, a small town some 50 kilometres from Caracas. A number of railway lines, contracted to German, English and local firms, joined the network of roadways: the line to La Guaira was laid down in 1883, thus overcoming a number of technical limitations caused by the big difference in levels between the city and its port; those of El Valle and Antímano also in 1883;

Figure 9.4 Frontispiece of the *Album de Caracas y de Venezuela* by Ramón Bolet, 1877. (*Source*: Archivo Biblioteca Nacional, Caracas)

the Central Venezuelan railway, which first arrived at Petare (1886) and then went on to Santa Lucía; and the train to Los Teques (1891), which, years later, would be extended to Valencia. Improvements in navigation and port infrastructure allowed the cabotage and interconnection of the nation's extensive coast. The telegraph network, which began in 1856 and was destroyed during the Federal War (1858–1863), was nationalized in 1875 and extended throughout the nation, reaching Colombia in 1882. In 1888, underwater cables were installed, facilitating the rapid communication of the country with the outside world and its reintegration into the world economic circuit.

With the country at peace and new access roads available, much of the capital's outskirts became occupied, being converted into areas for relaxation and pleasure. Sea, river and thermal water bathing spots, parks and squares were designed as places of elegance for the emerging bourgeoisie. Guzmán Blanco himself, would build a suburban villa in Antímano, a settlement some 9 kilometres from the centre of town, which would have recreational and cultural events under the management of French personnel specially hired for this purpose.

The world of consumption, with the desire for entertainment, was in sharp contrast to the world of agriculture and poverty and the precarious health conditions in which the large majority of the Venezuelan population lived. Silk dresses, flowers, perfumes, mirrors and many other French articles were exhibited in the fashionable stores in the city: *Paris Fashions*, the *Pharmacie Française*, the *Cable Français*, the *Boulangerie and Pâtisserie*, the *Salon du Monde Fashionable*, *Au Printemps*, *Librería Francesa* and the *Compañía Francesa*. Fashion and clothes were dictated from Paris through magazines such as *Semanario Familiar Pintoresco*,[12] translated in Spain.

By the nineteenth century, the state's increased skills in managing the national territory were accompanied by improvements in techniques of cartographic representation. Caracas, still far from having an urban plan, was reflected in different topographical plans which gave more precise information on the topography of the land and placed names on the territory. The Topographical Plan of 1875 which was made by the order of Guzmán Blanco (figure 9.5) is of special interest as it draws attention to the specific names given to the monuments constructed by the regime, places of civic beauty and order, which appear as parables of a good government. In the urban framework, churches are no longer indicated with the same intensity as new civic monuments and peripheral *haciendas* (estates).

Buildings in the Secular Republic

The new social order was secular, supposedly built on science in clear contrast to the colonial order, which had been centred on theology.[13] However, the religious cult was not totally eliminated but rather replaced by the introduction of the 'cult of the hero'. Several authors have argued that the cult of the Liberator and other leaders involved in the fight for independence has the same characteristics as a new theology.[14] A clear example is given by Guzmán Blanco, when in 1883, during the celebrations to commemorate the one hundredth anniversary of the birth of Bolívar, he proclaimed that:

The Liberator will see from his grave that we have learnt and are putting into practice the Republic which he bequeathed us; he will see that we have grown in all civilized manner; he will see that we have the virtue of patriotism and honesty and that nonetheless, with our own means that are still at our disposal, we will lead the Country with prosperity and speed to its great destiny.[15]

To achieve the desired prosperity and to 'civilize' Caracas, the government, apart from using patriotic and nationalist rhetoric, introduced a modern European agenda with basically French and English patterns. Order and progress, two liberal ideas, were the *leitmotifs*, while education, transport and infrastructure were declared as national priorities. Public works became essential governmental tasks and physical testimony of their agenda. In 1874, the Ministry of Public Works and its offices for 'Building and Embellishment of Towns' and 'Roads and Aqueducts' were created, and the State became the supplier or promoter *par excellence* of an extensive inventory of infrastructure (roads, bridges, telegraphs, aqueducts, gas lighting, electricity, railroads and tramways); buildings belonging to the Catholic Church and new cults (pantheon, temples, Masonic lodges, churches and cemeteries); civic monuments (statues and mausoleums); military and defence buildings (barracks and jails); government buildings (Presidential House, governmental palaces, municipal councils, post office and general archives); educational and cultural buildings (public schools, universities, libraries, exposition centres and museums); health installations (specialized hospitals); food centres (markets and slaughter houses); and recreational sites (boulevards, parks, thermal and sea baths, hotels, opera theatres, clubs and race courses).[16] As a result of this public building campaign, the old board and its surroundings were given new functions, types of

Figure 9.5
Topographical Plan of Caracas, 1875. (*Source*: Irma de Sola Ricardo. *Contribución al estudio de los planos de Caracas*. Caracas: Ediciones del Cuatricentenario de Caracas, 1967)

buildings, systems of transportation, social groups, real estate properties and places of public representation.

The secular stratum – including the cult of the civic heroes – was placed onto the traditional city in a form analogous to that in which Positivism was imposed onto Scholastic thought. The secular and anticlerical movements naturally led to the demolition of a number of religious buildings, especially convents and monasteries and the creation of new monuments consecrated to the heroes of civil institutions. Churches and seminaries were converted into museums, universities and civic monuments: the old church of La Santísima Trinidad (The Holy Trinity) became the National Pantheon; the church of San Pablo was demolished and in its place the Guzmán Blanco Theatre, known today as the Municipal Theatre (figure 9.6) was built; the San Mauricio

church was turned into the Santa Capilla, on a lesser scale than its Parisian counterpart; the San Francisco Convent was taken over by the university; the Concepción Convent was replaced by the Capitolio. A Masonic temple, under the patronage of Guzmán Blanco and designed, as were a large number of the buildings mentioned above, by Juan Hurtado Manrique, the regime's architect, appeared in the north of the city.

Based on an eclectic European pattern, the architecture was seen as a suitable instrument to give impetus to, and show the modernization of, the country. The massive acceptance and use of imported artistic styles emphasized the distancing from Spanish taste, the spreading adoption of a number of English and French furnishings in public and private works, and the creation of a new urban scene for the emerging bourgeoisie.

Figure 9.6 Guzmán Blanco Theatre, today the Municipal Theatre, *c.* 1880, anonymous author. (*Source*: Fundación John Boulton)

The New Space for the Citizens

As in other places, Caracas was the subject of a nineteenth-century tendency to 'improve different parts of the city with scenic areas for leisure and play'.[17] Therefore, urban space was designed as a 'vista' – creating a panoramic outlook of the city and from the city – where commemorative places and monuments were made to stand out in the layout. The new scale introduced by Guzmán Blanco modified the dimensional system of the city. The new 'pieces of the game' created an urban profile filled with landmarks – cupules, observation towers and pinnacles – which rose above the homogenous and anonymous level of the tiled roofs of buildings of the traditional city. There were also 'functional' buildings on the outskirts of the city like train stations, slaughterhouses, waterworks which gave a touch of monumentality to the peripheral areas.

The continuity of urban space and the figure/background relationship between the open and constructed spaces were also altered. For example, the Congress building, called the Palacio Federal (Federal Palace), whose plans were referred to earlier, was conceived of as an almost free structure, removed from the traditional alignment and surrounded by boulevards. The interior courtyard opened onto two sides and allowed one to see from one street into the next. This effect preceded the ideas of transparency found in modern twentieth-century architecture.

Nevertheless, in spite of Guzmán Blanco's attempts to bring Haussmann's ideas to Caracas, the grid and other traditional elements – such as the construction of low buildings, narrow streets and concentric order – remained the basic pattern to be found in the city. The nearest thing to an avenue of the Second Empire was Paseo Guzmán Blanco (Guzmán Blanco Promenade), an open space between the neo-classical Federal Palace and the neo-gothic University, with the equestrian statue of the leader in the centre (figure 9.7).

As would be expected, the central square in Caracas was not left out of the game of secularization and the celebration of national heroes and their victories. As anticipated, the square was renamed Plaza Bolívar. The statue of the Liberator, which was made in Munich and inaugurated in 1874, was placed in the centre of the space as a focal point of a diagonal walkway (similar to the one found in the Place Royale in Paris) and was designed by Roudier, a French architect. Besides its commemorative function, the plaza was recreated as a place of elegance and as a park, instead of maintaining its traditional role as market

Figure 9.7 Guzmán Blanco's Boulevard, in *Memorias del Ministerio de Obras Públicas*, 1876. (*Source*: Fundación John Boulton)

Figure 9.8 The Casa Amarilla in *Memorias del Ministerio de Obras Públicas*, 1876. (*Source*: Fundación John Boulton)

and agora. The different appearance of the space was probably an expression of modern European ideas of urban recreation, or the notions of leisure and *flânerie* among the emerging urban social classes, who were fond of the new manuals on courtesy and good manners. The old market was removed to the nearby San Jacinto square and the arcades which had been constructed by Governor Ricardos were demolished. Allegorical fountains were placed in the four corners of the square, representing no more and no less than the four seasons which were non-existent in the country. Gas lighting and benches, donated by leading figures, completed the furnishings in the square.

Apart from this, the surroundings were reformed in keeping with the patterns of the eclecticism at the time and also in accordance with the decorum which should prevail both in building construction as well as in public behaviour. These had been the object of town planning and urban design legislation. A presidential residence, the Casa Amarilla (Yellow House) was built to the west of the square, opposite the Cathedral, making the competition between the civil and religious powers obvious (figure 9.8). The northern side was devoted to public buildings, with a strong European flavour. To the south, the Santa Rosa de Lima Convent was remodelled in keeping with the neo-classical style and this housed the Palacio Arzobispal (Archbishop's Palace) and the Palacio de la Gobernación (Governor's Office).

Interlude between Centuries: Abandonment of the Board during the Belle Époque

The end of the nineteenth and the beginning of the twentieth century represented, to a lesser degree, the continuity of Guzmán Blanco-like proposals. Civil and military projects as well as ruptures and rediscovery of Guzmancism alternated during the regimes of J. P. Rojas

Paúl (1888–1890), R. Andueza Palacios (1890–1892), J. Crespo (1892–1898) and I. Andrade (1898–1899). At the same time, there was the consolidation of the commercialism of the local bourgeoisie, and the rise and fall of fiscal earnings, with an intense increase of foreign pressure to pay the external public debt, which substantially reduced the amount of funds allocated to public works, and resulted in no large-scale changes occurring in the city at the *fin-de-siècle*.

The arrival of new actors on the power scene, the Andeans Cipriano Castro and Juan Vicente Gómez, did not lead to any substantial changes to the development agenda. Very few 'novel' projects in the area of urban planning and public works were carried out in Caracas during the government of Castro (1899–1908), who had come to power under the slogan 'new men, new ideas, new procedures'. Perhaps, the beginning of the construction of the Academia Militar (Military Academy) building and the completion of the Ministerio de Hacienda (Exchequer) and the Teatro Nacional (National Theatre) were the most important. In 1902, Venezuela endured the blockade initially imposed by Germany and England, later joined by Italy, France, Holland, Belgium, Spain and Mexico. Having included the occupation of ports, the blockade would end only after mediation by the United States. This did not ease the international tensions, to the point that in 1908 diplomatic ties with the United States were broken, precipitating the end of Castro's regime and the beginning of Gómez's, who was his *compadre* (his son's godfather) and former right-hand man. The latter would rule the country for a period of twenty-six years (1908–1935), combining both liberal as well as social positivist elements – clearly seen in the works of intellectuals such as Pedro

Manuel Arcaya, José Gil Fortoul, Laureano Vallenilla Lanz and César Zumeta – as well as in the country militias' loyalty to their *caudillos*.

With Gómez, the defeat of the last regional caudillos would operate once more in favour of the concentration of power in the centre of the country and the search for the internal connection within the territory through the construction of roads and a more complete network of communications systems. In 1910, the *Comisiones Científicas y Exploradoras del Occidente, Oriente y Centro* (Scientific and Explorative Commissions of the West, East, and Centre) of the country were created, to study the roadways and the supply of potable water to the urban centres along the way. A law passed in the same year ordered the construction of a central roadway in each state with half of the budget coming from that allotted to public works in the country, which '. . . passing through the towns and convenient places would constitute the main roads of each federal entity for the export of fruit and commercial import products'.[18] In the same year, the construction of the Carretera del Este (Eastern Highway) of Caracas began, as well as highways from Caracas to Tuy, La Guaira and Barlovento, highways in Táchira, and the one from Maracay to Ocumare de la Costa. Construction of the Gran Carretera Occidental (Great Western Highway) from Caracas to Táchira – the state in which Gómez had been born – began in 1919, and was to be the main artery for the first national roadway system.

Other infrastructure and communication work was also carried out, such as the network of aqueducts and sewers, and cordless telegraph. There was also the diffusion of the hygiene debate in the country, with the creation of the *Oficina Nacional de Sanidad* (National Office for Heath) and the *Departamento de*

Ingeniería Sanitaria (Department of Sanitary Engineering).[19]

The capital extended its area of influence on a wider, regional level. The occupation of space on the coast for recreational purposes, which had been initiated by Guzmán Blanco, would extend to the sector of Macuto that was now connected by tramcars to the railway station in La Guaira, which was the main recreational centre for the inhabitants of Caracas.[20] It was in Macuto that prefabricated cottages were imported from the United States as antiseismic models made popular after the earthquake of 1900. The *El Cojo Ilustrado* magazine, which played a fundamental role in spreading cultural ideas at the time, noted that in the introduction of these models of North American architecture:

. . . It was the North Americans who have decided to introduce the 'frame house' to Venezuela. The first, put up on the site of La Guzmania, belonging to General Andrade, President of the Republic, has been erected by Mr. Duke. It is made up of 15 pieces and the frame is made of the best class of pitch pine available. The roof is made of wooden boards, pitch paper and roofing board.[21]

The beginning of oil exports allowed the city to become part of the worldwide market. For example, in the plan drawn in 1927, which was known as the '*Indicador Urbano*' (Urban Indicator), the city, or what was the most interesting about it, was enclosed in a circle surrounded by a number of texts which gave information on events such as the visit of Charles Lindbergh, which had occurred in that year (figure 9.9). A paragraph on the right side of the Plan read: 'Venezuelan life is still a little contaminated today by industrial busi-

Figure 9.9 'Urban Indicator' of Caracas, 1927. (*Source*: Irma de Sola Ricardo. *Contribución al estudio de los planos de Caracas.* Caracas: Ediciones del Cuatricentenario de Caracas, 1967)

nesses and foreign commerce . . . there is very little cosmopolitanism . . .'. Nevertheless, the products advertised in the *Indicador* were primarily cars, liquor, cigarettes, cash registers, radios and other items which were predominantly North American. This highlights the influence which the latter had on politics, business and the urban board. In contrast to the supposed isolation of the city, one of the most precise pieces of information on the Plan was that of a detailed survey of refrigerators in use in the city.

However, in contrast to what had occurred during the government of Guzmán Blanco and his immediate successors, official effort in the urban development of Caracas ostensibly decreased during the first few decades of the twentieth century. Instead, emphasis was placed on Maracay, a town about 100 kilometres from Caracas which functioned as a satellite city – a kind of tropical Versailles – for several years, especially from 1925, when Gómez decided not to return to Caracas, considering it a danger for his regime. Gómez's 'almost allergic rejection' of Caracas grew with the protest actions in 1928 by a group of a small urban bourgeoisie, who according to the historian Manuel Caballero:

[They] . . . are conspicuously urban, and extremely rural is the dominant *Gomecista* group. They are students, which means that they are learned, intellectual, almost the reserve of the boorish condition of the tyrant and his henchmen.[22]

As a result of establishing political power in Maracay, this urban centre was thereafter known as 'the Garden City', and an important amount of capital and public works, such as government buildings, military barracks, hotels, infrastructure and open spaces, were carried out there. In fact, the main public space created in Venezuela during the first few decades of the twentieth century is not to be found in Caracas, but in the Plaza Bolívar in Maracay. The office of the *Banco Obrero* (Worker's Bank), the first public housing agency in Latin America, was constructed in Maracay in 1928, for the purpose of building economic and hygienic houses for workers. This led to some urban expansion in popular sectors such as Urbanización Primera, in Maracay, as well as San Agustín, in Caracas – where, for the first time in the country, 200 houses were leased.[23]

Although it had been relegated to second place by the Gómez regime, Caracas continued growing slowly, mainly under the initiative of the private sector. The arrival of the tram car toward the end of the nineteenth century had pushed the expansion of the city to the south and had led to the creation of the first suburb, with single house units: El Paraíso. This residential area, known as the 'New City' was developed by the owners of the tram company along the main road which today is Páez Avenue. Better-off families moved to El Paraíso, thus beginning the abandonment of the centre of the city. This would also be magnified with the increase in the use of the automobile and the construction of new residential districts in the east of the city for the middle and upper classes, under the aegis of real estate promoters such as Eugenio Mendoza Cobeña, Luis Roche and Juan Bernardo Arismendi. The development of the Country Club, a residential district which had clearly been designed following the parameters of the North American suburb, around golf courses, was especially meaningful for this geographic and cultural migration. The American architect Cliff Wendhack was the designer of the Club House, while the office of Frederick Law Olmsted was in charge of the landscaping.

The plan 'Caracas and Its Surroundings', drawn by Eduardo Röhl in 1934, accurately

Figure 9.10 Aerial view of Caracas, taken by Eduardo Röhl, in March 1936 from a plane flying 4,000 metres. (*Source*: Fundación John Boulton)

captures the topography at the time and the wide areas of expansion in the city, sprawled in a vast territory which, at that time, was being photographed from a plane (figure 9.10).

This aerial view was a forerunner of the late-1930s efforts to produce the city's new cartography based on aerial photography.

The Return of Political Power to Caracas and the Formulation of Urban Plans

With Gómez's death on 17 December 1935, political power returned to Caracas and both the centralization as well as the concentration of activities in the capital, recommenced. In the absence of Gómez's restrictive attitude, the supremacy of Caracas would not be questioned again. Besides, the political power which returned to Caracas was not that of an agricultural but of a modern, urban State. Power would be wielded in and from a great city. All of this meant that the capital would take the greater part of the new riches from the country and increase its traditional domain over the rest of the nation with regard to population, political authority, economic strength and culture.

The capital, for its part, would receive an influx of changes fundamental to Venezuelan modernity: the transition from a poor country to a relatively rich one; from an agricultural to an oil and industrial economy; from a

rural to an urban society; from a low to a high demographic growth; from a provincial and homogenous community with few foreigners, to one which was cosmopolitan and heterogeneous; from an authoritarian to a democratic regime; and from an oligarchic and traditional community to a business-oriented and modern society'.[24]

The demography in the capital, which had continued to grow slowly after the Wars of Independence, reflect the importance that the city, and later the Metropolitan Area of Caracas, acquired with regard to the rest of the country (table 9.1). By the 1930s, Caracas had recovered its demographic primacy to that prior to the Wars of Independence, which was over 5 per cent of the entire country. In the meanwhile, the country was becoming urbanized, with the population as well as internal and foreign migration being centred on the big

Table 9.1 Population of Caracas and Venezuela.

Year	Population of Venezuela	Population of Caracas	Population of the AMC	Caracas as % of Venezuela	AMC as as % of Venezuela
1812	c.1,000,000	c.50,000	-	5.0	-
1851	1,429,498	34,165	-	2.4	-
1873	1,784,194	48,897	-	2.7	-
1881	2,075,245	55,638	-	2.7	-
1891	2,323,527	72,429	-	3.1	-
1920	2,411,952	92,212	-	3.8	-
1926	3,026,878	135,253	-	4.4	-
1936	3,364,347	263,358	-	7.8	-
1941	3,850,771	359,225	-	9.3	-
1950	5,034,838	495,064	790,456	9.8	15.7
1961	7,523,999	1,116,245	1,501,289	14.8	20.0

Source: Put together using data from several national censuses.

cities; benefiting what would later become the Area Metropolitana de Caracas (AMC, Metropolitan Area of Caracas), where, by the 1960s, one in every five Venezuelans would be living.

The demographic increase was accompanied by new forms for occupying the landscape. The desire for territorial domination evinced the necessity of adopting instruments which paved the way for geographical knowledge and modification of the environment. This reflected the continuation of the positivist discourse which prolonged the antimony between civilization and barbarism, both in urban planning and in fiction and the cultural imagination. It is not a coincidence that the key work in Venezuelan literature in the first half of the twentieth century is the novel *Doña Bárbara* (1929) by the social democratic leader, educator and writer, Rómulo Gallegos, who became President of the Republic in 1948. In the novel, the city gentleman, lettered and idealist, confronts and overcomes the deeply-rooted and obscure impulses of the wild untamed nature, manifested in the person of a barbaric woman.

Outside the literary sphere, the proposals for intervention in the territory were raised through urban and regional plans. The planning, as in the technical and cultural instruments of previous strata of Venezuela's urban modernization, had to be imported. Because of the lack of local expertise in planning and urban design, several foreigners were hired to prepare both the economic as well as the public works programmes and the urban plans for the city and the other urban centres in the country.

The establishment of planning practice, in terms of ideas and methodology, was realized through several important plans for the capital and the country at large: the February Programme, the Triennial Plan and a series of plans for Caracas from the end of the 1930s until the 1950s. Launched in February 1936, a few months after Gómez's death, the February Programme was the government's answer to the first irruption by city dwellers protesting against the public space. Presented by the

Interim President, Eleazar López Contreras, as a reply to the recent demands made by the population and as a methodological and rational way of organizing governmental activities, the February Programme was 'the first social and economic programme undertaken by the government in Venezuelan history'.[25] It was also the first national public speech broadcast on the radio, which indicates the increasing weight that the new communications media had in reaching the public at large. With the ultimate goal of *'sembrar el petróleo'* (sowing oil) as stated by the intellectual Arturo Uslar Pietri, spokesman for the regime (who coined this slogan meaning that Venezuelans should invest the oil income in order to boost other productive sectors, such as agriculture), the programme contained a number of initiatives in fields such as education, immigration, modernization of the armed forces, roads and public works, agricultural and political reforms.[26]

López Contreras himself presented the Triennial Plan for 1938–1941 before the Congress in May of 1938. The Triennial Plan was aimed at fulfilling the basic governmental objectives of 'rationalize, educate, and populate'. This plan, which followed the outline

established by the February Programme, has been considered the first programme where planning was aimed, through technical and precise objectives and goals, at articulating decision-making which is in contrast to the authoritarian forms of the previous governments.[27] The Triennial Plan pointed towards the notion of national planning as 'an important resource and an expression of the progressive modernization of the State'.[28]

Within this favourable climate for planning, a number of important steps concerning urban issues were taken. In May 1936, Elbano Mibelli, Governor of the Federal District, named a *Comisión de Tráfico Urbano* (Commission for City Traffic), made up of architects, engineers and real estate promoters, M. Mujica Millán, O. A. Machado, R. Domínguez and L. Roche, who put forward a proposal for public transport which would incorporate, among other things, an underground tram which would cross the centre of the city (figure 9.11). At the same time, a group from the *Colegio de Ingenieros* (College of Engineers) and from the Ministry of Public Works presented, through the well-known engineer Luis Eduardo Chataing, the outline of a plan for Caracas which included a study on land use

Figure 9.11 Manuel Mujica Millán's proposal for an underground tramway, Plaza Bolívar station, 1936. (*Source*: Graziano Gasparini y Juan Pedro Posani, *Caracas a través de su arquitectura*, Caracas: Fundación Fina Rojas, 1969)

and population density, a new road network, areas and spaces in reserve and a preliminary proposal for zoning. Although none of the proposals mentioned were sanctioned or adopted by government bodies, they were useful exercises in establishing a debate with regard to the theme of expansion and city transport.

Of greater importance was the creation of the *Comisión Municipal de Urbanismo* (CMU, Municipal Commission of Town Planning) in 1937, aimed at regulating urban development and 'finding logical solutions' to the funda-mental problems of the city.[29] A short while later, in April of 1938, the Government of the Federal District of Caracas created the *Dirección de Urbanismo* (DU, Direction of Town Planning), the first office in charge of urban planning in the country. Its task was to produce, with the help of a group of foreign advisors and under the supervision of the CMU, the *Plan Maestro* (Master Plan) for the city; an unprecedented initiative of general planning in the country's history since the colonial period.[30]

The Monumental Plan: Breaking with the Board, and Creating the New Centrality

France's 'techno-cosmopolitan'[31] and monu-mental urbanism would play a crucial role in late-1930s Caracas through the planning firm of Prost, Lambert, Rotival and Wegenstein; especially through the engineer Maurice Rotival (1892–1980), who was the most important foreign advisor in the programmes for the renovation of the city in the middle of the century.[32] Hired by Governor Elbano Mibelli, Rotival arrived in Caracas in 1937. After several months at work during which the French advisors collaborated with their Venezuelan counterparts, the so-called *Plan Monumental* (Monumental Plan) was presented to the Municipal Council in 1939, and was approved in 1940 in so far as the road system was concerned (figure 9.12).

The aerial vision of Rotival, who was himself a pilot, was strengthened in 1936 by the first series of aerial photographs of the city. The scope of the images provided inputs for the design of geopolitical strategies applied to urban planning, which was a characteristic of this engineer's approach. At the same time, he acknowledged the country's advantageous position and its rapid ascent, thanks to its earnings from oil, to become one of the richest countries in Latin America. His proposal

Figure 9.12 Cover of the Caracas Monumental Plan, 1939. (*Source*: Gobernación del Distrito Federal, *Revista Municipal del Distrito Federal*, No. 1, 1939)

shaped the search for comprehensive planned urban development, which had been receding under the pressure of sudden urban growth.

The *Plan Monumental* was accompanied by a group of plans and diagrams which represented all the possible scales of territorial and urban planning. It began with Caracas in the earthly globe, which meant an early recognition of the global nature of the territory and the appearance of regional cities, and ended with a perspective of the project for a market. The plan of the city was clear, with a main centre as the prevailing element of the urban image, which was symbolically connected with the interior and exterior of the country by great roadways.

The Plan described this image in grandiose terms:

The great City, with its lovely boulevards, parks, theatres, clubs etc. The outskirts, with the beautiful garden-cities and their sports clubs linked to the city through comfortable and beautiful arteries for rapid circulation.[33]

The territorial outline of separation between the centre and the peripheries was imbued with the theme of open space and an aesthetic associated with movement systems and gardens. This large, beautiful and extended city was compared to the face of an existing city which did not seem, however, so irregular and undesirable as to have required an operation which was typically Haussmannesque. In this respect, Governor Mibelli asserted that 'Leaving the city in its present state is the same as abandoning it to its own decadence', and although the city 'until the last years has conserved the physical aspects that we like . . . it is becoming an old and unhealthy city where only an unhappy population could live . . . [unless it is reconstructed and its layout modified and] giving it a consonant aspect in keeping with modern demands'.[34] As in other cities, it was assumed that 'the modernization could be achieved by placing a regular order on the urban web by providing good communication between the different parts of the capital and in improving the city's appearance'.[35]

'Sowing Oil': Public Works and Modern Architecture

The demands of a new and modern city were strengthened by appealing to functionalist elements, including the economy, hygiene, public opinion, tourism, lighting, transport and safety. These elements were clashing, theoretically, with the ornamental tendencies of traditional urban planning.

In spite of the functional rhetoric, the architectural images which accompanied the Plan were nearer to those postulated by *Beaux Arts* than by the tendencies of International Style. These tendencies had already made their debut in Caracas and were reflected in a number of private houses built in 1936 by M. Mujica Millán in the then suburb of Campo Alegre, and in some school buildings resulting from the agenda for the modernizing of the education system, as in Liceo Caracas, designed also in 1936 by C. Domínguez, and the Gran Colombia school, by C. R. Villanueva in 1939. The immense public works programme undertaken by the oil-exporting State which would boom in the following decades, would adopt the International Style for constructing important buildings in the nucleus of the *Plan Monumental* itself, as would be seen later on.

The Great Corridors of the Modern Period

Where there was a great degree of updating in the *Plan Monumental* was in the idea of the centre of Caracas as a multi-functional nucleus, developed along great corridors. Among them, the Central Avenue, now known as Bolívar Avenue, was the main corridor. Following the east-west axis along the narrow valley, this monumental avenue, inaugurated on 31 December 1949, questioned the concentric pattern of the city by imposing the French boulevard onto the grid and the system of squares which the Spanish urban planning had institutionalized in Latin America (figure 9.13). It should be noted that the idea of a great east-west artery had been put forward in the 1930s as one has only to look at the proposals, both made in 1936, by Ramiro Nava and Luis Roche, who were two of the promoters at that time concerned with urban planning themes, and who took the debate to the press in a number of articles in the *El Universal* newspaper. The former proposed two great perpendicular avenues – the Gran Avenida Bolívar (Great Bolivar Avenue) and the Avenida Urdaneta (Urdaneta Avenue) – 130 metres wide and 15 and 4 kilometres long, respectively. The two great avenues, which almost completely eliminated the original board layout found in Caracas, would greatly change the Cathedral, their meeting point, as three new façades would have to be constructed.[36] In the meantime, Roche, who was the least destructive of the two, suggested crossing the centre of the city a little more to the south, with the creation of a 36-metre wide avenue inspired by those of the Champs Elysées, which would continue on toward the suburbs along the Carretera del Este (East Highway), inspired by Broadway.[37]

The great avenues foreseen in the *Plan Monumental* epitomized the spectacular development and transformation of the public space which occurred in Caracas from the middle of the century and illustrate the forces which generated a new territorial, architectural and urban planning form through a complex process of negotiation in which urban planners, civil engineers, private promoters and governmental agencies were

Figure 9.13 The old grid system and network of roads, Caracas Monumental Plan, 1939. (*Source*: Gobernación del Distrito Federal, *Revista Municipal del Distrito Federal*, No. 1, 1939)

involved. This led to the introduction, in the sphere of an underdeveloped metropolis, of the urban experiences which characterize modernity and shape the individuals' perception. The modern experience changed the movement into an end in itself,[38] and this had important urban implications. The city stopped being 'a place of exile, protection and shelter and became an instrument of communication'.[39] In the case of Venezuela, the development of the communication systems allowed, on the one hand, the large-scale introduction of planning techniques and imported design guidelines and, on the other, the expression of the urgent need that the country and its elites had to import modernity. The great highways and avenues opened 'in the heart of an underdeveloped country, a perspective of all the enlightened promises held in the modern world'.[40]

This opening of the corridors was not free of complications. Throughout the twentieth century, problems were faced in adapting the existing city and changing it into a new organized city through new mobility schemes, as Haussmann had done in Paris in the nineteenth century. This occurred fundamentally because the old city was against the modern movement, as it was a symbol of the tradi-

tional and modest urban growth of colonial and republican times, whereas its structure clashed with the new demands for mobility.[41] In Caracas, the tensions between the old and new layout were often solved by the use of the bulldozer and large-scale demolition (figure 9.14). For this reason, the *Plan Monumental* foresaw, among other things, 'a new road plan based on a new layout',[42] which proposed the opening up of the congested city centre through the widening of the existing streets and the opening of diagonal arteries. The argument was that the network of traditional streets found in Caracas was of a regular layout, but inadequate for the volume of traffic in the emerging metropolis.

The 30-metre wide central road would end at two large open spaces: El Calvario hill to the west (where a square with a monument was proposed, a monument to Simón Bolívar and the new civic centre) and Los Caobos Park, in the east. Two groups of diagonal roads would connect the new roadways at each end. Due to its proportions, the avenue would provide symmetric and homogenous architecture, a monumental aspect to the city, similar to that found in the Champs Elysées in Paris, and Unter den Linden in Berlin, two examples given in the plan's text as models to

Figure 9.14
Demolition in the centre of Caracas, in the background the old Guzmán Blanco Theatre. (*Source*: Centro Simón Bolívar, *Acción sobre Caracas, c.* 1959)

be followed. The group would include a market square in front of the Guzmanian church of Santa Teresa, several diagonal arteries, a cloverleaf intersection of the avenue with the Norte-Sur 7 and a network of pedestrian paths which would join the central avenue to Plaza Bolívar. An organic analogy was the reason for this immense intervention:

It was required to create a spinal cord; to insert there the essential organism; to isolate and ventilate the communities; to shape the arteries, squares, and gardens on such a beautiful natural surrounding: to let flow the blood, and make an hypertrophied heart to beat regularly.[43]

It should be pointed out that in contrast to the massive public intervention into the old city centre, the *Plan Monumental* freed the extension of the city to private enterprise which had been becoming the key figure in the urban *ensanche* (expansion).

Conclusion

Rotival's departure for the United States, World War II and some local events led to changes in the *Plan Monumental* of 1939 which, nonetheless, continued providing a general outline for future developments in the city. The most important change was the creation of a group of residential buildings in El Silencio, instead of the Centro Cívico (Civic Centre) proposed in the plan. With this, housing, urban renewal and sanitary improvement of the degraded districts were placed at the centre of urban planning efforts. The residential activity moved from the background to the foreground.

With regard to urban planning, after the gap created by the war, in 1946 the *Comisión Nacional de Urbanismo* (CNU, National Commission of Town Planning) was created with the aim of preparing an updated plan. As had occurred in the previous decade, the CNU and the Venezuelan government required the services of foreign advisors in the field of urban planning. At that time, Rotival was hired once more as a consultant along with other important figures who worked in the United States, such as Francis Violich, José Luis Sert and Robert Moses.[44]

The new *Plano Regulador* (Master Plan),

aimed at a population of 1.7 million, was prepared in 1951 and presented in 1952. Although it repeated some elements in the image of the boulevards, wide spaces, rational circulation and monumentality, the *Plano Regulador* put forward up-to-date ideas of urban planning such as the principles of urban functionalism, and the division of zones, following the principles of the *Congrès Internacionaux d'Architecture Moderne* (CIAM). This gave rise to the creation of neighbourhood units and the separation of industrial, commercial and residential areas. Following this logic, the city was divided into twelve zones or communities, each designed on the base of several neighbourhood units. The urban planning acquired a less figurative and a more abstract character, so much so that the so-called International Style became usual in architectural representation. That would close another chapter or layer in the history of urban planning in Caracas, marked by the predominance of North American models.

The 'games' in the urban modernity entailed variable conceptions of territory, architecture and public space in Caracas. The following change occurred from the middle of the twentieth century, when the metropolis became the dominant force in the territory, modern architecture under the International Style prevailed with skyscrapers changing the city's silhouette, while the large corridors were constructed as a model for a new urbanism in which the avenue replaced the square as the public space *par excellence*.

NOTES

1. Romero, J. L. (1976) *Latinoamérica: las ciudades y las ideas*. Buenos Aires: Siglo Veintinuo Editores.

2. Sanoja, O. M. *et al*. (1998) *Arqueología de Caracas*. Caracas: Biblioteca de la Academia Nacional de la Historia.

3. Fernández, R. (1998) *El laboratorio americano, arquitectura, geocultura y regionalismo*. Madrid: Editorial Biblioteca Nueva.

4. Due to the non-existence of aboriginal urban traditions in Venezuela as there were in Mexico or Peru, it is possible to say that the influence of the first settlers was almost absent in urban matters. There were more than 25,000 Indians in Caracas, Valley of the Toromaynas, by the time of the Europeans' arrival, but in less than 25 years population had decreased to some 6,000 because of the natives' (resistance) war against the conquerors, aggravated by epidemic diseases. Caracas nomenclature retains many aboriginal names, which refer principally, as expected, to natural elements. Examples are found in the name of Caracas itself and others like Guatire, Catuche, Anauco, Baruta, Chacao and Petare. By contrast, artificial creations such as the grid and its parts, have Hispanic names.

5. Rossi, A. (1966, 1971) *La arquitectura de la ciudad*. Barcelona: Gustavo Gili.

6. The same kind of 'games' took place in other parts of the Venezuelan province and in the rest of Latin America, where the foundation of cities was both a symbolic declaration and a standard administrative procedure of an European power in its colonial enterprise within an unknown and very large territory. As a result, a uniform configuration appeared which bore a remarkable resemblance to Spanish settlements throughout the continent. The general form is an orthogonal grid, whose historical origin is as old as urban civilization. The guidelines of urban plans collected in 1573, during Felipe II's reign, in the so-called *Leyes de Indias* (Laws of the Indies), were the first modernizing effort that thereafter became tradition In Latin America.

7. The stratification of the population, established at the time of the first settlements, tended to be reproduced as the city grew. The urban elite, made up of an aristocracy or a high class of white landholders, most of them Creoles (also called the '*grandes cacaos*' [big cocoas] or '*mantuanos*') clustered around the Plaza Mayor. Meanwhile, less wealthy people – such as the newcomers from Spain, '*pardos*', Indians, and blacks – lived in areas more distant from the centre.

8. Caracas, like many other Hispanic foundations in the Americas, grew in a concentric way and along the paths leading to rural properties. As the time passed, the open form of the grid reinforced the strong relationship between the city and the country. See González, L and Vicente, H. (1992) Ciudades y haciendas. *Sartenejas*, 7, pp. 4–8.

9. A general process of modernization of the Spanish empire was undertaken under the Bourbon reformers, particularly during Carlos III's reign (1759–1788). This process, of French inspiration, led to many conflicts with the Catholic Church. In the Venezuelan case, reformers also wanted to punish the province for the 1749 rebellion. Ferry, R. J. (1989) *The Colonial Elite of Early Caracas. Formation & Crisis. 1567–1767*. Berkeley and Los Angeles: University of California Press, p. 246.

10. *Ibid*., p. 248.

11. Cunill Grau, P. (1987) *Geografía del poblamiento venezolano en el siglo XIX*. Caracas: Ediciones de la Presidencia de la República, Vol. 1, p. 445. It is worth noticing that, by 1821, the city's population was less than 17,000 people, about one-third less than the 1812 population.

12. Nazoa, A. (1967) *Caracas física y espiritual*. Caracas: Ediciones del Cuatricentenario de Caracas.

13. In Caracas, the tension between the State and the Church grew when the Archbishop Silvestre Guevara y Lira was expelled from the country (1870); the extinction of seminaries (1872) and the convents of the nuns (1874) was decreed, the creation of a Venezuelan Church independent of the Roman Curia was debated (1876), while the systematic demolition and recycling of religious buildings took place.

14. See Carrera Damas, G. (1969) *El culto a Bolívar*. Caracas: EBUCV; Castro L., L. (1987) *De la patria boba a la teología bolivariana*. Caracas: Monte Ávila.

15. Quoted in Esteva G., R. (1986) *Guzmán Blanco y el arte venezolano*. Caracas: Academia Nacional de la Historia, p. 1.

16. More detailed studies of the urban proposals of the

Guzmán era can be found in Gasparini, G. and Posani, J. P. (1969) *Caracas a través de su arquitectura*. Caracas: Fundación Fina Rojas; Galey, J. H. (1973) A City Comes of Age: Caracas in the Era of Antonio Guzmán Blanco, (1870–1888), *Boletín CIHE*, 15, pp. 77-113; Zawisza, L. (1988) *Arquitectura y obras públicas en Venezuela. Siglo XIX*. Caracas: Ediciones de la Presidencia de la República, 3 vols.; Almandoz, A. (1997) *Urbanismo europeo en Caracas (1870–1940)*. Caracas: Fundarte, Equinoccio, Ediciones de la Universidad Simón Bolívar.

17. Boyer, M. C. (1996) *The City of Collective Memory: Its Historical Imagery and Architectural Entertainments*. Cambridge, Mass.: The MIT Press, p. 34.

18. (1988) *Diccionario de Historia de Venezuela*. Caracas: Fundación Polar, 3 vols., Vol. 1, p. 319.

19. Almandoz, A. (2000) The shaping of Venezuelan urbanism in the hygiene debate of Caracas, 1880–1910. *Urban Studies*, 37 (11), pp. 2073–2089.

20. Macuto was the first planned area of the country, as a result of the combined efforts of public and private sectors. It was a product of an Executive Decree by Guzmán Blanco in March, 1884, according to which the owner of the land, Antonio Delfino, ceded to the government enough space for two public squares as well as to lay out streets and avenues. The government should plan and furbish the resort and provide the necessary public services to the new owners, who would buy their properties from Delfino, submitting to what the regulator plan established.

21. (1899) *El Cojo Ilustrado*, 8 (176), p. 285.

22. Caballero, M. (1994) *Gómez, el tirano liberal*. Caracas: Monte Avila, p.290.

23. The head office of the *Banco Obrero* moved to Caracas in 1936. In its first 17 years it produced 2,465 lodgings – an average of less than 150 units each year. The massive production would start later, in the 1940s. Between 1945 and 1958, 39,636 dwellings were produced, more than 3,000 a year. For more information, see: Instituto Nacional de la Vivienda (1988) *60 años de experiencia en desarrollos urbanísticos de bajo costo en Venezuela*. Caracas: INAVI.

24. González, L. (1996) Modernity and the City: Caracas 1935–1958. Unpublished Ph.D. Dissertation, Department of City and Regional Planning, Cornell University, Ithaca, NY.

25. Hellinger, D. C. (1991) *Venezuela: Tarnished Democracy*. Boulder, Colorado: Westview Press, p. 52.

26. López Contreras, E. (1988) Programa de Febrero, in *Documentos que hicieron historia. Vida republicana de Venezuela, 1810-1989*. Caracas: Presidencia de la República, Vol. II, pp. 183–195.

27. Guzmán P., J. E. (1983) *López Contreras: el último General*. Caracas: Gobernación del Distrito Federal, p. 30.

28. Tinoco, E. (1991) *Asalto a la modernidad. López, Medina y Betancourt: del mito al hecho*. Caracas: Academia Nacional de la Historia, p. 76.

29. Villanueva, C. R. (1950, 1966) *Caracas en tres tiempos*. Caracas: Ediciones del Cuatricentenario de Caracas, p. 21.

30. There is another initiative that can be considered as a pioneer effort in Venezuela's urban planning: the plan of Ciudad Ojeda, prepared in 1937. Ciudad Ojeda was created through a Presidential Decree on 19 January 1937, and projected by the urban planner and architect Cipriano Domínguez. It was conceived as the new city of the Oriental Coast of the Maracaibo Lake, replacing the old city of Lagunillas, which had been destroyed in a fire. According to the historian Eduardo Arcila Farías, modern urban planning started in Venezuela 'with the construction of Ciudad Ojeda, the first city that, under Republican Venezuela, was built by official disposition according to a preconceived plan, with all the requirements of a modern city, including domestic gas; this turned it into the first Venezuelan city that established the use of this product of hydrocarbon...' See Arcila Farías, E. (1974) *Centenario del Ministerio de Obras Públicas: influencia de este Ministerio en el desarrollo, 1874–1974*. Caracas: Ministerio de Obras Públicas, p. 267.

31. Term used by Rabinow, P. (1989) *French Modern: Norms and Forms of the Social Environment*. Cambridge, Mass.: The MIT Press.

32. Considered one of the founders of urban planning, Maurice Emile Henri Rotival, graduated from the École Central in Paris and was Professor in the School of Fine Arts at Yale University. Besides his experience of urban planning in Caracas, he coordinated or participated in the planning of New Heaven and New Britain, Connecticut; Winter Park, Florida; Reims and Paris, France; Algers, Algeria; Baghdad, Iraq; Madagascar; Guyana and Marruecos. The other active member of the firm in Venezuela was Jacques Lambert, with previous experience in Chile and Mexico; he was also a distinguished draftsman. Prost, the *Beaux-Arts* master, who contributed with the process of exportation of the French urban discipline to Africa and Asia, did not take active part in the urban planning of Caracas.

33. Gobierno del Distrito Federal (1939) *Revista municipal del Distrito Federal*, 1, p. 23.

34. *Ibid.*, pp. 14–15.

35. Çelik, Z. (1993) *The Remaking of Istanbul. Portrait of an Ottoman City en the Nineteenth Century*. Berkeley and Los Angeles: University of California Press, p. 158.

36. Nava, R. (1971) *Obras completas*. Madrid: Editorial Mediterráneo, pp. 789–810.

37. Roche, L. (1936) Embellecimiento de Caracas, *El Universal* (March 4), p. 3.

38. Sennett, R. (1996) *Flesh and Stone: the Body and the City in Western Civilization*. New York: W.W. Norton, p. 264.

39. Argan, G. C. (1984) *Historia del arte como historia de la ciudad*. Barcelona: Editorial Laia, p. 225.

40. Berman, M. (1988) *All That Is Solid Melts into Air. The Experience of Modernity*. New York: Penguin Books, p. 195.

41. Tafuri, M. (1977) Teorías e historia de la arquitectura (hacia una nueva concepción del espacio arquitectónico). Barcelona: Editorial Laia, pp. 80–81.

42. Villanueva, *op. cit.*, pp. 21–22.

43. Rotival, M. (1966) Caracas marcha hacia adelante, in Villanueva, *op. cit.*, pp. 172–182.

44. González, L. (1996) Modernity for Import and Export: The United States' Influence on the Architecture and Urbanism of Caracas. *Colloqui*, 11, pp. 64–77.

Urbanism, Architecture, and Cultural Transformations in San José, Costa Rica, 1850–1930

Florencia Quesada

Costa Rica's capital is a gay little city of uprising contrasts and contradictions . . . San José is anything but American in appearance and manners. On a very miniature scale it is Parisian. At all events, the streets, the stores and the people show a European stamp that is unmistakable.[1]

George Palmer Putnam (1912)

Todos advirtieron que en ellas se labraba un nuevo estilo de vida latinoamericano, signado, sin duda, por las influencias extranjeras pero oscuramente original, como era original el proceso social y cultural que se desenvolvía en ellas. Metrópolis de imitación a primera vista, cada una de ellas escondía un matiz singular que se manifestaría poco a poco.[2]

(Everyone noticed that in these metropolises a new style of Latin American life was being forged, without doubt marked by foreign influences, yet at the same time indefinably original, as were the social and cultural processes which developed within them. Metropolises of imitation at first sight, each concealed its own particular nuances which, little by little, would become apparent.)

José Luis Romero (1976)

In the second half of the nineteenth century cities in Latin America began a slow but continuous process of urban and cultural trans-formation, which José Luis Romero has called the birth of the bourgeois city.[3] The effective integration of Latin American countries into the world economy as primary producers – of coffee in the case of Costa Rica – was one of the fundamental reasons for the change. Cities, especially capital cities such as San José, changed in both size and form as a result of population growth, the creation of new means of transportation and new public services, and the altered lifestyles and leisure activities of the people in the public open spaces and improved areas.[4]

When North American traveller George Palmer Putnam visited San José on a journey through Central America in 1912, he encountered the results of this urban transformation. The irony of Putnam's opinion is that after comparing San José to Paris (with great imagination and poetry!) he added, among other things, that 'nearly all the buildings are of one story' and the 'sidewalks are absurdly narrow'.[5] Furthermore, Putnam showed only the fashionable and bourgeois side of the city, giving an incomplete picture of the contrasts and contradictions that also emerged in San José as a result of urban growth and social differentiation.

It was evident that San José's appearance as a colonial city had changed, a change particularly visible on the main avenues and streets. The introduction of new types of architecture in private and public buildings and the opening of new areas of development gave travellers like Putnam the impression of a small European metropolis. But the changes coexisted with or were built over the structure of a still very colonial city symbolized by the narrow sidewalks and single-storey houses which the traveller also mentioned.

This chapter analyses urban transformations in San José, Costa Rica from the 1850s to 1930s, highlighting the influences of European urbanism that led to the creation of a modern city in physical, architectural, and cultural terms. Three main phases of development can be distinguished in San José over this period. The first architectural and cultural changes were introduced from 1850 to the 1880s. The first urban shifts following modern principles were undertaken from the 1880s to 1900s. The 1910s and 1920s saw the consolidation of these developments and the geographic expansion of changes initiated in the last decades of nineteenth century.

This chapter begins by examining the origins and growth of San José in the eighteenth century and its establishment as capital of Costa Rica in the nineteenth century, which sparked a phase of cultural transformation that led to the city's first urban changes. Next the chapter describes the adoption of modern urbanism from the 1880s to 1930s, with new services, transportation, public and private infrastructure, spatial reorganization, growth, and social segregation. It also analyses the creation of public spaces such as parks and promenades and the new urban sociability which flowered there. The last section of the chapter outlines the transitions of the 1930s, which would lead to another phase of urban and architectural development in San José.

From Village to Capital

Most of the primate cities in Latin America were founded during the sixteenth century. San José is one of the few cases in Latin American urban history of a secondary village founded during the eighteenth century that became a primate city during the nineteenth century.[6] The traditional historiography of San José claims humble origins for the city, founded in 1737 when official and religious authorities required several families living in the Valley of Aserrí to form a village and build a small church on the site called La Boca del Monte. The first hermitage was completed in 1738 dedicated to the Patriarca Señor San José (Patriarch Saint Joseph).[7]

In spite of official support for the village's creation, settlement was precarious due, among other reasons, to the lack of water. It was not until 1776, when a new parish church and plaza were built one block north of the original centre, that a more defined urban structure developed within the city. During the last decades of the eighteenth century the streets and blocks were laid out according to the grid plan, which gave San José the imprint typical of most colonial towns in Latin America.[8]

However in San José the political and religious core was shared between the typical centre of colonial power – the main plaza and the parish church – and the city's original nucleus one block south. The construction of the Factoría de Tabaco (headquarters of centralized tobacco purchasing) and some of the State's most important public offices, such as the Palacio Nacional (National Palace) and the Congress, at the site of the original plaza helped anchor the State's political-administrative functions to that site during the nineteenth and twentieth centuries.

Another reason for the late urban consolidation of San José was the pattern of settlement that prevailed in Costa Rica's Central Valley before the production of coffee. According to Lowell Gudmundson the population was spread over a series of *caseríos* or small villages with a nucleated pattern of dwellings.[9] This nucleated settlement pattern facilitated social control by Spanish authorities and the exploitation of labour.

The construction of the Factoría de Tabaco in San José in 1783 and the later royal decision to assign monopoly tobacco production to the province of Costa Rica spurred the village's economic and demographic growth.[10]

After Independence local elites fiercely disputed which of the four cities of the Central Valley would become the capital. The *Batalla de Ochomogo* (Battle of Ochomogo) in 1823 gave San José a temporary victory over Cartago (the old colonial capital), Alajuela and Heredia. Tensions remained and in 1834 the *Ley de la Ambulancia* (Law of Peregrination) established the rotation of the capital among the four cities, a measure that ended a year later in the *Guerra de la Liga* (League War), which confirmed San José's predominance.[11] The official status of capital was given to the city in 1837 by Chief of State Braulio Carrillo.[12]

San José lies at an altitude of 1,200 metres, surrounded by mountains and small hills, on the western side of Costa Rica's Central Valley in a fertile plain between the rivers Torres and María Aguilar and other small tributaries of the river Grande de Tárcoles. Its position and the fertility of the soil were among the characteristics that most struck travellers during the nineteenth and early twentieth centuries. Green coffee plantations spread all the way to the borders of the tiny urban settlement, giving the impression of a village submerged in the greenery of its surroundings.

From 1840 onwards San José's successful production and commercialization of coffee gave the erstwhile small village the indisputable position as head of the country.[13] It became the political, economic, social and cultural centre of Costa Rica, and the node of communications. In sum, by 1850 San José was a dynamic coffee centre that was successfully inserted into the capitalist market, but its rural and colonial character was still evident in its physical appearance.

According to the plan of San José made by Nicolás Gallegos in 1851, which depicts the perfect colonial grid plan, the city comprised sixty-four blocks[14] which by 1864 housed 5,553 inhabitants.[15] Felipe Molina's description of the capital in 1851 captured its embryonic nature. 'The city is only now taking shape: there are no more than ten blocks extending from the main plaza and the rest of the residents [of the municipality] lived scattered in the surrounding fields' (figure 10.1).[16]

Architectural changes in the colonial city began just after Costa Rica was declared an Independent Republic in 1848. In 1850 the State centralized public works and a neo-classical language was introduced for the construction of the first public buildings of the young Republic. One of the key figures in this process was Prussian engineer Franz Kurtze, the first Director of Public Works, who encouraged the architectural modernization of public and religious buildings with the use of new construction materials such as brick instead of adobe, and hydraulic machinery.[17]

Kurtze came to Costa Rica in the 1850s with the *Compañía Berlinesa de Colonización* (Berlin Company of Colonization), one of the several colonization schemes promoted by the State to attract European population. He built many of the country's most important

churches and public buildings in the 1850s and 1860s. He was also in charge of the layout of many roads and the planning of new towns, such as Limón on the Caribbean coast.[18]

The Palacio Presidencial (Presidential Palace), the Teatro Mora (Mora Theatre) – the city's first theatre – the Cuartel de Artillería (Artillery Barracks), the Universidad de Santo Tomás (University of Saint Thomas), the Seminario (Seminary) – a religious high school for boys – and the first hospital, San Juan de Dios, are among the best examples of the transforma-

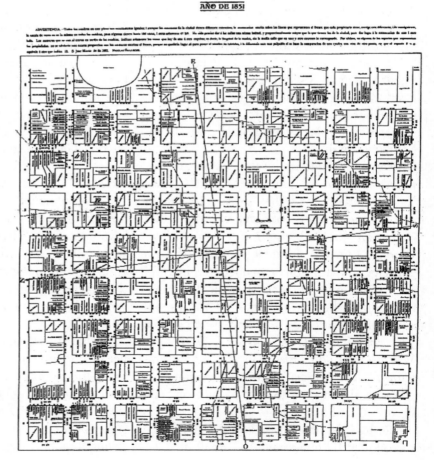

Figure 10.1 Plan of San José, by Nicolás Gallegos, 1851. (*Source*: National Archive of Costa Rica)

tion of the predominant architectural pattern of single-storey adobe buildings.[19] All of them, except the hospital, built on the western side of the city, were erected in the surroundings of the two main plazas.

At the same time a major process of cul-tural transformation and Europeanization, spear-headed by the coffee oligarchy, was underway. Services expanded, as the first hotels, restau-rants, stores, pharmacies, and clubs opened. Secularization accelerated. Consumption diver-sified. A more defined urban culture was born.[20]

From Capital to Mini Metropolis?

Though the process of cultural change began at mid-century, it was not until the 1880s that physical changes would transform the city's structure. The introduction of modern urban planning and design from Europe altered the colonial grid plan for the first time in that decade, breaking the hegemony of San José's two traditional centres (the cathedral and the original nucleus). As Steven Palmer has pointed out, this change was possible only when the wealth produced by coffee had matured and an urban bourgeois culture had begun to differentiate itself from the culture of other urban groups.[21]

Essential to San José's metamorphosis were the national political integration and administrative centralization promoted by the Liberals who took power in the 1870s. The adoption of a new urban model to shape a different concept of city was a conscious choice by Liberal elites, for whom European theories and practices were the sure road to civilization and progress. The emblematic Liberal project was the construction of the Ferrocarril al Atlántico (Atlantic Railway), begun in 1870 and not completed until 1890. This line became the most important route for communication and coffee exports to European markets, and the main railway sta-tion of San José became the epicentre of urban renewal on the north-east side of the city.

Transforming the capital in line with mod-ern principles was integral to the Liberals' political project: to build a nation-state. In the new boulevards and parks they erected monuments and statues promoting their civic and patriotic ideals (a point we return to below).[22] Local power in the shape of the Municipality also played an important role in promoting new infrastructure, developing new areas and maintaining some of the new public spaces such as parks. Public works were decentralized during the dictatorship of Tomás Guardia (1870–1882), who gave more power to the municipalities and in-creased the budget allocation for new services and infrastructure.[23]

As Jorge Enrique Hardoy has noted for many Latin American cities, Haussmann's ideas were used in a very fragmented way and limited to specific solutions and areas within the city.[24] Such was the case in San José where urban transformations throughout all the period of analysis were never part of a major urban project but rather isolated improve-ments that facilitated localized expansion. As a result, at the end of nineteenth century growth was concentrated to the north-east and the west and to a lesser degree in the southern part of the city. In 15 years San José almost doubled its size, from 153 blocks in 1889 to 259 in 1904 (figure 10.2).[25]

The following section traces the transformation of the capital through the development of public services and infrastructure and new public and private architecture. The influence of European urbanism permeated all of these, but modern urbanism would leave its strongest mark on the select new sector where luxurious residences, shady parks, and State buildings arose side by side, reflecting the new elite's ideal of the bourgeois city.

Figure 10.2   General view of San José. Postcard beginning twentieth century.

Public Services and Modern Infrastructure

Carl Schorske notes that one of the key elements of nineteenth-century urbanism was the creation of public services, 'the bone and muscle of the modern city'.[26] In San José after 1860 new public infrastructure and services burgeoned. A telegraph was installed in 1869.[27] Public telephones were in service for State offices in 1886, and by 1897 had been installed in San José and the most important cities of the Central Valley.[28]

In 1867 the engineer Angel Miguel Velázquez, commissioned by the State, started construction of an iron pipeline to carry potable water into San José, which was officially inaugurated in 1868 but completed a year later. In the first decades of the twentieth century a new sewer system was built and *acequias* (small streams) were channelled in conduits.

In 1884 electric lighting replaced the oil lamps in use since 1856 on some of the main streets of the capital.[29] A new power station built in the 1890s allowed the installation of incandescent lighting in private homes, and soon powered the trolley as well.[30]

The first trolley ran through the macadamized streets of San José in 1899. Owned by the Costa Rica Electric Light and Traction Company (an enterprise founded by Minor Cooper Keith with English capital), the trolley was a key change in city transportation because it allowed easy access to the suburbs and promoted the creation of new outlying neighbourhoods.[31] By 1922 trolley lines reached to the city's four cardinal points: west to the end of La Sabana Park (figure 10.3), east to San Pedro, north-east to Guadalupe.[32] The last line completed was to Plaza González Víquez, at the edge of the lower-class neighbourhoods in the south of the city.

The first automobiles arrived in San José around the turn of the century, and public buses were introduced in 1922.[33] From 1920 to 1930 many *carreteras* (roads) to other cities were improved, and the main streets of San José were paved between 1929 and 1930. As with the installation of electric lighting and potable water, the paving of San José's main streets began at the Atlantic Railway station and continued across town, ending up at La Sabana.[34]

Until 1889 streets were named for the most important building in the block or for a public figure, a colonial tradition replaced that year by a modern nomenclature of consecu-

tive numbering. In 1904 another nomenclature was introduced: streets (running north–south) and avenues (running east–west) were numbered progressively, odds to one side and evens to the other spreading outward from the city centre.[35]

As in many other cities in Latin America at the turn of the century, the expansion of infrastructure and public services in San José helped shape a new concept of the city, now renovated with a modern 'air'. Yet in the 1920s and 1930s ox-carts rolled over the streets of San José next to the tramways and automobiles, a testimony to the rural character that still prevailed in the capital and to the contrasts contained within the slow process of urban change.

Figure 10.3 Tramway in Paseo Colón. Photo: Manuel Gómez Miralles, 1922. (*Source*: National Archive of Costa Rica)

Specific Buildings for Specific Purposes

In 1907 José Segarra and Joaquín Juliá, two Spanish visitors to San José, interviewed former President Cleto González Víquez at his home, one of the most exclusive spots in San José in front of the Parque Morazán (Morazán Park). A member of the Liberal elite and an urban reformer, González Víquez held forth on the interests and goals of the State in relation to urban growth.[36] According to González Víquez health, aesthetics, and the status of San José as capital of the Republic all demanded the construction of certain buildings in order to be at the same level as other 'modern' capitals. Among the most important he mentioned were the public library then under construction, a new jail, the post office, and a new sewer system. As President, he declared, his aim had been to bring the benefits of hygiene and urban improvement to every corner of the nation (figure 10.4).[37]

From 1885 onwards Liberal elites did indeed promote the construction of varied infrastructure in the capital and other cities of the country as part of a social policy that united

hygiene, education, welfare, and control according to the new principles of modern urbanism. Two main phases of architectural and urban change can be distinguished in this process. The first ran from the 1880s until 1910, when an earthquake in the colonial capital Cartago destroyed the entire city and inspired new construction guidelines. The second, the 1910s and 1920s saw the consolidation of the variety of types of architecture introduced some decades before, but now built with new construction techniques and materials.

New 1890 guidelines for the construction of public works defined the *Dirección de Obras Públicas* (Public Works Department) more as a supervisor and technical advisor than a constructor. The State reinforced the relevant departments with many more professionals, European and Costa Rican engineers like Léon Tessier, Augusto Fla. Chebba, Enrique Invernizzio and Nicolás Chavarría, among others, and left construction work to private enterprises under a public tendering system.[38]

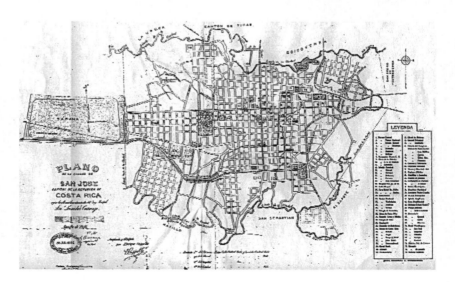

Figure 10.4 Plan of San José, by Leonidas Carranza, 1916. (*Source*: National Archive of Costa Rica)

Figure 10.5 Central Avenue. Photo: Manuel Gómez Miralles, 1922. (*Source*: National Archive of Costa Rica)

The State promoted the construction of new infrastructure but private investment, especially foreign capital, also played a major role in the process. From the 1880s onwards specific buildings were built for specific purposes for the first time in the city of San José, including hotels, pharmacies, clubs, stores, restaurants, banks, libraries, and theatres, which added complexity to the urban structure. The Central Avenue, the main commercial artery of the city, became the fashionable showcase for this variety of styles (figure 10.5).[39]

Thus between the 1880s and 1910s San José acquired a new covered market, an insane asylum (Asilo Chapuí), a national museum, schools (Edificio Metálico) and high schools (Liceo de Costa Rica, Colegio Superior de Señoritas), two hospices (for orphans and elderly people), a national theatre, a public library, and a penitentiary. These neo-gothic, neo-classical, and eclectic edifices became architectural landmarks in the urban development of San José (figures 10.6 and 10.7).

From 1878 to 1880 a foreign enterprise

Figure 10.6 Chapel Insane Asylum. Photo: Manuel Gómez Miralles, 1922. (*Source*: National Archive of Costa Rica)

Figure 10.7 National Library (*Source*: Fernando Zamora, *Vistas de Costa Rica*, 1909)

represented by Juan Myers and Jorge Clark, hired by the Municipality of San José, built a new public market for the city; in exchange they were granted usufruct of the building for 30 years.[40] The neo-classical edifice built with a brick and iron structure, with ample interior spaces and two storeys, inaugurated a new space for the daily purchase of food, vegetables, and fruits in San José and marked the abandonment of the main plaza's use for that purpose.

The insane asylum or Asilo Chapuí, built around 1890 on the street leading west to La Sabana, was another important public building which developed a new area in San José according to modern principles. Costa Rican architect Jaime Carranza designed the pavilions of the asylum, with all modern facilities and infrastructure surrounded by gardens filled with flowers and palms, and Rodolfo Bertoglio designed the neo-gothic chapel.[41] The garden suburb introduced with this building was then extended by the private villas which came to line the boulevard that ended at La Sabana.

The two main high schools built in this period – the Liceo de Costa Rica for men and the Colegio Superior de Señoritas for women – similarly spurred urbanization and development in the south-east area of San José. Founded in 1887, in 1903 the Liceo de Costa Rica was relocated to an eclectic edifice by the Italian architect Francisco Tenca, originally conceived for the House of Corrections. The Colegio Superior de Señoritas was designed by Costa Rican engineer Lesmes Jiménez, also in the eclectic style, and built between 1888 and 1893 (figure 10.8).[42]

As Ramón Gutiérrez has remarked, every single city in Latin America aspired to have a theatre as a proof of its urbanity and culture.[43] In San José those desires – promoted by the coffee oligarchy and the State – were fulfilled in 1897 with the inauguration of the Teatro Nacional (National Theatre).[44] An eclectic edifice built a few blocks to the east of the cathedral, the Theatre would surprise and delight travellers throughout the twentieth century and became the most important place for bourgeois socializing in the capital.[45] 'The crowning piece of Costa Rican extravagance, the National Opera House, which cost

Figure 10.8 'Señoritas' High School. Photo: Manuel Gómez Miralles, 1922. (*Source*: National Archive of Costa Rica)

a million dollars in this town of 20,000 people, is a tribute to their cultivated taste', wrote one visitor in 1914 (figure 10.9).[46]

The Penitentiary of San José, built from

1905 to 1908, introduced another type of architecture in this first period. The project was designed by Lesmes Jiménez in a neo-gothic style with the radial and panoptic

Figure 10.9 National Theatre or Opera House. Photo: Manuel Gómez Miralles, 1922. (*Source*: National Archive of Costa Rica)

model typical of its era. Overlooking San José from the right bank of the Torres river, linked to the city by a long avenue with ample sidewalks, the Penitentiary resembled an old medieval castle looming on the northwest limits of the capital (figure 10.10).

From 1880 to the 1900s major changes in architecture were continuously introduced in San José. The large buildings and variety of architectural types marked a fundamental but delimited urban transformation, contrasting with the single-storey houses that still characterized much of the small Costa Rican capital.

In 1910 an earthquake completely destroyed the old colonial capital of Cartago. That same year the Secretary of Public Works gathered the most important engineers and architects of the country to institute new construction methods that would mark a fundamental change in Costa Rican architecture.[47]

According to José Enrique Garnier and Heidi Venegas, the Liberal State used these changes after the earthquake to consolidate antecedent styles but with safer techniques for construction. Academic styles predominated but *mampostería reforzada* (reinforced masonry) and wood structures continued to be widely used in San José as in many other cities in the country.[48] This was a period of architectural transition which saw the beginning of the anti-academic reaction of neocolonial, modernism, and Art Deco.[49]

Figure 10.10 San José's Penitentiary. Photo: Manuel Gómez Miralles, 1922. (*Source*: National Archive of Costa Rica)

Beyond the Swamp: A New Area of Development

One of the biggest changes in the nineteenth-century Latin American urban landscape was the creation of boulevards – a key element of modern urban planning and design – in major cities. This was one of the urban principles exported from Europe, especially from Paris which had become the urban model followed around the world after Haussmann's reconstruction work in Paris under Napoleon III.[50] Promenades and boulevards opened new areas for social activities, becoming the public spaces of the city and the symbols of urbanity and power. They were also fundamental to the public health policies promoted by the State.

San José's best example of this new urban concept was Calle de la Estación (Depot Street) in the north-eastern sector, renamed the Avenida de las Damas (Avenue of the Ladies) when it was beautified and converted into a boulevard (figure 10.11).[51] This is an instructive example of how Haussmannic principles played out when applied in a small and peripheral capital.

The first period of development began in the 1870s with the construction of the first railway station, built for the line which would link the capital with other cities of the Central Valley (Alajuela, Heredia, and Cartago). Later a street was built to connect the station with the rest of the city, and a plaza was constructed in front of the station. The potable water pipeline and electricity lines installed along this street raised property values in this part of the city. The Dictator Tomás Guardia built his house in the south-west corner of the Plaza de la Estación (Station Plaza) at the end of the 1870s.

The second phase of development began around 1887 when President Bernardo Soto decreed the expropriation of parts of several properties. The swamp at the end of the avenue was drained and the area transformed into a complex of four parks, completed in 1890 (figure 10.12).[52] A marble statue brought from Italy with the figure of Próspero Fernández, a Liberal leader and ex-President, was placed in the middle of the four parks.[53] According to Ofelia Sanou the strategic position of the statue of Fernández at the end of the Avenue symbolized the triumph of the Liberal Reforms (1884), and was an indirect homage to the leader of the party which had planned and promoted this new space in San José.[54] Later the statue was removed to another part of the city, and a kiosk was built in 1910 as a bandstand for the celebration of *retretas* (evening military music) and concerts.

In 1891 the Central Valley railway was finally completed all the way to the Caribbean port of Limón. The station had become the entry point to the capital from abroad: a powerful stimulus to complete the beautifica-

Figure 10.11 Avenida de las Damas. Photo: Manuel Gómez Miralles, 1922. (*Source*: National Archive of Costa Rica)

Figure 10.12 Morazán Park (*Source*: Fernando Zamora, *Vistas de Costa Rica*, 1909).

tion of the area. In 1894 trees were planted all along the avenue, and a year later the old plaza in front of the station became the Parque Nacional (National Park).[55] The urban renewal promoted by the State was trumpeted in the grandiose inauguration of the National Monument that same year, with celebrations that lasted three days.[56] A bronze statue by French sculptor Henri Carrier-Belleuse, which allegorized the Central American countries' triumph over William Walker's Filibusters in the National Campaign of 1856–1857, was placed in the middle of the park (figure 10.13).[57]

In other words, Liberals conceived and used this street to promote bourgeois notions

Figure 10.13 National Park. Photo: Manuel Gómez Miralles, 1922. (*Source*: National Archive of Costa Rica)

of the modern city and the modern nation through the construction of monuments, statues, and public buildings.[58] The railway – symbol *par excellence* of the ideals of 'progress' and 'civilization' – both anchored and inspired this transformation. The central role given to the boulevard since its creation testifies to the importance of this new space, promoted by Liberals to serve as a new political and civic area breaking the hegemony of the old main plaza.[59] This tendency continued throughout the twentieth century: the Presidential Residence was moved at the end of the 1920s to occupy the former United Fruit Company headquarters facing the east part of the Parque Nacional, and in 1939 the Asamblea Legislativa (National Assembly) was moved from the old city center to the south-east edge of the Parque Nacional.[60]

The Avenida de las Damas and Parque Morazán became one of the most exclusive and expensive areas of San José, and land prices rose here between 1900 and 1930.[61] Many members of the elite, some belonging to the new bourgeoisie of politicians and immigrants who had made their fortunes in bananas, coffee, and sugar cane, built their houses in the surroundings of the park.[62] Many Consulates and International Legations also located around this area. These eclectic, Second-Empire, neo-classical and Victorian mansions, surrounded by gardens and secured by iron fences, were the backdrop for one of the most important public spaces in San José in the first decades of the twentieth century (figure 10.14).

According to Olsen, Haussmann justified his projects (the opening of broad boulevards planted with trees) as necessary preparations for bourgeois habitation, facilitating the westward exodus of the comfortable classes who were being pushed out of the centre by commerce and industry.[63] In this area of San José Haussmannic principles, although in a different context and small scale, were applied with the same results, promoting the settlement of wealthy classes around the most fashionable area of the city. This avenue and the

Figure 10.14 Cleto Gonzalez's house, Morazán Park. Photo: Manuel Gómez Miralles, 1922. (*Source*: National Archive of Costa Rica)

route to La Sabana Park were the two main boulevards that reflected modern European urbanism as emulated in San José.

Other buildings and parks were created near the Avenida de las Damas, such as the Edificio Metálico (Metallic Building) which housed San José's public primary school. The structure was designed by the Belgian architect Charles Thirion and constructed in Europe by the company Forges d'Aiseau (figure 10.15).[64] Inaugurated in 1897 the building symbolically capped the decade, embodying the era of technology, progress, and modernity in its provenance, its material, and its position in the city.

A few metres to the east, in the new Barrio Otoya, philanthropist Andrew Carnegie sponsored the construction of a neo-Hispanic building for the short-lived Central American Court of Justice in 1916.[65] In 1917 the plaza of the National Liquor Factory, which the Court overlooked – one of the few remaining colonial plazas in San José – was transformed into an elegant park called La Concordia (renamed Parque España [Spain Park] in the 1920s).[66]

Completing the green transformation of the area was the Parque Zoólogico Simón Bolívar (Simón Bolívar Zoological Park), inaugurated in 1921 in Barrio Otoya, abutting the Torres river. This became a centre of urban recreation for people from different classes.[67]

In 1908 the old railway station, a humble structure with a zinc roof, was replaced with a new building. According to Ana Luisa Cerdas citizens had protested to the Railway Company demanding a new building 'more in accordance with the century of lights'.[68] Apparently the old building was giving a bad impression of the Capital, especially to arriving travellers. The elegant new eclectic building with a Mansard roof, guarded by Mercury and Venus, far better expressed the ideals of modernity for the promoters and the residents in the surrounding area at the turn of the century (figure 10.16).

Angel Rama and Richard Morse argue that the Latin American city was not simply an imitation of European models: it is 'not mimetic but answers an inner logic'.[69] The evolution of the Calle de la Estación in San José exemplifies this, for the 'imported' urban planning

Figure 10.15 Metallic Building. (*Source*: Fernando Zamora, *Vistas de Costa Rica*, 1909)

Figure 10.16 Central Railway Station to the Atlantic. Photo: Manuel Gómez Miralles 1922. (*Source*: National Archive of Costa Rica)

and design was reinterpreted in the national and local context. We can identify in this street many of the modern principles: the creation of a tree-lined boulevard that started or ended with a statue or a monument, the installation of new public services and infrastructure, the construction of houses for the wealthy. But this urban development must be analysed in the historical context of this particular capital.

Though small in scale compared to major projects in Rio de Janeiro, Buenos Aires or Mexico City, this was the first major urban modern project for San José – and the one to which the majority of present-day San José's green spaces owe their origin. The Calle de la Estación (Avenida le las Damas) also would continue to reign as the launch point for the city's successive urban improvements, from

potable water and electric lighting at the end of the nineteenth century to street paving in the 1930s.

In sum the Avenida de las Damas, entryway to San José in the first decades of the twentieth century, played a major role in the city's urban transformation. Here among statues and monuments a new dynamic of urban segregation and sociability was inaugurated. Actions taken by the State, especially by the Liberals in power, literally prepared the terrain to transform the north-eastern part of San José into a showcase of modernity. What was a swamp in 1850 had been converted 40 years later into one of the most exclusive areas of San José, a centre of economic, social, political, and civic functions.

Green Areas: Parks and Social Spaces in the Bourgeois City

Parallel to the creation of boulevards was the proliferation of parks and squares in the capital beginning in the 1880s, promoted and maintained by the Municipality of San José.

The most important parks created in this period were the Central, Morazán, Nacional, Merced, Soledad, and España Parks; the huge area of La Sabana in the west; and the squares which replaced the old colonial plazas in front of the main churches of San José.[70]

As Richard Etlin points out, in modern urban planning and design parks and squares were thought to serve as reservoirs for pure air. Thus squares had to be placed at the intersection of several streets to be most effective. The ground in contrast was an important source of corruption for the air.[71] Such hygienic principles came to shape local urban politics, as witnessed by official arguments for the creation of a new park in front of the Hospital San Juan de Dios in 1905. Previously street vendors had used the area as a public market. State officials denounced this as a space of 'social rot', which they sought to convert into a 'source of clean air for the Hospital'.[72]

Across the city old colonial plazas that had continued serving as markets over most of the nineteenth century were transformed into parks, as in the case of the central plaza. The first step in the physical transformation of this plaza came in 1868 when the city's potable water system was officially inaugurated. To commemorate the occasion an iron fountain was placed in the middle of the

plaza and a fence installed to delimit the area of the park. Both were imported from England by the engineer Velázquez, in charge of the pipeline's construction (figure 10.17).[73] The Saturday market remained there for only one more year before it was relocated to the Plaza Nueva (New Plaza) and finally in 1880 moved to the new covered market.

The transformation of the central plaza into a park continued in 1885 when the Municipality of San José hired a private company to 'plant trees and gardens for the enjoyment and for the leisure of its inhabitants' in the Central Park.[74] One day before the park was officially inaugurated the State decreed that evening military band concerts (*retretas*) be celebrated there twice a week (figure 10.18).[75] Putnam described the importance of these activities in the life of the city in 1912:

> Music is the beginning and the end of the social life and amusement for the rank and file. Every one gets an extraordinary amount of pleasure from the many concerts that are given at the open-air band-stands in the plazas of San José.[76]

The old plaza thus became a promenade and a place for class-differentiated leisure,

Figure 10.17 Iron fountain Central Park, Harrison Nathaniel Rudd, 1890s. (*Source*: National Archive of Costa Rica)

Figure 10.18 Military band Central Park, Harrison Nathaniel Rudd, 1890s. (*Source*: National Archive of Costa Rica)

replacing the traditional market. The enclosure of this public space by the fence symbolized the new, segregated social dynamic. As Otoniel Pacheco, the editor of a City Guide, noted in 1895, the Central Park was 'the place of meeting of part of the *society* who comes here for special celebrations, Sundays and Thursdays in the afternoon and at night to hear the concerts of the military band'.[77]

As Richard Etlin notes, public parks were created not only to advance public health but also to teach elite habits of dress, morality and behaviour to the working classes.[78] Fashionable promenades in the public spaces of the 'civilized' metropolis became emblems of power and urbanity.[79] Such was the case in San José during this period. Urban elites attended the *retretas* in Central and Morazán Parks both for leisure and to promote ways of behaving, habits of dress, and proper moral values. Indeed the didactic display was integral to the pleasure parks offered them. Seeing and being seen were part of an urban bourgeois culture that established a series of social codes for public spaces. One North American traveller noted in 1925:

The pretty aristocrats are not secluded here as in some cities of Central America. They walk the streets in couples, trimly dressed in tailor-made clothes, are to be seen every afternoon in restaurants where tea is served in English fashion and stroll about the plaza later on listening to the fine band, and of course perfectly oblivious to the eyes of the young men strolling in the opposite direction.[80]

By the 1920s and 1930s the *retretas* of the Morazán Park showed greater social differentiation than those of the Central Park, reflecting the new dynamic of social segregation in this part of the city.[81] The old kiosk, destroyed some years before, was replaced in 1920 with a new concrete structure known as the Temple of Music, the perfect setting for the celebration of *retretas* (figure 10.19).[82]

Morazán Park was composed of four gardens, separated by streets, with the kiosk at the centre, and this physical delineation became a stage for displaying the social divisions of urban society. The garden in the southern portion of the park, in front of the house of former President Cleto González, had a brick-covered open area and was for middle and high classes. The garden on the northern side had only dirt ground to walk

Figure 10.19 Temple of Music. Photo: Manuel Gómez Miralles, 1922. (*Source*: National Archive of Costa Rica)

on and was for the low classes – servant girls and workers. The boundaries were rarely crossed; the two promenades coexisted but rarely mixed.[83] This social differentiation was evident to North American traveller Dana Gardner Munro, who wrote in 1914:

On Monday and Friday evenings, Mary and María Luisa and I always went to the *retreta*, a concert by the army band in the Morazán Park. There was also a concert on Wednesday in the Central Park, usually with better music, but few of the *gente*, the 'principal families', went then because the crowd was considered too mixed. The Morazán Park was divided by cross-streets into four sections, and the *gente*, by custom, had one of these to themselves.[84]

According to David Scobey, promenades help us understand how the dialectics of class and gender in the city worked in public, since promenading delineated a public space of class exclusion and gender mixing. Flirting through established signals, men and women established relationships, but only with those of the same social status. For young women of the elite it was a respectable and safe public space for socializing with their own kind. The promenade ritual was repeated twice every week. Women circled around the outside and men walked in the opposite direc-

tion in the centre, all stepping to the invigorating tunes of the military band.

The Calle de la Estación was another place to promenade in this period, with a more exclusive character but similar dynamic. This was, as Scobey says, 'sociability in motion, perpetual motion, people passing each other back and forth repeatedly, actors and spectators in a tableau of orderly circulation'.[85]

The Parque Morazán and the Calle de la Estación, the newly transformed areas of the modern city, exemplified also the new process of urban segregation which created settings for sociability and differentiated leisure, and turned the public sphere into a stage on which hierarchy and social legitimacy were reaffirmed. Different classes shared this space with distinct, but linked, dynamics.

The *retretas* and promenades of San José marked public space as respectable according to bourgeois values, allowing elites to differentiate themselves from the rest of the society. Such practices are fundamental for understanding the urban and social fragmentation of the late nineteenth and early twentieth century city.[86]

New Social Segregation

The gradual movement of elite groups away from their traditional locus near the main plaza towards the suburbs was another important change spawned by the new urbanism and the social and economic transformations. As Scobie notes, such movement determined the direction of urban expansion in capitals and major cities throughout Latin America.[87] Meanwhile popular neighbourhoods began to appear in the less expensive areas of the city, geographically opposite those of the elite. These trends altered patterns of urban segregation, breaking the hierarchical concentration of power around the main plaza and introducing a new dynamic of settlement.

As we have already seen, San José's upper-class families began to move north-east in the 1890s following the drainage of the swamp and the creation of Morazán Park and Avenida de las Damas. The process was consolidated further north during the first decades of the twentieth century with the creation of new elite neighbourhoods such as Amón, Otoya, and Aranjuez, clearly segregated from the rest of the city.[88]

In 1892 French businessman Amón Fasileau-Duplantier presented a project to the Municipality to extend the city to the northern limits of San José. He proposed developing a zone that was then mainly pasture, next to the coffee plantations his family owned.[89] This initiative would be the beginning of the first elite residential neighbourhood consolidated in the first decades of the twentieth century. Barrio Amón exemplified the city's new social and architectural segregation. Its residents – families headed by professionals, businessmen, bureaucrats, and coffee and banana plantation owners – would develop a distinct bourgeois culture.[90]

The houses built in Amón reflected the complex process of adoption and reinterpretation of European styles blended with multiple local traditions. New styles appeared, such as Victorian, neo-colonial, Moorish, and especially eclectic (figure 10.20). Single-

Figure 10.20 Amón neighbourhood. Photo: Manuel Gómez Miralles, 1922.

storey houses, abutting the sidewalk colonial-style but constructed with new materials and ornamentation, rubbed shoulders with the new types of architecture.

New construction materials such as brick (instead of adobe) and wood, and in a few cases metal, allowed the development of more elaborate styles. The front garden secured by an iron fence was introduced in Amón but would be more extensively used in neighbouring Otoya (figure 10.21).

The interiors also show the mixture of old and new in the organization of space, with a strong post-colonial influence. Over the nineteenth century there had been a gradual change in the interior distribution typical of urban adobe dwellings. The *zaguán* (long hallway) was introduced in adobe houses as the central axis, permitting a greater specialization and a gradation from public to private spaces, separating social and family activities.[91] Amon's houses shared this general pattern of internal distribution, with even greater specialization thanks to their modern infrastructure such as electricity and sewers. The house reflected urban bourgeois culture in the use and decoration of the spaces: the living room

– the public space of the house – was the most elegant, and the family's wealth and status was here on display in a visual language consciously adopted from Europe.[92]

In colonial times the south of San José became home to the city's poor, with the establishment of La Puebla.[93] At the turn of the nineteenth century the southern and western sides of San José saw the birth of the first working-class neighbourhoods: Rincón de Cubillos, Laberinto, Turrujal, Colección, and others.[94]

In 1900 José C. Zeledón and Julio Alvarado, two well-known San José businessmen, bought a piece of land on the southern limit of the city. Their project included not only the urbanization of the area for working-class housing (one of the first private initiatives of its kind) but also the construction of a textile plant, a sawmill and other small factories for the production of soap. In the 1920s Minor Keith and Adolfo Carit (a prominent Costa Rican doctor) donated money and land for the foundation of other popular neighbourhoods nearby. The development of these neighbourhoods to the south, in opposition to the elite neighbour-

Figure 10.21 Otoya neighbourhood. Photo: Manuel Gómez Miralles, 1922. (*Source:* National Archive of Costa Rica)

hoods in the north-east, was part of a new urban segregation that would consolidate the southern part of the city for industry and lower-class housing until the present day.[95]

As Hardoy has noted elsewhere, philanthropic initiatives like the neighbourhoods of Carit and Keith were partial and dispersed solutions within the city, and not part of a major urban plan. Like other Latin American cities, official initiatives did not include any public projects for infrastructure or housing for working classes.[96] In contrast to north-eastern San José, there was hardly any State development in the southern part of the city in this period. The Liceo de Costa Rica, a public high school for boys, was among the few public works built here; Plaza González Víquez (1925) was another. Living conditions were precarious, especially in the *chinchorros*, two-storey dwellings divided into single rooms rented separately, described by Costa Rican author Carmen Lyra as offering 'two or three overpopulated square meters where up to ten people live and sleep'.[97] Basic services such as electricity and potable water were introduced for the first time in the 1910s in the most central popular neighbourhoods.[98]

The inauguration in this area of a second railway station in 1910 – this time for the new line to the Pacific port of Puntarenas – did not bring the flowering of boulevards and parks that the Atlantic Station had brought to the eastern part of the city. The growth of several sawmills and other industries in its surroundings determined land use in this part of San José.

Meanwhile the construction of villas and chalets at the two main entrances to the city (San Pedro del Mojón to the east and Mata Redonda to the west) in the first decades of the twentieth century marked the beginning of suburban bourgeois settlement. The street to La Sabana Park became another main axis of development: a site for Sunday afternoon promenades, a favourite destination for elite automobile owners or for rented carriages.[99] As Dana Gardner Munro described it in 1914:

One of the attractions of San José was the Sabana, an open meadow about three fourths of a mile square on the outskirts of the city, reached by an electric trolley. One family always drove around and around the Sabana in one of the few motor cars that had thus far reached Costa Rica.[100]

Yet the tram also allowed different classes and ages easy access to this space of social activity and sport, and thus it was not limited to the elite classes.

The 1930s: Modernism and Urban Growth

If the Avenida de las Damas symbolized the urban ideals of the turn of the century, Paseo Colón (Colón Avenue) to the west announced key features of the urban and architectural development of the 1930s and 1940s (figure 10.22).

Paseo Colón, inaugurated in 1932, was a 12-metre wide boulevard decorated with benches, pergolas, and a 10-metre obelisk in honour of Christopher Columbus (placed in the middle of the boulevard).[101] Many important public and private edifices were built in modernist and neo-colonial styles along the boulevard during the 1930s and 1940s, such as the Echandi Pavilion, an annex to the Hospital San Juan de Dios erected in 1934, and many elite residences.

The most important landmark in the area

Figure 10.22 Paseo Colón. Postcard, 1930s.

was the first airport of San José, built between 1936 and 1939 at the end of the avenue on the eastern side of La Sabana Park. Designed by Costa Rican architect José María Barrantes, the terminal was a mixture of neo-colonial language with great liberty and modernist lines.[102]

Paseo Colón became the new entryway to San José in the 1930s, and connected the city with La Sabana Park. If at the turn of the nineteenth century visitors reached San José mainly by train, and were greeted by the Calle de la Estación, in this period they began to arrive by aeroplane at La Sabana Airport, and enter the city along the tree-lined, ample boulevard of Paseo Colón.

As Garnier and Venegas have noted, the decision to build the airport at one end of Paseo Colón accorded with the ideals of European urbanism, in which large boulevards served as the axes which organized the public spaces of the city.[103] Thus following the same principles which inspired the Avenida de las Damas, in Paseo Colón those ideas were applied on a bigger scale and in a period of urban and architectural transition which heralded a new phase of urban growth.

The decades of 1930 and 1940 witnessed the introduction of North American and European modernist architecture in San José, suited to the new official architectural programmes of the public and private sector.[104] The incorporation of modernist language or international style into the architectural landscape of the city was mixed with other tendencies such as neo-colonial or Hispanic, Art Deco, and more.

The State used modernist language to build new infrastructure such as schools and hospitals and to respond to the social demands and popular movements that emerged during this period. Several architects had a major influence on this new phase of urban and architectural development, among them José María Barrantes, José Francisco Salazar, and Paul Ehrenberg.

José María Barrantes, a self-taught Costa Rican architect, worked for the State beginning in 1928 and was involved especially with the construction of most Costa Rican public schools during this period.[105] His production of religious buildings was also prolific, especially churches inspired more by neo-classical language.[106]

José Francisco Salazar was a Costa Rican

architect trained at the School of Architecture in Santa Clara, California. After graduating in 1912 he moved to New York and worked for some years at the firm George B. Post & Sons. In 1915 he returned to Costa Rica and began producing intensively, developing between the 1920s and 1930s the neo-colonial and modernist styles in public and private buildings in San José.[107]

The German architect Paul Ehrenberg was another key figure in the development of modernism in San José in this era, whose importance grew at the end of 1940s and 1950s. Ehrenberg graduated in 1926 from the *Technische Hochschule* in Munich and came to Costa Rica in 1929, hired by the German construction company Ways and Freitag, after several years in Seville, Spain.[108]

Conclusions

In 1927 San José reached 50,580 inhabitants – 11 per cent of the country's population – with one of the highest rates of growth of all the Central American capitals.[109] According to Carolyn Hall the primacy of the city can be seen in the fact that between 1864 and 1927 its population increased by an annual average of 2.8 per cent when the rest of the country was growing between 1 and 2 per cent per year.[110] The small colonial city of the second half of nineteenth century had become by 1930 a bigger, more complex, and more segregated society.

In general terms the most important feature of urbanism in San José throughout the period was the European influence visible in each phase of the city's growth. The adoption of modern urbanism was limited to specific areas of the capital, and brought the first alteration and expansion of the grid-plan that had dictated the morphology of San José.

Another characteristic was the absence of general urban planning in the development of San José. Expansion and growth were uncoordinated results of the *ensanchamiento* or overflowing of colonial urban limits. Throughout the twentieth century San José has grown in a process of spontaneous expansion and occupation of spaces. Consequently it lacks an urban hierarchy or defined urban structure and presents severe problems of uncontrolled growth, a lack of a clear architectural identity, and high pollution levels caused by heavy traffic.[111]

The leaders who transformed the urban landscape in the last decades of the nineteenth century aimed to erase the Spanish colonial image. The uniform colonial city of adobe houses and tile roofs had to be replaced by individual buildings with eclectic styles in order to create a new city with a European façade. As we have seen, this goal was indeed realized along the main streets and avenues of San José and in select new areas of development.

The urban renewal of the nineteenth century promoted and encouraged a new dynamic of social segregation that broke the monopoly of the two traditional centres of power (the original nucleus and the cathedral) and created other public spaces of importance in the city. Enjoying *de facto* public subsidies in the form of infrastructure investment, private builders created new neighbourhoods for the wealthy in the northeast quadrant and at the city's eastern and western edges.

The beginning of a new dynamic of urban segregation was best exemplified in the surroundings of the Parque Morazán in the 1890s. In the following three decades urban development centred north of this area, in Amón, Otoya, and Aranjuez. To the west suburban bourgeois villas flourished along the boulevard to La Sabana Park and in Mata Redonda, and to the east the suburb of San Pedro del Mojón developed. These trends were consolidated during the 1930s and 1940s.

The Calle de la Estación, the transformed colonial plazas, and the new shady parks all set the stage for the development of a new urban bourgeois sociability in San José at the end of the nineteenth century. In green spaces like Central and Morazán Parks – each with its kiosk, benches, gardens, and statues – social distinction was enacted, witnessed, and reproduced in popular activities such as the *retretas*.

On the *other* side of the city the first initiatives for the development of working-class neighbourhoods came from private investors, as in the case of Laberinto, Keith, and Carit, and later on Barrio Luján. In general terms the working classes were excluded from the project of the 'modern city' and received few benefits from the urban transformations and public improvements.

The modern communication and transportation infrastructure helped develop new ways of living. First the trolley, then automobiles and public buses promoted the development of many outlying districts in San José. They also offered easy access from the city to the suburbs where big parks such as La Sabana were built, and Sunday afternoon promenades became a widespread custom. The wealthy and most privileged made the trip not on public transportation but in the first automobiles, introduced in San José by the turn of the century.

The European urbanism adopted at the end of nineteenth century had a long-term effect on the growth of the capital across the twentieth century. In particular, the sharp segregation of elites from the rest of the urban classes, begun in this period, has never diminished. A century later the capital's rich live secluded in their luxurious condos, far from the *tugurios* (slums) that surround the Metropolitan Area.

NOTES

1. Putnam, G. P. (1914) *The Southland of North America. Rambles and Observations in Central America during the year of 1912*. New York: The Knickerbocker Press, p. 6.

2. Romero, J.L. (1976) *Latinoamérica: las ciudades y las ideas*. México: Siglo XXI, p. 250.

3. *Ibid.*, chapter 6.

4. For other cases in Latin America see Gutiérrez, R. (1983) *Arquitectura y urbanismo en Iberoamérica*. Madrid: Ediciones Cátedra, chapters 18 and 19; Pineo, R. and Baer, J.A. (ed.) (1998) *Cities of Hope. People, Protests, and Progress in Urbanizing Latin America 1870–1930*. Boulder: Westview Press; Needell, J. (1988) *A Tropical Belle Époque: Elite Culture and Society in Turn-of-the-Century Rio de Janeiro*. New York: Cambridge University Press; Llanes, L. (1993) *1898–1921: La transformación de La Habana a través de la arquitectura*. La Habana: Editorial Letras Cubanas; Scobie, J. (1974) *Buenos Aires: from Plaza to Suburb, 1870–1910*. New York: Oxford University Press.

5. Putnam, *op. cit.*, pp. 66–67.

6. Hardoy, J.E. (ed.) (1975) Two Thousands Years of Latin American Urbanization, in *Urbanization in Latin America: Approaches and Issues*. New York: Anchor Press, p. 45.

7. González Víquez, C. (1958) San José y sus comienzos, in *Obras Históricas*. San José: A. Lehmann Librería e Imprenta, p. 477.

8. Bustamente, T. (1996) *La ciudad de San José. Ensayo histórico*. San José: Municipalidad de San José, p. 84.

9. Gudmundson, L. (1990) *Costa Rica antes del café. Sociedad y economía en vísperas del boom exportador*. San José: Editorial Costa Rica, p. 43.

10. Molina, I. (1991) *Costa Rica (1800–1850). El legado colonial y la génesis del capitalismo.* San José: Editorial de la Universidad de Costa Rica, p. 76.

11. *Ibid.*, p. 310.

12. Bustamente, *op. cit.*, p. 94.

13. Molina, *op. cit.*, p. 301; Vega, J.L. (1988) San José: tenencia de la tierra y nuevos grupos sociales en el siglo XIX, in Fernández, R. and Lungo, M. (comps.) *La estructuración de las capitales centroamericanas.* San José: Educa, pp. 162–181.

14. Archivo Nacional de Costa Rica onwards ANCR, Maps and plans, #4201, 1851.

15. Gudmundson, *op. cit.*, p. 183.

16. Molina, F. (1851) *Bosquejo de la República de Costa Rica, seguido de apuntamientos para su historia.* New York: Imprenta de S.W. Benedict, p. 51.

17. Sanou, O. and Quesada, F. (1998) Herencia, ruptura, y nuevas expresiones arquitectónicas (1841–1870), in Fonseca, E. and Garnier, J.E. (eds.) *Historia de la arquitectura en Costa Rica.* San José: Fundación de Museos del Banco Central, pp. 151–217, pp. 156–212.

18. *Ibid.*, p. 214.

19. *Ibid.*, pp. 151–166.

20. For an analysis of the cultural change see Molina, I. and Palmer, S. (eds.) (1992) *Héroes al gusto y libros de moda. Sociedad y cambio cultural en Costa Rica (1750–1900).* San José: Editorial Porvenir-Plumsock Mesoamerican Studies.

21. Palmer, S. (1996) Prolegómenos a toda historia futura de San José, Costa Rica. *Mesoamérica, 31*, pp.198-202.

22. Palmer, S. (1990) A liberal discipline: inventing nations in Guatemala and Costa Rica, 1870–1900. Unpublished PhD Thesis, Columbia University, New York. For a general analysis of the liberal period see Salazar, O. (1990) *El apogeo de la República liberal en Costa Rica 1870–1914.* San José: Editorial de la Universidad de Costa Rica; Vargas, C. (1991) *El liberalismo, la iglesia y el estado en Costa Rica.* San José: Guayacán.

23. Sanou, O. and Quesada, F. (1998) Orden progreso y civilización (1871–1914). Transformaciones urbanas y arquitectónicas in Fonseca and Garnier (eds.), *op. cit.*, pp. 219–317, p. 224.

24. Hardoy, J.E. (1995) Teorías y prácticas urbanísticas en Europa entre 1850 y 1930. Su traslado a América Latina. *DANA Documentos de Arquitectura Nacional y Americana, 37/38*, pp.12–30.

25. González Víquez, C. (1905) *Apuntes estadísticos sobre la ciudad de San José.* San José: Imprenta de Avelino Alsina, p. 3.

26. Schorske, C. (1981) *Fin de siècle Vienna. Politics and Culture.* New York: Vintage Books Edition, p. 26.

27. Calvo, J.B. (1887) *Apuntamientos geográficos, estadísticos e históricos.* San José: Imprenta Nacional, p. 135.

28. ANCR (1890) Serie Fomento, 11 March, 1897, f. 210. For a study of the telephone see Núñez, F.M. (1925) *Iniciación y desarrollo de las vías de comunicación y empresas de transportes en Costa Rica.* San José: Imprenta Nacional, pp. 203–207.

29. Manuel Dengo and Luis Batres installed the first electric plant for public lighting in Aranjuez, in the north-eastern side of San José. Initially the lines for electric lighting began in the street of the railway station descending to the Carmen Church and then to the Central Park of San José. Quijano, A. (1939) *Costa Rica ayer y hoy.* San José: Editorial Borrasé Hermanos, p. 605.

30. This plant was constructed in Anonos. ANCR (1890) Serie Municipal, No. 4002, 2 May 2, fs. 1–4.

31. Minor Cooper Keith was one of the most important capitalists in Costa Rica. He built the railway to the port of Limón on the Caribbean coast. In exchange the State gave him a millionaire concession of 300,000 hectares of land along the railroad, where he started banana production. In 1899 he founded the United Fruit Company. For a study of the trolley in other Latin American cities see Rosenthal, A. (1998) Dangerous Streets: trolleys, labor conflict, and the reorganization of public space in Montevideo, Uruguay, in Pineo and Baer (eds.), *op. cit.*, pp. 30–52.

32. The trolley line to Guadalupe, inaugurated in 1909, promoted the urbanization of many districts in San José such as San Francisco and Calle Blancos. Enríquez, F. and Avendaño, I. (1991) *El cantón de Goicoechea: un reencuentro histórico-geográfico 1891–1991.* San José: Instituto de Fomento y Asesoría Municipal, p. 74.

33. Bustamante, *op. cit.*, p. 230.

34. ANCR (n.d. in the original) Maps and Plans, # 4487.

35. ANCR (n.d. in the original) Serie Municipal, No. 1141. This document compares the new nomenclature for streets, avenues and plazas adopted in 1904 with the older system of 1889.

36. Cleto González Víquez a prominent lawyer of the political elite called El Olimpo, was one of the best symbols of the triumph of Liberal reformers. He was

Minister of Public Works, President of the Supreme Court, and two times President of the Republic (1906–1910, 1928–1932), among many other public posts. González also published several works concerning the history of San José and was actively involved in sanitary and philanthropic activities. For further analysis of social policy in Costa Rica see Palmer, S. (1996) Confinement, Policing, and the Emergence of Social Policy in Costa Rica, 1880–1935, in Salvatore, R. and Aguirre, C. (eds.) *The birth of the Penitentiary in Latin America. Essays on criminology, prison reform, and social control, 1830–1940*. Texas: Texas University Press, pp. 224–253.

37. Segarra, J. and Juliá, J. (1907) *Excursión por América. Costa Rica*. San José: Imprenta de Avelino Alsina, p. 248. Another traveller mentioned in this period that sanitation was the hobby of the President Víquez 'whom the weekly Life – for San José includes in its free press a humorous weekly- always pictures with a mosquito on the top of his bald head'. Palmer, F. (1913) *Central America and its problems*. New York: Moffat Yard and Company, p. 203.

38. Sanou and Quesada, *op. cit.*, p. 224.

39. One traveller described in 1910 the attractive shops in San José: 'imported dainties for the palate reappear in the store windows after being absent since leaving the City of México'. Palmer, *op. cit.*, p. 203.

40. Sanou and Quesada, *op. cit.*, p. 232.

41. Ponce, J. B. cited by Sanou and Quesada, *op. cit.*, p. 256.

42. Sanou and Quesada, *op. cit.*, p. 237.

43. Gutiérrez, *op. cit.*, p. 430.

44. For an analysis of the architecture and process of construction see Fischel, A. (1992) *El Teatro Nacional de Costa Rica. Su historia*. San José: Editorial del Teatro Nacional.

45. Fumero, P. (1996) *Teatro público y Estado en San José. 1880–1914*. San José: Editorial de la Universidad de Costa Rica.

46. Palmer, *op. cit.*, p. 204 and Palmer, *op. cit.*, p. 206. For a vision of the other side of the modern bourgeois city, see Marín, J.J. (1994) Prostitución y pecado en la Bella y Próspera ciudad de San José (1850–1930); and Palmer, S. (1994) Pánico en San José. El consumo de heroína, la cultura plebeya y la política social en 1929, in Molina, I. and Palmer, S. (eds.) *El Paso del Cometa. Estado, política social y culturas populares en Costa Rica (1800-1950)*. San José: Editorial Porvenir-Plumsock Mesoamerican Studies, pp. 47–73, pp. 191–224.

47. González, L.F. (in press) *Luis Llach Ll. En busca de las ciudades y la arquitectura en América*. San José: Editorial de la Universidad de Costa Rica.

48. Garnier, J.E. and Venegas, H. (1998) La arquitectura en la primera mitad del siglo XX, in Fonseca and Garnier (eds.), *op. cit.*, p. 325.

49. Garnier and Venegas, *op. cit.*, p. 325.

50. Marchand, B. (1986) *Paris, histoire d'une ville XIXe-XXe siècle*. Paris: Éditions du Seuil, Loyer, F. (1994) *Paris XIXe siècle. L'immueble et la rue*. Paris: Fernand Hazan. For other cases in European cities see Olsen, D. (1986) *The City as a Work of Art*. New Haven: Yale University Press; and Schorske, *op. cit.*, pp. 24–115.

51. The name came from the trees '*dama*' planted alone the boulevard but also because it was one of the most popular promenades in the afternoons especially for youngsters of the urban elite in the beginning of the twentieth century. Sanou, O. (1999) El Paseo de las Damas. El índice iconográfico del gobierno liberal y el nacimiento de la ciudad moderna, 1871–1914, in Córdoba, S. (ed.) *La ciudad y sus historias*. San José: Editorial de la Universidad de Costa Rica, pp. 125–141.

52. ANCR (1888) Colección de Leyes y Decretos. San José: Imprenta Nacional; ANCR (1887) Acuerdo No. LXXX, June 7th; and No. XXIV, September 15th.

53. Sanou, *op. cit.*, p. 131.

54. *Idem.*

55. ANCR (1894) Serie Fomento, No. 4400, June–December.

56. (1897) *Las fiestas del 15 de septiembre de 1895*. San José: Tipografía Nacional, p. 157.

57. For an analysis of the monument see Fumero, P. (1999) *Fiesta y develización. El Monumento Nacional, setiembre de 1895*. Alajuela: Museo Histórico Juan Santamaría; and Lemistre, A. (1988) *Dos bronces conmemorativos y una gesta heroica: La estatua de Juan Santamaría y el Monumento Nacional*. Alajuela: Museo Histórico Juan Santamaría.

58. Palmer, S. (1992) Sociedad anónima, cultura oficial: inventando la Nación en Costa Rica (1845–1900) in Molina and Palmer (eds.), *op. cit.*, pp. 169–196; Sanou, *op. cit.*, p. 128.

59. Nevertheless the Parque Central (Central Park) and the Cathedral continued to play an important role in the public sphere of San José, and do so to this day. See Low, S. (2000) *On the Plaza: the Politics of Public Space and Culture*. Texas: University of Texas Press.

60. This civic status had prevailed until the present. In

the 1990s a postmodernist building for the Tribunal Supremo de Elecciones (Supreme Electoral Tribunal) was built on the site of the old presidential house in the western part of the Parque Nacional.

61. Salazar, L.G. (1986) *Formación del espacio social de la ciudad de San José: Proceso de apropiación del territorio urbano (1870–1930)*. Unpublished M.Sc. thesis, Postgraduate School, University of Costa Rica, p. 130.

62. The former president Cleto González Víquez, built his house in front of the Morazán Park. For an analysis of its dwellers see Sanou, *op. cit.*, pp. 132–133.

63. Olsen, *op. cit.*, p. 143.

64. Stols, E. et Bleys, E. (eds) (1993) *Flandre et Amérique latine*. Anvers: Fonds Mercator, p. 362.

65. Upon the Court's dissolution in 1919 the building was ceded to the State. Today the 'Casa Amarilla' (Yellow House), as it is called because of its peculiar colour, is the Ministry of Foreign Affairs of Costa Rica.

66. This park was inaugurated by the Dictator Federico Tinoco in 1917 to promote *la concordia* (harmony) between citizens after the *coup d'etat* he led in that same year. In 1919 he was thrown out of power and the new political forces renamed the park as España (Spain) in commemoration of the 100 years of Independence (1821). Tristán, G. La plaza de la Fábrica. *Album de Granados*. Biblioteca Nacional de Costa Rica, n.d., n. ed, p. 262.

67. Vargas, G. and Zamora, C. (2000) *El patrimonio histórico y arquitectónico y el desarrollo urbano del distrito Carmen de la ciudad de San José 1850–1930*. San José: Ministerio de Cultura Juventud y Deportes, p. 153.

68. Cited by Cerdas, A.L. (1988) El Ferrocarril al Atlántico y su estación en San José. *Boletín Informativo del Centro de Investigación y Conservación del Patrimonio Cultural*, 5 (1), pp. 30–33, p. 31.

69. Rama, A. (1984) *La ciudad letrada*. Hanover-New Hampshire: Ediciones del Norte, p. 116; Morse, R. (1984) Peripherial cities as cultural arenas (Russia, Austria, Latin America). *Journal of Urban History*, 4, pp. 423–452, p. 441.

70. La Sabana was built thanks to a legacy to the city made by the priest Manuel Antonio Chapuí in 1783, in the area called Mata Redonda. Bustamante, *op. cit.*, p. 83.

71. Etlin, R.A. (1994) *Symbolic Space. French Enlightenment Architecture and its legacy*. Chicago: Chicago University Press, pp. 10–11.

72. ANCR (1905) Memoria de Gobernación y Policía. San José: Tipografía Nacional.

73. ANCR (1868) Informe de Gobernación, Fomento, Justicia, Guerra y Marina, pp. 29 and 32.

74. ANCR (1885) Serie Municipal No. 2297, Memoria del Cantón de San José, f. 11.

75. ANCR (1885) Colección de Leyes y Disposiciones Administrativas, Acuerdo No. XCVII. San José: Imprenta Nacional.

76. Putnam, *op. cit.*, p. 85.

77. Pacheco, O. (ed.) (1895) *Guía comercial*. San José: Imprenta Nacional, p. 160. In the case of the Central Park in New York, since 1860s wealthy New Yorkers defined the new public park as their own. They established an unwritten set of social rules for use on the park drives. Wealthy New Yorkers spatially constituted themselves as a class each afternoon; Rosenzweig, R. and Blackmar, E. (1992) *The Park and the People. A History of Central Park*. Ithaca: Cornell University Press, pp. 212–216.

78. Etlin, *op. cit.*, p. 201.

79. Scobey, D. (1992) Anatomy of the promenade: politics of bourgeois sociability in nineteenth-century New York. *Social History*, 17, pp. 205–227, p. 210.

80. Elliot, L.E. (1925) *Central America. New Paths in Ancient Lands*. New York: Dodd, Mead and Company, p. 223.

81. Quesada, F. (2001) *En el barrio Amón. Arquitectura, familia y sociabilidad del primer residencial de la elite urbana de San José, 1900–1935*. San José: Editorial de la Universidad de Costa Rica.

82. The Costa Rican architect, José Francisco Salazar, inspired in the 'Temple of Love and Music' of Versailles built the kiosk. Vargas and Zamora, *op. cit.*, p. 196.

83. Quesada, *op. cit.*, p.209.

84. Munro, D.G. (1983) *A Student in Central America, 1914–1916*. Middle American Research Institute. Publication No. 51. New Orleans: Tulane University, p. 5.

85. Scobey, *op. cit.*, p. 215; Quesada, *op. cit*, 212.

86. Scobey, *op. cit.*, p. 204.

87. Scobie, J. The growth of Latin American Cities, 1870–1930, in Bethell, L. (ed.) (1986) *The Cambridge History of Latin America*. Vol. IV, 1870 to 1930. Cambridge: Cambridge University Press, pp. 233–265.

88. Quesada, *op. cit.*, p. 71.

89. Amon Fasileau-Duplantier was the brother-in-law of Hipolite Tournon, another French businessman who by that time was one of the most important coffee planters of the country. He controlled a large percentage of the production, commercialization and transportation of the coffee to the European markets. Peters,

G. (1979) La formación territorial de las grandes fincas de café en la Meseta Central: un estudio de la firma Tournon (1877–1955). Unpublished undergraduate thesis, School of History, University of Costa Rica, San José. Quesada, *op. cit.*, p. 72 and 75.

90. Quesada, *op. cit.*

91. *Zaguán* (long hallway) came from the Arab word *ustuwan* introduced to America by the Spanish colonization. Quesada, *op. cit.*, p.163.

92. Quesada, *op. cit.*, p.165.

93. Bustamante, *op. cit.*, p. 80.

94. Gómez, J. (1924) *Homenaje a don José C. Zeledón.* San José: Imprenta Trejos Hnos., pp. 72–73. By 1905 one of the workers' newspapers mentioned that 'many were the workers that are buying a piece of land in that area (south of the city), soon we will have a real workers' neighborhood'. *El Noticiero*, March 7, 1905, cited by Oliva, M. (1985) *Artesanos y obreros costarricenses, 1880–1914.* San José: Editorial Costa Rica, p. 66.

95. Abarca, R. et al. (1990) San José-ensanches (1900-1959). Un análisis evolutivo de la ciudad. San José: Seminario de Graduación-Escuela de Arquitectura, Universidad de Costa Rica, p. 161; Cerdas, J.M. (1994) Condiciones de vida de los trabajadores manufactureros de San José 1930–1960. Unpublished M.Sc. thesis, Postgraduate School, University of Costa Rica, San José.

96. Hardoy, *op. cit.*, p. 21. In 1954 an autonomous institution related to urban planning and construction, the *Instituto Nacional de Vivienda y Urbanismo* (National Institute for Housing and Urbanism), was created for the first time in Costa Rica.Vives, *op. cit.*, p. 399.

97. Cited by Altezor, C. (1986) *Arquitectura urbana en Costa Rica. Evolución histórica 1900–1950.* San José: Editorial Tecnológica de Costa Rica, p. 26.

98. In 1939 the State founded the first institution for popular housing called the *Junta Nacional de Habitación (National Board of Housing)*, and some individual houses were built in San José. But it was not until 1942 that the State began a social housing project called the *Cooperativa de las Casas Baratas de la Familia* (Cooperative of cheap houses for the family) as a response to the many social movements and reforms of the 1940s. The first lower-class housing project called Ciudadela Calderón Muñoz was built in Zapote. Vives, (1998) Una arquitectura para el cambio, in Fonseca and Garnier (eds.), *op. cit.*, p. 387.

99. Quesada, *op. cit.* p. 229.

100. Munro, *op. cit.*, p. 5.

101. Altezor, *op. cit.*, p. 32.

102. Garnier and Venegas, *op. cit.*, p. 346.

103. *Ibid.*, p. 347

104. Altezor, *op. cit.*, p. 30.

105. He also designed (among dozens of works) the new presidential house (later the Legislative Assembly) in a neo-colonial or Hispanic style, the *Banco Nacional de Seguros* (National Insurance Bank), and the Hospital Calderón Guardia (Calderón Guardia Hospital) with a pure modern language. Altezor, *op. cit.*, pp. 157–159.

106. Altezor, *op. cit.*, p. 177.

107. Some of the best examples in San José are the Temple of Music, Club Unión (Union Club), the Legation of México, and many hospitals and health institutions, such as the Echandi Pavillion (an annex to the San Juan de Dios Hospital in Paseo Colón). Salazar also designed the health complex for the Ministry of Health, many private houses for elites, and a new modernist building for the Pacific Station. Altezor, *op. cit.*, pp. 193–194.

108. Among some of his most important works are the Palace, Lux and Ideal movie theatres, Almacén Borbón, Schyfter and Trejos González buildings, and dozens of high-class dwellings. Altezor, *op. cit.*, pp. 223–248.

109. Samper, M. (ed.) (1991) *El censo de población de 1927: Creación de una base nominal computadorizada.* San José: Oficina de Publicaciones de la Universidad de Costa Rica, p. 63; Fernández and Lungo (comps.), *op. cit.*, p. 72.

110. Hall, C. (1985) *Costa Rica. A Geographical Interpretation in Historical Perspective* Dellplain Latin American Studies, No. 17. Boulder and London: Westview Press, p. 131.

111. It was not until 1949 that for the first time a project for the development and urban planning of the capital was made by Anatole Solow (the Head of the Division of Housing and Urban Planning of the Pan American Union), hired by the State and the Municipality of San José. The most important recommendations made by Solow were the creation of a Metropolitan Area (including all the cantons in the surroundings of the city), improving the street layout, the creation of more boulevards, and the delimitation of specific zones for industry, residence, recreation, etc. Cited by Altezor, *op. cit.*, p. 35.

Conclusions

Arturo Almandoz

As the Argentine thinker Néstor García Canclini pointed out some years ago, Latin America's 'hybrid culture' throughout the twentieth century can be explained historically in terms of the different times of arrival of modernity as a stage, modernization as a process of social change and modernism as cultural and intellectual projects.[1] This lack of correspondence among the different components of modernity is partly due to Latin America's peripheral and subordinated position in Western capitalism since colonial times, a subjugation that was traditionally denounced by the theorists of dependence as an economic and political handicap that supposedly prevented the Latin republics from cultural autonomy. However, as this book has tried to demonstrate on the basis of a cultural approach to the transfer of urbanism, there certainly are hybrid manifestations in the domains of the capital cities' architectural fabric and urban culture, in which one can track the peculiarity of Latin America's own search for progress and civilization from the mid-nineteenth century, followed by modernity, modernization and modernism until the middle of the twentieth.

Included in the agenda imported from Europe by national elites since the early republican time, the reforms that underpinned Latin America's urban planning were but one set of ideas amongst a more extensive baggage of urban culture – a fact which is essential to an understanding of the emergence of the technical discipline during this period in most of the countries.[2] This cultural approach to the question of transference has allowed us to identify the continuity of a Europeanized era in the history of major Latin American capitals, both in terms of urban culture and planning breakthroughs. Manifestations of this era obviously were more conspicuous in the major capitals of the expanding economies of the nineteenth century, such as Buenos Aires, Rio de Janeiro and Santiago, than in countries such as Peru, Venezuela and Costa Rica, which were developing more slowly and so were less attractive to the capitalist networks of the North Atlantic bloc. In this respect, it is interesting to note that the post-colonial ranking of Latin American economies brought about a new hierarchy amongst their capitals according to the speed with which they adopted urban ideas and models from abroad. As pointed out by Pérez Oyarzun, Rosas and Ramón,

Buenos Aires became a reference for Santiago, while the latter was a model for Lima, thus confirming the loss of primacy of the early viceregal capital in post-colonial Latin America. At the same time, in the case of smaller cities such as Caracas or San José, the transfer of urban models from Europe was less evident, thus their historical research has often to make use of non-spatial examples, as is shown in the different levels of representation analysed by González and Quesada.

As proof of the continuity and importance of urban modernization throughout the period considered in this book, we can look at the institutions, buildings and districts created during the early reforms of the republics, and which maintained their prominence until the mid-twentieth century. This continuity can be illustrated, for instance, in the Ministries of Public Works created after administrative reforms which tried to modernize the apparatus of colonial times in Mexico, Chile and Venezuela. These new institutions pioneered the urbanization of the vast and wild territories of the young republics. At the same time, the Europeanization of the bourgeoisie's urban life was epitomized in new types of buildings exhibiting unprecedented styles: theatres such as the Colón in Buenos Aires, the Tacón and Villanueva in Havana, the Municipal in Santiago, Caracas, Rio and São Paulo, or the Nacional in San José, all of which became the elites' social venues for nearly a century; commercial *passages* and arcades that, together with the new hotels, spread a bustle of business activity in the centres of Buenos Aires and Santiago and in the Murallas of Havana . . . Also during this era many modern areas emerged out of the colonial *damero* – the northern district in Buenos Aires, Arquitectos in Mexico City, Vedado in Havana, Jardim América and

Jardim Europa in São Paulo, Amón in San José, El Paraíso in Caracas. There, the commercial and industrial bourgeoisie could exhibit the features of a residential modernity imported from industrialized metropolises: architectural eclecticism, sanitary regulations, new building systems and a suburban culture that had been unknown for the dwellers of the crowded *conventillos, vecindades* or *callejones* of central districts. While breaking the hegemony of the colonial centres, these upper-class *urbanizaciones* or *colonias* also initiated the process of urban expansion and social segregation that would lead to the teeming metropolises, as McMichael Reese's analysis so clearly demonstrates.

Perhaps with the exception of Havana, where Spain's stronger and longer presence led to the adoption of the *ensanche* model of Cerdá and architectural combinations typified by Segre, in most of the Latin capitals the *grands travaux* of Second Empire Paris were the explicit or implied reference for local and national governors. Anticipated by Tacón's reforms in Havana and Pedro II's in Rio, Torcuato de Alvear in Buenos Aires, Vicuña Mackenna in Santiago, Guzmán Blanco in Caracas, Pereira Passos in Rio, can be seen as more or less successful variants of Creole Haussmanns who acted from different scales of local or national power. Similarities with the Haussmann's urban surgery are theoretically significant in the case of the Chilean capital, where the publication of Vicuña's *La transformación de Santiago* seemed to forecast the principles of the Baron's *Mémoires* at the end of the nineteenth century. Even though some aspects of the sanitary debate were discussed in cities like Rio from the 1820s – almost as early as in Europe – it must be remembered that not all the Baron's principles had arrived in nineteenth-century Latin

America. The European debates on hygiene and finance were apparently not included in the first Haussmannesque wave of ideas which arrived in Latin America; they were to be adopted by the end of the century, and in a different way.

The progress and civilization envisaged by liberal governments of the nineteenth-century republics paved the way for their capitals' incorporation to the 'Bella Epoca'. Spanning a broader period of time than European *Belle Époque*, Latin America's *Bella Epoca* prolonged the refinement imported from the Old World throughout the capitals, particularly in the domain of urban culture, from the 1890s until well after World War I. Although this influence was not always evident in the urban renewal of minor capitals, it underpinned the sanitary and planning reforms pursued by national governments in the municipal domain, as was proved by the examples of Buenos Aires, Caracas, Lima and Rio. The latter are also examples of how medical debates anticipated the codes of urban modernization even before architecture. Still within the *Bella Epoca*, as Pérez Oyarzun and Rosas show for the case of Santiago, the centennial celebrations of Independence were a sort of turning point for architectural and urban debates in the capitals, since they evinced a conflict between nineteenth-century aesthetic ideals and twentieth-century social and political demands. This was a dilemma faced by most of the proposals elaborated by foreign visitors to the capitals, including Bouvard's projects for Buenos Aires and São Paulo, Forestier's proposals for Buenos Aires and Havana, and later, Agache's plan for Rio. In architectural terms, most of these proposals were inspired by the academic principle of 'building aesthetic' – the concept emphasized by Gutiérrez in his

analysis of the case of Buenos Aires – the most visited and studied capital during Latin America's *Bella Epoca*. Also in this respect, one can generalize da Silva Pereira's idea that, in terms of the eclecticism of the urban design, the nineteenth century lasted in the *Cidade Maravilhosa* until the first decade of the twentieth, which can certainly be said of most of Latin America's capitals seduced by *Beaux-Arts* grandeur.

Principles and institutions for planning began to change throughout the 1930s, when more technical concepts and methodologies emerged in the plans elaborated for most of the Latin American capitals. Paradoxically, the consolidation of *urbanismo* was not so evident in Le Corbusier's sketches for Buenos Aires, though his proposal for Rio was perhaps better focused. But the contextualization and the concern for implementation were mature traits already present in Hegemann's proposals for Buenos Aires, Prestes Maia's plan for São Paulo, Brunner's for Santiago and Bogotá, and Rotival's for Caracas. Backed by local groups of professionals returned from Europe and North America, or who had studied in the new schools of architecture, this was also the phase when these foreign pioneers helped to found the new institutions and professional practice of planning – as was clear in the outstanding example of Brunner in Chile and Colombia.

To some extent it was true that, in a continent still seduced by the last vestiges of *Beaux-Arts*, some of these plans ended as late examples of what Bardet labelled as '*Haussmannisme amélioré*'. As the ambassadors of French *urbanisme* did in the colonies of Africa or Asia – which Gwendolyn Wright demonstrated in her beautiful book[3] – in cities like Buenos Aires and Rio, Havana and Caracas, the French designers acted as ambassadors for the '*mission civilisatrice*' of which they were in charge. Though they might be more *avant garde* when working at home, the visitors tempered their potentially disruptive modernity for the sake of a monumentality they thought to be more suitable for the Latin American republics, some of whose capitals still sought to realize their academic aspirations which originated in the nineteenth century. Da Silva Pereira demonstrates part of this dilemma very well by contrasting the proposals of Agache and Le Corbusier for Rio: the former saw modernity as a question of style, and not as a technological and cultural change. This misconception can perhaps be applied to other European representatives of academic urbanism in Latin America.

When Violich saw, at the time of his journey in the early 1940s, that French training and influence had been abandoned by Latin American planners, he was witnessing the end of that European-oriented cycle of urban culture and models. Its place had been taken by a more functional and modern rationale of urban planning which came under the aegis of American modernity. Le Corbusier's second proposal for Buenos Aires and Sert's for Havana were examples of that shift, to be crowned in Lucio Costa's master plan for Brasilia. But this later era of Latin American urban and regional planning, which was to see the city fabric obliterated for the sake of rational and abstract principles, is beyond the scope of this book. It is a period which has been explored for Europe and North America in terms of both planning theory and practice,[4] while Latin America's planning history during the second half of the twentieth century remains to a great extent undiscovered. Let us hope that this book will lead to that new search.

NOTES

1. García Canclini, N. (1992, 1995) *Culturas híbridas. Estrategias para entrar y salir de la modernidad.* Buenos Aires: Editorial Sudamericana, p. 19

2. Some of the ideas in this chapter explore hypotheses hinted at in the conclusions of my book (1997) *Urbanismo europeo en Caracas (1870-1940).* Caracas: Fundarte, Equinoccio, Ediciones de la Universidad Simón Bolívar. The book is the translation of my PhD thesis, Almandoz, A. (1996) European Urbanism in Caracas, 1870s–1930s, Architectural Association School of Architecture, Open University, London.

3. Wright, G. (1991) *The Politics of Design in French Colonial Urbanism.* Chicago: University of Chicago Press.

4. Taylor, N. (1998) Urban Planning Theory since 1945. London: Sage; Hall, P. (1988, 1994) *Cities of Tomorrow. An Intellectual History of Urban Planning and Design in the Twentieth Century.* Oxford: Blackwell; Hall, P. (1974, 1992) *Urban and Regional Planning.* London: Routledge.

∝ Index ∾

Note: Figures are indicated by *italic page numbers*, notes by suffix 'n[ ]'